# THE TECHNIQUE
*of*
# THE MOTION PICTURE
## CAMERA

**THE LIBRARY**
**OF COMMUNICATION TECHNIQUES**

THE TECHNIQUE OF FILM EDITING
*Karel Reisz and Gavin Millar*

THE TECHNIQUE OF FILM ANIMATION
*John Halas and Roger Manvell*

THE TECHNIQUE OF FILM MUSIC
*John Huntley and Roger Manvell*

THE TECHNIQUE OF FILM AND TELEVISION MAKE-UP
*Vincent J-R. Kehoe*

THE TECHNIQUE OF TELEVISION PRODUCTION
*Gerald Millerson*

THE TECHNIQUE OF THE SOUND STUDIO
*Alec Nisbett*

THE TECHNIQUE OF DOCUMENTARY FILM
PRODUCTION
*W. Hugh Baddeley*

THE TECHNIQUE OF THE TELEVISION CAMERAMAN
*Peter Jones*

THE TECHNIQUE OF SPECIAL EFFECTS
CINEMATOGRAPHY
*Raymond Fielding*

THE TECHNIQUE OF TELEVISION ANNOUNCING
*Bruce Lewis*

THE TECHNIQUE OF THE MOTION PICTURE CAMERA
*H. Mario Raimondo Souto*

THE TECHNIQUE OF EDITING 16 mm FILM
*John Burder*

THE TECHNIQUE OF THE FILM CUTTING ROOM
*Ernest Walter*

THE TECHNIQUE OF SPECIAL EFFECTS IN TELEVISION
*Bernard R. Wilkie*

THE TECHNIQUE OF LIGHTING FOR TELEVISION
AND MOTION PICTURES
*G. Millerson*

# THE TECHNIQUE OF THE

# MOTION PICTURE CAMERA

*by*

## H. MARIO RAIMONDO SOUTO

FOCAL PRESS

*London and New York*

*Manuscript translated by*
H. M. Grierson-Rodriguez


*First Edition 1967*
*Second Revised and Enlarged Edition 1969*
*Reprinted 1971*
*Third Revised and Enlarged Edition 1977*
*Fifth Impression 1978*


Text set in 12 pt. Photon Times, printed by photolithography, and bound in Great Britain at The Pitman Press, Bath

# CONTENTS

*To my Mother*

# INTRODUCTION TO THE THIRD EDITION

Seven years have elapsed since the second revised and enlarged edition of this book was published. During this period, the hardware used in shooting a film has developed considerably. Motion picture camera technology has also evolved further and new, lighter, equipment of greater precision with more refinements has replaced, or is replacing, instruments which were standard in the industry for decades.

This updated, considerably enlarged, third edition continues the original objective of the book: to provide a description of the motion picture camera in its wide range of construction variations, a listing of the characteristics of equipment used in all main film making centres of the world and handling methods, maintenance and use of these complex instruments. For this revision, new sections have been added to the book, other sections have been enlarged, and several camera models have been omitted since they are no longer used in the industry.

To acquaint the reader with the latest innovations on the market more than twenty new cameras are described. However, although the latest improvements are vital in providing a clear picture of modern hardware available to the industry, the author has also added to the descriptions of vintage cameras—a subject of great interest to many people working in films.

This third edition also provides additional information concerning shooting techniques, operation and maintenance. Further matter has been added to the tables. Thus this third edition should prove a most efficient and practical source for the reader who wants to become acquainted with all possibilities afforded by the main instrument in motion picture making.

Montevideo, Uruguay, 1976          H. MARIO RAIMONDO SOUTO

# INTRODUCTION TO THE REVISED EDITION

MANY innovations have appeared in world markets on this book's subject matter in the year and a half since the first edition. Besides updating the material, this second edition penetrates deeper both into the camera's design, as well as into its evaluation, application, servicing and related techniques.

Thus, more construction details of the various components are given, the operating principles of others are explained and historical notes are given on their development.

This edition also includes more information on various techniques in which the motion picture camera plays an important role. The basic concepts of equipment for time-lapse cinematography, cine-radiology and kinescopic recordings are described in the corresponding section.

It was also considered useful to provide descriptions of the techniques for inspecting the camera and checking breakdowns and troubles. The best methods developed by manufacturers and scientific institutions are described, as well as some simplified tests which the cinematographer himself can carry out where there are no specialised workshops at hand.

The camera is of course dovetailed with motion picture production and direction. Introductions into those subjects are included, showing how the choice of equipment affects production costs, and giving pointers on film language for the benefit of operators when they are faced with the twofold responsibility of also directing the film.

An attempt is also made to humanize what was previously an exclusively technical description, by adding historical notes on famous items of equipment used for shooting films which are now classics. These notes highlight the relationships between man and instrument, which has been typical of this profession.

Montevideo, Uruguay, Nov. 1968    H. MARIO RAIMONDO SOUTO

# INTRODUCTION

OF the many books written on the seventh art, very few deal with the techniques of professional film making, and in these the space devoted specifically to the instrument that made motion pictures possible is very scant indeed.

Most of today's well-established directors of photography, camera operators, assistants, and newsreel cameramen have attained an inside knowledge of their equipment in a manner similar to mediaeval apprenticeship, that is, after mastering each phase in turn, by step-by-step promotions in their scale of responsibilities. Continuous hard work and the instruction of more experienced colleagues eventually give them a thorough familiarity with the more readily available instruments. But even the most highly reputed cameramen are often unaquainted with instruments used by colleagues abroad, or with facilities provided by the foreign manufacturers.

Perhaps even more frustrating than this was the fact that there was no concentrated and readily available source of information to the budding cameraman on the instruments he would handle, nor on the best techniques for operating them.

The increasing development of international co-productions requires many cinematographers to travel abroad where they face equipment with which they have had no experience. Moreover, the mushroom growth of low budget and "new wave" production units, incorporating a large proportion of new and young blood into the industry, has increased the number of those interested in learning thoroughly the techniques of this branch of the cinema.

Television, too, has created an enormous demand for filmed material for filling time-gaps and this, in turn, has considerably increased the need for skilled operators. The 16 mm gauge has become professional to such a degree that camera makers have concentrated their attention on this medium and have come out with a succession of new instruments to meet this specific demand.

A specialized source of information on the subject was therefore urgently needed. The author hopes this volume fills the gap. His intention in writing it was to provide readers in the field of TV and motion pictures with a source of information, comprehensive and concise, on the professional cinematographer's main tool—the camera.

For many reasons, specifically scientific instruments have been left out. Their operating principles are generally totally different from standard cameras. They are used only by very few scientific investigators and the mechanisms and characteristics of many are carefully guarded secrets.

This book gathers together widely scattered information and the know-how of experienced cinematographers for the benefit of newcomers to the art, and provides them with a descriptive roster of the cameras most extensively used in Europe and the American continent. It is hoped that this work will help all those interested in becoming acquainted with the "innards" of the instruments, and in obtaining practical hints on their operation and maintenance. The experience of skilled cinematographers, as well as the author's, have been summarized in the technical chapters as well as in the final chapter on shooting techniques.

However, this book is not intended only for cinematographers. The author trusts that other specialists in the film production industry—producers, directors, laboratory workers, specialized camera mechanics, documentary film makers and others, will find useful information to apply to their specific tasks, and that they will thereby derive a wider and more exact comprehension of the industry's basic instrument.

The author takes pleasure in acknowledging the generous contributions from equipment manufacturers mentioned in the text: *Arnold & Richter A.G.; Arriflex Corporation of America; Bach Auricon Inc.; Beckman & Whitley Inc.; Bell & Howell Company; Consortium Pathé; Eclair International Diffusion; Etablissements André Debrie, Federal Manufacturing & Engineering Corp.; Houston Fearless Corp.; James A. Sinclair Co.; John M. Wall Inc.; Mitchell Camera Corp.; Producers Sales Corp.; Paillard S.A.; Rank Precision Industries Ltd.; The Animation Equipment Inc.; S.D.S. Aerospace Systems; Technicolor Corporation; Vinten Ltd.*

They have all kindly provided technical information on their products as well as most of the illustrations in this volume. Special acknowledgement must be extended to *Messrs. F. & B. Ceco; Camera Service Center; S.O.S. Photo-Cine-Optics Inc.; Unitalia Film and A.U.R.Y.T.C.;* as well as to *Warner Brothers, Pathé Laboratories Inc.* and *Twentieth Century Fox Studios*, who were kind enough to give the author access to many of the facilities and equipment and to supply all the information that was asked of them.

Thanks are also due to the American Society of Cinematographers for the use of reference material in the *American Cinematographer Manual* and the *American Cinematographer Magazine*.

Finally the author wishes to thank *Mr. Daniel Arijon* for his valuable help in the preparation of several sections, to *Mr. Carlos Cabrera* for cooperation in preparing the art work, and to the translator *Mr. H. M. Grierson-Rodriguez* for his careful work and useful suggestions in drawing up this English language version.

Montevideo, Uruguay, 1967          H. Mario Raimondo Souto

# ACKNOWLEDGEMENTS

This third edition has been made possible thanks to the cooperation of the following persons, companies and institutions, who were kind enough to afford the author access to their equipment, facilities, technical information and permission to reproduce material or illustrations.

Ets. Pierre Angenieux, France
Mr. Daniel Arijon
Mr. Jean Pierre Beauviala, Aäton Cinematographie, France
Prof. Jaroslav Boucek, Academy of Arts, Czechoslovakia
Birns & Sawyer, Inc. USA
Canon Inc, USA
Departmento de Medios Tecnicos de Comunicación, Universidad de la República, Uruguay
Mr. A. Coma, Eclair International, France
Mr. Jose Domenech, Spain
Mr. Bruno Furini, Cinecitta Studios, Italy
A. Gordon Enterprises Inc, USA
Imphulphysik GmbH, German Federal Republic
Instituto Tecnologico de Educacion Audiovisual, Uruguay
Maison Brant Frères, France
Mr. Jacob G. Monroy, Cine Precision Engineering Co, USA
Pathé-Movie-Sonics, France
Photo-Sonics, Inc, USA
Red Lake Laboratories, Inc, USA
Mr. E. Shultz and Mr. P. Haferkorn, Arnold & Richter AG., German Federal Republic
Society of Motion Picture and Television Engineers, USA
Mr. Hans Vos, Filmpartners, Holland
Mr. Peter Waldek, Cinema Products, USA
Mr. Enrique Wallfisch, Lowe Producenter, Argentine
Wilcam Photo Research, USA
Mr. Ted de Wit, Carillon Films, Holland

# THE MOTION PICTURE CAMERA

THE motion picture camera employs the basic principles of still photography. The fundamental difference lies in the fact that while the still camera is designed only to print a single image on the film at each exposure, the motion picture camera is built to effect multiple successive exposures, thus accomplishing a photographic breakdown of motion.

To achieve such results, a complicated precision mechanism must be included inside the darkened chamber where the image is formed on the film. This mechanism is placed within a strong and light-tight, but easily accessible, body.

Until 1920, camera bodies were built mostly of wood and the mechanisms of bronze, with the key parts in steel. But the characteristics of these materials greatly impaired performance, since ambient atmospheric conditions and rough and continuous wear and tear reduced their efficiency considerably.

Nowadays, manufacturers have obviated such difficulties by building camera bodies in special pressed steel or aluminium alloy, which provide great strength combined with light weight. Light-excluding problems have been solved by means of sealing strips and special-action hinges and locks. Mechnical wear has been eliminated by making moving parts with special alloy steels or fibre. Moreover, the shape of the camera has been improved, as well as its appearance, by sophisticated finish on outside surfaces.

## Mechanical Unit

The mechanical principle of the modern motion picture camera has been developed from that of those earlier models which blazed the trail for today's cinematography. To make its study easier, the complete system can be broken down into two mechanisms, each with an individual task but with a common purpose.

The first mechanism has the task of drawing the unexposed film (or raw stock) from the storage chamber, and after exposure, driving it into a similar one for exposed film. This mechanism runs continuously.

The other mechanism is an intermittent one whose function is to arrest sections of film, called frames, one at a time, behind an opening or *aperture*, on which the camera lens focuses an image of an object in the outside world. Operating in combination with this intermittent mechanism, a *shutter*, placed in front of the film obscures the light from the lens each time the film is drawn down to the next frame.

*Continuous drive*

Since the intermittent drive alternately holds the film stationary and moves it rapidly downwards, it would be impossible to feed the film directly into it without snatching and tearing. To avoid this, slack loops of film are formed above and below the intermittent mechanism (often called a *gate*), so that the intermittent and continuous drives can be combined.

The continuous drive of the film is effected by means of sprocket wheels whose teeth penetrate the film perforations, thus causing it to move smoothly and steadily. The steadiness of the film flow is assisted by having an adequate diameter of sprocket wheel, designed so that several teeth simultaneously penetrate the perforations of the film wrapped round it.

Moreover, to cope with the constant and continuous action, in which the teeth penetrate into and withdraw from the perforations at a given angle, the teeth are given a tapered rounded shape so as to avoid damage to the perforation edges. Large sprockets generally have 32 teeth (or even up to 40 for wide-screen film) and run at 180 r.p.m. for 24 frames per second. In cameras provided with more than one sprocket wheel, each wheel may have 8, 12 or 16 teeth. The size of the sprocket is also determined by the camera design and how the film travels. Most sprocket wheels are provided with a stripper near the edge of the teeth to keep the film from wrapping round the sprocket if the teeth should accidentally hook up the perforations. Specially located rollers guide the films towards the other sections of the mechanism.

Adequate penetration of the teeth into the perforations is ensured by pressure rollers, which do not press the film, but merely prevent the perforations from slipping out, or from meshing less teeth than

16

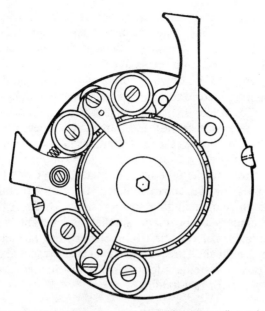

Fig. 1. Bell & Howell's 32-teeth large sprocket with pressure rollers and strippers.

were originally designed. The pressure rollers contact the film only in the area of the perforations and not at the central part where the image is formed, to avoid damaging this surface. Pressure rollers are designed to open up so that the film can be easily threaded. Unless the rollers are replaced in their working position the camera access door cannot be closed. This avoids damage to the film and mechanism if the roller is incorrectly reclosed or if the film is not properly threaded. Some camera manufacturers have introduced devices for opening all pressure rollers simultaneously when working with more than one sprocket, especially in the case of hand held cameras used by newsreel cameramen, for whom fast and sure threading is essential.

Within the camera, film travels from one magazine chamber to the other by one of two methods. The first method, whereby the film travels lengthwise in the same plane all the time, is known as *single plane travel*. This means that the magazine chambers have to be in the same plane, too, but when working with large film loads the magazines must be placed outside the camera body itself, and keeping them in the same plane adds considerably to the bulk of the instrument. Single plane travel is used by most camera manufacturers in America as well as by some in Europe. It simplifies camera

17

construction and allows for easy loading. Continuous drive is effected either with only one combined-action sprocket working simultaneously on top and below or two smaller-diameter sprockets placed for feed and take-up respectively.

The other method is known as *three plane travel* and was first used by the André Debrie company when trying to reduce the size of the camera. To attain this, they placed the magazine chambers within the camera, side by side and thus in two different planes. By this method the film leaves the feed chamber in one plane, passes to another plane on going through the film gate and into a third plane when being drawn to the take-up chamber. Three plane travel was extensively used by European makers (Debrie, Askania, Eclair, Prevost, Vinten, etc) including the Russians (Rodina) because it enables the camera to be made smaller and permits the use of separate magazines. However it complicates the mechanism and makes loading difficult. Three-plane travel is at presented applied in coaxial magazine systems adopted by many makers to simplify storage and allow for fast loading.

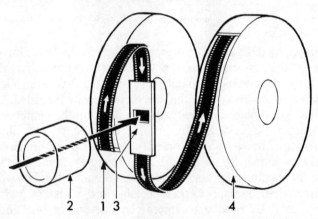

Fig. 2. Three-plane travel as in Debrie Parvo or coaxial magazines. (1) Supply chamber, (2) lens, (3) film gate, (4) take-up chamber.

*Intermittent mechanism*

The intermittent drive is the most delicate of all the components in the camera's mechanism. As explained above, its function is to expose frames of film in rapid succession behind the aperture or film gate. This is achieved by means of a series of coordinated motions which can be roughly broken down as follows:

(i)    a downward pull of 19 mm ($\frac{3}{4}$ in.) for 35 mm film and of 7·62

18

for 16 mm film, effected by a shuttle with one or more claws which penetrate the film perforations. This places the film frame behind the aperture;

(ii) retraction of the claws from the perforations. Immediately afterwards the shuttle starts its upward motion, while the film frame is held steady behind the aperture;

(iii) after the shuttle's upward displacement is completed, the claws penetrate the film perforations and start the cycle over again.

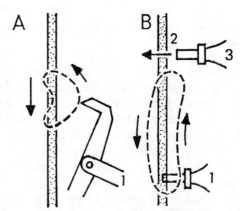

Fig. 3. Detail of displacement pattern of two different types of shuttle. (A) Typical 16 mm camera claw shuttle; (B) shuttle and pin registration system; (1) shuttle; (2) film; (3) pilot pin.

Synchronized with the intermittent motion of the shuttle, another mechanism completes this operation, ensuring the exact registration of the photographic impression by holding the film steady during the period it remains motionless in order to record the image.

Once the film has been placed in position by the shuttle claws and these are withdrawn to start the cycle over again, one or two *register pins* or *pilot pins* immediately penetrate the perforations close to the aperture. Their purpose is to steady the film completely so that the image is printed on a steady surface, free of jerks or vibrations.

But the pilot or register pin also adjusts the placing of the film in relation to the aperture. In mechanisms where the pilot pin moves towards the perforation, the latter is not always in its exact position. Therefore, in many instruments the pin is cone-shaped. As it completes its travel, the perforation edge bears on the pin's surface and the film shifts to its correct position. The pin's travel is designed so that it remains completely motionless while the film is being exposed. All this is effected at very high speed within the short lapse afforded by the next action of the shuttle and that of another mechanism called the shutter which we shall study further below.

Another system for registration known as the *fixed pilot pin* was introduced in the early 1900s, by Arthur Newman, from an idea suggested by one of his mechanics, called Woodhead. It works on the principle of a register pin fixed on the film gate at a side of the aperture; registration is effected when the film seats on the aperture plate and is kept steady by one or two pilot pins penetrating the perforations. This method depends on a special movement of the film instead of the pilot pin(s). The fixed pilot pin was used on all Newman Sinclair cameras and was improved upon by the Bell & Howell Company for their studio cameras. Because of its effective registering and minimum wear, it is still used on many special-effects cameras.

Registration devices may act on both or on only one side of the film. When they work on both sides, horizontal accuracy is attained by the pin on one side while that on the other side effects vertical registration. Pilot pins working on only one side of the film effect vertical registration, while horizontal correction is effected by side pressure devices mounted in the film gate. This method is used on many 35 mm cameras, and is practically standard on 16 mm equipment. Pilot pin systems are used mainly on studio cameras, owing to their complex mechanism, but they give an image steadiness of 0·001 mm. On comparing this value with the 0·02 mm steadiness obtained by cameras without register pin, we understand why images taken with cameras with register pin show a much better definition and can be combined in multiple exposures with no apparent blurring round the edges.

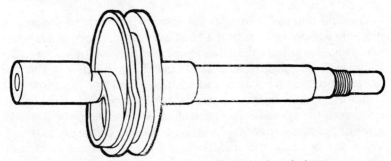

Fig. 4. Typical characteristics of eccentric in professional standard camera.

The design of the intermittent mechanism has undergone many modifications since the primitive devices constructed by Lumière and Edison. Most intermittent drives and many moving register pins work on the basis of an eccentric. Figs 4 and 7 give some idea of the variety of eccentrics in use and the many different ways in which they are made to work and are combined with other mechanical methods.

A study of today's shuttle and register pin movements leads to the conclusion that the design of any such mechanism is very closely connected to the individual personality of each camera manufacturer. Consequently, to identify each system one must refer to the make and model of the camera using it.

MITCHELL CAM AND GEAR MOVEMENT. The intermittent drive designed by the Mitchell Camera Corp. for their Standard, High Speed and 16 mm camera (not SSR 16 model) is based on the properties of the *Trezel* cam to operate within a frame which makes up the shuttle. The upward or downward movement of the shuttle is achieved by the displacement of a fixed shaft along a groove in the shuttle.

The shaft of the cam is also the shaft of a gear wheel which meshes into another of the same dimensions and in its turn, drives the register pin movements. The object of the latter is to drive the pins into and then withdraw them from the film perforations, under the action of a second cam on a frame which is part of a sliding shaft.

The whole mechanism achieves two objects. First, an intermittent shuttle motion whereby four claws (two on each side) penetrate the film perforations and pull the film down by the height of one frame.

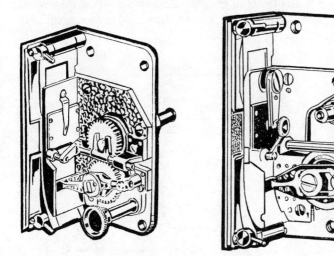

Fig. 5. *Left.* Mitchell cam and gear movement. *Right.* Mitchell eccentric movement.

In co-ordination with this, two register pins (one on each side), actuated by the registration mechanism, penetrate the perforations when the film is motionless, and thus ensure its steadiness during the exposure period.

MITCHELL ECCENTRIC MOVEMENT. When sound filming requirements called for a noiseless camera, the Mitchell Corp. engineers had to change their cam and gear mechanism for a less noisy one but working with the same degree of precision. The new design of mechanism was introduced about 1930 in the NC model and incorporated later in the Studio BNC and recently in S35-R (Mark II) and BNCR. The outstanding feature of the new mechanism was that gears were reduced to a minimum thus eliminating a large portion of the noise so that scenes could be shot with direct sound recording, without any danger that the microphone would pick up any camera noise, at least at medium distances.

Figure 6 shows the main shaft of the unit (1), running at a number of revolutions equivalent to the film speed, and provided with an eccentric (2) at one of its ends. The eccentric is provided with a shaft which ends up in a cube shaped block placed inside the frame of the pull down arm (3). The right hand side of the frame is connected to the housing (4) of the eccentric by means of a rod (5). The left hand side end of the housing is provided with a part jutting out which operates in a housing (6) built into the plate of the whole unit.

When the main shaft (1) rotates, the housing (4) of the eccentric is

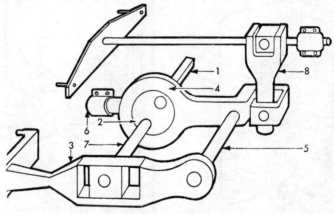

Fig. 6. Simplified diagram of the operation of the eccentric mechanism in Mitchell NC, BNC and BNCR cameras. (1) Main shaft, (2) eccentric, (3) pull-down arm, (4) eccentric housing, (5) connecting rod, (6) housing, (7) shaft, (8) operating rod.

moved, providing an eliptical displacement of the frame (3) by means of the shaft (7). At the opposite end of the frame where the claws are placed, a magnified elliptical travel is obtained which drives the film down the film gate. The housing (4) also starts the register pin moving by causing an elliptical travel at the bottom end of the rod (8), which is provided with a frame at its top end to drive the long horizontal rod of the register pins to and fro.

This shuttle mechanism ensures maximum registration: in the first place, it is provided with four claws (two on each side) which give fast and even film travel; two register pins are used, the non-sound track pin fully fits the perforation hole, while the other fits the perforation hole in the vertical plane but is smaller horizontally to allow for film shrinkage.

All parts of this mechanism are machined and lapped to 0·0001 in. accuracy. Register pins are ground lapped and polished to 0·0005 in. accuracy, this being also the tolerance value estimated for the shuttle travel.

BELL & HOWELL SHUTTLE & PILOT PIN MOVEMENTS. The intermittent drive of this American-manufactured camera was created about sixty years ago by *Mr. A. S. Howell*. A special feature of this mechanism is its ingenious fixed pilot pins, that is to say, two small registration pins jutting out from, and forming an integral part of the aperture plate. During its vertical travel, the film is not pressed but is allowed to run freely driven by the shuttle claws. When the shuttle completes its vertical displacement, a pressure plate seats the film on to the aperture plate and the fixed pilot pins penetrate two perforations.

After the frame is exposed the pressure plate is withdrawn and the film is free again to repeat the cycle.

Another characteristic of this mechanism is that shuttle, pilot pins and aperture plate are all contained within a single interchangeable assembly called "Unit I", which is used in all standard B & H Model 2709 cameras. It can run at speeds up to 32 frames per second (f.p.s.), but can be easily interchanged with another, similar unit specially designed for high speeds, thus making the camera capable of operating at a wide range of speeds.

BELL & HOWELL ECCENTRIC MOVEMENTS. For their Filmo and Eyemo cameras, the Bell & Howell Company designed a new drive mechanism located on the same plane as the aperture plate, that is to say, at right angles to the movements studied above. The intermittent

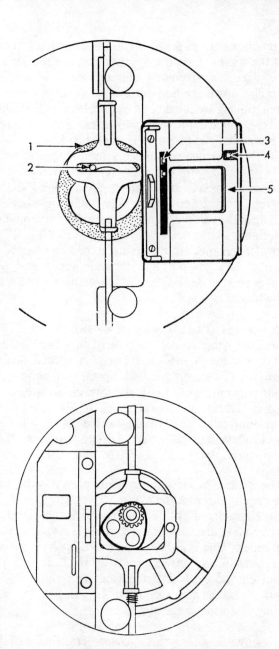

Fig. 7. *Top.* Action of eccentric pin on a shuttle frame, in a Traid manufactured camera, similar to the Eyemo. (1) Cam, (2) shuttle, (3) shuttle claws, (4) register pin, (5) aperture plate. *Bottom.* Use of a three-sided eccentric working on a similar principle upon the intermittent mechanism of the Filmo camera.

motion is obtained by the rotation of a Trezel eccentric within a shuttle frame with sliding shafts. The penetration or withdrawal of the shuttle claws into or from the film perforations, is effected by the rotation of a disc of unequal thickness acting upon the shuttle. In some special models, this assembly is complemented by a pilot pin fixed at the side of the aperture to provide greater film steadiness.

NOISELESS DRIVE SYSTEM. About 1939/40, Robert Stevens, Charles Miller, D. B. Clark and G. Laube were working on the design for the 20th Century Fox camera. In connection with the in-

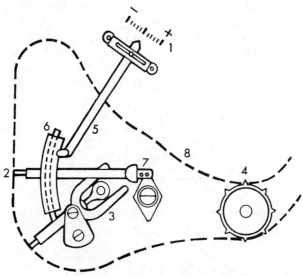

Fig. 8. Diagram of Eclair's adjustable register pin system. (1) Calibrated scale; (2) register pin displacement; (3) shuttle; (4) main sprocket; (5) lever; (6) adjusting bearing; (7) oscillating or swivel bearing; (8) film.

termittent mechanism for it, they successfully carried out research and trials to achieve the elimination of noise at its source. Their investigations were aimed at reducing the weight and size of the parts with a fast shuttling travel in order to adjust speed-increase and decrease values, thus minimizing vibrations which produce most of the noise. These concepts were applied to a movement which operates as follows: an eccentric with a very accurately designed shape is provided with a pin which drives a sliding sleeve; within this sleeve there is an arm at one end of which the take down pin is held; the pin moves forwards and backwards as it bears on the edge of the eccentric, while the arm, provided with a pivot at its other end, produces the pull down as it slides within the sleeve. At the same time, a scroll cam acts upon two register pins which hold the film steady behind the aperture.

The extremely silent operation of this movement, eliminating noise at its source, made any form of cumbersome and heavy blimping unnecessary; unfortunately, other manufacturers did not adopt this efficient and practical mechanism.

ADJUSTABLE REGISTER PIN SYSTEM. One of the most interesting design improvements of recent years is that achieved by the French engineers *Coutant* and *Mathot*: a device for adjusting the stroke of the register pin. This system was applied to the mechanism of the Eclair Camé 300 Reflex, and it comprises a lever which effects a fractional displacement of the position of the register pin by means of an adjustable bearing. The value of the displacement can be read on a scale, and it is allowed for by an oscillating bearing. Thus, the distance between the register pin and the shuttle claws is adjusted ac-

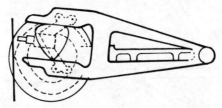

Fig. 9. Arriflex IIC movement with its heart-shaped cam claw system during 60° rotation of cam.

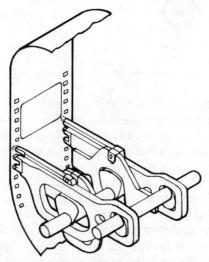

Fig. 10. Arriflex BL movement with four claws and two pilot pins. This movement was specifically designed for the new silent and hand-held studio camera produced by this company.

cording to the pitch of the film perforations. Such adjustments bring about not only maximum image steadiness but also minimum movement noise, as well as an appreciable reduction in maintenance.

Early in 1963, The Mitchell Camera Corporation brought out a device for the intermittent mechanism of their NC and BNC cameras, which achieved the same end, although based on a different mechanical concept. They called it the "vari-stroke control".

The adjustable register pin is an important contribution towards solving the problem of film steadiness in warm climates where film tends to shrink.

*Film gate*

This is the part of the camera in which raw stock is placed behind the aperture in order to print the image. On passing through the gate, the film tends to steady its run in order to reach the aperture without vibrations. This steadying is effected by side pressure devices which control the film's travel and help to obtain registration of the take, specially in cameras without register pins.

In different cameras the film gate is built either all straight, or partially curved, or with a curve only at the place where the shuttle claws act. In some instruments the film gate is very long (up to ten frames) while in others it is half that length. Such differences depend

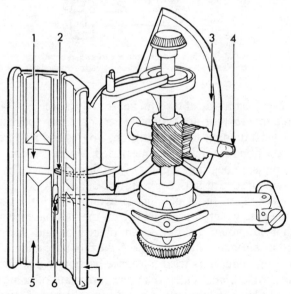

Fig. 11. (1) Film gate, (2) pilot or registration pin, (3) mirror shutter, (4) shutter shaft, (5) film channel, (6) shuttle claw, (7) pressure plate.

27

on the shape of the camera and where the continuous drive is located.

The main elements of the film gate are undoubtedly the interior surfaces of two separate parts, the aperture and pressure plates. The aperture plate is of course the one with the aperture in it and on

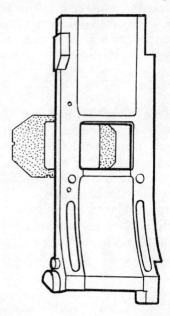

Fig. 12. Aperture plate of Mitchell Camera. Note bottom curve where shuttle claws operate, as well as two holes below and on both sides of aperture where register pins operate. The part jutting out is a gelatin filter holder.

which the emulsion side of the film bears in its travel. For the latter it is essential that this surface should be very carefully polished so as to avoid the least damage to the emulsion. To this end all parts in contact with the film are thickly chrome plated. Moreover, contact at the central (emulsion bearing) section of the film is reduced by building this part with a strip at both edges jutting out slightly so that the film should bear only at the edges. The pressure plate is the other inner face of the gate which presses lightly on the film base (rear face) in order that it should be flat when placed behind the aperture. Although its surface is in contact with the film base and not with the emulsion, manufacturers tried to reduce friction to a minimum here also, using rollers and slides. The pressure plate of some cameras presses the film intermittently, only during the period of exposure, thus reducing friction appreciably and improving registration.

28

To facilitate threading and to afford easy access, some film gates are made so that the pressure plate is hinged by a special device to the aperture plate and opens up backwards. Thus the operator can quickly check that the gate is clean and brush off the emulsion deposits frequently built-up there.

To adjust the instrument to requirements of special shooting processes, the aperture of 35 mm cameras must often be changed from standard (sound) to silent, or panoramic, or "scope" apertures. To facilitate this, manufacturers frequently provide for interchanging apertures, either the film gate complete or only the aperture plate.

Many cameras are provided with a slot on the front of the film gate to take filters or masks. This concept has been further refined in cameras like the Mitchell or the Newall by adding, besides the filter slot, a device with masks which can be regulated from the outside and which up to a certain extent controls the size of the aperture, by blocking the image formed on the film plane.

*Shutter*

The shutter mechanism is synchronized with the intermittent drive, so that each frame of the film, after exposure to the light rays, is obscured from them while it is being pulled down and the next frame is taking its place. A simple shutter takes the form of a rotating disc occupying the reduced space available between the film and the lens. The opening of this disc is so situated that the film is covered while it is in motion. In different cameras this opening is given angles ranging from 120° to 230°, the larger angles corresponding to faster pull-down movements.

Several camera makers have built their instruments with a large diameter shutter with its shaft placed as far away from the aperture as possible, to reduce exposure time, while maintaining a considerably wide shutter opening angle.

There are other shuttering systems besides the rotating disc. One is the *guillotine*, which consists of a small plate travelling up and down in front of the aperture, under the action of an eccentric coordinated with the shuttle mechanism. The disadvantage of this system is that exposure time cannot be regulated. Another type is the "focal plane" shutter used only on the Akeley camera; it consists of a narrow cylinder band running round the camera body, which is also cylinder shaped. Its characteristics allow for very wide openings.

Some cameras provide shutters with openings which can be

adjusted by means of a control placed on the outside, from maximum angle to zero. This affords the camera operator a high degree of control of film exposure without utilizing the lens diaphragm, and its facilitates the shooting of fast moving subjects.

The shutter opening control is generally a lever placed either behind or at the side of the camera, sliding over a calibrated scale. Some improved camera models complement the reading on this scale with a miniature reproduction of the shutter which is synchronized to the main shutter mechanism. It reproduces the actual shuttering opening and its position relative to the camera aperture, at all times.

As demands for a system of focusing and framing through the taking lens became insistent, manufacturers designed a new type of shutter rotating on an axis at an angle of 45° to the plane of the film and the lens. The side facing the lens is silvered, so that when it is in the closed position, the image formed by the lens is reflected into a magnifying optical system. This allows for framing and focusing through the taking lens itself. Further details of this device, known as a reflex viewfinder, will be found in the section on framing and focusing devices (p. 44).

*Recording unit*

Cameras designed for simultaneous image and sound recording are provided with a unit for recording the sound track on the film itself, either by the magnetic, the optical process or both. The inclusion of this unit demands the incorporation of means, such as compensating rollers and an inertia flywheel, to counteract the effect of the intermittent movement of the film and thus ensure the steadiness of the film's travel through the sound gate. The recording unit is installed on or very near the flywheel; and may consist of either two magnetic heads (one for recording and the other for reproduction) or, in the case of optical recording, a device to project the modulated beam produced by the galvanometer. The recording head must be placed so that the standard distance from image and sound is maintained between the aperture and the point where sound recording is effected.

The generalized application of magnetic sound recording has appreciably simplified the recording unit on many sound-on-film cameras, and has brought about the appearance of detachable units which are easily installed on the camera. For example, on the Arriflex 16 BL a module is used comprising a plate designed for rapid mounting on the camera. The plate houses the magnetic recor-

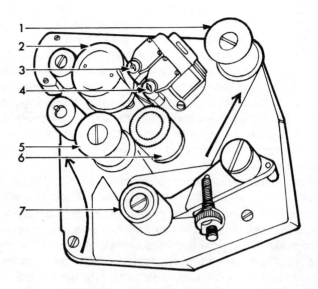

Fig. 13. Arriflex BL sound module (1) Guide roller, (2) brake roller, (3) playback head, (4) recording head, (5) guide roller, (6) sound roller with flywheel, (7) compensating roller.

ding and playback heads, a roller with a large inertia fly-wheel, a tension roller, and several guide rollers. On Auricon cameras, the module is of small size, it needs no tools for mounting and the flywheel is built into the camera itself.

Some makers have carefully studied the problem of sound recording with hand-held cameras and have found that fast panning, jerky movements and rough handling in general, affect the quality of recorded sound considerably. Consequently they have devised systems to make up for problems arising from jerky camera movements. For example, the Bolex 16 Pro-Commag is provided with two flywheels running in opposite directions. Another finding of such studies resulted in savings on the magnetic heads by avoiding wear when not in use.

All sound-on-film cameras are connected to a transistorized amplifier with an easily read large-scale volume indicator as well as volume controls for different microphone channels, equalizing switches, devices for testing the state of batteries and bias and a selecting switch for different working positions.

*Built-in exposure meter*

The concept of having an exposure meter built into the camera

31

first arose in amateur cinematography, as a helpful resource to simplify setting the correct aperture for the scene. Several German and Austrian manufacturers introduced it as a novelty in 8 mm, 9·5 mm and 16 mm amateur cameras with varying degrees of success. The new metering system was based on one of three construction principles: hand operation, semi-automatic, and automatic. In the first of these methods the exposure value information is supplied by the pointer of a microgalvanometer moving over a scale calibrated in stops which is seen in the camera viewfinder. After reading the indicated diaphragm value, the operator must set it on the corresponding ring of the camera lens.

In the semi-automatic system, an opening for the photoelectric cell on the front of the camera is provided with a diaphragm coupled to the diaphragm of the lens. The pointer of the microgalvanometer is also seen through the camera viewfinder. It does not travel over a graduated scale, but is provided with a single marking. The correct exposure is achieved when the microgalvanometer pointer indicates a particular mark. This is achieved by turning the diaphragm ring on the photoelectric cell which simultaneously operates the lens diaphragm. A rheostat allows the instrument to be adjusted according to the sensitivity of the film.

A driving system operating the lens diaphragm ring directly was the next development which led to the complete automation of the operation. As the years went by, the built-in exposure meter, in one of its three forms was adopted by manufacturers of amateur cameras to simplify film making as a hobby. The methods described were adapted to up-to-date reflex viewfinders on 8 mm and Super 8 mm cameras with great success.

For some time professional film makers resisted the application of this system to their 16 mm and 35 mm cameras, as it was considered the cameraman's responsibility to determine exposure himself taking into account the many factors demanding minor adjustments. However, several special types of work, such as newsreel and film reporting and subjects seen under variable or indeterminate lighting show the advantages of this refinement. This is particularly true in situations where speed is vital, such as shooting from aircraft and underwater.

Many 16 mm cameras have been provided with this built-in control and some manufacturers have coupled exposure meters in 35 mm cameras for specific requirements. Two of the most outstanding systems are the Arriflex and the Coutant.

## Arriflex TTL exposure control system

This system has been designed for 16 BL, ST and SR cameras as an optional accessory. The exposure reading is taken from the image supplied by the taking lens. It therefore has the advantage of taking into account the light transmission factor of the lens and any variations determined by filters, extension tubes for close-up photography, etc. The main feature of this system is that there is no translucent body (prism or semi-silvered mirror) between the lens and the film which could impair the quality of the image reaching the film.

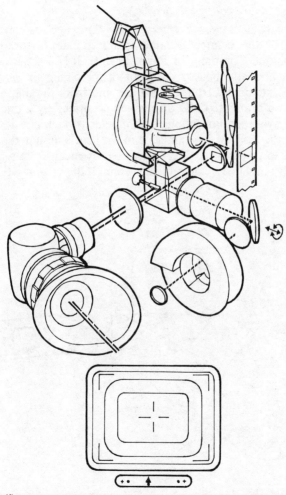

Fig. 14. Arriflex exposure control device diagram showing the light path for viewing or meter reading.

The image is reflected by the shutter mirror during the shuttering period and in to the viewfinder system for the exposure measuring unit.

This is installed on the camera door and uses a complex optical system consisting of several lenses, four prisms, a CdS type cell, a microgalvanometer and a neutral density wedge. The operator reads the exposure value in the viewfinder. On the front part of the camera door there is a regulator to combine the sensitivity of the film, with the shuttering time and the camera speed (fps.)

*Coutant exposure control device*

This instrument was created some time ago by one of the designers of the Cameflex camera and is manufactured by the Kinotechnique Company of Paris, France. It is a separate instrument which is attached to the front of the Cameflex camera and works independently from the shutter and from the diaphragm. It comprises a graduated ND disc which is rotated by a micromotor regulated by a cadmium sulphide photo-electric cell. The device is installed at the front of the camera and the lens is mounted on it. The image taken through the filter is diverted by means of a reflector at 45°, and is amplified by an optical system. It then reaches the photo-

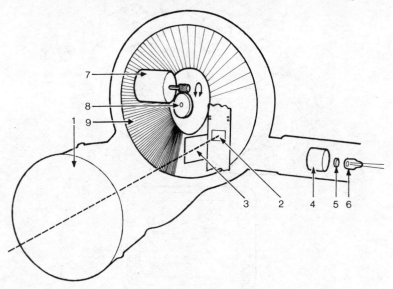

Fig. 15. Coutant exposure control device. 1: lens; 2: film; 3: front surface; 4: photocell; 5: collecting lens; 6: electronic cell; 7: micromotor; 8: gears; 9: graduated ND disc.

electric cell which regulates the current operating the micromotor by means of photoresistence. The density of the ND graduated disc ranges from 0 to 4 in an extra thin layer, and its surface is free from diffraction. The complete attachment comprises a main unit, a galvanometer, and a system with controls and connections to the power source.

The Coutant exposure device is favoured for use in scientific work such as missile tracking, macroscopy, study of the atmosphere, aerial cinematography and all other situations where the constant changes of light intensity requires continuous modifications to exposure values.

### Motor

In most professional-type motion picture cameras the mechanism is driven by an electric motor. Until recently some portable cameras were spring driven, with a capacity of about fifty feet of film in 35 mm cameras, and about twenty-two feet in 16 mm cameras, each time the spring was wound.

As the electric motor is the principal source of power for the film camera, its design has been developed so that it will operate the mechanism at a very constant rate, with the minimum effort. Such steady running is essential in order to maintain the exposure of the film with a high degree of constancy. Other vital characteristics are:

(i)  instantaneous start-up at rated speed,
(ii)  capacity for running without excessive heating,
(iii)  capacity for continuous and constant operation.

Such characteristics vary according to the type of motor. There are three types of motor widely used for camera drive:

(i)  the synchronous motor,
(ii)  the interlocked motor,
(iii)  the variable speed motor.

Synchronous and interlock motors are generally provided with a soundproof covering to make them completely noiseless. Their main characteristics are:

(i)  constant speed,
(ii)  noiseless running,
(iii)  capability of precise synchronization with similar motors driving sound recorders or background projectors.

The speed of synchronous motors is necessarily in direct ratio to the frequency of the alternating current fed to it. They are generally bulky and consequently heavy and are usually employed when direct sound recording must be effected while shooting. Their capacity for synchronizing with other equipment driven by the same power source results from their design and construction characteristics; the induction coil of such motors produces a magnetic field in the armature; thus if two motors are adequately connected their armatures will rotate synchronized with such magnetic field, just the same as if their shafts were mechanically coupled.

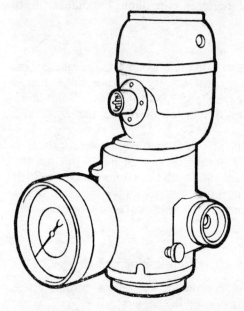

Fig. 16. Mitchell variable speed motor which is detachable from the camera and incorporates its own speed regulator in the form of a rheostat.

Normally, synchronous motors work with 3-phase, 220 v. 50 or 60 Hz, AC. However, there are single-phase, 110 v. models. When shooting at the studio, the power source is obtained directly from public utility line, or own generating plant, but when this is not available, from portable generators. In the latter event, it is essential that the frequency of the AC generated should be perfectly constant in order to keep the camera speed steady.

Interlock and synchronous motors have similar characteristics. At present the former are used only for back projection shots and for focus remote control.

Induction motors are also used by some camera makers. Their speed is constant but they are not synchronized to the frequency of the AC feeding them. Their drive power is quite high in relation to

36

their size. Generally they are designed to run at 24/25 f.p.s. only, and they are used with many cameras for direct sound recording.

The variable speed motor is noisier, since it is not provided with sound proofing protection, and it is used for shooting without sound recording. It incorporates a special rheostat which regulates the operating speed from a minimum of four frames per second, to fifty or more f.p.s.

Certain models also include a tachometer to indicate the speed at which the camera is running.

Special models have recently been marketed, utilizing transistor systems in order to ensure that speed is maintained constant to a high degree. These motors are combined with others incorporating signal generators inserted in their circuits, and are employed in new methods for synchronizing image and sound. Among these units, the DC servo motor is best known. This is a small sized unit containing a

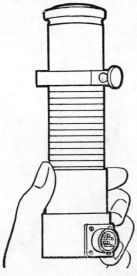

Fig. 17. Kinotechnique motor for Cameflex with transistorized speed regulation. This is typical of the light weight and precision provided by modern techniques.

source which generates magnetic pulses at a determined frequency. These are compared by an electronic unit to a similar signal coming from a crystal. Should there be a difference between such signals the motor is automatically corrected and a constancy of 0·001% is achieved. Some models allow for selecting speeds and thus working as a variable speed motor, but these must have a high degree of constancy. The main advantage of this type of motor is that it can

37

function without cables for synchronizing which affords easy camera handling.

Motors are generally separate units from the camera and in many cases can be easily mounted on it, and easily interchanged. They generally incorporate the starting switch, as well as a socket for the feed cable. They run with either single, two-, or three-phase, AC, or DC, at voltages varying according to make and model, ranging from 8, 12, 16 or 24 volts for DC from battery source, or 90, 110 or 220/230 v. with AC for studio running.

SPRING DRIVE. Spring (or mechanical) motors work on similar principles to the drive of gramophones early this century. They are generally built into the camera body and operate under a spring (or two in some cameras) held in tension by a complex gear set. Speed is regulated by a special governor working by centrifugal force. The governor can be adjusted from the outside by means of a dial, in order to select the most convenient speed, and its action on the mechanism does not allow speed variations greater than 4 per cent of the pre-set working speed.

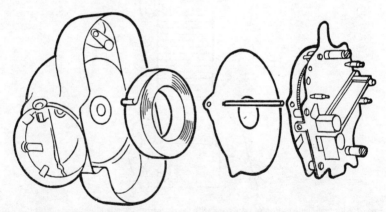

Fig. 18. Method of fitting the spring drive in the Bell & Howell Filmo. Note how the shape of the camera is governed by the design of the various mechanisms.

The spring is wound by turning a handle, which can be quite long in some cameras, or a collapsible, non-rotating winding key. In some instruments like the Cameraflex and the Konvas Automatic, the spring drive was an easily installed separate unit. Nowadays, spring drive tends to be discontinued because of its excessive weight and bulk, as against modern lightweight, midget electric motors.

38

# Camera controls

The camera controls and indicating instruments are the elements which enable the camera to be operated, and they provide information on how it is running. These components are located either behind or at the side of the camera, and they are of great help in handling the camera properly while it is operating. The main controls are:

*Starting switch*

The starting switch is installed either on the motor itself or on the feed cable. In general it consists of an adequately dimensioned toggle switch, with protection devices to avoid accidents while handling the camera. Spring-driven cameras are started by pressing on a push-button which releases the mechanism lock.

*External focusing control*

In most studio cameras, focusing is effected by means of controls geared to the lens focus ring. Such controls are calibrated to a high degree of accuracy, and they are located for easy use by the assistant camera operator.

*External iris control*

Besides the external focusing control, some European cameras are provided with a similar device to adjust the diaphragm without touching the lens. This control uses interchangeable plates and can be applied to any type of lens.

*Variable shutter control*

As explained above, the shutter opening control is effected by means of a lever sliding over a scale which can be calibrated each ten degrees from maximum to minimum openings (as in the Mitchell and Newall cameras) or with special calibration (Debrie cameras).

*Automatic dissolve control*

This is an additional feature provided on the most up-to-date studio cameras. It comprises two push-buttons which close or open the shutter automatically thus producing a dissolve or fade effect at the beginning or at the end of a take, over a length of film of about five feet.

*Footage and exposed-frame counters*

These are small counters connected to the main movements,

which indicate the amount of exposed film. The frame counter is used for special work requiring such information. In some cameras the footage counter is of a simpler type connected to a lever inside the film storage magazine, which bears on the roll of film.

In some studio cameras the counters have their own light source to facilitate readings when the lighting level is low. Counters are provided with a knob to turn them to zero when changing the film magazine.

### Built-in telemeter (rangefinder)

This is an accessory to the focusing control whereby the camera assistant can obtain exact focusing without using a measuring tape.

### Magazine footage counter

This is a dial indicator showing the amount of exposed film and the amount remaining in the feed magazine chamber. It is very useful since it allows immediate readings of raw stock and exposed film, data which the camera assistant must fill in on his photographic report sheets.

### Exposure speed indicator

The work speed of the camera is controlled by the electric motor itself (if it is a variable-speed motor), and is indicated by the rheostat markings, as well as by a detachable speed indicator. In some cameras, this speed indicator or tachometer is built in, while in others it is coupled to the motor. Their scales are calibrated in frames per second.

### Automatic safety switch

Many cameras designed for direct sound recording, run so noiselessly that if any mishap should occur inside (oversize loop, film running off the track) the operator will not realize it. Therefore an automatic device is provided whereby the slight pressure of the mis-carried film acts upon an adequately placed plate which stops the camera automatically. In some cameras, this is complemented by a warning light on the outside. The automatic safety switch is used in the best studio cameras or sound-on-film cameras.

### Spirit level

This small item is of great use to the operator when mounting the camera. Since the camera's position must be changed frequently for

40

shooting from different angles, the adjustment of the tripod or mounting element must be modified, and consequently it is essential to check the level of the camera. These instruments are located either in front of or behind the camera, and they can be either spirit-levels or oil-filled levels.

## Viewing system

The viewfinder is an optical system working in combination with the camera lenses and providing the operator with an exact view of the image being recorded on the film. Many years hard work have been put into the search for a viewing system which would show an image of the field as framed by the aperture and taken by the shooting lens.

The first such cameras were built in France. Framing was obtained through the thickness of the film or by withdrawing it from the camera aperture and substituting a piece of translucent material. When camera manufacturing crossed the Atlantic, American manufacturers introduced the camera side-framing viewfinder working independently of the taking lens. Thus the camera was for the first time able to move, and could be panned and travelled. This improvement was soon widely accepted by all cinematographers, and Europeans immediately started to manufacture their cameras with a side viewfinder, since the new system saved time and made for far greater convenience with all types of framing. The main European viewfinder conceived on these lines was the Orthoviseur developed by Debrie for their Parvo T and Super Parvo cameras. With the progress of research, the viewing and focusing system of the modern camera has become more and more elaborate. The different viewing systems which are found on a wide range of cameras are the following.

### Side viewfinder

This is the type used in some old portable camera models. It is fixed to the side of the camera and is carefully centred in relation to the camera aperture. It affords an image obtained through an optical system of small lenses, which is a replica of the taking lens. Some cameras have these viewing lenses mounted on a small turret so that, by displacing the tube's eye piece along a calibrated scale, the operator can correct for parallax, which is the angle formed by the different viewing positions of the tube and the taking lens.

## Monitoring viewfinder

This viewfinder is known as a monitor since its work is complementary to a focusing and framing device through the taking lens. It is also placed at the side of the camera and produces an upright image correct from left to right. The size of the image is $1\frac{7}{8} \times 3\frac{5}{16}$ in. (47 × 84 mm) which allows more than one person to look at it at the same time.

The image obtained is projected by a short focal length optical system (consisting of a wide angle lens and a porro prism) upon a ground glass. The size of this image is controlled by means of separate masks which are inserted in a slot, or by four masking (or graticule) lines which are adjusted externally by means of knobs, so as to reproduce the field actually taken by the camera lens. The graticule system also allows the operator to see what is happening just outside the effective field, so that he can prevent unwanted objects appearing in the picture.

Other characteristics of the monitor viewfinder are automatic focusing control, and easy panning while keeping the operator's head away from the camera and with both eyes open, as well as

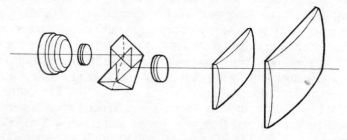

Fig. 19. Optical design of a side viewfinder showing a wide angle lens, a porro prism, a magnification crystal and a large ground glass.

checking the field covered by the various lenses. These range in focal length from 25 to 152 mm in the 35 mm gauge camera, and from 13 to 75 mm (approx) in the 16 mm gauge model.

Among well known monitor viewfinders are those made by the Mitchell Corp., as described above. Messrs. Bach-Auricon, Maurer, Bell & Howell, and Maier-Hancock have also produced monitor viewfinder models, devised specially for 16 mm cameras. Monitor viewfinders are seldom used on up-to-date cameras, except for heavy studio equipment. They are being replaced by devices with TV screens.

42

## Viewfinder through taking lens

The operator requires the image framed in the viewfinder to be exactly the same as the one being recorded on the film, and this necessitates a focusing and framing device free from the parallax problems encountered with side viewfinders. The search for these qualities led to the development of a mechanical device for framing and focusing, which displaces the film from behind the taking lens and places a ground glass in its stead, on which the image is projected.

Two important manufacturers adopted this system: the Mitchell Camera Corp. in the U.S.A. for all their early models, and Ets. André Debrie in France for their Parvo and Super Parvo cameras.

The Mitchell Corp. used a method developed by John E. Leonard and subsequently improved. Basically, it consists in displacing the camera body to one side so that a special lens focusing system may be placed behind the camera taking lens; the image projected on the lens can be magnified from 5 to 10 times, thus obtaining good focus control. This displacement (often called *rackover*) is achieved by building the camera in two parts. The *camera base* is fixed to the tripod and the taking lenses are mounted on it. The *camera body* comprises the film drive mechanism, the magazines and the viewfinder, and it is displaced over slides on the base by means of a rackover handle. By displacing the camera body so that the viewfinder is placed behind the lens, the framing obtained is perfect, since it is effected through the taking lens and the aperture through which the film is exposed.

The method adopted by the Debrie company was developed from

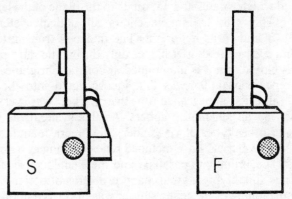

Fig. 20. (S) Front view of rackover type camera in shooting position; (F) the same camera in focusing position.

a principle introduced by the Russell camera and was based on the sideways rotation of the aperture together with the film, simultaneously placing an identical aperture with a ground glass behind the lens. A permanent optical system affords a magnified upright image correct from left to right, either through the film itself or through the ground glass. The aperture switchover mechanism is simply and instantly operated by means of a knob behind the camera (or on top of it in the Parvo mod. L).

When this system was developed, framing and focusing through the film was common practice. To facilitate the work of the operator and to prevent his being momentarily dazzled, a thick black cloth was used around the optical tube, in the fashion of old-time photographers. When emulsions became more sensitive, necessitating an appreciable closing of the lens diaphragm, and with the advent of colour film with its black anti-halo coating, focusing and framing through the film became increasingly difficult.

*Reflex viewing*

Viewfinding by displacing the film and substituting a ground glass does indeed provide an accurate image devoid of parallax, but it is not practical when shooting a moving subject. We have seen that when framing by this method, the camera cannot be operating, and if panning or travelling has to be effected, the operator must use the monitor viewfinder as a guide.

To obviate this problem, August Arnold, engineer of the German company Arnold & Richter, developed in 1931 the ingenious reflex viewfinder system. Reflex viewing signifies the viewing of an image as reflected by a shutter whose blades are silvered on their front surfaces, and which rotates at a 45° angle to the plane of the lens and of the film. This reflected image enters an optical system which magnifies it and turns it upright. The image is transmitted to the operator's eye by the shutter blades only during the short period the shutter is closed, but it is maintained at constant brightness.

The reflex viewfinder was first incorporated into the Arriflex camera, and its appearance on the market was very widely welcomed by all cinematographers. As this system was evidently superior to other types of viewfinder, all camera manufacturers in Europe, and America, have included reflex viewing systems in their cameras. They eliminate parallax, and the elements needed to correct it, thus simplifying a great many problems of design.

The positioning of the reflex shutter was improved upon by some other manufacturers. For example: Debrie and Eclair have placed

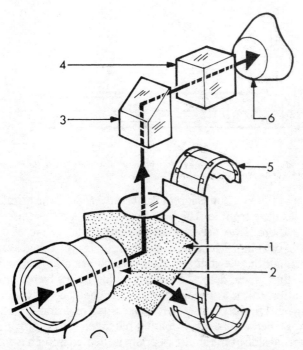

Fig. 21. Reflex shutter. (1) Mirrored shutter blade; (2) taking lens; (3) prism; (4) viewfinder tube prism; (5) film; (6) eyepiece.

the shaft of the shutter beneath the lens, so that the blades blank out the frame from side to side, which facilitates quick panning by reducing the stroboscopic effect. This layout also permits reflection of the image from the wide side of the aperture, instead of from the narrow side as in the Arriflex. This method of mirroring allows for the use of extremely wide angle lenses and permits the design of more convenient camera shapes.

A different type of reflex viewing system has been adopted on some cameras, such as the Pathé, Bolex, and others. It consists of inserting a semi-reflecting mirror between the lens and the aperture, at an angle of 45° to the optical axis. This mirror splits the light rays forming the image, some of which are diverted to the reflex viewing system, while the rest continue straight through the aperture.

The semireflecting mirror may be either a thin specially-treated crystal foil or the face of a specially conditioned prism. By both methods 8% of the light is reflected. The foil system, as compared to the prism, has the disadvantage of producing a double image on the magnifying viewing glass. The secondary image is produced by the

45

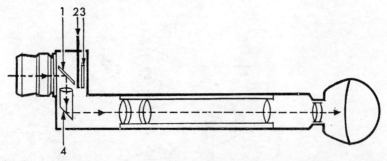

Fig. 22. Method of operation of a reflex system with mirror at 45°. (1) Semi-reflecting mirror, (2) shutter, (3) plane of the film, (4) prism.

other face of the foil, but as it represents only 15% of the primary image, it gives little trouble. The loss of light through this mirror is so small that there is no need to compensate for it by increasing the diaphragm opening. Moreover, sufficiently bright images are obtained through the viewfinder, images which are also free of flicker, this being the typical defect of reflex viewing by a silvered shutter.

A variation to the rotating reflex shutter has been introduced in the Japanese Doiflex Camera. It makes use of a focal plane disc shutter, together with a reciprocating balanced reflex mirror. Close to the external side of the shutter a prism is located in such a way that when the shutter blocks the film aperture, the prism comes down into place completing a reflex viewing optical system. As the shutter opens, the prism is elevated, interrupting the reflex vision, and the film aperture is revealed to expose the film frame behind.

A useful auxiliary device for the reflex viewing and focusing system is the periscopic viewer, which allows for swivelling in all directions and thus for viewing from any position. Some makers, (e.g. Eclair) have built this device into the camera itself, while others such as Arnold & Richter supply it as an accessory for their Arriflex cameras. A highly novel device has been designed and built in the U.S.S.R. which consists of a flexible cable connected to a special viewing mask for the operator. The operator can view from any position in relation to the camera by means of this cable, which makes use of the principle of coherent fibre optics.

### Reflex TV monitor

The gradual growth of reflex viewing systems has been the result of continuous efforts made to obtain a sharp image, exactly framed and with freedom of vision for the operator. A new step in this process has been to apply electronics to optical cinema equipment

46

by adding a closed-circuit TV camera to the reflex optical viewing systems of some film instruments.

This allows the scene being shot to be viewed remotely from the camera itself on TV monitors placed in a part of the set away from the main event being covered. This in turn facilitates a constant view of the scene as it is being recorded on film. The film director and the director of photography can therefore watch the scene simultaneously through the taking camera, and as these TV signals can be recorded on video tape, the whole scene can be played back immediately to decide the corrections to the camera movement or the action of the players that both may want to introduce. This in certain conditions provides more economical production of a film. It also permits both technicians to operate several cameras at the same time, with precise viewing of what all of them are taking, even to the point of starting and stopping the cameras from the central console where viewing is effected.

Film production using these methods is just beginning, and opens the way to innumerable possibilities for a more dynamic and efficient use of the cine camera.

The electronic viewing system has been applied both to studio and to hand-held cameras. The system generally comprises a small vidicon-type television camera built into the motion picture camera. The television camera records the image supplied by a reflex viewer on to a ground glass. Alternately some equipment uses a beamsplitter prism supplying two images. One is directed to the optical view finder of the motion picture camera and the other is directed to the small television camera which transmits that image through a cable to a monitor. This system requires an optical finder with a very bright image to compensate for the loss in the video system and to afford a good television image. But the inclusion of an electronic camera also brings about certain disadvantages. For example, one of them is that when the camera is operating, either of each two fields is analysed on a darkened target. To overcome this, a complex synchronization system has been built, as well as a self-adjusting variable amplification device to eliminate the resultant blinking as much as possible.

This method was applied to the Aäton camera by its maker J. P. Beauviala with excellent results. This camera is very easy to handle, and the mechanical layout of its elements allows for a easy installation of the video unit, which is interchangeable and is driven by its own power source. The controls for operating the video unit and the HF transmitter are installed in the power source itself. This is fitted to a special belt worn by the camera operator. The camera is connected by only one cable. The signal from the video viewfinder is of the standard type and is transmitted to the video recorder through a cable of 75 ohms, or through a RF transmitter.

In the case of other hand held cameras, like the Bolex 16 Pro, part of the viewfinder is removed and is replaced by an electronic viewfinder. The image may be viewed on a monitor which can be placed a considerable distance away from the camera.

The Mitchell Company some time ago introduced the System 35 for its Mark II camera. This consists of a special blimp, the main door of which houses a one-inch vidicon tube with a negative field-flattener cemented to its face. The camera directly feeds the electronic viewfinder, which is normally mounted on the camera door but can be turned for viewing from any position on or off the camera. The viewfinder is a standard five-inch TV monitor modified to have 450-line horizontal resolution and designed for minimum size and weight. To the cameraman or his assistant, this unit displays a bright, crisp, high-resolution picture free from parallax and appreciable flicker.

The Arnold & Richter Company has built a special unit, known as the "Electronic Cam", into a blimp which houses the Arriflex IIC camera with 1000 ft. (300 m) magazine and a coupled electronic unit. This is a Plumbikon camera installed on the door of the blimp, an optical system catching the image from a beam-splitting prism, a light flux compensating system based on a rotating disc which maintains the same amount of light whenever the camera is running or stopped, and a monitor installed behind the blimp with a seven inch rectangular screen with a large number of controls, including gamma corrector. The Electronic Cam system is very elaborate and generally comprises three motion picture cameras and a camera control desk with four monitors for direct supervision and editing of the material shot. The equipment operates with a standard of 625 lines and an interlaced ratio of 2:1.

## Detachable camera parts

*Film supply system*

The chambers or the compartments where the raw stock and the exposed film are stored are known as magazines. Early in the history of motion pictures, the magazines were housed inside the camera body, and largely governed its shape. Three main systems were evolved: one, introduced by Debrie in 1908 in the Parvo camera, another used by most of the makers in the United Kingdom, and a third adopted by Duval, the French mechanic who developed the Pathé camera.

The Debrie system was the most compact of the three: the two magazines were placed vertically and parallel within the camera box and turning on the same shaft. The size of the camera was thus greatly reduced and it gave the instrument a box shape similar to the still photo camera which the Eastman Kodak Company was making so popular at the time in their specific market. For many years Debrie cameras maintained this arrangement in their Parvo and Super Parvo models and, similarly, other makers in Italy, Great Britain, and the Soviet Union utilized this method for housing magazines. But since it implied certain limitations this design concept has been discontinued over the past few years.

In the first instruments produced by British makers, the magazines were placed one on top of the other, inside the camera body, which thus became very bulky. Famous instruments like the Moy, the Williamson, the Darling and the Newman Sinclair were good examples of this system which has now been discontinued.

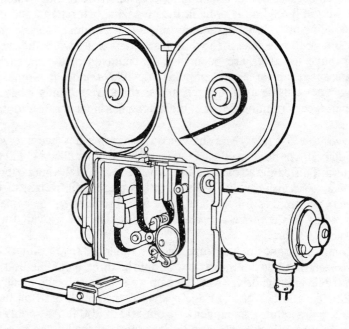

Fig. 23. Typical arrangement of a motion picture camera. Standard double compartment magazine opened, and classical arrangement for threading the film.

When, in 1905, the Pathé Fréres Company launched into the market the camera which made them famous, one of its features was the magazine position, which was totally different from previous systems. Two separate magazines were mounted on top of the camera body and this was so widely accepted by cinematographers, that some years later Bell & Howell Company in America adopted and improved on this system for their new all-metal camera: a double chamber magazine placed on top of the body, which nowadays has been adopted by most camera manufacturers. This system is driven by belt transmission to the take-up chamber. The film comes out and goes into the two chambers through slots provided with plush rollers to avoid light leaking in and also to protect the emulsion. Some models are provided with a device which closes these slots automatically when the magazine is detached from the camera body.

Another special type of film storage is known as the magazine camera; it is used mostly with lightweight cameras and houses the continuous drive in the magazine. One of the first cameras to adopt this system was the Akeley, designed for scientific explorers and news cameramen. The outstanding characteristic of this system is that all the threading is done in the magazine beforehand and thus the loading on o the camera takes only a few seconds. This is a great advantage to newsreel men who must often reload while the events they have to cover are occurring. Instruments of the magazine-camera system are very popular nowadays, and in some the magazines can be interchanged in less than five seconds while the camera keeps running. Most of the magazines incorporate a footage counter.

Over the last few years the coaxial magazine has become very popular. It was conceived as a independent unit installed behind the camera. This camera construction allows the size of the magazine to be reduced considerably. It also lightens the overall weight of the camera and makes for fast and easy film threading in the camera. According to the makers, coaxial magazines can be provided with two access doors.

One is for raw stock storage and the other for take-up film. We have seen that coaxial magazines adopt the three-plane-method for film travel and the drive from the camera is always mechanical.

Finally, another film storage system is the spool, used on hand held cameras and with capacities from 100 to 200 ft. As spools are supplied with black protective leaders they can be loaded into the camera or interchanged in daylight.

# Camera Lenses

The lens is an optical device with the function of imaging the subjects within its field of view in a controlled or regulated manner in the plane of the film at the aperture.

The size of the image produced by the camera lens is regulated by its *focal length*. This is the distance from a point within the lens when focused at infinity, to a plane perpendicular to its axis where a clear image is produced.

A lens produces a circular image and the rectangle of the aperture fits the circle. In still photography, lenses are classified as *normal*, *wide angle* or *telephoto*, when their focal lengths are, respectively, about the same, smaller or greater than the diagonal of the aperture covered by the image. In motion picture photography, however, such classifications are applied with focal length values twice those of still photography. In the six gauges used nowadays in cinematography, the following are normal lenses:

| Film gauge: | 8 mm | 9·5 mm | 16 mm | 35 mm | 65/70 mm |
|---|---|---|---|---|---|
| Focal length: | 13 mm | 20 mm | 25 mm | 50 mm | 85/100 mm |

Normal lenses cover a medium field and the images produced are similar in their proportions in respect to the frame, to those produced by human sight. Wide angle lenses cover an ample field of view, which appreciably reduces the proportions of the elements making up the image. On the other hand, telephoto lenses cover a limited field but magnify the elements in the image considerably.

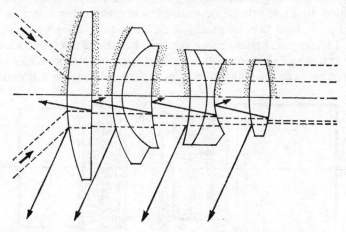

Fig. 24. Lengthwise section of lens showing path of light rays through crystal elements and internal reflections. Shaded parts on elements denote their anti-halo treatment.

Important progress has been achieved in the last few years, in the quality of image produced by still photography and motion picture lenses. These improvements are the result of new and very complex mathematical formulae made possible by the use of electronic computers, the production of new types of glass, the application of anti-reflective coatings on the faces of the lens elements (which improves image contrast), and the combination of glasses to improve colour rendition (apochromatic lenses).

Lenses for cinematography are made in several contries. The best known makes are: Astro, Schneider, Kilfitt, and Zeiss in the German Federal Republic; Eastman, Bausch & Lomb, Century, Elgeet, Panavision, and Wollensak in the U.S.A.; Kern-Paillard in Switzerland; Angenieux, Berthiot and Kinoptik in France; Dallmeyer, Ross and Taylor-Hobson in Britain; Canon, Cosmicar, Kowa, Nikon, Prominar, Sun and Komura in Japan; and Foton in the Soviet Union.

*Lens mount*

The individual lenses making up the optical unit are installed in a special metal holder called the lens mount. Its task is to house the complete lens and provide an adequate means to effect micro-metric displacements of the various elements along the same axis. The mounts are built with a series of specially connected brass or duralumin cylinders.

A lens for cinematography is generally provided with two rings: one regulates the displacement of the various optical elements in relation to each other (focus ring), while the other controls the passage of light rays by means of an internal iris (diaphragm ring). The focusing ring acts upon a section of a helical pitch thread; this ring is marked all round with a scale of values corresponding to distances between the plane of the film and the subject; the calibrations

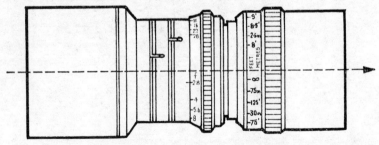

Fig. 25. Lens for motion picture camera in its mount, with focusing ring and diaphragm (iris) ring.

may be in feet, or in metres or both. In lenses of a short focal length these values start off from very short range (a few inches) and infinity is reached with only a short turn. On the other hand, lenses of long focal length start off from a minimum of more than six feet and the ring must be turned a long way to reach the other end of the scale.

The diaphragm or iris ring is calibrated in "f" or "T" values. The "f" values correspond to a mathematical determination of the capacity of the lens to admit light rays, and are obtained by dividing the focal length by the diameter of the image-forming light beam. "T" values allow for light losses in the lens caused by absorption, reflection, etc. and are therefore more accurate than "f" values and are very useful when working with lenses comprising a large number of elements e.g.: zoom lenses.

Filters and lens hoods (sunshades) are generally installed at the front end of lenses where the barrel is provided with a screw-in thread. The other end of the lens barrel fits into the camera. There are several methods of attaching the lens. Some 16 mm cameras allow for the installation of lightweight lenses with "C" type thread, but this method is not effective with heavier items. Each manufacturer has conceived individual mounting methods, according to the

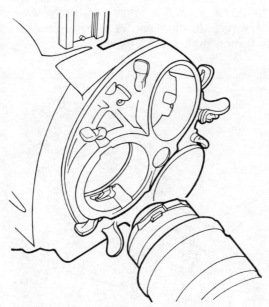

Fig. 26. New design of camera and lens mount specially conceived for the long and heavy zoom lenses.

characteristics of each model. Many 35 mm cameras use the bayonet principle, while others use the helical thread system or guides and retaining devices. Sometimes lenses can be interchanged among cameras from the same maker but more often this is only possible with the aid of adaptors sold by camera accessory dealers.

*Mounting the camera lenses*

The mounting of lenses on the 35 mm camera is effected by either of two methods. One method is single mounting, and is used with only one lens. The other consists of mounting several lenses on a rotating disc or spyder arm called a lens turret.

The single mount system is used on heavy studio cameras, to meet sound-proofing and remote-control-focusing requirements. It is also used on portable cameras requiring simplified lens positioning and light weight.

Some cameras have a single zoom or vari-focal lens which cannot be interchanged. Part of this long lens is built into the camera body so as to afford a better balance of the instrument and also achieve a more functional shape. The application of these concepts to semi-professional 16 mm cameras is a consequence of their many advantages proved over years in amateur 8 mm instruments.

The lens turret method is more frequently used on standard cameras. The turret usually carries three or four lenses which are placed in position by means of clips which fit into grooves in the turret.

Some turrets are star shaped and the lens sockets have been

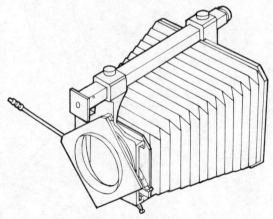

Fig. 27. The adjustable bellows allows the hood to shield lenses of differing viewing angles. Figure shows matte box and sunshade of Arriflex 16 ST camera.

designed with the lens axes divergent, so that they do not interfere with each other's fields.

## Sunshade and matte box

This assembly is an essential accessory to the camera. It is intended mainly to protect the lens from reflections, while it also allows for the insertion of filters and masks.

The assembly generally comprises a boom and adjustable bellows, with accessories for its extension and retraction. Some of these sunshades are built so that they can only be used with lenses of medium angle, and must be interchanged with a more open type when using wide angle lenses.

## Camera construction concepts

Cameras at present available on the market are designed for a wide range of different purposes. These camera types can be grouped under the following main headings: studio cameras, noiseless portable models, field cameras, lightweight cameras, sound-on-film cameras and special purpose instruments.

## Studio cameras

For many years studio cameras have been a heavy construction designed for sync sound shooting on a separate strip and mainly, save for a few exceptions, for shooting 35, 65 or 70 mm gauge film.

They are provided with many refinements such as noiseless running, an intermittent drive system with register pins, the use of large film capacity magazines (1,000 ft. or 300 m for the 35 mm format) external controls for lens focus, variable shutter, dissolve device, automatic safety switch, monitor viewfinder and a back projection synchronization device. It is, therefore, a high cost instrument and is used in slow and costly shooting programmes where high technical quality is imperative—i.e. for large budget films. Instruments like the Mitchell BNC, BNCR, Panavision Studio, Cinema Products XR-35, Druzhba, Mir or Camé 300 Reflex are good examples of studio cameras.

In design a studio camera, makers aim to combine a high grade of performance with all available devices to facilitate easy handling and operation. Problems of size and weight are disregarded, but care is taken to obtain the highest precision in recording the image (with double claw shuttle and register pins on both sides of the film), a totally noiseless drive, and a wide range of resources to comply with an increasing number of technical requirements. Such cameras are therefore usually housed in bulky bodies where the film drive mechanism is installed on shock absorbers to reduce vibration and silence mechanical noise. The body usually has separate castings for the mechanical unit, for the magazine housing, and even for the drive motor housing.

In most studio cameras the magazines are placed on top, the motor on one side and the various controls and the viewfinder eyepiece behind the camera. The monitor viewfinder is on one side while at the front there is only a single lens to reduce the risk of escaping noise. This lens is connected to external controls to regulate focus and is protected, in some models, by a sound dampening device which also supports the sunshade and matte box/filter holder.

Figure 28 shows a classical design adopted by several makers of heavy studio cameras. The drive motor is generally of the synchronous or crystal controlled type. It is coupled at right angles through helicoid gears to the shaft of the intermittent drive system. The coupling is usually of resilient type because the motor is normally interchangeable in order to adapt the camera to different requirements. The intermittent drive shaft drives the shutter and the main sprocket through helicoid gears on the transmission shaft,

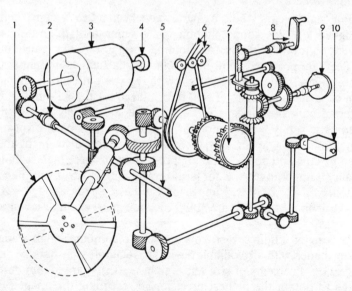

Fig. 28. (1) Variable shutter, (2) resilient coupling, (3) drive motor, (4) manual movement turning knob, (5) shaft to the intermittent mechanism, (6) magazine drive, (7) main sprocket, (8) variable shutter lever, (9) dissolve device, (10) film and frame counters.

while another gear shaft operates the tachometer, the shutter opening adjustment and the dissolve device.

*Noiseless portable cameras*

Recent studio instruments have been designed to maintain the most important of the above characteristics, but within a much smaller volume and lighter weight, making the camera suitable for shoulder operation. This improvement has been made possible by progress in modern technology and has radically changed concepts of the possibilities and limitations of studio cameras, and therefore of film production economics.

*Field cameras*

This term has been applied to the instrument which provides

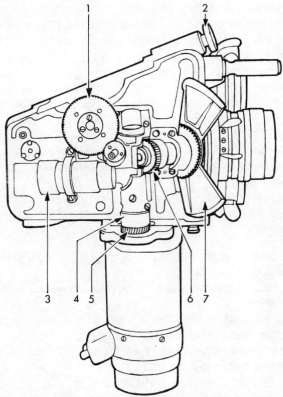

Fig. 29. (1) Intermediate gear, (2) knurled knob for securing magazine, (3) tachometer, (4) housing for vertical shaft, (5) vertical shaft with gear, (6) gear for shutter, (7) mirror reflex shutter.

many of the facilities of the studio camera, but which is not totally noiseless and which also lacks some of its refinements. Until a few years ago these instruments were used for shooting silent takes outdoors, or by adding a blimp, in the studio. They are or were cameras of medium weight, as for example, the Mitchell, Vinten, Windsor, etc. Their mechanism is generally similar to that of the studio cameras. More recent trends in portability have tended to eliminate the distinction between the two types.

*Lightweight cameras*

For many years lightweight camera designs were mainly aimed to satisfy the demands of news coverage. After the Second World War two such cameras, the Arriflex and the Cameflex which fulfilled the urgent requirements of low budget film makers, also proved to be flexible enough for many other types of production. Their wide acceptance for over twenty years in the production of shorts and feature films clearly demonstrated that an efficient but easily carried instrument was vital for bringing agility to film production. Mobility has become an increasingly important factor in reducing production costs to a minimum. The design for this type of camera must therefore take into account functionality, good registration quality, wide operational scope and multiple accessories, but also maintain small weight and volume, so that the instrument can be easily handled and carried by only one person. These priorities gradually evolved over the years for 35 mm cameras but were also adopted for 16 mm instruments when this format gained wider acceptance in the professional field.

The mechanical design of such cameras has varied considerably with each particular instrument. However, general tendencies can be noted as follows:

(i)  the camera body volume is strictly the sum of its different component elements;
(ii)  efforts are made to make the mechanical system as simple as possible;
(iii)  ease for holding with the hands with a marked tendency to use the operator's shoulder as support;
(iv)  use of pre-threaded magazines, especially of the coaxial type which are the most compact;
(v)  a reduction of the size of the drive motor;
(vi)  the instrument is conceived as a basic unit, to which accessories are added to increase its operational possibilities.

## Sound on film cameras

A demand created by television for a camera to simultaneously record image and sound on the same film, determined the design of special 16 mm cameras for this purpose. The camera had to run noiselessly and record sound by optical or magnetic means on the film. The nature of the work also required a relatively lightweight instrument. Technological evolution in this specific field led to the increasing use of easily removable magnetic (rather than optical) recording units which allowed the camera to be applied to other purposes, and also the adoption of the double system to cater for editing requirements. The camera too, tended to be lighter. The result was a self blimped camera adequate for all types of work, with many refinements and capable of recording sound on the film itself and for support on the shoulder. This camera is very suitable for shooting documentaries with direct sound recording, for covering conferences and interviews, or for silent shooting. Self blimping was the most complex technical problem to solve and it was achieved by reducing gears to a minimum (for example, the Eclair 16 NPR uses the same shaft for the motor and for the shutter). Or it was done by using a compact body acting as a blimp in which all the camera mechanism is mounted on a single platen which is acoustically floating within the housing in order to absorb the noise of the running motor—limiting it to a minimum of 31 dB, as in the case of the Arriflex 16 BL. This design concept arises from the maker's desire to place no limits on the mechanical possibilities of the intermittent drive system. In other aspects the design of these instruments does not differ from the principles set out above.

## Special purpose cameras

Special purpose cameras cover a wide range of uses and requirements and consequently their design and basic mechanical concepts are determined by the purpose to which each camera will be applied.

## Camera accessories

Besides the camera, the shooting of a film requires a number of accessory elements, which widen its possibilities considerably.

## The tripod

THE TRIPOD LEGS. In order to provide a firm and portable base to mount the camera on, early cinematographers adopted the well-

59

known photographic tripod, and to this they subsequently added a head with certain mechanical characteristics. The tripod still keeps its original design, but is now stronger; it must be at the same time durable, stable and easily adjusted.

The tripod comprises three legs of wood or metal. Wood is more commonly used. Many operators prefer metal legs, generally made of duraluminium because of their resistance to rough handling, humidity and very low temperatures. Wooden legs are made of specially treated beech or maple, because of their strength, light weight, and flexibility. Each leg is tipped with aluminium shoes provided with a spur and steel point to avoid sliding.

The overall length of the legs varies with the model, and the tripod height is adjusted by extending or retracting the legs. The most common tripod heights are 7 ft. 3 in. (220 cms.) fully extended, and 4 ft. 3 in. (130 cms.) with retracted (collapsed) legs. Besides the standard height tripod, there is a specially low model, known as the "baby", whose legs are about half the length of the standard ones, for very low level shots ("worm's eye" views).

THE TRIPOD HEAD. One of the most important parts of the tripod is the head, on to which the camera is mounted, and from which it

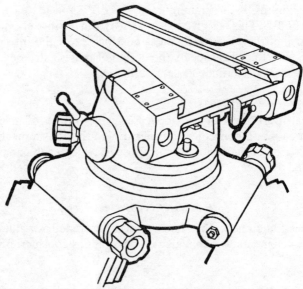

Fig. 30. Friction tripod head. Note the female dovetail for mounting the camera, typical of French cameras.

should be capable of swivelling in all planes. There is a large variety of tripod head designs, amongst which four are widely used.

(i)   the friction head,
(ii)  the gyroscopic head,
(iii) the gear head,
(iv)  the fluid head.

All four are easily disassembled and interchanged.

The friction head is the commonest, since it is easy to operate, light in weight, and affords smooth movements. As indicated by its name, it is provided with friction surfaces treated with special grease to provide the smoothest possible movement.

The gyroscopic or gyro head is more elaborate and of heavier build. Its outstanding feature is the easy operation for panning, especially on fast moving subjects, liable to alter their direction. Its mechanism consists of a gear system which turns a flywheel, damping out irregularities in the panning motion. Another feature is its adaptability to any tripod position, which allows the camera to be set level without having to adjust the length of tripod legs. This feature is so much of a help that it has been adopted on other types of head. This level adjusting device known as the floating bowl, consists of a half sphere which is part of the tripod head and an adjustable clasp round it which is a part of the leg hinge casting. When the clasp is loosened the half sphere can be moved about in its seating and the head can be adjusted to various angles. With the help of the spirit level on the tripod head the operator can adjust the position without the need to adjust the length of the leg. This method was devised by Carl E. Akeley in the silent movie era for his famous camera. But despite of its many advantages it was neglected until recently.

The gear heads are the bulkiest. They are used with studio cameras and are provided with a large number of improvements

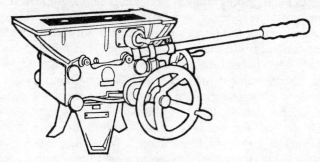

Fig. 31. Heavier studio camera gear head. Horizontal and vertical movements are by rotating the handwheels.

which make them very easy to operate. Their design is based on the action of a mechanism controlled by hand-operated wheels, which drive the horizontal panning and vertical tilting actions through racks and gears. They are built to give a very smooth and easy panning action.

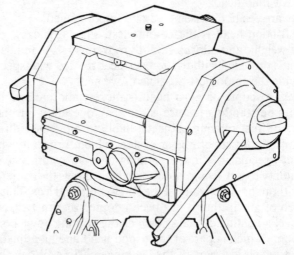

Fig. 32. O'Connor fluid head specially suited for heavy studio cameras.

The tripod head known as the fluid head appeared on the market more recently. It consists of two factory-sealed units containing a special fluid. One of the units is for panning while the other is for tilting. They afford great ease of action and smooth operation, with similar results to the gyro head.

*Hydraulic pedestal*

The old still photography tripod, adapted and improved for motion pictures, has recently been joined by a competitor which may in the future turn out to be its substitute. It is a hydraulic pedestal of similar dimensions to the tripod, and which is also collapsible, compact for easy transportation and with a device for adjusting its height. The instrument, made by the O'Connor Company of California, allows for a new method for supporting the camera, which is different from that of all its forerunners. The instrument is known as the Hydro-ped and consists of a sturdily built magnesium alloy column which can be rapidly extended, by turning a handle, up to a height of 60 in. Its hydraulic system allows for setting level on any ground and it can be folded down to a minimum length of 30 in. for easy transportation. The desired tripod head is installed at its top end, and the makers claim that it is four times as steady as a standard tripod when panning or tilting. It is designed for use with equipment weighing up to 100 lbs. Its own all up weight is less than 20 lbs.

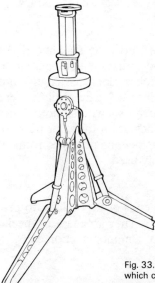

Fig. 33. The Hydro-ped, a sturdily-built magnesium alloy column which can be rapidly extended by turning a handle. Its hydraulic system allows for setting at level on any ground.

*Rolling tripod*

The camera position must be changed continually while shooting a film. In a studio the rolling tripod or camera pedestal is very often used, as it permits repositioning of the camera without dismounting it.

The rolling tripod is very similar to the standard tripod, but it is provided with a three-wheel rolling attachment, allowing the unit to be moved along.

The camera pedestal or rolling support is a much heavier and more elaborate device. It consists of a metal column provided with a device for raising the camera, and has a specially designed wheel assembly, control lever, position fixing device, etc. Camera pedestals are widely used in European cinema and TV studios. The best known manufacturers are Houston Fearless in the United States, Eclair International Diffusion and André Debrie in France, and Vinten Ltd. in the U.K.

### Gimbal tripod

When shooting on board ship, this tripod is used to keep the head level and steady, no matter what the direction of rolling. The steadying and levelling effect is produced by a device based on the Cardan principle. It is of rugged construction and is immediately identified by the heavy weight suspended between the tripod legs.

### Spider

This is a very simple device which ensures the stability of the tripod. It consists of three metal or wooden arms which open up to form a star or "Y". Each arm has notches along its length, into which the points of the tripod legs are inserted. The spider is very useful for shooting in the studio or on locations with smooth floors where tripod legs tend to slide. Another device for the same purpose is the triangle. It is less compact than a spider and not so convenient to move about. Both, however, are widely used.

### Suction cups

These are sometimes installed on the ends of tripod legs, to prevent them sliding on highly polished floors. They are made of special anti-slide material, and have the shape of common suction cups.

### Hi-Hat

Very often while shooting a film it is necessary to take shots almost from floor level or with the camera placed where one cannot install a tripod. On such occasions the camera with a tripod head is mounted on a hi-hat. This is a metal device of about 8 in. (20 cm.) overall height, with three legs which are provided with holes or slots for fixing it to the base or floor where the camera is to be installed (car, aeroplane, travelling truck or dolly, etc.)

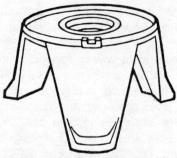

Fig. 34. Hi-hat with its three legs for standing on the floor and provision for a tripod head, it allows limited tilt but full pan movement.

## Camera wedge

As its name indicates, this accessory allows for the inclination of the camera at greater angles than those allowed for by normal tilting with the tripod head. It is mounted on the tripod head and the camera is then installed on it at an angle to the horizontal. There are different models with fixed and adjustable angles.

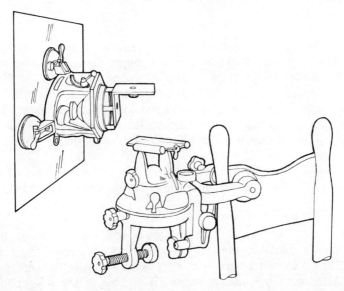

Fig. 35. *Left.* Samcine Limpet mount device, capable of fixing the camera to either flat or curved surfaces by means of high efficiency suckers. *Right.* Eclair two-way clamp unit that can be clamped to a chairback or in similar places.

## Special camera mount

Modern film work makes increasing use of accessories which allow the camera to be mounted at various positions and levels and on any type of vehicle without having to resort to the complex installations which were necessary not so long ago.

This idea was first championed by Eclair when they introduced a metal tripod for the Cameflex, with a detachable head which could be fixed easily by a system of clamps to readily available supports such as a door or window frame or even to the back of a chair.

These special mounts have been improved over the past few years. High efficiency suction pumps (some of them with a pressure indicator to prevent damage of the equipment) are capable of fixing the instrument to either flat or curved or irregular surfaces, whether on cars, aeroplanes, boats, windows or walls. These attachments have been designed generally for cameras weighing from 20 to 40 lb. Their accessories are specially designed to allow the camera to be levelled (whatever the position of the special mount) after it is installed. The most outstanding of these special camera mounts are the Limpet, Super Grip, Power Grip, Keeline and those manufactured by Samuelson Film Service Ltd.

*Barney*

The Barney is a flexible cover for the camera, to dampen noise and to protect it from extreme high or low temperatures. It is made from several layers of insulating materials, such as kapok, fibreglass, aluminium foil, etc. The outside cover is generally of heat-reflecting white leather. Heating elements are provided inside the cover which allow the instrument to run with outside temperatures as low as $-60°$ F. The heaters work at 110 v., with power ranging from 55 to 255 watts.

Barneys are easily installed and are made fast by means of zip-fasteners. Allowance is made for operation of camera controls.

*Blimp or soundproof cover*

Normally the speech of feature films is recorded while the scene is being shot. Early in the era of sound filming, one of the many problems the cinematographers were faced with was the noise made by the camera mechanism which, if audible to the microphone, ruined the recording. This brought about the appearance of the soundproof booth, popular in Hollywood in the early thirties. Although this solved the problem at the time, it was not very practical, as the operator and crew had to be shut up with their camera in the booth.

At the insistent request of studio technicians, several manufacturers substantially modified the mechanical movements of their cameras to make them less noisy. Though such modifications did not totally eliminate noise, they made it possible for cameras to be used more freely on the set when protected with noise dampening covers. These later pioneered the way for today's soundproofing systems, of which the best known is the blimp.

The blimp is manufactured as an accessory to cameras which are specially designed to shoot while recording speech and sound directly. They consist of bodies of aluminium or magnesium alloy (light and highly resistant materials), lined with several layers of rubber foam combined with plastic foam and/or glass wool. All doors are

66

generally lined with the same layers and they close hermetically, so that the camera is practically floating inside the blimp. The blimp design allows for a number of operations to be carried out from outside. These are:

(i) lens diaphragm and focus changes,
(ii) starting switch and speed changes,
(iii) shutter opening control,
(iv) direct framing and focusing, etc.

Of course, these characteristics vary with each camera and model and the way it is operated.

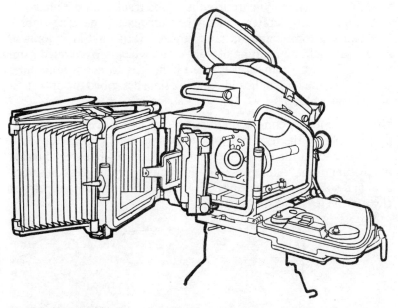

Fig. 36. Arriflex blimp with all doors open showing construction characteristics and connections of outside controls.

In most cases the blimp door needs to be opened only for changing the magazine and threading the film. As for sound-proofing, a well built blimp will not allow noise seepage at any recording levels, even when using a highly sensitive microphone directly in front of it.

*Camera slate*

At the beginning of each take a *slate* or clapper board marked

67

with pertinent data is placed in front of the camera to record such information as:

(i)   number of the scene, and take,
(ii)  whether it is an interior or exterior,
(iii) date,
(iv) number of sound recording,
(v)  name of film,
(vi) director, and
(vii) director of photography.

On top of or under this slate there is a hinged section, which can be opened, and closed suddenly to produce a loud crack. This serves as a reference mark to synchronize the sound track with the images.

The numbering is often done by interchangeable hanging slabs.

However, some cameras are provided with built-in automatic slates, with self-illuminating placards, and which are operated from behind. The Fox camera was one of the first to adopt automatic slating. The makers of the old Kinevox slate described the operation of theirs as follows:

"As the camera is coming up to speed, an optical arm is raised into position before the lens. A trip button is manually operated, sounding a buzzer at the same time as a marking line appears alongside the picture of the slate. These simultaneous operations establish optical and sound sync markings. The slater arm then instantly drops clear of the lens and shooting begins."

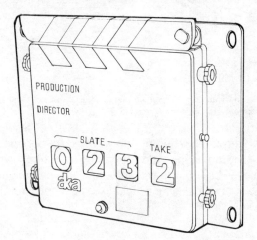

Fig. 37. Modern automatic slate manufactured by Allan King Associates in the U.K.

68

Among the most recent slates is the Kingklapper, produced in the U.K. by Allan King Associates. The Kingklapper is a modern slating system comprising a signal generator with light synchronization fed from dry cell batteries housed within the unit. The numbering system is controlled from both sides. A cable carries the synchronizing pulses to the recorder. A pulse generator operates the light and the synchronous pulsation simultaneously. The light is very bright and can be used in sunlight without any difficulty at all.

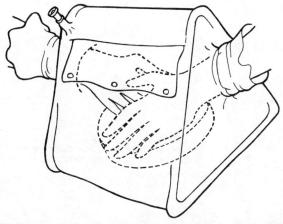

Fig. 38. Changing bag of new design ideal for working in direct sunlight.

*Changing bag*

This accessory is used for loading magazines, an operation which can be carried out anywhere, even in direct sunlight. The changing bag is essential when shooting far away from a darkroom, and has been used since the very early days of photography. It is a close-mesh, black fabric bag, satin lined. At one end it is provided with two sleeves with elastic cuffs. At the opposite end, an opening allows the magazine and film to be placed inside, and a double zipper makes a light-tight seal.

Changing bags vary in dimensions from the small size, 27 × 25 in., to a large model, 34 × 44 in.

*Cameraman's tape*

A roll of special adhesive tape is the cameraman's standby. It will seal film cans, fix or fasten cables, secure the photographic report to the can sent to the laboratory, mark references on the floor for the actor's movements, indicate on the magazine cover the type of film loaded in it, and so on. It is made in different colours and dimensions.

69

*Measuring tape*

This is a common measuring tape used by the camera assistant to determine the distance from camera to subject in order to make correct focus adjustment. It is usually calibrated in feet and inches.

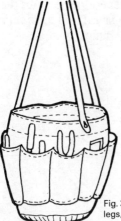

Fig. 39. Ditty bag, leather bag hanging under the tripod head between its legs, for holding items such as light meters, tools, measuring tape, etc.

*Ditty bag*

This name is applied to a leather bag hanging under the tripod head between its legs. It is a safe and handy place to keep items which are being used continuously, such as light meters, measuring tape, tools, and so on.

## Mobile supports

*Travelling truck*

The travelling truck is one of the most important accessories available to the cinematographer. Modern production techniques demand that the camera be moved during shots and for smooth flowing results a special mobile platform is required.

With the travelling method the camera is propelled along a straight line at any angle to the subject. For this purpose it is mounted on a solidly constructed truck with four or more wheels, and this vehicle runs on parallel guides.

The design of the truck, wheels and guides varies considerably with the maker and model, but the whole assembly should have a high degree of stability and steadiness, smooth rolling and facilities for mounting heavy camera equipment and carrying one operator.

Travelling trucks in use at present are built according to two systems, one adopted in Hollywood and the other in Europe. The Hollywood travelling truck is provided with pneumatic tyres, sometimes used at very low pressures to seat better on the guides, rolling on wooden parallel guides with a flange.

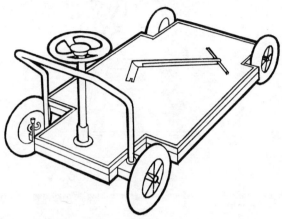

Fig. 40. Typical lightweight travelling truck with a platform large enough for camera, operator and focus puller.

The other type of truck is widely used in France and Italy. This features ball-bearing-mounted steel tyre wheels, with a groove along the tyre. The wheels roll on a rail system with $1\frac{1}{2}$ in. piping, in two-metre lengths, one end of which fits tightly into the open end of the next length.

The platform of a travelling truck must be heavily constructed in order to make it steady, and it must be fitted out to mount lights, hi-hats, etc.

*Dolly*

This is a special and more elaborate truck for travelling shots, allowing a very wide variety of camera movements. It is provided with an hydraulic mechanism (sometimes a spring and gear mechanism) which operates a boom at the end of which the camera is installed, thus raising or lowering it, and pivoting it at different angles. The boom can be manually controlled, and the vehicle must be of heavy and solid construction. It usually has five wheels.

Among the different types of dolly the most elaborate is the well known crab-dolly. This vehicle is provided with hydraulic controls,

71

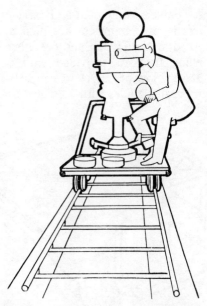

Fig. 41. A popular European system for travelling shots using grooved steel tyres running on an easily assembled piping track.

usually placed at the rear, allowing for movements of any kind as all wheels can be steered in any direction. Thus the operator can combine diagonal movements, turns round curves, turns at right angles, etc.

Some widely used dollies and crab-dollies are

(i)     Houston Fearless Panoram Dolly,
(ii)    N.T.C. Hydrolly,
(iii)   Moviola Crab-Dolly,
(iv)    J. G. McAlister Crab-Dolly,
(v)     Vinten Pathfinder Type 1,
(vi)    Edmonton Camera Dolly,
(vii)   Colortran Crab Dolly
(viii)  Elemack Spyder Dolly.

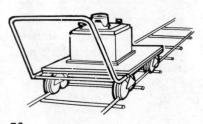

Fig. 42. Another view of the rail system. Note the method of mounting the hi-hat and the bar used by the pusher.

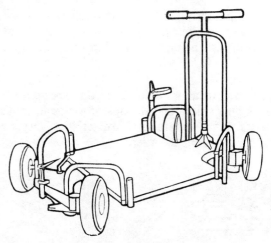

Fig. 43. A more elaborate light travelling truck or dolly with pneumatic tyres and steering for crab movements.

The compact Elemack dolly is manufactured in Italy and has been widely accepted, not only in that country, but elsewhere in Europe and in the U.S.A. Its design allows for placing its four double wheels in twelve possible combinations, carrying two operators on it, and it

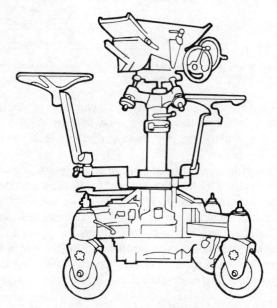

Fig. 44. Elemack camera mount widely used in studios in Hollywood and Europe.

73

is capable of going through doors and other narrow openings. The Elemack Dolly accepts the Jonathan Jib Arm Assembly, an accessory to convert the unit to a medium size crane.

*Crane*

The crane used in film studios is a complex item of equipment which affords the camera and the operator an enormous facility of movement. Its dimensions and characteristics vary considerably since it is generally made to order.

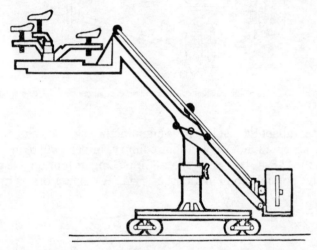

Fig. 45. A crane with special wheels adapted for use on rail system. It has a counter-weight and parallelogram arm system to maintain a level platform.

The base of the crane is a very heavy vehicle, to which is attached a long boom, which is the crane's main feature. At the end of the boom there is a platform that always remains level, whatever the position of the boom.

On this platform facilities are provided for installing the camera and three seats: one for the director, one for the camera operator and another for the camera assistant.

The crane movements are obtained by means of electric motors driving an elaborate mechanical and hydraulic system. Balance is maintained by counter-balance weights at the other end of the boom.

Some models have total automatic control, allowing the camera operator to raise, lower or swivel the crane from his seat on the platform.

This item of equipment is very much in use for spectacular films where the camera equipment must move over large sets, or for very complex outdoor location takes.

Among crane manufacturers are:

(i)   Houston Fearless Corp.;
(ii)  Chapman Studio Equipment, and others in the U.S.A.;
(iii) Newall Baby Crane and Samuelson Mighty; Master; Major, Maribon, Midway; Mini in the U.K.
(iv)  A.T.C. Gina Crab-Dolly in Italy.

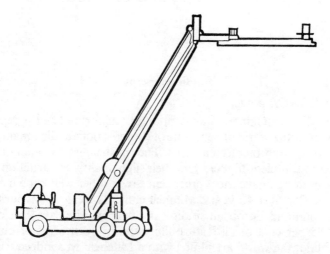

Fig. 46. Chapman Titan Crane: largest American-made crane. Note the six-wheeled truck.

## 1. REFERENCES

[1]  Alvar, M. F., *Tecnica Cinematográfica Moderna*, J. M. Yagües, Madrid.
[2]  Gregory, C. L., *Motion Picture Photography*, 2nd ed., Falk Publishing Company, New York (1927).
[3]  Newman, A. S., Camera Mechanics Ancient and Modern, *Journal of the Society of Motion Picture Engineers*, No. 5, p. 534 (1930).
[4]  Spottiswoode, R., *Film and its Techniques*, University of California Press, Los Angeles (1951).
[5]  Valera, J. A., *Arte y Tecnica Cinematográfica y Television*, Editorial Albatros, Bs. Aires (1944).
[6]  Weisse, Harold, Die Kinematographische Kamera, Springer Verlag, Vienna (1955).
[7]  McKay, H. C., *The Handbook of Motion Picture Photography*, Falk Publishing Company, New York (1927).

# SURVEY OF 35 MM CAMERAS

## Studio cameras

*Mitchell BNCR model*

The Mitchell Camera Corporation of California has the reputation all over the world of being one of the most outstanding manufacturers of motion picture cameras. Their instruments came into the market in the silent film era and their high quality construction and excellent design gave them precedence over other well known competitors. For over 40 years, Mitchell cameras were the favourite in Hollywood and European studios and over many years the slogan that "85 per cent of all feature films shown in theatres or on TV throughout the world are filmed with a Mitchell' was indeed true.

The first Mitchell camera on the American market in 1920 introduced the "rack-over" system conceived by John E. Leonard, a cameraman. Soon its excellent construction and design established its outstanding reputation. As time went by, improvements were made to the original model. A better intermittent mechanism drive was fitted (employing eccentrics and new materials). The appearance of sound films led to the semi-noiseless NC model. The year 1934 saw the birth of the BNC model, with its compact noise dampening devices built in. The BNC also comprised all the latest refinements of a studio camera at that date, but was sold extensively only in 1938 when one of the large Hollywood studios (Warner Brothers) bought a considerable number. The first two important films for which the BNC was used, were *Wuthering Heights* in 1939 and *Citizen Kane* in 1941, both photographed by the famous Gregg Toland.

Long after the famous BNC studio camera was established in world markets, the Mitchell Company in 1967 launched their

BNCR Model which, together with the classical features of the BNC camera, now included a reflex viewing system, an even more silently running mechanism, and a unit at the front with specially treated glasses to dempen the noise from the new reflex shutter.

The BNCR was the first Mitchell Studio camera which was not built on the principle of two separate units for racking over, as in previous models, since reflex viewing made this complex system unnecessary.

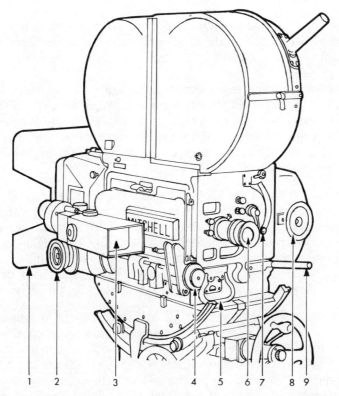

Fig. 1. (1) Sunshade, (2) focusing dial, (3) viewfinder, (4) focusing dial, (5) carrying handle, (6) reflex viewing eyepiece, (7) hand dissolve lever, (8) manual movement turning wheel, (9) carrying handle.

*General description.* The BNCR camera consists of a blimp type body housing three main units: an inclusive Mitchell NC mechanical unit, the drive unit which is an interchangeable motor, and the 1,000 ft. magazine which is housed on top of the camera. On the front of the camera there is a noise dampening device for the lens with sufficient space for zoom lenses and with specially treated glasses which avoid losses in the image quality. All these devices dampen the running noise of the instrument to levels below 24 dB.

INTERMITTENT MOVEMENT. This is the classic Mitchell intermittent movement created by this company at the birth of sound films and used over many years in the NC, BNC and Mark II cameras. The movement consists of a shuttle and register pin mechanism driven by an eccentric, the film being pulled down by means of two claws penetrating the perforations at either side of the film. After the film has travelled the height of one frame and has stopped, register pins penetrate one perforation at each side, steadying the film during the exposure period.

A pressure plate presses the film firmly against the aperture, and the 0·0015 in. clearance between pressure and aperture plates allows for the travel of two films at a time for bipack systems, or of a single film allowing for overlapping splices. Aperture plates with different sized apertures can be interchanged; the standard aperture is 0·868 in. × 0·631 in. (22·09 × 15·92 mm.).

MOTOR TRIP SWITCH. Should the film break on being taken up after exposure, or should there be faulty threading, or any other form of failure in the take-up, an oversized loop will be formed in the back of the camera body. This presses against a plate, tripping a switch which opens the motor circuit and stops the camera. This avoids damage to the delicate precision movement of the intermittent drive and tells the operator that the camera is not working properly.

VARIABLE-OPENING SHUTTER. The BNCR camera is provided with a stainless steel, segmented shutter which runs syncronized with the normal shutter of the camera. The latter comprises two blades on a single shaft. Its maximum opening is 175° and it can be closed in calibrations of 10° each by means of a swivel-handle knob sliding over a scale on the back of the camera. Just below this knob and scale a miniature shutter reveals at a glance the shutter opening and the relative position of the shutter with respect to the aperture. The normal shutter of the BNCR camera is of the automatic dissolving type, allowing fade-ins and fade-outs by pressing one of two buttons.

LENSES AND LENS MOUNT. In the Mitchell camera lenses are held in position by bayonet type lens locks. They are provided with rings for external focus control. The BNCR, like the BNC model takes only one lens at a time. The lenses carry special markings which, on mounting, must be made to correspond with determined positions, so as to synchronize for parallax and focus if the side viewfinder is used.

MOTOR. Mitchell BNCR cameras like the BNC model, are driven by interchangeable motors attached to the right hand side by means of two screws and a retaining latch. Thus the motors can be interchanged very quickly. The motor is positioned with its shaft in the horizontal position and parallel to the axis of the camera. Transmission is by means of a reduction gear at right angles to the shaft and camera axis. A switch is provided so that it will be acted upon by the oversize loop buckle-trip. All motors are provided with sockets for connecting the leads from the power source, to facilitate a quick change-over of motors when necessary. A range of motors is supplied for the requirements of this camera. They are: *Synchronous*: 110 V. AC 60 Hz, single phase; 110 V. AC. 50 Hz, single phase; 220 V. AC, 60 Hz, 3-phase: 220 AC, 50 Hz, 3-phase; 220 V. AC. 3-phase, interlock; *Multi-duty* 220 V. AC, 60 Hz, 3-phase; 96 DC; *Variable-speed* (requires a special motor door) 110 V. AC/DC, 60 Hz; 110 V. AC/DC, 50 Hz; 12 V. DC.; *Animation motor* 220 V. AC, 60 Hz (3-phase); 96 V. DC; 110 V. AC, 60 Hz or 50 Hz.

COUNTERS. An exposed footage counter and an exposed frame counter are built into the back of the camera, with zero reset knob on the camera interior at the left-hand side.

REFLEX VIEWFINDER. The main feature of the Mitchell BNCR model is its reflex viewing system. The R at the end of the designation signifies reflex. The image seen through the viewfinder is very bright and is produced by a segmented shutter made of highly polished stainless steel. The standard feature for critical focusing in previous models is maintained, that is to say, the image is ten times magnified. The shutter runs at 720 r.p.m., which eliminates blinking and vibrations and provides dynamic balance. A system of baffles eliminates the possibility of light coming through the viewfinder eyepiece.

VIEWING TUBE. This item is provided with a large diameter eyepiece which provides a bright, easily visible image of five times standard frame size. It may be enlarged up to ten times for critical focusing but only with a reduced field. The image reaches the viewer by means of a mirror at 45°, parallel to the blades of the reflex shutter. The ground glass on which the image is formed is placed between the reflex shutter and the mirror. Near the eyepiece the plane of the image is changed again by means of two prisms in order to position it again along the optical axis of the lens. The viewing tube also holds the green and amber filters which are classical in other models of this make. Two buttons control their insertion or withdrawal from the field. The image seen through the amber filter corresponds to panchromatic film, and the one seen through the green filter corresponds to orthochromatic film though such controls have little application today.

VIEWFINDER. Though the reflex viewfinder provides a parallax free image and allows for continuous focus control, the Mitchell BNCR camera is also provided with the projected image side viewfinder. Many operators prefer this item as it allows rapid framing and camera movement such as tracking and panning, and is provided with automatic parallax control (for lenses with eight different focal distances) and automatic focus control. Two rubber matte-adjusting knobs are situated in the top and left side of the viewfinder.

SPECIAL FEATURES. The Mitchell BNCR is provided with many refinements for special work.

*Automatic dissolve*

Two buttons are placed on the left side of the shutter opening control. The top one closes the shutter creating a fade-out over a 4 ft. film length; the bottom button opens the shutter, producing a fade-in over the same film length. *Miniature shutter.* This is a replica of the focal plane shutter of the camera which reproduces its actual opening and allows for checking at a glance; it is very useful in some special effects, such as back projection. *Filter holder:* In this model filters can be inserted in different ways—in front of the aperture (gelatine filters) or in front of the lens by means of the special filter holder for 3 × 3 in. or 4 × 4 in. when using wide angle lenses. *Four-way mattes:* the camera has a built-in, four-way matte system controlled by two knobs. *External focus control:* three focusing dials with vernier adjusting knobs are placed on both sides and behind the camera to facilitate the work of the focus puller. *Power plug for zoom lens motors:* low voltage, DC, power to operate zoom lenses automatically. *Self-lighting front block:* this block dampens the noise made by the mechanical movement of the reflex shutter and is self illuminating to allow the lens scale to be read through the corresponding window and for quick changes to be made.

## Adaptations of the BNC model

Since the Mitchell BNC camera is still standard equipment in many studios around the world some companies in the United States have designed instruments to adapt it to reflex viewing. In some cases the changes are slight and refer only to the viewing system, but one company has redesigned some of the basic features of the instrument. It is useful to analyse these adaptations.

CONVERSION BY CINEMA PRODUCTS DEVELOPMENT CO. In 1968 this company developed a thorough readaptation of the BNC model, for which those responsible, Edmund M. Di Guilio, Niels G. Patersen and Norman S. Hughes, were given the Technical/Scientific Award.

The main feature of the readaptation is an optical block with a beam-splitter based on a glass pellicle, 0·010 in. thick with a high-efficiency, antireflective dichroic coating in several layers, which reflects 30 per cent of the image received through the lens and allows the remaining 70 per cent to pass through to the film. Although this signifies some loss in film exposure, several advantages are obtained, in particular: noiseless running, continuous image free of flicker, and very simple design. This reflex system brings about the changes in the viewing system which are similar in some aspects to those of the BNCR camera. The blimp covering the whole instrument has also been changed for another which is more compact, of modern design and attractive finish. The rack-over mechanism has of course been eliminated, the eyepiece of the viewfinder is made larger, a system is provided for inserting filters in the viewfinder which is controlled from behind the camera and, moreover, the system allows for the insertion of a compact TV closed circuit system. Another improvement is a silent running motor of special design to operate zoom lenses. Many Mitchell BNC cameras have been adapted by this company under the name of SPR (Silent Pellicle Reflex) for studios in the U.S.A., U.K. and other European countries.

F & B/CECO CONVERSION. This American company has for many years specialized in adapting BNC and NC cameras, among other lines in the motion picture instruments industry. Their system is also based on a thin treated film placed at 45° to the plane of the film, which causes a loss of light of less than 1/5 stop. The adaptation is carried out in little more than a month and implies no changes in the body of the camera except for elimination of the rack-over mechanism. The quality of the image obtained is identical to that produced by the standard BNC or BNCR cameras.

## Cinema Products XR-35

A new studio camera has recently appeared, made by the Cinema Products Company of California. Film makers from all over the world first saw this instrument at the 1972 Photokina Show at Cologne, West Germany. It was designed by the outstanding technical team which had merited the Hollywood Academy Award for their adapted reflex system for Mitchell BNC cameras.

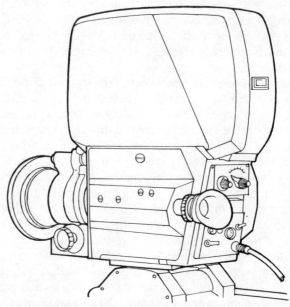

Fig. 2. The new Cinema Products XR-35 studio camera, instrument of compact design, with reflex viewing and multiple refinements.

GENERAL DESCRIPTION. The XR-35 camera is a compact instrument, 21 × 14 × 22 in. (0·53 × 0·35 × 0·56 cm), for shooting with direct sound recording on a separate strip. Its single unit, sound blimped magnesium body houses the mechanical unit, the drive motor, and the magazine. The camera controls are placed at the rear. The general characteristics of this camera make it very suitable for high efficiency work, it runs at very low noise level, and it can be carried by only one person.

INTERMITTENT MECHANISM. This is the classic Mitchell mechanism driven by cams, with a four claw shuttle (two on each side of the film) and two register pins (one on each side of the film). The unit was specially redesigned to allow for adjustment in the

82

stroke and the position of the shuttle claws on twin axes in relation to those of the register pins. This also reduces camera noise considerably and makes the mechanism adaptable to variations in the raw stock due to temperature and ambient humidity.

SHUTTER. This camera is provided with a reflex shutter, with variable opening from a minimum 5° to a maximum 180°. The opening is easily adjusted by a control on the panel at the rear of the camera.

VIEWING SYSTEM. Reflex system either by a mirror shutter which closes automatically at the viewing position, or, at buyer's option, by the reflex pellicle method. The viewerfinder is of the fixed type with a large-opening eyepiece, adjustable for different dioptres. Built-in devices enlarge the image considerably, and adapt it to the requirements of the anamorphic system.

MOTOR. This is placed at the side of the camera and runs at voltages ranging from 28 to 36 v, DC. Running speed can be adjusted from 4 to 32 f.p.s. The speed is governed by a crystal system which renders it very constant. Light and sound signals will immediately indicate if the motor runs "out of sync". Connection to the power source is by means of a separate cable with an eight-pin Canon connector. The on-and-off switch is placed at the control panel on rear of the camera.

MAGAZINES. Magazines are installed on top, inside the sound blimp body, by opening only one door. The magazines are of special design, of the QUAD (quick acting displacement) type, which allows for quick reloading and with a 1,000 ft. (300 m.) film load capacity. A built-in counter indicates the load situation at all times. A window on the sound blimp body permits this indicator to be read when the magazine is in position.

LENSES. This camera takes lenses with Mitchell BNCR lens mounts. The focus ring is easily adjusted by two controls placed one at each side of the instrument. A compact sunshade can be mounted on the front of the camera supported by two, rapid fitting, parallel booms which hold it from one side.

OTHER FEATURES. There is a built-in, filter holder disc, placed in front of the lens, for six gelatine filters; a control panel with self-lighting footage counter; lighting inside the camera; built-in spirit level; recessed camera handles. The all up weight is 93 lb. (42 kg.).

ACCESSORIES. A very useful accessory is the 30 v. 7 amp battery.

## Filmovy Prumysl Model Ark-1A

Cameras have been manufactured in Czechoslovakia since early in the history of motion pictures. Experiments were carried out there shortly after the First World War to determine if they could produce these instruments on an organized, industrial level. The trials were so successful that, shortly after, while film makers in other European countries were using cameras with wooden bodies, the Czechoslovakian film industry was working with the the first cameras to be made with an all metal body. The Czech Slechta cameras, which later became famous, sold extensively abroad under the name of Cinephon. Film makers in many countries used Cinephon cameras which were noted for their excellent construction and advanced design; the best known models were the BH and the BR.

After the Second World War Filmovy Prumysl, a government company, took over the Slechta establishment and therefore, the production of a wider range of technical equipment for motion pictures. Over the last few years they have manufactured many types of camera, amongst which the ARK-1A for studio work, the ERK-1 for outdoor work and the TK-3 for special effects, puppet or cartoon films are outstanding.

The ARK-1A camera was designed to make the utmost use of as little space as possible. It is intensively used at the Barrandov and Gottwaldov motion picture studios. A 94 × 47 × 46 cm blimp houses the mechanism for driving the film and the magazines contain 1,000 ft. (300 m.) of film. The high precision intermittent system uses register pins to achieve a steadines of 0·005 mm, or better, both horizontally as well as vertically. The viewing system is of the reflex type through the shutter and the image can be seen through a viewer with either a single or a double eyepiece. The shutter is variable from 0 to 170°. The 3-phase 220 v, 50 hz motor is housed within the instrument and is suitable for synchronous running. The back of the camera holds a panel with an on-and-off switch and indicating light, and an milliammeter scale indicator. Other controls at the rear or at the side of the instrument allow adjustment of the shutter opening, the lens focus and the levelling of the instrument. At the front, a special unit allows for interchanging the lenses, installing filters and also acts as a sunshade. The ARK-1A camera takes Cooke Speed Panchro lenses with different focal distances and its running noise is below 28 dB.

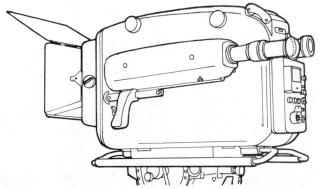

Fig. 3. Filmovy Prumsyl Ark-1A of compact design manufactured in Czechosolvakia.

## Eclair Camé 300 Reflex camera

This camera was designed by the French engineers Coutant and Mathot and is manufactured by Eclair International Diffusion. It is a blimped, all metal, heavily built but compact camera. The body is of box shape and its front consists of a fixed plate provided with a specially treated glass through which light reaches the lens. Lenses with the special mount designed by the camera makers can be installed by means of this plate, and it furthermore affords easy access to the variable shutter control.

The intermittent drive consists of a two-claw shuttle with adjustable register pin; the adjustment for this is marked on a calibrated scale. It can operate in reverse, and under any working conditions the registration is highly accurate.

The new adjustable register pin system obtained an award from the Superior Technical Committee of the French film industry and many European operators have praised its advantage for multiple exposure takes, and for shooting in tropical regions where film frequently shrinks.

VIEWING SYSTEMS. The Camé 300 Reflex camera is provided with three different viewing systems:

(i)   an integral, bright image, reflex viewfinder, with reflecting blade shutter placed at a 45° angle;
(ii)  direct viewing through film;
(iii) side or monitor viewfinder with parallax correction.

Generally the reflex viewfinder is the one most in use, and its tube swivels in order to facilitate viewing with the camera in awkward positions.

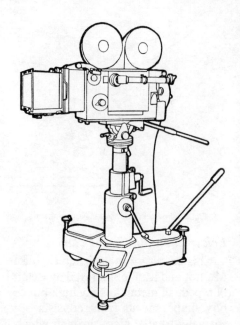

Fig. 4. Eclair Camé 300 Reflex mounted on a rolling pedestal manufactured by the same company.

OTHER CHARACTERISTICS. The magazines are for 300 metres (1000 ft.) of film, and they are externally attached and are interchangeable (raw stock magazine and exposed film magazine). The magazines are provided with mechanical transmission for normal and reverse drive.

The variable-opening shutter is calibrated from 180° to zero.

The camera is driven by an interchangeable electric motor, bayonet mounted at the rear, which can be either synchronous, 3-phase, for 220 v., 50/60 Hz, or variable speed from 22 to 26 f.p.s. at 24 v. DC.

The single lens mount is of the bayonet type. The minimum focal distance is 18 mm, but under certain conditions one can use 14 mm lenses. An extendible bellows sunshade and a matte-box are installed in front of the lens.

Other features of this camera are:

(i) exposed film-length counter in metres,
(ii) speed indicator,
(iii) automatic slating device,
(iv) threading safety switch,
(v) special warming system for working in extreme cold conditions,
(vi) synchronization socket for back projection.

86

## Panascope Model Mini-B

In mid-1975 a new, compact, self-blimped studio camera made its appearance.

With the name of Panascope the Cine Precision Engineering Co of California launched the new concept of a small studio reflex camera designed by its president, Mr. Jacob G. Monroy.

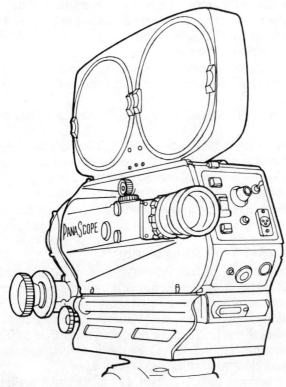

Fig. 5. Rear view of the Panascope studio camera designed by Jacob G. Monroy, with Mitchell NC compensating link positive registration movement. This 26 lb. camera includes all the features of the larger and heavier cameras in use today.

Some of the features of this lightweight, compact and silent motion picture camera are: A BNC-R compensating link positive pin registration movement; battery operated DC crystal controlled motor with variable and 24 and 25 f.p.s. sound speed; follow-focus unit with a quick camera release riser base; 200, 400 and 1000 ft. displacement type quick release film magazines; a quick-lock matte box and hand grip with built in switch for hand-held operations; an LED electronic film footage counter; buckle trip switch; self-aligning and rattle free magazine film spools; convenient threading knob; BNC-R bayonet-type lens lock; a built in dovetail in the front of the camera to accommodate zoom lens supports, sunshades, matte boxes and other accessories.

The camera is driven by PIC timing belts and has all sleeve bearings, rotating mirror shutter and reflex viewing. The mid-rib of this camera which accommodates the entire moving mechanism, including the optical system, is suspended and completely isolated by rubber shock mounts from the camera box or soundproof housing which acts as a blimp. For hand held operation the camera is quickly released from the riser base and the standard door with the viewing tube is replaced by a special door which has a short erect image viewfinder.

The conversion from studio to hand held mode takes less than one minute.

The viewing system houses two filters (one for contrast and one for colour) and also a knob for 5 and 10 times magnification to enlarge the image of the subject being photographed. In the back of the instrument are controls for starting and stopping the camera, selecting film-speeds, light signals, synchronization devices, and connectors. The total weight of this camera is 26 lb. and has a db rating of 27.

## Druzhba and Mir Soviet studio cameras

The Soviet motion picture industry has expanded considerably over the last twenty years, which has encouraged a parallel progress in the production technology of instruments to feed its requirements. The 39 motion picture studios, many laboratories and specialized institutions all over the USSR have produced more than 200 feature films a year, and 2000 "shorts" in the newsreel, documentary, educational, cartoon, scientific and other fields.

The vast internal Soviet market has determined an intensive production of the most varied range of instruments, among them, cameras. Most of these instruments have been designed by engineers of various government divisions, such as the Cinematographic Equipment Construction Workshops, at Leningrad and Moscow (C.K.B. and M.K.B.K.), the Moskinap Unions and the Leningrad Optical Mechanical Organization (L.O.O.M.P.). The design of these instruments is not outstanding for any important innovations and they are the same construction principles as many makes in the western world, but one must note their excellent quality and a recent tendency to improve the lines and the finish of the instruments. The Druzhba and the Mir cameras are two of the most versatile in-

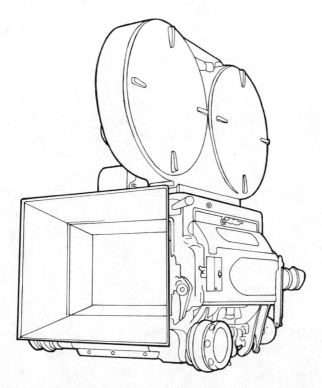

Fig. 6. Druzhba Soviet studio camera of similar design to the Mitchell BNCR.

struments in use at present and have displaced older models like the Moskva, not provided with reflex viewing.

The Druzhba is very similar to the Mitchell BNCR, as is evident from its shape, almost identical intermittent drive, reflex viewing through the shutter and lens, focus controls, lens hood with matte box, 170° variable shutter, side viewfinder with automatic parallax correction, 1000 ft. magazine, automatic dissolve, 24 dB sound level at 3 ft. (1 m.) and several other details.

The Mir camera is produced in two versions: one for 35 and another for 70 mm, to cover studio camera requirements in the two gauges. It is provided with a shuttle and register pin mechanism similar to the Mitchell, with a reflex viewing system, and with provision for reverse running. It is driven by a 3-phase, 220 v, synchronous motor, as well as another special motor to drive the 1000 ft. magazine. It is supplied with all the refinements of a studio camera, such as focus control, sunshade and matte box, etc. As with

89

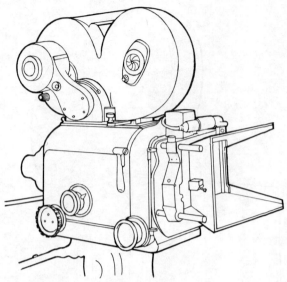

Fig. 7. Mir Soviet-made studio camera supplied in two versions: for 35 and 70 mm film gauges.

all modern Soviet cameras, the Druzhba and the Mir are painted an attractive light grey.

### Panavision cameras

Panavision Inc. is a well known American firm which has developed an up-to-date means of wide-screen filming, through its processes called Ultra-Panavision 70, Super Panavision 70, Panavision 70 and Panavision 35. For this last system it has created a modern studio camera, the Panavision Silent Reflex, with all refinements required by the latest techniques. These cameras are not for sale; they are hired together with Panavision lenses, equipment and the firm's services with headquarters in U.S.A. and U.K. Their most outstanding characteristics are: four-claw shuttle mechanism (two claws on each side of the film), double register pins, shutter with a variable opening from 0 to 175°, reflex viewfinder built into the camera access door, interchangeable servo motors, externally-placed blimped 1000 ft. magazines, side viewfinder with automatic parallax correction, remote focus control, and special design Panavision 35 mm lenses.

### New Panaflex Silent Reflex

The most outstanding of this line of cameras, is undoubtedly the new Panaflex Silent Reflex introduced in 1972, after many years of research and testing. This instrument is an excellent exponent of the multipurpose concept, since small changes and additions will make it either a light, hand-held camera with magazine at the rear for supporting on the operator's shoulder, or a semi-portable field camera for outdoor shooting, or a studio camera with all its refinements.

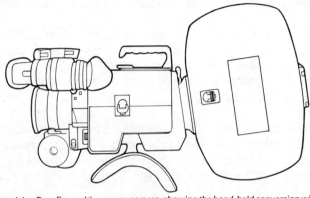

Fig. 8. Panavision Panaflex multi-purpose camera, showing the hand-held conversion with 250 ft. magazine.

DESCRIPTION. The heart of this camera is the mechanical unit comprising the intermittent drive mechanism, the continuous drive sprocket and the standard motor placed at the side. The magazines are installed either behind or on top. A single lens is mounted at the front of the camera, on which there is also a shutter-reflex viewing system. When the instrument is used for studio work, a base plate is installed underneath, which allows for the installation of a monitor viewfinder, with automatic parallax correction. The whole system runs silently.

INTERMITTENT MECHANISM. This is removable, with double fork pull-down claws and register pins engaging with the perforations on both sides. It is provided with a pitch and strobe adjustment system. The intermittent mechanism includes a film gate which, like that of the Mitchell, is provided with a slot for inserting mattes and filters; the film gate is easily removed to facilitate cleaning.

SHUTTER. Variable-opening in segments of 10° from a minimum 40° to a maximum 200°. Shuttering time 1/43 sec.

MAGAZINES. Either single or double chamber, for installing either behind or on top of the camera body. The single chamber magazines are of the compact type for 250 ft. (76 m.) or 500 ft. (152 m.) film loads and are suitable for supporting the camera on the shoulder. The 1000 ft. (300 m.) magazines are of the double chamber type and those, too, can be installed either behind the camera body or on top and are suitable for working with the instruments as a studio camera. They are of the beltless type, driven by separate torque motors.

VIEWING SYSTEM. Reflex viewing by means of mirrored shutter, providing a bright image magnified six times by an internal zoom device. The viewing tube can rotate 360°, has built in filters for viewing and contrast, an unsqueezed image device, and an automatically closing eyepiece.

LENSES. Bayonet type single mounting. The lenses are adjusted by geared controls on both sides of the camera. A rigid sunshade can be mounted in front of the lens. This shade may be adjusted and allows for installing different types of filters. Various models of sunshade are supplied.

MOTOR. The standard motor of the Panaflex is crystal-controlled at 24 or 25 f.p.s. The running speed can be varied from 6 to 32 f.p.s. A special pulse generator for synchronizing with the sound recording runs at 50 or 60 Hz. Power for the motor is supplied from 24 v. Panavision batteries, each of which has sufficient capacity for the camera to run up to ten 1000 ft (300 m) film magazines.

CONTROLS AND ACCESSORIES. The camera is supplied with a projected image monitor viewfinder with automatic focus and parallax correction, self-lighting digital type footage counter and tachometer; battery load indicator; speed indicator in the finder; shutter opening hand control behind the camera; built-in on-and-off switch; film-inching-knob; running speed variation switch; padding for supporting the camera on the shoulder; hand-grip with trigger switch; noiseless running. The all up weight is 25 lb. (11·3 kg.) with medium sized magazine.

### Noiseless portable cameras

*Arriflex 35 BL*

The first motion picture cameras came out some 80 years ago. The instrument was developed slowly but steadily through the early years; but improvments came with increasing rapidity and so that now every day seems to bring astounding changes. The trend towards low cost film production has affected camera design, making today's popular instruments light in weight and of relatively low cost to be within the reach of independent producers. Technological progress has strived to achieve a seemingly unobtainable goal: a 35 mm camera with the advantages of the latest 16 mm instruments, light weight and silent running.

For many years professional motion picture crews had become accustomed to the idea that a silent 35 mm camera could only be a heavy studio instrument for high cost feature films. Their use signified loss of time in transporting a complex instrument requiring elaborate conditions for operating; they implied more personnel for upkeep, high rental or long amortizations. When hand-held instruments became popular and blimps were designed for them, camera makers had taken a great step forward: the weight and volume of the instruments were cut to half. But still there was some 80 lb. (35 kg.) to move around.

This contrasted with the light, silent-running 16 mm instruments that were appearing at that time, but it also showed that the goal was now within reach.

Admittedly, 16 mm film takes up half the volume required by 35 mm and it runs at a slower speed, so it was easier to control noise. But it had been done.

After 3 years' trials the Arnold & Richter Company of Munich managed to solve the complex technical obstacles to achieving the long-desired instrument. They built a light, silent-running 35 mm camera suitable for hand-held shooting as well as for precision quality studio work. The prototypes of the new camera were shown at the 1970 Photokina. In spite of the large number of orders from all over the world the makers wanted to achieve an instrument as near perfection as possible, specially as regards silent running. They redesigned the mechanics of the prototype until the running noise was reduced to an equivalent of 5 dB. With this and other changes which further improved the instrument in even minor details, the new camera reappeared at Photokina in 1972 before an avid market which had already appreciated its qualities.

GENERAL CHARACTERISTICS. The Arriflex 35 BL is a very compact, small size camera of long shape and comprising the unit housing the main mechanism, a 400 ft. (120 m.) coaxial magazine placed behind the main unit and the lens blimp at the front. The

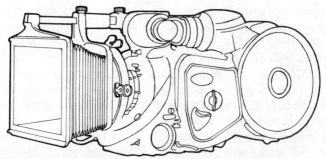

Fig. 9. Arriflex 35 BL camera, silent-running multi-purpose camera suitable for hand-held shooting as well as for precision quality studio work.

camera complete is $19\frac{1}{4}$ in. (54·6 mm.) long, $10\frac{1}{2}$ in. (38·1 mm.) wide, and 9 in. (22·8 mm.) high. These dimensions unusual in a noiseless 35 mm camera, make it ideal for hand-held shooting. Its long shape is ideal for shoulder support and its weight (20 lb. 8 oz., approx 9·3 kg.) is well within acceptable standards for portable instruments.

The main goal of the makers was to turn out an instrument with high precision image recording suitable for shooting with direct sound recording on a separate strip, and light enough to compare with the self-blimped 16 mm cameras. These goals were fully achieved.

INTERMITTENT DRIVE. The intermittent mechanism is of a totally different design from those used by this company in their previous models. It was specially designed for high quality registration, and for running up to 90 f.p.s. It also runs both forward and in reverse. The mechanism is based on two shafts acting on four cams, two on either side of the film, which drive two shuttles with two claws each for each sector of the perforations, and two register pins, one on either side. This provides horizontal and vertical registration. The intermittent unit was designed as a rectractable block to facilitate threading the film through the film gate and cleaning the aperture plate. The high quality registration achieved (between 2 and 3 $\mu$) not only produces a very steady image with high definition, but also allows for special effects, such as travelling matte and multiple exposure.

VIEWING SYSTEM. As in all Arriflex cameras, the 35 BL is provided with a reflex viewing system based on a mirrored double blade shutter with 180° opening placed under the aperture so that the blades shutter horizontally to reduce the stroboscopic effect when panning. The viewfinder is of the swivelling periscopic type, close to the top of the instrument so that when the camera is supported on the operator's shoulder, he can easily place his eye to the eyepiece and adjust it to his convenience. The periscope can swivel up to 120°. The optical system provides a very bright image enlarged $6\frac{1}{2}$ times. The ground glass can be easily interchanged for others with different composition areas.

MAGAZINES. In this camera they are installed behind the camera body and have a built-in continuous drive mechanism based on two sprockets placed in the throat of the magazine. The magazine is of the coaxial type with the raw stock chamber placed side by side with the take up chamber and it is provided with a supply footage indicator. The magazine is detached from the camera body to be reloaded independently and is attached again with a film loop of the required dimensions. Guide rollers are placed at the end of the throat. The magazine is attached to the camera body mechanically and a special device ensures that it is properly positioned.

The standard magazine holds a 400 ft. (120 m.) film load, but the makers also supply models for 1000 ft. (300 m.).

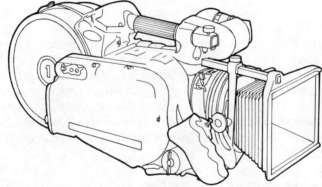

Fig. 10. Side view of Arriflex BL showing the camera hand-grip, transportation handle and panel of controls.

MOTOR. The camera is driven by a motor directly connected to the shaft of the intermittent mechanism. This specially designed motor is housed within the camera body and its speed is controlled by a crystal for 50 Hz and 60 Hz, to run at 24 or 25 f.p.s. An electronic device supplied as an accessory allows filming speeds to be varied from 5 to 30 f.p.s. The motor runs at 12 v. DC. Among its many refinements there is a device with a sound and visual signal in the viewfinder to indicate when the motor is running out of synchronism.

LENSES. The Arriflex BL takes only one lens mounted on a special Arri steel bayonet mount. Heavy lenses such as zooms require lens support gadgets. When very short focal length lenses must be used it is necessary to install those designed for Arriflex Model IIC. A sunshade and filter holder can be installed in front of the lens with two positions for either 3 or 4 in. filters. Behind this there is another rotating filter holder for polarized filters.

LENS HOUSING. As this is a blimped camera a special lens housing must be used to dampen the noise transmitted through the taking lens. This housing covers the lens all round and also acts as a external focus control, as well as for installing filters. Diaphragm and focus settings can be easily seen through a window on the lens housing.

FILM GATE. The film gate of this camera is interchangeable and is provided with a removable pressure plate, both of which are easy to inspect and clean.

CONTROLS. The controls are placed on different positions of the camera. The tachometer is near the door which provides access to the inside of the camera; the footage counter zero reset button is placed above the tachometer. The focusing handle is on the lens housing. The lever for manual shutter advance is on the access door. There is a panel for power connections to various electronic systems, Pilotone, etc. On the side of the camera there is a small panel with a mode selector switch, a fuse, and a volume regulator for "out of sync" buzzer. The on-and-off switch is placed on the camera hand-grip.

OTHER FEATURES. An accessory allows for filming at up to 100 f.p.s. Multi-camera synchronization is allowed for; Pilotone synchronism system; safety-switch with sound signal; system for slating on the film for sync sound speed; 25 to 125 W load for speeds between 25 to 90 f.p.s.; 28 dB noise level.

## Mitchell Mark III

This camera was brought out by the Mitchell Company in 1972 and is the latest offer to film makers of a noiseless, portable instrument with many facilities. It was designed on totally new lines except for the intermittent system, which is the classic mechanism adopted by this company for most of their instruments. The camera was conceived for hand held shooting, as well as for different applications in features or documentary films.

INTERMITTENT MECHANISM. This mechanism works on the system of cams which move a four-claw shuttle (two claws on each side), and with two register pins, one for each line of perforations. It is the same mechanism as that used on Mitchell NC, BNCR and Mark II cameras. It could run efficiently at speeds up to 120 f.p.s. A manual advance knob places the shuttle in position for threading the film. The intermittent mechanism consists of a removal unit which also includes the film gate. A feature which differs from other models of this company is that the continuous film drive with its large sprocket is not combined with the intermittent mechanism but is installed in magazine instead.

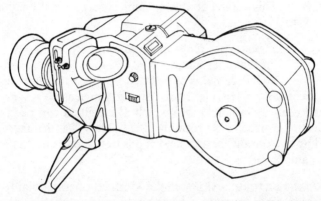

Fig. 11. The new Mitchell Mark III, lightweight and portable silent camera for studio work.

VIEWING SYSTEM. The viewing system is the reflex type with a mirror shutter, specially treated to give a reflectivity of 96 per cent. The bright image obtained is seen in a finder giving a 6·2 times enlargement. The eyepiece can be corrected for characteristics of individual eyesight. The optical system includes an easily inserted neutral density filter to help with judging contrast. The optical system ground glass can be interchanged for shooting with different aspect ratios.

MAGAZINE. The standard magazine of the Mitchell Mark III is of the coaxial type for 400 ft. (120 m.) film loads. It is attached behind

97

the camera body and does provide a long shape suitable for supporting on the operator's shoulder. The magazine has a built-in, continuous drive sprocket and works on the pre-set-loop method. A door on each side affords easy access to both raw stock supply and take-up chambers. The magazine is rapidly installed on the camera body by means of the bayonet attachment.

DRIVE MOTOR. The variable speed motor is built into the camera and uses a 28 v. DC power supply. It is regulated by a crystal. Operating speeds are 8, 16, 24, 25, 28 and 32 f.p.s. A 50 or 60 Hz signal generator is built into the motor circuit for synchronizing by cable. When the motor is "out of sync" an alarm system will operate an indicating light seen in the viewfinder. The motor is internally synchronized so that whenever it stops, the shutter will be in the viewing position. The crystal system affords a speed regulation with a precision of 15 parts in one million.

SHUTTER. This is the variable opening type, externally adjustable from 20° to 170°.

LENS AND SUNSHADE. Only one lens can be mounted at a time with a three-lug bayonet mount. It also allows lenses for Mitchell Mark II and S35-R cameras to be fitted. A special support supplied as an accessory is required for using zoom lenses. A very light sunshade can be mounted into which $4\frac{1}{2}$ in. filters can be inserted. The sunshade also holds a rotating filter holder. The sunshade is supported by two parallel booms held in position at one side on the front of the camera.

SPECIAL FEATURES. Although the Mark III offers similar features to those on other equipment made by this company, there are some extra refinements: hand-grip with on-and-off switch, easily accessible shutter control, self-lighting footage and frame counters, automatic slate marking a signal on the film at the zone of the aperture synchronized with the sound signal sent to the magnetic tape recorder, zoom operating switch on the hand-grip, adjustable and padded shoulder support and special viewer for framing from difficult positions.

### Field cameras

*Filmovy Prumysl Model Erk-1*

This camera is the up-to-date version of the well known Cinephon

BR which was widely used at the Barrandov, Gottwaldov, Kudlov and Koliva studios in Czechoslovakia, as well as by film makers in Poland and other countries in eastern Europe.

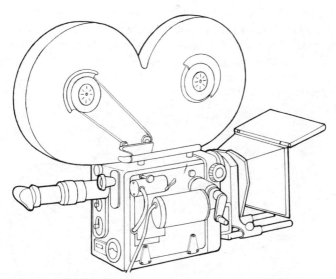

Fig. 12. Filmovy Prumysl Erk 1 field camera manufactured in Czechoslovakia and widely used in the studios of that country.

This model is suitable for all types of work which does not involve direct sound recording during shooting. The camera is of standard design with film travel on only one plane. It measures 32 × 22·5 × 24·5 cm. and comprises a film drive unit with an access door on each side and with a double chamber magazine on top for 500 ft. (150 m.) or 1000 ft. (300 m.) of film with belt drive. The drive motor is placed on the right hand side of the instrument and it can be either synchronous, 3-phase for 220 v. 50 Hz, with a 70 watts power rating, or a variable speed motor for 12 v. DC with 60 watts power rating. Both of these motors are of small dimensions.

The outstanding characteristics of the ERK-1 are its reflex viewfinding system, affording a very bright view through a periscope type finder easily adjusted to any position that the operator requires. A sunshade and matte-box is mounted on booms at the front of the camera. At the rear there is a footage counter, a frame counter, a milliammeter, and a spirit level.

## Lightweight cameras

### Mitchell S35R (Mark II) reflex camera

In 1960 the Mitchell Camera Corp. introduced a new camera known as the Mark II. This was the result of fruitful research to fulfil the demand of the movie industry for a multi-purpose, noiseless, light camera, with a reflex viewfinder, which would be easily adaptable to studio work. To achieve this, the Mitchell company first designed and produced an experimental model, the R-35, and put it in the hands of camera operators, directors of photography and producers, so that they could try it out.

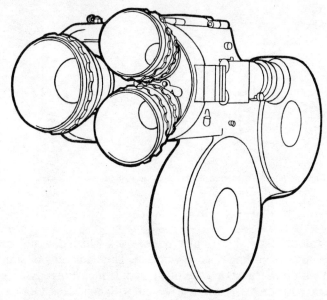

Fig. 13. The Mitchell R-35 reflex, a trial model which was tested by cameramen working in the film production industry.

After a year's trials during which the new features were tested out one by one, the Mark II was launched, taking into account the suggestions derived from the experimental runs. The result is a finely finished, easy-to-carry camera of modern design, capable of running at a wide range tf speeds up to 128 f.p.s., just by changing motors, and which furthermore can easily be turned into a studio camera by merely attaching accessories.

The intermittent movement is similar to that of the Mitchell NC and BNC, and consists of a two-claw shuttle working with two register pins, one at each side of the film.

100

The intermittent unit is easily disassembled for quick interchange when required.

The Mark II incorporates reflex viewing for the first time in a Mitchell camera. The very bright image is reflected by polished stainless steel blades placed at a 45° angle to the film, these blades being rotated by the shutter shaft. The shutter is of the focal plane type, and its opening can be adjusted from 170° to zero, in segments of 5° each. The optical tube of the finder magnifies the image up to 10 times to afford critical focusing, and inside it there are filters which provide a very great help in studying lighting in the subject. The field of view is larger than covered by the lens, so that the operator can see unwanted subjects just outside the frame. The ground glass on which the image is projected can be easily interchanged to suit the aperture size being used.

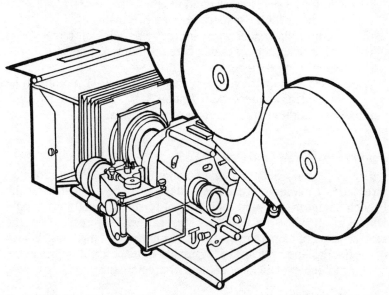

Fig. 14. Mitchell Mark II with 1000 ft. top mounted magazine, special sunshade and matte-box and viewfinder.

The Mark II is loaded with film by means of an external 400 foot magazine, which is secured by an attachment plate on to the underside of the camera, at its rear, so that it rests on the operator's shoulder for hand-held shooting. The magazines take 100 ft. or 200 ft. daylight spools or cores for 400 ft. dark-room film loads. When a larger film-load is needed the typical 1000 ft. Mitchell magazine is installed on top of the camera or slant-back by means of adapter.

101

Interchangeable motors are supplied to drive the new Mitchell camera: 12 v. DC, 24 v. DC; 110 v. DC or AC (all for speeds ranging from 1 to 70 f.p.s.). Moreover there are synchronous motors of the following characteristics: single-phase 110 v., 60 Hz; 3-phase, 220 v., 50 Hz; 110 v. AC for animation filming; and 115 v. AC for high-speed shooting.

A sync-pulse built into the camera affords synchronization of camera operation with certain types of sound recorders working on this principle.

The lenses are specially made by the American firm of Bausch & Lomb and are installed by means of a special mounting (either single or on a lens turret, at choice) which can be combined with a manual focusing control.

Other characteristics of the Mitchell Mark II are:
(i)   slot for inserting masks and filters,
(ii)  mount for taking a special design of sunshade,
(iii) monitor viewfinder with automatic parallax correction,
(iv)  hi-hat when the magazine is rear mounted,
(v)   blimp of modern design,
(vi)  closed circuit television system with built-in monitor tube and video-tape recorder (System 35),
(vii) water-tight cover for submarine shooting.


## Eclair Cameflex M3 camera

One of the most outstanding innovations in the field of motion picture camera manufacture was the design of the Cameflex by the French engineers Coutant and Mathot for the Eclair International Diffusion. It was the result of several years research on the requirements of camera operators and on the combined possibilities of mechanics and optics. The originality of its conception lies in the attempt to achieve the ideal camera characteristics:

(i)   light weight,
(ii)  high precision,
(iii) functional shape permitting easy handling,
(iv)  extremely fast loading,
(v)   capacity for taking different drive motors,
(vi)  wide range of applications.

With these aims in view, the Cameflex 35 was designed and built, and subsequently the Cameflex 16/35, the former having obtained an award from the Hollywood Motion Picture Academy.

The history of the Cameflex has a long tradition of ingenuity and perseverance behind it. The makers, Eclair of Paris, started work last century as a motion picture studio, and later as a laboratory.

In 1909 the company started producing cameras which were widely accepted in Europe and the USA. Among the many instruments they produced was the Cameraeclair famous for its six lens turret, and the hand-held Camerette.

When sound films appeared, a new model was produced to record image and sound simultaneously on separate films. During the Nazi invasion of Paris in World War II, the Eclair Co. was immediately occupied and fruitless attempts were made to make the technicians of the company produce a camera for the German Film Service (UFA). Some time later, Eclair engineers started secretly to conceive an ideal instrument for all types of work, designed on the basis of totally different concepts from those applied at the time. These were kept secret and put into practice only after the war. The first units were manufactured in 1947 and obtained a prize at that year's Venice Biennial Festival. The "nouvelle vague" (new wave) surged in France through this instrument, which is also extensively used in Britain, in continental Europe (both East and West), the Soviet Union, India, and Latin America. In the USA it has a circle of addicts and it is known there as the Camerette, in honour of its old time ancestor.

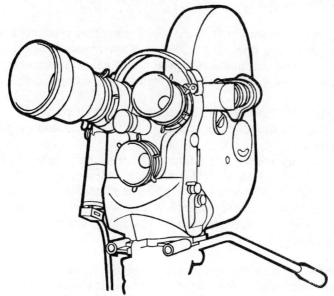

Fig. 15. Eclair Cameflex CM3 with self-contained magazine.

DESCRIPTION. The outstanding feature of the Cameflex lies in the principle of the magazine camera system.

Certain mechanical devices are included in the magazine which permit the film to be threaded in the magazine itself, instead of through the camera. This principle had previously been applied to some 16 mm cameras, but was now improved so that even the continuous drive and the two loops are included within the magazine.

FILM DRIVE. The intermittent drive consists of a two-ratchet claw shuttle movement installed inside the camera body, and two pressure pads mounted in the magazine. Two spring-loaded guides acting on the loops in the magazine keep the film moving at a continuous and uniform rate. The patent registration principle of the Cameflex produces a remarkably steady image and allows for a wide range of temperature fluctuations with resulting film stretch or shrinkage.

The continuous drive which forms the loops consists of a single sprocket with several pressure rollers on top and beneath, making up an assembly installed in the magazine.

LENS TURRET. The lenses are bayonet-mounted on a spider turret, with diverging optical axes. The minimum focal length is 18 mm. The turret is rotated by hand, the taking lens being the one on the arm pointing down.

SHUTTER. The shutter is of the variable opening type, adjusting from a maximum opening of 200° to a minimum of 40°. It was designed so that the shutter blades stop the light rays very near the focal plane, which produces a very high degree of image definition.

VIEWING SYSTEM. The Cameflex viewing system works with mirror surface shutter blades, a large magnification and eyepiece adjustment.

The viewing system can be pivoted horizontally, upwards and downwards, so as to allow for framing and focusing from any camera position. Moreover, viewing can be effected with either right or left eye by rotating the eyepiece. A special shutter shuts light out of the viewfinder when not in use, to avoid the possibility of light seeping through to the film.

MOTOR. The standard motor of the Cameflex is of small size and is installed on the right hand-side of the camera. It also acts as a hand-grip. It is of the variable-speed type and works at 6/8 v., its rating being 55 watts. It is easily interchanged with other motors of similar dimensions, either for 24 v. DC or synchronous 110/220 v. For special processes an attachment is supplied for hand operating with a crank, affording speeds of either 1, 8, or 16 frames per turn.

APERTURE PLATE. The plate with standard sound aperture (868 in. × 631 in.) is of chrome plated steel. The Scope model of this camera is provided with a 0·937 in. × 0·735 in. aperture.

MAGAZINES. Three magazines sizes are supplied for the Cameflex: 100, 200 and 400 ft. respectively. The 100 ft. magazine, with 3⅝ in. spools can be loaded in daylight but the others must be loaded in a darkroom or changing bag. As explained above, the continuous drive movement is situated inside the magazine, which thus constitutes the second most important unit in the camera. The magazines are easily attached to and detached from the camera, thus allowing for changeover to different types of emulsion with negligible loss of film (about 2 in.), at the same time simplifying the record of exposed film, as each magazine is supplied with its own built-in footage counter.

SUNSHADE AND MATTE-BOX. The sunshade of the Cameflex is built throughout of light metal alloy or, recently, in bellows form and is carried on two parallel rods which can be attached to the camera base; masks can be fixed on its front to reduce the field of view. The two-slot matte-box allows for the insertion of 3 in. × 3 in. filters and masks. Gelatin filters can also be inserted in a slot in front of the aperture.

CONTROLS. The controls are incorporated in various parts of the amera: the footage counter (in meters) is built into the magazine; the magnetic speed indicator is placed at one side, below the aperture; the shutter-opening adjusting knob is placed on one of the sides of the camera, and the switch is built into the motor.

BLIMP. The Cameblimp is a soundproof cover built of light metal alloy which permits the use of the Cameflex with 400 ft. magazines for direct sound recording. The Cameflex is installed on a sliding plate in the blimp, and the different functions are directly connected, either by rods or by flexible cables, to external controls on the outside of the blimp. The external controls provided are:

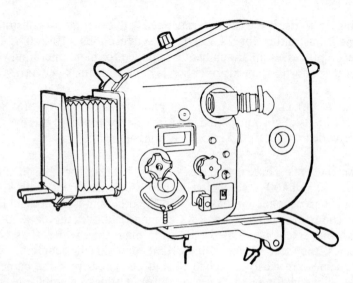

Fig. 16. Cameblimp. Visible are the controls for focusing and diaphragm, peepholes for observing footage indicator and tachometer, and the reflex finder.

(i)   diaphragm control,
(ii)  focusing control,
(iii) shutter control,
(iv)  reflex viewing,
(v)   footage counter,
(vi)  speed indicator window.

An extendible square-section bellows sunshade can be attached in front of the blimp. The Cameblimp including camera and 400 ft. magazine weighs approximately 100 lbs.

ANAMORPHIC LENS SCOPE MODEL. The manufacturers have released a model of the Cameflex called the Scope which allows for shooting with anamorphic lenses. It differs from the standard model in that:

(i)   the dimensions of the aperture are $0 \cdot 937 \times 0 \cdot 735$ inches ($18 \cdot 67 \times 23 \cdot 80$ mm) (see p. 268) to suit Cinemascope or standard anamorphic ratios; the aperture dimensions can be modified by means of interchangeable plates;
(ii)  a de-anamorphic viewer may be fitted to afford direct viewing through the anamorphic taking lens, but showing an un-squeezed image. As in the standard model, this is a reflex viewfinder, but larger;

(iii) a special turret with one of its arms adapted to the anamorphic lens and corresponding aperture, while the other two arms are adapted to standard aperture.

The CM-3-T model of recent development allows the use of the Techniscope system by providing a quick change from four perforation pull-down to two perforation pull-down.

Single perforation pull-down for 16 mm is also available in the 16/35 mm model.

*Arriflex camera mod. IIC*

In 1936 the German camera manufacturers Arnold & Richter A.G., introduced this excellently designed instrument, with its then revolutionary reflex viewing by means of a shutter placed at a 45° angle to the plane of the film. The first models were provided with 120° opening shutter, circular motion intermittent drive, and a rigid sunshade attached to a square shaft. Although its general design has been adhered to, improvements have been gradually added, and today, the mechanical system generally is improved. The shutter opening has been increased to 180°, the intermittent movement has been changed for one giving high quality registration, a new optical

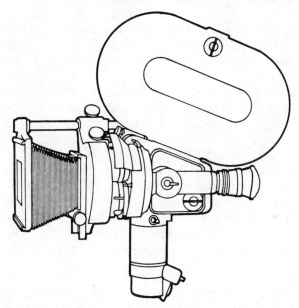

Fig. 17. Arriflex 35 Model IIC, with reflex viewing system and combined motor and handgrip and three-lens turret.

107

system has been adapted for the viewfinder so that the resulting image is of greater brightness, and an extendible sunshade replaces the former rigid one. The most recent innovations are a variable opening shutter and the possibility in certain models of interchanging viewfinder masks and blimp for use with 400 and 1000 ft. (120 or 300 m) magazines.

Many important cameras were made in Germany over the years, but the most outstanding is, no doubt, the Arriflex, created by Arnold & Richter. Established in 1917 as laboratories and accessory makers, they brought out their first camera, the Kinarri, in 1925. Long research by the heads of the company, August Arnold, an engineer, Dr. Robert Richter and Erich Kaestner, led to their ingenious viewing system in 1931. After testing the principles on prototypes, they came out with the now famous Arriflex.

Designed mainly for news coverage, it had the sad task of recording the rise and fall of Hitler's regime: the Axis pacts, the invasion of France, the Russian Disaster, Mussolini's death, the Nuremberg trials. Many World War II documentaries include much German material shot with Arriflexes.

In spite of the war, many of its innovations leaked through to West Europe and America. From 1943, the almost identical American "Cineflex" (known as the PH-330), was made for the Armed Forces. The first Hollywood feature film employing the Arriflex, "Dark Passage" (1945), was directed by Delmer Daves, who had tried them out before, testing captured enemy material for the US Forces.

Arriflexes started crossing the Atlantic commercially in 1947, and Robert Flaherty was one of the first to adopt them for his "Louisiana Story" (1948). Some time later their makers could hardly cope with ever-increasing orders. It became standard equipment with the BBC, the Italian RAI, Polish Film News, and film units of the US Armed Forces. The Arriflex is used in many documentaries, commercials and "new wave" productions all over the world. Many film historians mention this camera as the tool of new-generation film makers the world over. When the government of the People's Republic of China decided to manufacture their own cameras, they set up a factory in Nanking to turn out an instrument identical to the Arriflex.

GENERAL DESCRIPTION. The shape of the Arriflex is asymmetrical and its compact body in the form of a right-angled triangle holds the film drive mechanism; the reflex viewfinder tube is mounted on the outside of the access door. The cylinder shaped motor is attached to the camera base and acts as a hand-grip. The three-lens turret can be rotated by means of three small wing grips (one for each lens), which also indicate the lens which is in the taking position. The taking lens is protected by either a rigid or an extendible-bellows sunshade with matte-box for holding three 3 in. × 3 in. (76 × 76 mm) filters. The compact film magazine is externally attached, and includes a built-in footage counter. Other controls, such as the on-and-off switch, speed indicator and variable shutter control, are placed at the side or the rear of the camera. The resulting instrument, a light-weight, medium-size camera, is perfectly suited to hand-held shooting, but at the same time is easily adapted to high quality studio work by adding the relevant accessories.

FILM DRIVE. Two sprockets built into the magazine effect the continuous drive of the Arriflex, both for film supply and take up. On attaching the magazine to the camera, a gear in the continuous drive movement meshes with the camera's main drive, thus providing mechanical power transmission from the latter.

The intermittent drive movement is a precision mechanism which produces images with a high degree of registration stability. It is based on the action of a "dwelling-time" shuttle which at the end of its downward stroke steadies the film for recording the image.

The aperture plate is combined with the pressure plate to form a hinged door which opens inwards and affords easy access for threading the film and cleaning.

VIEWING SYSTEM. As explained previously, the Arriflex was the first camera to incorporate a viewing system of the reflex type. When the shutter is in the closed position, its blades, set at an angle of 45° to the optical axis of the lens, reflect the image on its mirror glass outer surfaces on to a ground glass with vertical louvres to eliminate reflections falling on the film emulsion. An optical magnifying system (improved in the latest model II-C) shows this image exactly as it is recorded on the film when the shutter is in the open position. The ground glass is interchangeable and is marked to indicate the aperture it corresponds to. The viewing optical system is installed on the camera access door, and is furnished with an eyepiece having a rubber eyecup and adjusting ring for individual eyesight. In the latest model, the pressure of the eye on the eyecup opens an automatically closing shutter to protect the film from light coming in through the viewing system. When sighting the scene through the viewfinder before shooting, a small knob on the right-hand side of the camera is turned by hand to rotate the shutter and close it. The image shown through the reflex viewfinder is upright and correct from left to right, and is magnified $6\frac{1}{2}$ times.

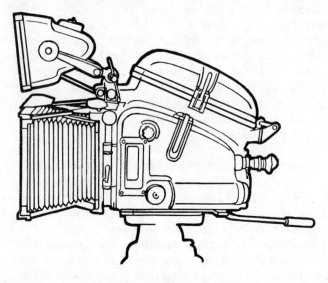

Fig. 18. Arriflex converted for studio use by adding the Model 400 blimp with full external controls, and blimp basher attached.

MOTORS. The motor of the Arriflex is also the handgrip. It works at 16 v. in the latest models, and draws about 4 amps when working with a full film load. It is provided with a rheostat at the lower end for adjusting the operating speed, which is read on a built-in speed indicator, scaled from zero to 50 frames per second. The rheostat itself is calibrated from 1 to 9, a scale which furnishes a basis for operating-speed determination, given a constant voltage. Speeds greater than 32 f.p.s. can be attained by exchanging the motor for another one specially designed for running at speeds up to 80 f.p.s.

Two switches are provided for starting and stopping the motor. One is of the push-button type, located near the motor socket, for short hand-held takes. The other is a toggle switch for long takes, or when operating on a tripod. The latest models are supplied with a switch for reverse drive, located near the power cable socket.

When the camera is operated in synchronism with a sound recorder, the variable speed motor must be changed for a synchronous one. A governor-controlled motor, or a transistor-controlled constant speed motor can also be used. The synchronous motor is a larger unit than the other ones, since it comprises a built-in

110

footage counter, and a safety switch which is installed in the camera to switch off the power in the event of stoppage.

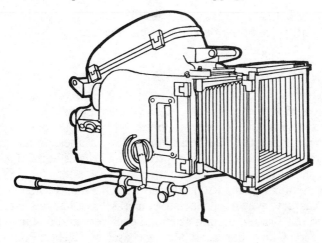

Fig. 19. Right-hand view of Model 400 Arriflex blimp with matte-box and sunshade.

ACCESSORIES. Of the accessories supplied by the manufacturers for this camera, the most important is probably the blimp. There are two models of blimp, for 400 ft. and 1000 ft. magazines. Both are built according to the most up-to-date sound-proofing techniques and are of streamlined functional shape. The 400 ft. model encloses the camera with synchronous motor and magazine for 200 ft. or 400 ft. colour film, or 500 ft. b & w. It is supplied with external controls for focusing, observation windows for lens markings, adjustable sunshade and matte-box. The 1000 ft. model converts this hand-held camera into equipment capable of turning out studio work. One of its outstanding features is that it will take 1000 ft. rolls of film in Mitchell or Newall magazines; the magazine includes a special adapter with the continuous drive sprocket, guides etc. A small torque motor assures trouble-free take-up in the 1000 ft. magazine by means of reduction gears and a double friction belt. The controls furnished with the 1000 ft. blimp are the following:

(i)   three focus controls (located at both sides and behind the camera),
(ii)  knob at front for diaphragm adjustment,
(iii) direct observation windows for lens marking,
(iv)  pulsating pilot light,

111

(v)  sound signal when safety switch is operated,
(vi) dial for rotating shutter manually.

Among the many other accessories for this camera, the periscope attachment to the finder deserves special mention; its use is briefly described in Chapter 5.

### Newman Sinclair Autokine cameras

The James A. Sinclair Co. Ltd, of London, of longstanding reputation in the photographic field, has for more than 60 years produced a series of excellent motion picture cameras for documentary, commercial and newsreel filming. Two of these models may still be found in many short film production centres and animation benches in the UK and other countries.

Since Arthur Newman started producing them in the first decade of this century, Newman Sinclair cameras have had an excellent reputation in Britain, among scientific explorers and documentary film-makers. One of the first models was used by Herbert Ponting to shoot his Antarctic expedition. They were also taken on J. Noel's Mount Everest expedition, and their efficiency was also proved under different climates and difficult conditions by the Royal

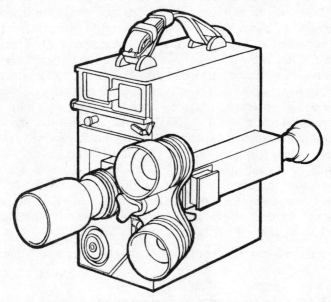

Fig. 20. Newman Sinclair Model N, made in duralumin showing the lenses mounted on divergent axes.

Geographical Society and the New York Zoological Society. A hand-held, spring-driven model known as the "Autokine" appeared in 1928 which also won great acceptance among cinematographers. Robert Flaherty shot his famous "Man of Aran" in 1933 in lonely Inishmore Island off the west Irish coast mostly with this camera. When Basil Wright travelled east and climbed the dangerous Sri Pada peak to shoot "Song of Ceylon" in 1934–35 he also relied on this instrument to produce one of the classics of documentaries. This camera was almost the standard tool of a large portion of British documentaries produced at that time by the film units of the Empire Marketing Board and the GPO under the leadership of John Grierson.

The identifying characteristic of the Newman Sinclair camera is its box-shaped duralumin body ($9\frac{1}{2}$ in. $\times$ $4\frac{3}{4}$ in. $\times$ $9\frac{1}{2}$ in.). Six models were produced: the M, the D, the E, the G and the N, as well as a high-speed model. The intermittent movement produces a very steady registration. It comprises a shuttle acting on a sector of the perforations, and a fixed pilot pin at the lower, right-hand corner of the aperture. In recent models viewing is effected through a bright-image reflex finder. In previous models a side-placed finder provided the viewing system which was parallax-corrected and had an interchangeable front lens. These old models also incorporated direct viewing through the film by means of a special prism optical system.

The film is carried in internally-mounted, double-compartment 200 ft. magazines. Normally the shutter has a fixed opening of 160°, but the manufacturers can supply a shutter variable up to 170°.

Newman Sinclair cameras are driven by two springs which can be wound either at the beginning of the take or when the camera is running. The capacity of the springs ensures that 200 ft. of film is driven at constant speed with a single wind. For sound synchronization work, either a synchronous or variable speed motor can be used. Both types of motor include a speed indicator and sound sync-pulse, and are for 230 v. AC.

The lenses are mounted on a divergent-axis, three-lens turret (model N), four lens turret (model D) or single mounted lens (models G and E), by means of a special sliding plate. Other characteristics are:

(i)   operating from 10 to 32 f.p.s.,
(ii)  weight approx. 17 lbs.,
(iii) special sunshade with matte-box for 3 in. $\times$ 3ins. filters.

## Newman Sinclair P/400 camera

This interesting camera was introduced in the early sixties and is the most recent in the range of hand held cameras manufactured by the James A. Sinclair Company. This instrument is totally different in shape and design from previous models. Few units were manufactured and these were sold in the U.K., USA and the Netherlands. Its users, short film makers, point out its advantages as an ideal portable camera for multiple exposures and other work requiring high efficiency in image quality. The 35 mm P/400 if fitted with the special built-in motor unit and is of very compact design. A normal 12 volt battery is used for the standard motor. Synchronous and other special motors are available for sound recording.

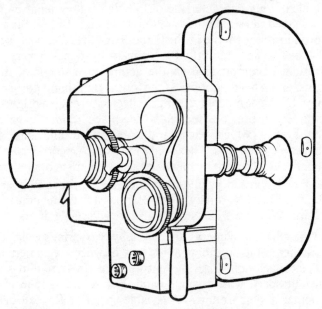

Fig. 21. Newman Sinclair Model P/400 with three-lens turret, reflex viewing and detachable magazine.

REFLEX VIEWING. This is by mirror shutter of robust construction, surface specially treated to enable cleaning and dust removal to be undertaken without damage to the reflecting surface.

OFF-SET TURRET FRONT. This is of special design and strong construction. The positive locking instantly effected by a central knob ensures perfect optical registration with all types of lenses. There is

114

accommodation for three lenses, wide range of focal lengths from 10 mm, also for the latest zoom lenses.

DOUBLE REGISTER PIN AND CLAMPING TYPE FILM GATE. Such a system ensures exceptional picture steadiness and, being of full size, prevents any possibility of film cramping. With this gate the film can be run in reverse for special effects.

FILM MAGAZINES. Available for 200 or 400 ft. and fitted with footage gauge, they have a simple push-on fitment. There are special magazines for running film in reverse with take-up on both spools. The magazines are fitted with internal sprockets for constant film loop.

LENSES. The lenses are fitted into standard Newman Sinclair Type N Focusing Kine mounts having fixed back register. They are interchangeable with all the later models of Newman Sinclair cameras.

## 16/35 mm model

A special model of this camera with interchangeable film gates can be used for both 16 mm and 35 mm. The makers have designed a special blimp enclosing the complete camera for shooting with synchronous sound recording. Fitting the camera into the blimp is quick and positive.

## Sputnik Soviet camera

In 1962, the Soviet film equipment industry developed this new in-

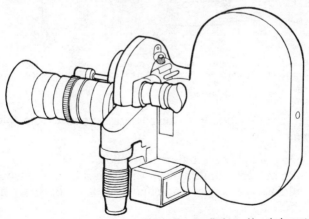

Fig. 22. Sputnik Soviet newsreel camera with reflex viewfinder and handgrip controls.

strument, its design having been specially aimed at film reporting and newsreel shooting.

It is provided with a three-lens turret and a shutter installed at 45° to afford a reflex image, with variable opening from 160° to zero. The reflex viewing system is through an optical tube which can be adjusted to the position of the camera operator. It can take 200 or 400 ft. magazines of the automatic type. A 5–8 v. DC electric motor drives the film at speeds from 8 to 40 f.p.s.

Perhaps the most interesting novelty introduced by this camera is its ingenious controls system. All of them being installed in the camera handgrips, they enable the operator to change focus, rotate the lens turret and start the motor.

### Konvas Automatic Model IKCP Soviet camera

The Konvas Automatic is undoubtedly one of the most widely known and highly reputed Soviet made cameras, which the Mashpriborintorg Company of Moscow has placed in the internal market and in the Comecon. It is an instrument of very sturdy and simple construction, suitable for many types of work, especially in the province of short films. Some aspects of its design resemble those of the Eclair Cameflex.

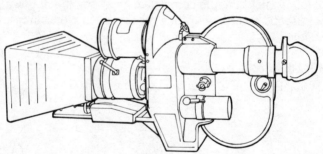

Fig. 23. The Konvas Automatic, a Russian camera extensively used in shorts and newsreels. This 12 lb. camera was used during the flight of Vostok II by astronaut Titov for obtaining shots of the earth.

GENERAL DESCRIPTION. The camera comprises the following main units:

    (i)    body of lightweight aluminum alloy,
    (ii)   film movement mechanism with one-side single claw,
    (iii)  mirror-type single-vane shutter with an open segment of 150°,
    (iv)  three lens not-divergent turret,

116

(v) 6 v. DC electric motor,
(vi) built-in non-swivelling viewfinder with a 5 × magnification,
(vii) tachometer.

The magazine has a capacity of 200 and 400 ft. and comprises the pressure plate, the film drive and the footage counter. When the magazine is mounted on the camera, the frame of the film gate on the camera body enters the magazine film gate and the registering frame contacts the film gate frame. This registers the film in a single plane and brakes it after being moved by the film movement claws.

The DC electric motor has a rated power of 12 W and is attached to one side of the camera. Two hand-crank drives are available for special requirements. One is for single frame exposures and is mounted in a bushing of the camera body. The other is mounted and clamped on the camera in the same way as the electric motor or the spring drive and is for normal speed.

The Konvas Automatic has several accessories such as matte-box and sunshade, anamorphic headpiece with two detachable lenses in special mounts and sunshade for shooting wide screen films, tool kits, etc.

### Sound-on-film cameras

From the birth of sound films to the upsurge of TV, a large number of cameras appeared which recorded sound directly on the film band itself or on a separate film. They were conceived to cover the new possibilities open to news filming with the advantage of directly synchronizing sound and image to cover conferences, interviews, etc.

Many American and European manufacturers made models specifically designed for this purpose. We recall the Sound Cameraeclair with image and optical sound in separate bands; the Akeley Sound widely used in America and which appeared for a long time in the head titles of the MGM newsreel; the Wall used by many newsreel companies the world over, the sound versions of the Mitchell and the Newall, the Vinten Sound, the German Fernseh, and the Soviet Era 1.K.O.S. of more recent production.

TV, with its daily crop of news, hastened the downfall of 35 mm newsreels and cameras of this format are no longer used. The instrument described below deserves special attention because it is the only 35 mm camera in a new double system version still used in some places applying the modern technique of recording sound on a separate perforated magnetic film.

## Double system: Arricord camera

Arnold & Richter, makers of the Arriflex, produced some time ago this model to fill the need of newsreel camera operators for picture and sound recording on separate film and magnetic tape.

The Arricord comprises a special blimp housing an Arriflex 35 with 400 ft. magazine in one section, and a recorder using $17\frac{1}{2}$ mm perforated magnetic tape in a separate section. Both elements are mechanically coupled to ensure perfect synchronization of picture and sound recording.

The camera section is furnished with external controls for focusing and iris diaphragm. Reflex viewing is retained by extending the finder tube through the rear of the blimp. Reading of the tachometer is through a window close to the finder eyepiece.

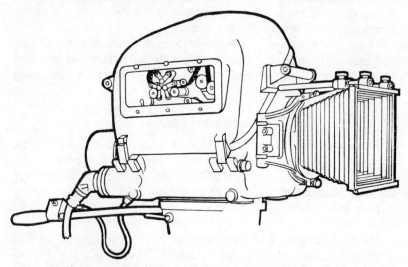

Fig. 24. Arricord double-system camera to record magnetic sound incorporating an Arriflex camera with 400 foot magazine.

Constant speed drive at 24 f.p.s. is supplied by interchangeable motors for either 24, 110 or 220 v. An extendible bellows sunshade with matte-box protects the lenses against reflected light; it is adjustable for lenses of different focal length.

The sound recording section houses a magnetic recorder carrying 500 ft. of perforated tape and works with a Klangfilm amplifier. Other features are:

(i)   built-in illuminated indicators,
(ii)  phone-type dial to operate shutter,

(iii) footage counter,
(iv) built-in ammeter,
(v) earphone plug for listening to recorded sound,
(vi) electronic slate.

## Wide screen cameras

*Technirama camera*

The Technirama process was developed by the Technicolor Corporation and was in use until some years ago. Its basic principle is the squeezing of a scene by an anamorphic prism block to print lengthwise on a 35 mm negative which travels horizontally. This system is similar to Vistavision, (see page 121), but has the added advantage that the picture can afterwards be reduced and turned 90° to convert it into a squeezed 35 mm film image, or it can be reprinted on 70 mm stock.

The use of a very high quality optical system, plus the advantage obtained by reduction, produces an image of high definition, free of graininess, and without distortion.

Technirama was based on the old "three-strip" Technicolor camera (see page 202).

The beam-splitter prism was replaced by a wide aspect ratio aperture for an 8-perforation frame, and the bipack system intermittent movement by a horizontal movement in which the film was moved forward 8 perforations at a time.

The optical system was designed by Professor Bouwers of the Oude Delft Company of Holland. It consists of a combination of interchangeable primary lenses with a split rhombohedral prism with specially cut faces producing an anamorphic coefficient of 1·5 to 1 constant over the whole picture area and giving excellent definition.

The primary lenses were chosen from among different makes with the intention of obtaining a similar degree of definition, resolution and apochromatic quality. These comprise: 50 mm Leitz Summicron, 75 and 100 mm Cooke Taylor Hobson, and 135 mm Canon.

Primary lenses can be focused by the Selsyn motor remote control, as originally installed in the 3-strip cameras, or by individual control on the side of the camera.

Viewing is effected by a through-the-lens finder, and by an automatic parallax-corrected monitor viewfinder installed on the side of the camera.

Magazines are mounted side by side and have a capacity of 2000

119

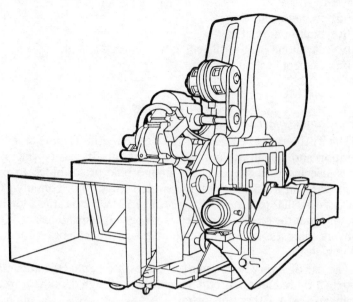

Fig. 25. Technirama camera using an anamorphic optical system and horizontal film travel for lengthways images on 35 mm film.

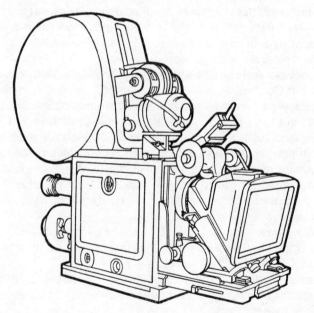

Fig. 26. Another view of the Technirama camera. Observe the elaborate system for driving the magazines.

ft. They are driven by a special torque motor with friction pulley transmission, thus eliminating film snatch when starting, and overrun when stopping.

The driving motor is installed at the rear, and can be interchanged; the models supplied are of the synchronous type for AC or DC, three-phase, and for 220 or 96 v.

For filming with direct sound recording, a special large volume soundproof blimp is used, which is a modification of the 3-strip camera blimp, and is further provided with a special sunshade and other improvements.

More recently, a lightweight model of the Technirama camera has been introduced. It is of smaller volume, takes 1000 ft. magazines and allows the use of three primary lenses of 50, 75 and 100 mm focal length. For underwater shooting, the makers supply a watertight shell furnished with external controls, floats and stabilizers; this shell is built to withstand high water pressure and allows the camera to be very easily operated down to a depth of 230 ft.

## Vistavision camera

The Vistavision system was developed by Paramount Studios of Hollywood, and makes use of an 8-perforation horizontal frame on 35 mm film. Vistavision is in many ways similar to the Technirama system just described. Most of the Vistavision cameras were produced by The Mitchell Camera Corp., and though the system is now obsolete, some of the cameras are still in use for matte shots and for producing transparencies for back projection.

Lenses are single mounted and their focal length varies from 21 mm to 152 mm. The shutter is of the variable opening type, with a maximum of 190°.

The film drive mechamism is a development of the Mitchell intermittent movement. The film travels horizontally from left to right exposing 1·485 in. × 0·991 in. frames which cover eight perforations and have an aspect ratio of 1·96 to 1.

Viewing is effected directly through the taking lens by mechanically displacing the camera body, complemented by a Mitchell monitor viewfinder on top of the camera provided with vertical parallax correction.

Magazines are equipped with their own drive motors and take a film load of 2000 ft.

The Vistavision camera is driven by a special synchronous motor installed with its shaft placed horizontally at the back of the camera.

121

Its rating ranges from 96 to 220 v. and it is provided with reverse drive.

The most important accessories are:

(i) special design of blimp enclosing the complete instrument,
(ii) Selsyn motor remote focuse control,
(iii) sunshade.

*Vistavision field camera*

The intermittent movement of this camera is similar to the Mitchell NC and BNC models. The shutter opening is fixed at 162°. Viewfinding is by means of a parallax-corrected finder equipped with a small turret holding several lenses installed on top of the camera.

The 400 ft. double-chamber magazines are mounted behind the camera. The instrument is driven by a lightweight variable-speed motor working at 28 v.; a built-in rheostat allows the camera to be operated at speeds from 12 to 24 f.p.s. For outdoor shooting, a DC supply can be fed from portable batteries. For special process work the motor can be interchanged for a 96 v. motor.

The Vistavision field camera weighs about 20 pounds, and therefore can be easily hand-held for locations where studio cameras cannot be employed.

## Vintage cameras

With the progress of film technique, many excellent cameras have become obsolete. Examples of these, built in the period between 1920 and the coming of sound, are still doing stalwart work in scientific and technical institutes and laboratories in Europe and Latin America. Good specimens may still be found for sale or on exhibition in museums and some camera stores and are fast becoming valuable collectors' items. In a short tabulation such as this, many less well-known makes and models must necessarily be omitted.

*Akeley*

Many critics consider that the twenties and the thirties were the golden age of motion pictures. Together with a large output of fiction films, many industrial and "travel" productions were made, and the major world events of the time were recorded. For the latter items, cinematographers had available a wide range of cameras made in the USA and in several countries in Europe. Britain was making Darling cameras, Williamsons, Newman Sinclairs, Cinchros and the Moy-Omnias used by Ernest Shackleton in his Antarctic expedition. In

France the Debrie Parvo and the Eclair were already reigning while in Germany they were making the Askania, the Bamberg, the Ernemann, the Zeitlinger, the Maurer & Waschke and the Ika Kinamo. We have already seen some of the instruments which acquired wide fame in America and still maintain their reputation; we shall see a few others yet, but at that time one of the most popular instruments was undoubtedly the camera designed by Karl E. Akeley, an outstanding American scientist, inventor, lecturer and sculptor.

Akeley was curator of the New York Natural History Museum, who sent him to Africa to study animal life in that continent and record on film. He took with him several camera models that were popular at the time. But he did not succeed in obtaining an effective filmed record of the expedition owing to the requirement for a camera that was immediately available in optimum operating condition and able to follow fast movement. On returning he tackled the design of an instrument capable of overcoming the difficulties he had suffered. He achieved an instrument which broke away from most of the established concepts at that time, and which include many improvements to follow rapid moving subjects.

The new Akely camera soon became a favourite with newsreel cameramen and documentary producers (Robert Flaherty took it to the Arctic in 1922 to shoot his first film "Nanook of the North"). It sold so well that for a long time its manufacturers could not cope with an increasing build up of orders. And when Hollywood returned to Africa with first-rate cinematographers like Fred Parrish and for spectacular feature films like "Trader Horn" (1932), the Akeley was in the front line, challenging the same difficulties that a few years ago had led to its creation. The camera's outstanding characteristics were: all metal, circular-shape body; focal plane shutter with 230° opening; intermittent movement with effective steadiness, the claw working on one side of the film only; framing and focusing system using a lens identical to the taking lens, with focus control and easily adjusted eyepiece; a 200 ft. magazine with built-in sprocket for installing inside the camera. It was crank-handle driven, but during World War II was adapted to take electric drive.

*Cameraéclair*

This camera was manufactured by Eclair and became well known for the many facilities in afforded to the cinematographer for special effects and process work. The lens turret mounted up to six lenses. Framing and focusing through the taking lens was effected by means

123

of a mechanical device which placed a special viewfinder behind the aperture. Up to 400 ft. of film was loaded by means of magazines mounted inside the camera body. The camera was driven either by crankhandle or by constant speed electric motor, and counters were supplied for indicating exposed footage, exposed frames and crankhandle turns. The camera was equipped with sunshade and matte-box, built-in rangefinder, etc.

### Newman Sinclair Standard

We have seen that Newman Sinclair cameras held a prominent position in British cinematography. The 400 ft. model was one of the first items this firm produced about 1910 and was widely used during World War I. It was also used on the trips made by the Duke of Windsor (then Prince of Wales) to Africa and South America, and by the well known explorer Major A. Radcliffe Dugmore, as well as by other cinematographers and explorers of that time, like Cherry Kearton, Harry Burton, Paul Rainey, and others. It went on a Mount Everest expedition with Capt. J. Noel and returned years later in Houston's flight. Throughout the years it maintained its reputation for its resistance to hard treatment and efficiency under all climates.

It was one of the first cameras to be adapted to take a smallsize, battery-driven electric motor. Among its features the following are noteworthy:

(i)   automatic fade-in and fade-out,
(ii)  three different systems for focusing,
(iii) bright finder for critical framing,
(iv)  variable opening shutter,
(v)   intermittent drive with pilot pin registration.

It was driven by either crank-handle or electric motor and had a striking appearance since it was built of polished duralumin plates.

### Askania Model Z

Over a period of many years, Askania Werke A.G. of Berlin manufactured a series of cameras for professional cinematography, of which the most outstanding was the Z model. The characteristics of this camera were very similar to Debrie Parvo.

The demand for the Askania Z led to its mass-production for several years while it was the instrument preferred by many European operators and documentary film-makers. It was the camera most used by Karl Vass to shoot notorious Nazi propaganda films like "Triumph of the Will" (1936), as well as "Olympiad" (1938), by Leni Riefenstahl. Many of these cameras covered the scenes of vast masses in these films. Leni Riefenstahl once employed up to 45 camera operators. At the same time, political films were being shot with Askania Z instruments in Italy, where the same system of simultaneously covering a scene with many cameras was applied. The Askania Z was well accepted in Italy, where it can still be found on animation benches and producing titles at some laboratories or documentary films for producers such as the well known Institute Luce.

The basic characteristics of this camera were very similar to the Debrie Parvo; its basic differences from the latter were the body finish, the lens hood and matte-box, the viewing system with double eyepiece, and critical framing effected only through the film.

## Prevost

The motion picture industry became important in Italy during the silent era, and consequently many Italian manufacturers produced models of 35 mm cameras. Amongst them should be mentioned the Micro of the Societa Micromeccanica of Milan, the Standard camera produced by the Fotovita Company, also of Milan, and the Teck by the Serra Company of Turin.

But the Italian camera that was most widely accepted and sold in international markets was undoubtedly the Prevost made by the Attilio Prevost Company. This instrument was first produced in 1922 and was based, like many other designs on the principles of Joseph Debrie's Parvo L. However the Prevost boasted several improvements in form and mechanical design.

The lenses and lens mounts had been designed for quick changeover and furthermore allowed for shifting the lens along the optical axis. A diaphragm and iris system provided for special photographic effects. Fade-ins and fade-outs were produced by a variable shutter ope ing. Critical viewing was achieved through the taking lens with the loss of only one frame. The filmload was carried in separately mounted 400 ft. magazines. The other characteristics were similar to the Debrie Parvo L.

## Institute Standard

Created in 1910, the New York Institute of Photography has acquired international reputation in teaching the arts of still photography and motion pictures. Distinguished professors and cinematographers like Herbert C. McKay, ARPS, Peter Milne, Carl

Louis Gregory, FRPS and many others transmitted the most severe standards of cinematographic techniques to several generations, through this Institute and its associated Falk Publishing Co. Many of the cinematographers, who have become active in the industry, whether commercial, documentary or newsreel were produced by the Institute's publications, correspondence courses or practical lessons at its own premises.

To cover the requirements of specialized tuition and the demand of its pupils, and "shorts" producers, the Institute decided to undertake the production of a low-priced, lightweight, multi-purpose camera. It was designed by the Institute's director, Carl Louis Gregory, together with Herbert C. McKay and William Nelson and it was manufactured at the Wilart Cinema Corporation's workshops, a firm which was already well known for the streamlined design of their cameras. The new instrument was called the Institute Standard and was widely used for cinema students in the east coast of USA.

Its outstanding features were its four-lens turret, choice of fixed or variable opening shutter, high efficiency intermittent and continuous drive, critical viewfinding through film, 400 ft. double chamber magazine, etc. This camera introduced a concept now generally applied throughout the motion picture camera industry: that of a basic unit improved and complemented by accessories. The camera was sold with a single lens and small magazine, and could be gradually added to by means of a lens turret, large capacity magazines, rangefinder, etc.

## DeVry

Over many years, the De Vry Co. won a reputation in the American market for its motion picture projectors, particularly the portable 35 mm model, which sold to many Armed Forces all over the world. Early in the twenties, hand-held, spring-driven, lightweight cameras were very scarce; the most popular was the B & H Eyemo which had recently appeared and was selling very well. This persuaded the De Vry company to design a compact 35 mm gauge instrument, conceived for newsreel cameramen and exacting amateurs. It consisted of a leather-covered metal box of small dimensions weighing about nine pounds. Its main characteristics were:

(i)    single mounted interchangeable lens,
(ii)   fixed opening (135°) shutter,

(iii) spring-driven motor,
(iv) daylight-loading 100 ft. spools of film.

The De Vry was much used by newsreel operators and the Allied Forces during World War II.

The company also built a camera for direct recording image and sound by the optical process, either on one or two strips. This camera obtained a very poor acceptance, but some of its concepts were later adopted by John M. Wall in his famous sound camera.

## Universal and Box cameras

The Universal and Box cameras were very popular instruments for newsreel shooting, commercials and documentary films during the second half of the twenties. They were low-priced cameras of simple design built of seasoned wood as was usual at the time. The Universal carried a 200 ft. film load in square metal magazines, internally mounted. It was turned by a crank-handle. The Newton-type viewfinder was installed on top of the camera and was protected against reflections. The variable opening shutter could be adjusted from the back of the camera. The Universal was equipped with a 3-lens turret, and critical focusing was effected by a viewing system through the film.

The British-made Box camera was supplied in different models but its characteristics were very similar to those of the Universal.

## Cunningham combat camera

Of all instruments of this type, the one which best deserves the name of combat camera is undoubtedly the Cunningham. It was designed with painstaking research by the U.S. Government, for use by film reporters covering the combat fronts in World War II. Its main features were:

(i)   magnesium alloy body with rifle-butt shoulder pad and pistol grip;
(ii)  special turret with shockproof lens mountings;
(iii) intermittent movement consisting of a 2-claw shuttle and register pin, which together with the continuous drive were included, in 200 ft. magazines;
(iv)  viewfinder on top of the camera with frames for four different lenses;
(v)   drive by electric motor for variable speeds from 16 to 32 f.p.s.

The camera could be operated in the taking position by grips and controls located within easy hand reach. Outstanding characteristics of the Cunningham were its sturdy construction and its anti-reflection treatment of all surfaces and components.

This instrument was conceived by Harry Cunningham and was manufactured by the American Camera Co., of Hollywood, and it is believed that Gregg Toland participated in its design on returning from shooting the well known "December 7th" war documentary. Military restrictions on this camera, known as the PH-530 PF, were withdrawn in 1954 and it then appeared for sale in the American market.

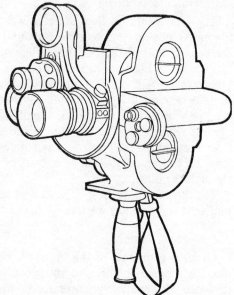

Fig. 27. Bell & Howell Eyemo Model "Q" camera. Note the 3-lens spider turret.

## Bell & Howell Eyemo

In the motion picture industry, the Bell & Howell Co. had become world famous for their Standard Camera which for the first time included in this type of instrument, an all metal body, an externally placed double chamber magazine, an excellent intermittent drive with register pins, and an all-ball-bearing mounted mechanism. For many years it was standard equipment with all Hollywood studios and the minion of many cinematographers. In 1923 this company decided to step into the 16 mm gauge market (which had been actively promoted by the Eastman Kodak Co.) for exacting amateurs, and launched their Filmo camera. This instrument won such widespread approval that the makers decided to apply the same design and

128

characteristics to the professional 35 mm gauge. They called their new model the "Eyemo" and it was conceived for use by newsreel cameramen, scientific explorers and documentary producers. Its spring drive had so many advantages over the then reigning crank-handle, that it was universally adopted by documentary film-makers. During World War II it was one of the standard instruments used by the Allied Forces and was still a leading lightweight camera until a few years ago.

## Bell and Howell model 2709 camera

For the past forty years or so, the Bell & Howell Co. of Chicago have produced a first-rate camera with high precision register, offering excellent possibilities for process and high-speed filming. Production has now been discontinued but the camera is still often used in process work, as well as for animation and optical printing.

The intermittent movement of this camera is known as Unit I, and works with two register pins fixed at the side of the aperture which achieves a very high degree of registration steadiness. The Unit I intermittent movement can be exchanged for another one designed to operate at higher speeds up to 200 f.p.s.

Viewing is possible through the taking lens by displacing the camera body sideways while the lens turret remains in its rigid posi-

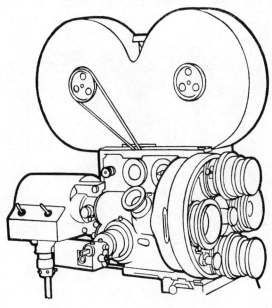

Fig. 28. Bell & Howell Model 2709 seen from the side.

129

tion. A parallax-corrected monitor viewfinder allows for framing and focusing while shooting.

In the older models of this camera, viewing was by rotating the lens turret till the taking lens was placed before the fixed position viewing tube at the camera side where the other controls are placed.

The shutter is of the variable opening type, ranging from 170° to zero.

Film is loaded by means of double compartment magazines attached to the camera top. The camera is driven by interchangeable motors of 115 v. AC or DC, or for 12 to 24 v. DC, for outdoor working.

Among other features of the model 2709 are:

(i)   the four-lens turret,
(ii)  automatic dissolve,
(iii) shutter opening indicator,
(iv)  capacity for adaptation to bipack systems,
(v)   slot for inserting masks and filters.

## Debrie Parvo and Super Parvo Cameras

In 1900 Joseph Debrie founded his company to specialize in making equipment for the newly born motion picture industry. They manufactured one of the most sought-after film punching instruments of the time. Their products were acquired by the best

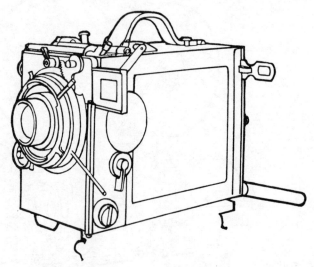

Fig. 29. Debrie Parvo L camera, which provides three different methods of viewfinding.

known manufacturers—Thomas A. Edison among them. In 1905 they produced the first professional printer, and in 1908, Joseph Debrie, together with his son André, designed the first Parvo camera.

The Parvo (meaning compact) introduced the box-shaped concept in order to reduce bulk. It was readily accepted by cinematographers and through the years many models were turned out on the basis of the same solidly built bronze mechanism and specially treated wooden body (five-layer walnut). Years later the first all metal (aluminium) model appeared, and other improvments were gradually added, e.g. focusing device, automatic dissolve, etc. With the coming of sound films, many adaptations were made, leading to the model "L" which soon attained wide popularity.

Debrie-made instruments gave international renown to the French camera industry, and more than eight thousand were sold in world markets. In America the Parvo competed with the then reigning Bell & Howell and was extensively used all over Europe in a large portion of films made in Britain, France, Spain and Italy. In the Soviet Union, Serge Eisenstein employed Parvos in many of his productions shot by Edouard Tissé. It was the typical instrument of the new-born cinema industries in Asia and South America, too. The popularity drove manufacturers in other European countries to copy the most important characteristics of the Parvo.

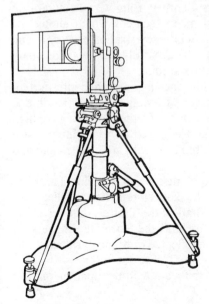

Fig. 30. Debrie Super Parvo Color camera on a rolling pedestal.

The Super Parvo appeared in 1932 equipped with a noiseless movement conceived specially for shooting sound films. This camera immediately outdated all previous cameras with sound padding covers, since it was almost noiseless but of compact size, being one of the smallest and most easily handled cameras taking 1000 ft. (300 m.) magazines. It is interesting to point out that the Super Parvo was an elaboration of the then well-known Parvo 120, brought about by the requirements of a large film capacity to compensate for the new filming speed of 24 f.p.s., needed for sound filming. The ancestor of the Super Parvo was the Parvo "T"; it consisted of a model similar to the Parvo "L" with capacity for 1000 ft. magazines. This model had to be enclosed in a special blimp provided by the makers due to its noisy operation.

At the time when Debrie enlarged the magazine enclosure in order to take 1000 ft. magazines, a sound padding cover was added. In 1941 a reflex viewing system was added and a high precision film drive movement was adopted, together with a special shutter and high quality internal optical system. The different models of this camera were widely used for many years by studios all over the world.

*20th Century Fox camera*

This camera was built by the Simplex Company under the instructions and requirements of 20th Century Film Corp. studios in 1939/1940. The studios wanted an instrument which should be noiseless, relatively light in weight, of high registration precision, and easy to operate. The camera was so successful that it was for many years standard equipment in the Fox studios.

The heart of the Fox camera is its specially designed intermittent mechanism whose absolutely noiseless running makes it possible to dispense with blimping, and which has the further advantage of high operating speed and light weight. It is based on the principle of a single-claw shuttle working in combination with an eccentric pin and cam, and two register pins.

Viewing is effected through the taking lens, or by using a monitor viewfinder. By moving a handle, the camera body is swivelled over an angle of 75° on the axis of the shaft of the shutter; this swivelling places the focusing tube directly behind the lens. The image seen through the monitor viewfinder is a reflected one, and parallax is corrected automatically.

The shutter opening is variable from a maximum opening of 200° to a minimum of 45°.

The magazines are attached externally, and are of the two-compartment type holding 1000 feet of film. The Fox camera is driven by a motor specially adapted to different types of supplies, which is attached to the rear of camera. This camera is provided with an automatic slating device, focusing control, synchronizing control for back projection, and other features.

## Cameraflex

During the Second World War, the Cameraflex Corporation of New York manufactured a camera which was very similar to the Arriflex Mod. I, and was known as the Cineflex. A few more than two hundred units were manufactured for the U.S. Air Force. Shortly after the war the manufacture of this instrument was discontinued. The main differences between this camera and the Arriflex were the following:

(i)  removable motor to be placed at one side of the camera,
(ii)  gelatin filter holder placed behind the film gate,
(iii)  double chamber 400 ft. (120 m.) magazine,
(iv)  spring-driven motor as an optional accessory,
(v)  Goerz Apogar lenses with built-in sunshade.

## Wall camera

This camera was manufactured by John M. Wall Inc. of New York, and was designed to cover the requirements of newsreel operators for simultaneous image and sound recording. It is of sturdy construction and the outstanding feature is its optical recording on the same film that carries the image.

Standard lenses for this camera were manufactured by Bausch & Lomb with focal lengths of 35, 50, 75 and 152 mm. The sound recording system is independent of the camera and is easily installed. The variable shutter opening is adjusted up to a maximum of 170° (190° in some models) by a knob located on the right-hand side of the camera.

The high-precision intermittent movement was specially designed, and can be easily interchanged.

In its general principles the viewing system is similar to that of the Mitchell camera.

The camera body is displaced sideways so that a special focusing and framing tube is placed behind the taking lens.

When the camera is in the operating position, the tube acts as a side-mounted viewfinder; it is parallax-corrected at the eyepiece and is

133

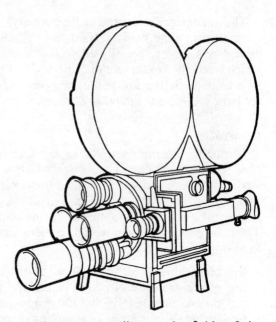

Fig. 32. Wall camera with built-in single-system sound recording.

provided with different masks corresponding to the fields of the different apertures.

The 400 ft. or 1000 ft. double chamber magazines are installed on top of the camera. Drive is supplied by a constant speed, 12 v. motor, with speed control at the back of the camera by a rheostat and tachometer.

## 2. REFERENCES

[1] A.S.C. Cinematographic Annual, edited by Hall & Hall, Vol. I and II, Hollywood (1930).
[2] Cameron, J. R., *Sound Motion Picture Recording and Reproducing*, 8th edn., Cameron Publishing Company, Florida (1959).
[3] Mascelli, J., *American Cinematographer Manual*, 1st edn., A.S.C., Hollywood (1960).
[4] Rose, J. J., *American Cinematographer Hand-book and Reference Guide*, 8th edn., Hollywood (1953).
[5] Lutz, E. G., *The Motion Picture Cameraman*, Charles Scribner's Sons, New York (1927).
Wyn, M., *Initiation aux Techniques du Cinema*, Eyrolles Ed., Paris (1956).

# SURVEY OF 16 MM CAMERAS

For many years, 35 mm film was the accepted standard gauge for professional film making, while 16 mm was used almost exclusively by advanced amateurs and a few professionals for scientific and other specialized work. The great upsurge of television with the consequent profusion of specially shot documentaries and news films, brought widespread popularity to 16 mm, adopted mainly because of its lower cost. Thus, though 35 mm is still standard for feature films and large-scale TV serials, the number of professional units working with 16 mm has now outrun the 35 mm units.

Technical developments over the past twenty years have contributed to provide TV film units, and especially TV news cameramen, with a wide range of equipment to carry out their tasks rapidly and effectively. Manufacturers in the U.S.A. and Europe have taken great pains to design cameras with the characteristics required by TV coverage: light weight, high precision, sturdy construction and ease of operation.

Increasing demand in an ever extending market has forced manufacturers to improve their products constantly in order to incorporate the very latest developments as they appear from the research stage. Although in some cameras the original basic design has remained, new manufacturing processes open up infinite possibilities for the future.

## TV requirements

From the long list of makes and models manufactured today, this survey covers only the instruments which TV crews and documentary film units use most frequently, to the extent that they have now become standard equipment.

TV coverage usually falls into one of three categories: on-the-spot coverage, the elaborated documentary and the interview, which implies simultaneous recording of sound and picture. Film production in each category makes different demands on the equipment, which must therefore be selected according to the type of work.

In the first category, cameras must be of small size, minimum weight and, consequently, their film capacity is limited to 100 or 200 ft. (30 to 60 m.). The inclusion of a zoom lens with a not-too-wide range considerably simplifies the task of changing to different focal lengths and frees the operator from the task of rotating the turret. Electric motors built in to the camera body are a great improvement over the much heavier spring drive which also limits the length of the take.

The filmed documentary calls for a number of further refinements in the camera. In the first place, it must be able to take 200 or 400 ft. magazines. A reflex viewfinder is also vital for this type of film, because of the rapid and exact framing and focusing it provides.

The variable opening shutter is also a useful feature for shooting fast-moving subjects and compensating for different film emulsion speeds.

A variable speed electric motor, a matte-box and a sunshade to allow shooting against the light, are other useful features.

*Sound processes*

Simultaneous recording of image and sound, required by interviews and similar films, can be done by magnetic recording of sound on a track positioned next to the picture which is being recorded (single system), or recording on a separate tape or film (double system). The simplicity of single-system recording makes it the most effective medium when the material must be on the air very shortly after filming. This is the standard system for TV news programmes. It is when the material must be carefully edited that the double system shows its advantages.

Besides a focusing and framing viewfinder through the taking lens and a rod drive mechanism, cameras for double-system sound recording must be able to run noiselessly and must be provided with effective sound synchronism. This can be achieved by interlock or synchronous motors, or by pulse or tone generators.

## Silent 16 mm cameras

*Bell & Howell Filmo*

Until ten years ago this camera was standard equipment in 16 mm newsreel on-the-spot coverage. Even today it may still be found in use, due to its sturdiness and ease of transportation.

The "70" series of this make comprises six different models: DA, DL, H DR, SR and HR; the latest three of these include several refinements which considerably improve their ease of operation and general appearance.

The body is a single-piece aluminium alloy pressing, whose shape is determined by the main internal element, the drive mechanism and the film chamber. The sturdiness and rigidity of the body frame make possible a precision fitting of the different parts of the mechanism.

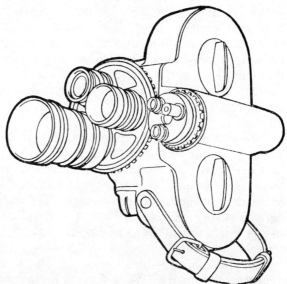

Fig. 1. Bell & Howell Filmo 70-DR newsreel camera with geared viewfinder turret and matched lenses.

INTERMITTENT DRIVE. This mechanism comprises a cam operating a single claw shuttle, which penetrates into and withdraws from the film perforations at a right angle so as to avoid any up-and-down disturbance of the film. This produces a steady image without the use of a register pin.

SPRING DRIVE. Between 19 and 22 feet of film can be exposed with one winding of the spring, and a constant speed is ensured throughout the run by a high-speed governor. The intermittent shuttle is complemented by the two sprockets making up the continuous drive, which are gear-connected to the film take-up. The pressure

137

rollers on the sprockets are interlocked so that on opening them up, the film gate is also opened. Thus a single operation makes the camera ready for threading.

speeds. This camera can be operated at seven speeds: 8, 12, 16, 24, 32, 48 and 64 f.p.s., controlled by a dial on the side of the camera.

FILM STORAGE. Two classical type 100 to 120 ft. spools, one for supply and the other for take-up, are mounted on corresponding spindles inside the camera body.

LENS TURRET. Three lenses can be installed on the turret by means of C type thread mountings. When the turret has been turned, a safety device prevents the camera being started if a lens is not correctly in front of the aperture. In the DR, SR and HR models of this series, the taking lens turret is gear-connected to a turret on the viewfinder, so that the change of lens is synchronized with a change of viewfinder.

VIEWFINDER. Viewfinding and framing of the picture are done solely by a side viewfinder fixed on the camera access door and provided with a three-lens miniature turret corresponding to the three taking lenses. The finder's eyepiece is fitted with a control ring to adjust it to the operator's eyesight. The finder also allows for parallax correction down to 3 feet. The magnified image it provides is very bright and of the same proportions as that recorded on the film.

CRITICAL FOCUSER. When focus adjustment must be effected through the taking lens itself, its diaphragm must be opened fully and the turret rotated 180° to place it before a small critical focuser. The focus can then be checked by means of a small circle showing part of the image.

FOOTAGE COUNTER. Located on the side of the camera, near the speed control, the footage counter is a disc which can be set directly by hand. It is scaled from zero to 100 feet and its calibrations allow for the length of leaders at the beginning and end of the spool.

CRANK HANDLE. The Filmo camera can be driven by means of a crank handle inserted into a hole provided for that purpose. This allows for continuous drive of the film, regardless of the 22 ft.

138

maximum of the spring. Reverse drive can also be effected with the crank handle, but this winds the spring, which restricts the length of reversing. A frame counter indicates the number of frames exposed or reversed. The crank handle exposes 20 frames at every turn.

*Paillard Bolex H-16 Models*

This renowned Swiss-made camera is extensively used for news coverage in many European countries as well as by some TV stations in Europe and North and South America. It is precision built, with a fine quality of finish.

The body incorporates the drive spring and the film drive mechanism. As with other hand-held cameras, the film is loaded inside the body by means of two spools holding up to 100 ft. of film perforated on one or both edges.

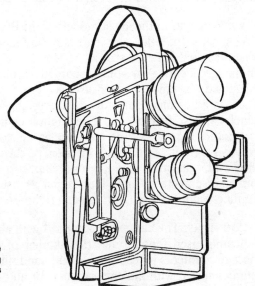

Fig. 2. Bolex Paillard with fade device attached and showing lever-operated triple-lens turret.

INTERMITTENT DRIVE. This is a precision mechanism with a registration pin to ensure image steadiness. It is interlocked with the two continuous drive sprockets to form a combined automatic threading mechanism. This provides fast and foolproof threading, a great convenience to any TV cameraman working under pressure.

SPRING DRIVE. The spring is wound by means of a relatively long crank handle, and with each complete winding $16\frac{1}{2}$ feet of film can be

139

exposed. A small battery-driven electric motor is provided, whose light weight makes it ideal when taking hand-held shots of long duration. An interlocking device disconnects the spring from the mechanism, so that the latter can be driven either by the electric motor or by the crank. The latter, provided with a constant speed governor, also makes possible reverse drive. A speed selector allows operation from 8 to 64 f.p.s.

LENS TURRET. The turret takes three lenses with C type mounting. It is rotated by a lever, and is provided with a device for holding it fast when heavy lenses are used.

FILTER SLOT. As with most professional cameras, the Bolex allows for the insertion of gelatin filters between the lens and the aperture, through a slot located at the side of the turret.

VIEWFINDER. In the latest models of the Bolex, the manufacturers have included a reflex viewing system by means of a beam-splitter prism inserted between the taking lens and the aperture. This gives an image identical to that recorded through the aperture, but magnified six times, and ensures accurate framing and focusing. There is adjustment for individual eyesight at the finder eyepiece, which can also be closed to avoid light seeping in.

Another side viewfinder, known as an "octameter" because it provides eight focal ranges, is installed on the camera access door. It shows a bright image and has a parallax correction device and a 10 mm supplementary lens. This finder is used when precision of framing is not essential, but image brightness is important.

COUNTERS. The camera is equipped with an elaborate system for indicating used footage and the number of exposed frames. The footage counter is placed on the right hand side of the camera and is interconnected with the camera door for automatic resetting.

VARIABLE-OPENING SHUTTER. The shutter is of the variable opening type, which is a help in exposure control and when shooting fast-moving subjects. The opening can be adjusted by means of a sliding lever to give 1/65 second exposure at 24 f.p.s. when fully open, to 1/640 second when 3/4 closed. An accessory allows for automatic fade-ins and fade-outs over 28 or 40 frames.

OTHER ACCESSORIES. A wide range of accessories can be supplied by the makers, providing the camera operator with a large number of

140

facilities. Among them are 400 ft. magazines (for H16 RX-5 model), a constant-speed electric motor Type MST, a light-weight rechargeable battery, a pistol grip with trigger starter, cable releases which are very handy when using a zoom lens, and underwater container and an adjustable sunshade and matte-box.

## Bolex HRX-5

In response to the demand of TV producers for long takes with sync. sound, Paillard S.A. have produced a new Bolex model, the HRX-5, with accessories which include a 400 ft. magazine, a special motor and a portable battery. The camera itself is little changed from the standard Bolex model, but is built to take interchangeable magazines, though it will also accept 100 ft. spools.

THE 400 FT. MAGAZINE. This is a single chamber magazine for laboratory rolls or spools of up to 200 ft. It is attached on top of the camera, and its base is provided with a light-trap at the film slot, so that no light will seep in when the magazine is removed from the camera. The magazine is driven by its own drive motor, and is provided with a counter reading unexposed footage.

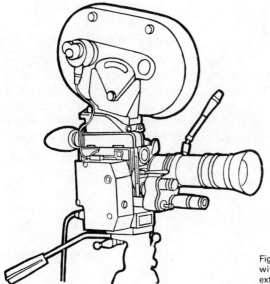

Fig. 3. Bolex H-16 Model RX-5 with 400 ft. magazine and external motor.

CONSTANT SPEED MOTOR. The new MST motor is the most important innovation of the HRX-5. It weighs only 2 lb. Its constant speed derives from an armature which rotates at a speed controlled elec-

141

tronically by a centrifugal governor. It is available in three models (24, 25 and $16\frac{2}{3}$ f.p.s.) for commercial films or U.S. TV, for European TV, and special work respectively.

The 24 and 25 f.p.s. models are provided with a frequency generator to facilitate sound synchronization by means of a pulsed signal. Consequently, when ordering, the buyer must specify the type of magnetic synchronizing head used: Pilotton, Neopilotton, Perfectone or Rangertone.

The MST motor runs at 11 to 15 v. DC, and is provided with connections for the magazine motor and for the special starting switch (other than the one built into the motor) which can be operated from the hand-grip or by remote control.

BOLEX BATTERY. This is a 10-cell, nickel cadmium battery (Saft-Voltablock), weighing $3\frac{1}{2}$ lbs, and rated at 12 v. The unit also comprises a charger for connecting to AC at 100 to 250 v. and 50/60 Hz with voltmeter, and which also acts as "buffer" and thus allows the camera motor to be connected while the battery is being recharged. The capacity of the battery is enough to shoot twenty-five 100 ft. spools or five 400 ft. magazines.

## Bolex H-16 EBM Electric

This is one of the new models from the Paillard Company. Its basic unit is very similar in shape and size to the models described above. The outstanding difference is its built-in motor which is electronically controlled for variable speed filming from 10 to 50 f.p.s. as well as sync sound filming with sync pulse generator or crystal. Motor power is generated by a small rechargeable battery located in the handgrip. A fully-charged battery provides power for 2,400 feet (720 m.) of film. A light in the rear of the camera indicates when the battery needs recharging.

Other special characteristics of this model are:

(i) simple and rugged bayonet mount, capable of holding heavy lenses with practical lock ring and safety device for rapid changing of lenses,

(ii) unlimited film rewind in 100 (30 m.) camera for double exposure by means of rewind crank,

(iii) 170° shutter opening,

(iv) moulded handgrip, perfect for handheld filming and carrying the camera. It forms a base for mounting the camera on tripod,

142

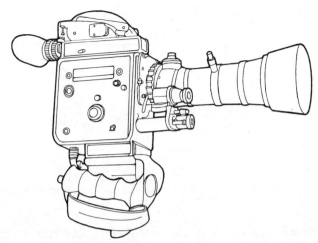

Fig. 4. The new Bolex model H-16 EBM Electric with its built-in motor electronically controlled and a small battery located in the handgrip.

(v) sync pulse generator accessory producing a sync pulse signal of 1·2 v and 60 cycles, which is transmitted to the tape recorder by means of the coiled cable, and recorded on the tape by the sync pulse head.

Otherwise, the camera is built to the same design concepts as the models described above. Together with 400 ft. (120 m), magazine, handgrip and take-up magazine motor, it weighs 12 lb. (approx 5·45 kg.).

*Bolex H 16 EL*

This is the latest model introduced by this company. It has the following main features: built-in electric motor with crystal control for wireless sound; automatic slating with sync-pulse generator; 13× reflex finder with light-emitting diodes to indicate correct exposure; strong safety zoom lens mount; electronically controlled single frame facility; 400 ft. magazine mount; rechargeable battery mount; silicon built-in cell for exposure device, etc. The camera retains the general appearance of previous models.

*Bolex 16 Pro*

This Bolex camera is totally unlike its predecessors in conception and appearance, and incorporates the most up-to-date ideas in automation, viewfinding, and hand-holding.

143

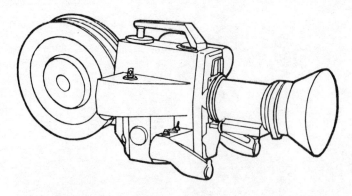

Fig. 5 Bolex 16 Pro camera designed for hand and shoulder support, with reflex viewing and through-the-lens exposure control.

GENERAL CHARACTERISTICS. This camera has been conceived fundamentally for hand-held shooting, although provision has also been made for tripod mounting. The 400 ft. coaxial magazine has been designed to provide adequate support on the shoulder. At both sides of the camera body there are hand-grips with switches for starting the motor and controlling the various devices.

The reflex viewing system using a revolving mirror shutter is so arranged that the image is always visible, even when the camera is stopped.

There is a × 20 magnifier for ease of critical focusing, and the swivelling periscope eyepiece. The diaphragm setting can be read through the finder.

MOTORS. The camera is driven by a 12 v. Synchro-Vario type motor installed inside the camera body. It provides both forward and reverse drive, as well as single-frame and its speed range is from 10 to 50 or 100 f.p.s. according to the model.

The motor speed is regulated by means of transistorized governors. The double function claw intermittent movement gives a very steady image.

Three servo motors may be operated without moving the hands from the grips.

The third motor is designed to automatically set the diaphragm in accordance with the prevailing light conditions. This motor is controlled by light through the lens (the TTL method) deflected from the viewfinder. This device allows for a film speed range of 12 to 1600 ASA, and a running speed of 12 to 100 f.p.s. according to the model, as well as single-frame exposure.

144

The lightweight, easily inserted magazines take either rolls or daylight-loading spools. When the film run is nearing its end, the operator is warned by a red lamp.

The camera is usually equipped with an Angenieux $f.2 \cdot 2$ 12–120 mm zoom lens, or a Schneider-Variogon $f.2$ 16–80 mm zoom lens.

Other lenses can also be used, and the mounting is of the bayonet type and of rugged design. The lenses are provided with special rubber sunshades.

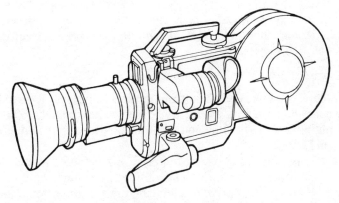

Fig. 6. Front view of the new Bolex Pro showing the multiple camera controls situated in the handgrips.

Other features are: changing running speed while filming with automatic adjustment of diaphragm, pushbutton power focusing, the ability to see the area surrounding the field covered by the lens, fade out by pushing button, production of fade-in, production of lap dissolves, rewind film without covering lens, minimum image flicker on viewing, automatic threading, slate on tape and film automatically, instant change of film magazine, right or left eye viewing, connection for sync-pulse recording, 100 c/s to 50 c.s. pilot signal, 132° shutter opening, perfect camera operation from −4° F to +120° F, knife incorporated for cutting partially exposed film, motor with quartz frequency emitter, etc.

The Paillard Company makes four models of the Bolex Pro:

16 Pro Sepmag
16 Pro Commag
16 Pro-100 Sepmag
16 Pro-100 Commag

The first model is the standard one. The second model, the Commag,

145

is supplied with a magnetic head for direct recording on film with a high efficiency pre-striped track. The Pro-100 Sepmag is the standard model with the additional possibility of running up to 100 f.p.s. for special shooting such as sports, games, scientific work, where slow motion is essential. Finally, the 16 Pro-100 Commag model allows for both running at 100 f.p.s. and for direct sound recording.

ACCESSORIES. The most important accessories provided are: battery with control unit and charger, amplifier for magnetic recording on the film itself, radio microphone and receiver, "monopod" for hand-held shooting, × 15 magnifying eyepiece, electronic viewfinder, tachometer.

*Arriflex ST camera*

Arnold & Richter, German camera makers since 1917, have for many years had a reputation for well designed instruments to cover the requirements of scientific and documentary film units and news-reel cameramen.

The first 16 mm camera made by this firm was the ST model. The shape of its body is compact and designed for hand holding. It houses the intermittent drive mechanism, the reflex viewfinder, and space for the film, while the lens turret is mounted on the front. The body is a single-piece, light alloy casting, weighing no more than $6\frac{1}{2}$ lbs.

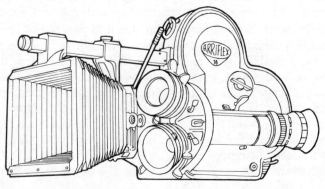

Fig. 7. Arriflex Mod. 16 ST can be converted for recording single-system magnetic sound recording with Gaumont Kalee recording equipment.

INTERMITTENT DRIVE. This mechanism comprises a single-claw shuttle pulling down on one side of the film, and a register pin to steady the film during exposure. All parts are made of high quality

146

steel and are precision balanced and finished to ensure image steadiness.

FILM GATE. The pressure plate is spring loaded to ensure freedom from weaving and breathing. All surfaces in contact with the film are of alloy stainless steel with hard chromium plating. The pressure plate is hinged to allow access directly to the aperture and to the film guides.

REFLEX VIEWFINDER. This type of viewfinder with all its advantages of rapid focusing and accurate framing was first introduced on the Arriflex in 1936 and has been adapted to the 16 mm cameras. It produces a very bright image, even when the diaphragm is stopped down for shooting. The optical tube gives a 10 × magnification. The eyepiece is adjustable, and is closed automatically when not in use, to prevent fogging.

LENS TURRET. The turret takes three lenses with mountings of special design (identical to those for the Arriflex 35). Minimum lens focal length is 5·7 mm. The turret is compactly designed with divergent lens axes so that their fields will not interfere. To change lenses, the turret is rotated by pressing on wing grips jutting out of the turret edge, with inscriptions on their rear faces to indicate which lens is in the taking position.

CONTROLS. Located at the back of the camera: tachometer calibrated from 0 to 50 f.p.s.; footage counter and frame counter, both with zero reset knob.

MOTORS. The Arriflex ST is driven by an electric motor of small size which can be easily installed and interchanged to suit the operator's need. The standard motor is rated at 8 v. DC, and is provided with a reostat for adjusting the camera speed from 4 to 48 f.p.s. It can also reverse at any speed. The following motors can also be supplied: synchronous motor for 110 or 220 v., 50 or 60 Hz driving the camera at 24 or 25 f.p.s.; governor-controlled motor for 8 v., also running at 24 or 25 f.p.s., and stop-frame equipment for animation.

ACCESSORIES. The makers produce many accessories for these cameras which turn it into a complete studio instrument. Among the most important are the following:

(i) the 400 ft. magazines which can be mounted in a slot on top of the camera, and can take 200 ft. or 400 ft. spools. An easily-detachable separate motor drives the take-up spool and is connected automatically to the camera power supply when the magazine is attached to the camera; these magazines are fitted with their own footage counters;

(ii) the blimp for this camera is very complete: it is equipped with a device for focus control and an extension for the reflex viewfinder tube and is designed to allow for the attachment of external magazines (as above), and for inter-changeable motors;

(iii) periscope viewfinder attachment which swivels in any direction and allows the operator to view through the finder tube when standing in almost any position in relation to camera and subject.

*Arriflex Model M*

The wide popularity attained by the Arriflex 16 ST led to the introduction of two new 16 mm models, the M and the BL.

The M model is designed on the basis of the "magazine-camera" principle introduced on the Arriflex 35 in 1936. The motor is

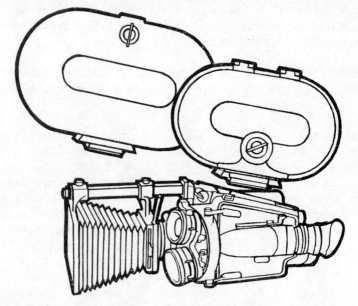

Fig. 8. Arriflex 16-M, with 200 and 400 ft. magazines. It has a built-in pilot-tone generator for synchronizing sound.

mounted on the camera body which houses the intermittent drive mechanism. The interchangeable magazine unit carries the continuous drive sprockets. After threading in the magazine the loop is inserted into the camera when attaching the magazine.

The other characteristics of the camera, such as the bright image reflex viewfinder, tachometer, frame and footage counters, lens turret with divergent axes, register pin, intermittent movement, etc., remain the same as for the ST model previously described.

However, in order to meet the needs of modern sound synchronization systems, together with certain specialized requirements, the makers have added several new facilities.

BUILT-IN TONE GENERATOR AND SLATING MECHANISM. This device allows for sound filming by synchronizing the camera to the sound recorder through the tone generator. A frame or its edge is exposed as reference between the sound track and the film at the start. To employ the pilot-tone generator built into the camera body, one of the special 24 or 25 f.p.s. motors must be used.

THREE CONNECTOR SOCKETS. These are located at the rear of the camera and are:

(i)    socket for the 5-pin plug of the pilot generator;

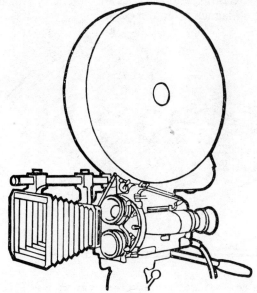

Fig. 9. Arriflex 16-M with 1200 ft. co-axial, double compartment magazine.

(ii)  socket for the 3-pin plug for parallel connection to the camera feed circuit (for special purpose work);

(iii) empty space for installing 2- to 12-prong connections for scientific work.

THE 1200 FT. COAXIAL MAGAZINE. This magazine is of ingenious design, with the two film spools mounted on the same axis, so that a large film capacity is enclosed in a comparatively small space. At sound filming speed 1200 ft. of film gives 30 minutes of continuous shooting, often a necessity when covering conventions and conferences, and in certain types of scientific work in which frequent reload must be avoided.

MOTOR TRIP SWITCH. An item usually found only in more elaborate cameras, this acts as a safety switch which stops the motor in the event of film jamming inside the camera.

*Arriflex model BL*

The BL model of the Arriflex 16 mm line has become one of the most widely used cameras in the field of documentary film making and for television report work. It combines the characteristics and advantages of the M and ST models, as described above, but has the added advantage of a noiseless running mechanism, use of zoom lenses of special characteristics, and facilities for double or single sound recording using a magnetic sound module.

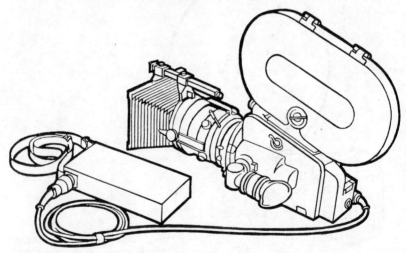

Fig. 10. Arriflex 16 mm BL model with battery in separate case and shoulder strap.

CAMERA BODY. The body consists of a unit mounted on a single platen which is floating acoustically within the camera housing in order to isolate the noise of the running motor. In this way, the intermittent system has a noise level of no greater than 31 dB.

FILM TRANSPORT MECHANISM. This is the same as that used in other models, with a single claw shuttle and register pin.

LENS MOUNT. The great improvement in the image quality of zoom lenses has brought them into almost universal use. The Arriflex BL, therefore, has been provided with a single mount design for zoom lenses, with their own special housing which limits motor noise. Several models of zoom lens with housing are available: Angenieux $f$ 2·2, 12·5–75 mm; Angenieux $f$ 2·2, 12–120 mm; Angenieux $f$ 2·2, 9·5–95 mm or Zeiss Vario Sonnar $f$ 2·8, 10–100 mm. The lens housing provides facilities for lens controls with scales for diaphragm and focusing. On the front of the unit there is an extendible bellows sunshade and matte box. In view of the weight of the complete optical unit the lens mount is of rugged construction in steel. Zoom lenses can be operated automatically by a motor with controls set on the handgrip.

MOTORS. The motors are interchangeable and are positioned on one side of the camera. The motor is connected to the camera mechanism by two gears. The standard motor is for 12 v. DC, running at 3000 r.p.m. for a camera speed of 24 f.p.s. By interchanging the gears the camera speed can be changed to 25 f.p.s. The motor is provided with a governor to maintain a speed constancy within a limit of 1·5%. A special device to change the running speed can be supplied as an accessory. There are models which the Pilotone signal corresponds to 60 c/s instead of 50 c/s. The company supplies synchronous motors for 100 to 240 v, and 50 or 60 c/s.

CONTROLS. The main controls and connections are sited at the rear of the camera. These are a 0 to 50 f.p.s. tachometer, four digit foot counters with zero reset button, a socket for connecting the battery cable, earphone connection socket, Pilotone socket, indicating lights to show when the camera is running, another to show when the sync mechanism is running and another for the edge-marking system. The on-off switch is placed on the body of the motor.

151

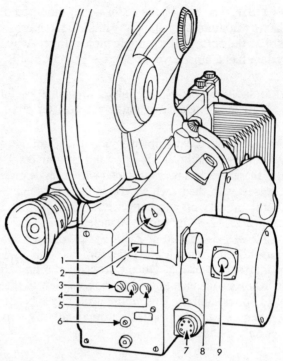

Fig. 11. (1) Tachometer, (2) footage or metre indicator, (3) start marking lamp, (4) operation control lamp, (5) manual scene control lamp, (6) earphone connection, (7) camera motor connection, (8) zero reset, (9) toggle switch.

VIEWING SYSTEM. This is identical to all other Arriflex 16 models, viewing through a mirror shutter at 45° of the plane of the film. The image is seen through a swivelling periscope viewing system with automatic closing eyepiece which can be adjusted to any operation position and allows for viewing with either the left or the right eye. An accessory can be added to raise the viewing axis for shoulder operation. The image obtained is bright and is conveniently enlarged (× 10) and permits focusing with ease. The ground glass can be interchanged for one with grids, TV safe area, cross hairs, etc.

MAGAZINES. The camera takes the usual type of magazine made by this company for 200 and 400 ft. loads. These have a built-in drive system and blimp and are of the single chamber type. They are provided with a footage counter calibrated in feet or metres, according to buyer's needs. A loop of film from the magazine allows rapid threading.

152

BUILT-IN EXPOSURE CONTROL SYSTEM. At the request of users a built-in exposure control device can be added to the Arriflex BL which measures light values over an area equivalent to 50 per cent of the 16 mm field. This is built into the viewing system and indicates the exposure in the viewfinder. The meter uses a CdS cell and has a film speed setting range from 16 to 500 ASA. The controls of this system are on the front end of the camera door.

SINGLE-SYSTEM SOUND MODULE. This camera allows for easy installation of a module containing a recording head, a playback head, and inertia flywheel and several guide rollers. By this means sound can be recorded on the magnetic track which is coated on the film. A transistorized amplifier has been designed for this purpose and is provided with two sockets for a pair of low impedance microphones with individual speech/music switches, gain control, and modulation meter.

ACCESSORIES. As in the use of other models made by this company, there is a wide range of accessories for the BL to meet the most varied requirements and to adapt the camera to any kind of work. Among them are an oscillator for tape recorder, 1200 ft. coaxial magazine, carrying handle, pistol grip with trigger release, filters, carrying and storage cases, shoulder pod and batteries.

## Arriflex SR

This is the most recent offspring of the Arnold & Richter Company in the 16 mm camera line. It is the result of further advances in camera technology which set new standards in speed of operation, compact design, mobility and operational comfort.

GENERAL CHARACTERISTICS. This is an extremely compact camera, weighing only 11 lbs. It is designed for hand-held shooting and supporting on the shoulder without tiring the operator. Its makers claim that it is the first camera ever designed to achieve a perfect operational symmetry. Consequently it allows for total control with either the left or the right hand. It also allows for viewing either with the left or the right eye and can be operated from any position. Thus, it is suitable for all kinds of work: TV reporting, documentaries, scientific films, and so on.

MAGAZINES. These are the coaxial, double chamber type for either 200 or 400 ft. loads and allow for rapid exchange and loop control.

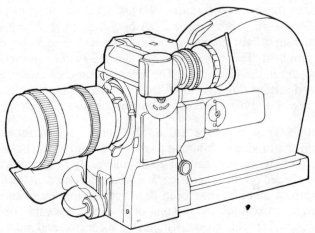

Fig. 12. Arriflex Mod. SR, the latest offspring of the Arnold & Richter line of 16 mm cameras.

The magazine is provided with the pressure rails, while the aperture plate is in the camera body. Daylight reels can be used.

INTERMITTENT DRIVE. Positively controlled pull-down claw and registration pin.

VIEWFINDER. There is a 180° mirror reflex shutter. The viewfinder tube can be rotated and swivelled in three planes with complete image position compensation. The viewfinder image therefore remains upright and correct left-to-right in every eyepiece position.

MOTOR. The camera uses a high performance 12 v. DC motor with built-in crystal control for 24/25 f.p.s. synchronous sound filming with any type of tape recorder which is fitted with a crystal generator. A warning light is visible in the camera viewfinder and lights up with loss of synchronization. The motor is also equipped for slave operation. Various filming speeds (from 24/25 to 50 f.p.s.) can be set with an accessory control mechanism. An electronic stopping device always brings the mirror shutter into the viewing position when the camera is switched off.

BUILT-IN EXPOSURE CONTROL. This system uses a built-in CdS follow-pointer exposure meter (equipped for fully automatic exposure control over a range of film speeds of 16 to 500 ASA). A + 2 $f$-stop indicator in the viewfinder allows exposure control within the permissible film contrast range.

154

LENS MOUNT. Arriflex bayonet mount for one single lens is fitted.

OTHER FEATURES. These include quiet blimp-free operation for synchronous sound filming, spacer gate, gelatine filter slot behind the lens, automatic lens diaphragm with internal release from the camera (therefore focusing is always possible with the lens wide open).

## Eclair NPR (Noiseless Portable Reflex)

When Eclair of Paris conceived their new design of 16 mm camera, they broke away from long established concepts in camera making. In the first place, they abandoned the classical system of installing the film magazine on top of the camera, and instead attached it at the rear so that it rests on the operator's shoulder. This coaxial magazine (i.e. with both film spools on the same shaft) houses the camera's continuous drive mechanism; thus threading takes place in the magazine instead of in the camera body.

As in the firm's Cameflex 35, (see p. 102) the magazine is very quickly attached to the body, even while the instrument is running, which is important when switching to different types of emulsion, and when there is a need to save seconds at critical moments.

Framing and focusing are by a reflex viewfinder taking its image from a variable shutter made of Lucite, with brightly plated outer surfaces. As the image field on the ground glass is 20% greater than

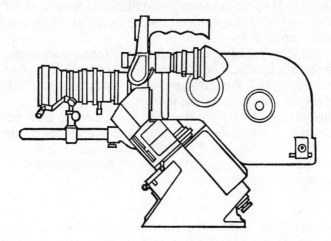

Fig. 13. Eclair 16 NPR camera, a self-blimped instrument basically designed for hand-held operation.

that of the aperture (whose field size is marked by a rectangle with the TV safe area engraved on it) the operator can check the subjects that will come into the frame or are just out of it. The image on the finder is very bright and is twelve times magnified. The finder allows for sighting with either right or left eye, and as it can be swivelled 360° it is very useful for "candid camera" shots, where the operator has his back to the subject.

Eclair make a special point of the careful research behind the design of each part of the camera. This can be appreciated in the position of the shutter shaft below the aperture, so that the shutter blades close the aperture in a horizontal direction, i.e. from one side to the other, thus working like the focal plane shutter in many still cameras. This layout permits faster panning free of stroboscopic effects.

Various types of motor are available for driving this camera. The standard one is a transistor model for 12 v. DC with constant speed regulation, and it comprises a pulse generator for synchronizing the camera with Perfectone or Nagra type recorders. Other available motors include a variable speed type, an AC synchronous motor, and one with a crystal speed control.

The outstanding characteristic of this camera is its careful engineering, which provides in effect, noiseless running without sacrificing portability by the use of blimps. This has been achieved by simplifying to the utmost the noise producing components in the mechanism. These mechanical modifications have created the camera's particular shape, which contributes to its convenience for hand-held shooting.

The supply and take-up compartments of the separate magazines are placed side by side. The raw stock can be supplied in 100 or 200 ft. spools, or in 400 ft. darkroom loads. Footage counters (either in feet or metres) are built into the magazines.

Many accessories are provided for this camera to meet various requirements. Among them are: sunshade and matte-box, hi-hat, magnetic sound recording system built in a special case, 1200 ft. magazines, and a case for carrying camera assembled ready for immediate use.

### Eclair ACL

The ACL Eclair camera is the latest model produced by this well-known French company. It is a crystallization of their efforts to achieve a high efficiency, portable camera with all the advantages obtained from modern technology. The result has been a complete success: it is of a simple mechanical design and is very versatile, while it retains all those facilities which are accepted and even demanded by present day cinematographers, such as: snap-on magazines, reflex finder with a field of view greater than the image, silent mechanism, etc.

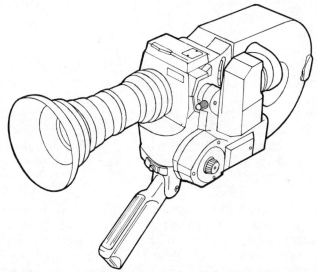

Fig. 14. Eclair ACL. Highly portable camera with all the advantages obtained from modern technology.

GENERAL CHARACTERISTICS. The camera has a small body housing the drive mechanism, reflex shutter, the film gate, the lens mount, and the drive motor. The magazine, with the continuous drive mechanism, is provided with a pressure plate for attaching to the camera body.

MOVEMENT. A wedge-shaped claw is mounted beside the film aperture. The claw movement is controlled by an eccentric and a fixed cam and rendered positive by the use of a counter cam. According to the manufacturer the definition and steadiness obtained is of the highest professional standards.

SHUTTER. Plane shutter of large diameter placed just in front of the film and with an opening of 175°.

REFLEX VIEWING. This is achieved with an oscillating mirror. The reflecting surface of the mirror is glass, attached to a magnesium

157

support. The viewfinder provides an exceptionally bright image which allows precise and easy focusing with the fastest films. As on the Eclair NPR 16, the ground glass gives a field of view greater than the recorded image which helps avoid the possibility of the intrusion of microphones into the picture area. The viewfinder rotates through 360° and an accessory extension enables the operator to use the left eye for operating.

LENS MOUNT. Universal lens mount for "C" mount lenses or steel TS mount screws to permit the use of Cameflex, Arriflex, Mitchell or Nikon mount lenses.

MAGAZINE. The snap-on co-axial magazine of the Eclair ACL is designed to take 200 ft. reels on a 2 in. (50 mm) core or 100 or 200 ft. (30 or 50 m) daylight loading spools. The magazine is arranged with the supply side on the left and take up on the right. A film counter indicates the amount of unexposed film remaining.

MOTOR. This is a crystal controlled brushless motor developed for space applications, and runs silently on 12 v, DC battery power. It is a Hall effect motor, absolutely static-free, and will not add hash to radio microphone signals. It runs at 24 or 25 f.p.s. depending on the frequency of the crystal used. The crystal is located under the small motor cover. Also available: variable speed, 12 v. DC, not silent motor.

OTHER FEATURES. Pilotone module for tape recorders not equipped with crystal control, semi-automatic light meter built in to the camera, behind the lens slot for gelatine filters, bellows matte-box with rotating filter holder, sound recorder connection, automatic clapper, adjustable handgrip, sound level comparable with Eclair NPR 16, power consumption less than 0·8 amp, weight 7·7 pounds (3·5 kg.) without lens.

## Beaulieu R 16B (PZ)

In the early fifties, Marcel Beaulieu introduced into the European market through the Electro-Technique-Mechanique Company, a 16 mm camera which was outstanding for its novel design features. With the years 16 mm and Super 8 Beaulieu cameras have been distributed all over the world. An incredibly high number of cameras in both gauges are manufactured in the company factory at Romoratin, France, to meet the demands of all kinds of filmmakers.

The R 16B (PZ) is one of the most complete among 16 mm portable instruments, and is, consequently suitable for many kinds of film work.

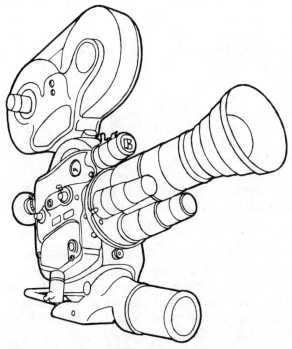

Fig. 15. The Beaulieu R 16 (PZ) compact instrument, intended for all-purpose shooting showing the 200 ft. magazine.

GENERAL CHARACTERISTICS. The R 16B (PZ) is a compact instrument, intended for all-purpose shooting. The smart body is a one piece casting in a very light but shock resistant alloy. The various controls are easy to identify and most of them are situated on one side of the camera.

INTERMITTENT DRIVE. Hard steel single claw pull-down of elliptical action.

VIEWFINDER. The reflex viewing system gives a very bright image even at small diaphragm settings. The camera uses a 45° angled, mirrored, reciprocating shutter working on the guillotine principle. The image on the viewfinder is 10 × magnified. It is very bright due

159

to a new type of viewing screen developed by Eastman Kodak and the eyepiece can be adjusted to the operator's individual eyesight.

PHOTOCELL. Gossen CdS cell is built into the viewfinder system with an indicator needle in the viewfinder. There is an automatic or semi-automatic exposure system with servo motor to open the diaphragm ring to the correct setting. Film speed setting ranges from 10 to 400 ASA.

MOTOR. The mechanism is driven by a small speed-regulated 6 v. DC motor with a range of 2 to 64 f.p.s. which can also be reversed to provide special effects. A built-in tachometer allows the filming speed to be adjusted. There are eight calibrated speeds: 2, 4, 8, 16, 24, or 25, 32, 48 and 64 f.p.s.

CAMERA CONTROLS. There is a footage counter, graduated in feet and metres from 0 to 100 which also reverses, a trip control (normal or frame by frame) and remote control by cable and radio.

LENS TURRET. This may be for single or three-lens mounting. Reglomatic autocontrol unit: the Reglomatic system consists of a transistorised micro-motor which is geared directly to the diaphragm ring in response to commands given by the light sensitive cell of the built-in exposure meter. The focal range of the zoom lens can be also varied by means of the Reglozoom.

FILM CAPACITY. The Beaulieu takes 100 ft. daylight-loading spools, but also has provision for the attachment of 200 ft. double compartment external magazines with built-in micro-motor and footage counter.

ADDITIONAL FEATURES. Built-in mechanical sync pulse connection device for controlling input voltage, ease in hand-held shooting due to light weight and pistol grip with built-in rechargeable NICad battery, battery supply socket, 50/60 Hz sync sound connection. Among available accessories are an intervalometer for precisely timed stop-frame exposures, fixed turret, camera base, matte-boxes and extension tubes.

*Mashpriborintorg Mod. 16 CII-M Soviet Camera*
The Russian motion picture industry has produced a 16 mm camera for professional work and it is used in that country for film

reporting and productions for television. It is a compact camera (195 × 215 × 320 mm) and, together with the lenses weighs 11 lb. (5 kg.). Its construction affords maximum ease for the operator, whether for hand held shooting or use on a tripod. The camera can take a wide range of fixed focus or zoom lenses which are mounted on a divergent turret with capacity for three lenses. A bellows sunshade and matte-box is installed in front of the lenses.

Viewing is by means of a mirror shutter with a pair of unbreakable plastic blades with variable opening ranging from 30° to 170°. Special devices eliminate the image flicker in the viewfinder while shooting. The image is ten times enlarged and the operator can use either the left or the right eye.

The variable speed electric motor is installed behind the camera, can be regulated from 12 to 48 f.p.s. and allows for reverse drive. A tachometer placed behind the camera indicates the running speed. The main novelty of the design is the use of loaded magazines for 100 ft. (30m.) spools which house the built-in continuous drive mechanism and the exposed film counter. These magazines are mounted behind the camera. The camera body is similar in shape to the Arriflex 16 ST.

### Doiflex

The Japanese camera industry, already famous for its still photo and 8 mm motion picture cameras, has entered the international

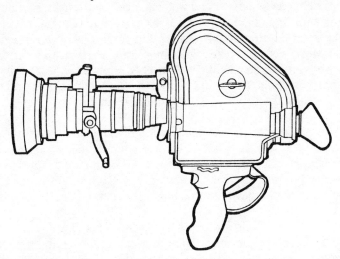

Fig. 16. Doiflex camera with a reflex viewing system and three-lens turret, shown here with a zoom lens attached.

161

market with a new 16 mm camera designed to cater for the requirements of TV newsmen as well as documentary and industrial film-makers. It was one of the first Japanese attempts in the field of professional motion picture cameras.

Of compact design, sturdy construction and excellent finish, the Doiflex incorporates typical modern professional characteristics: very bright reflex viewing by means of a special device synchronized with the focal plane shutter, shuttle and claw pull-down mechanism and register pin, three-lens turret with "C" mount lenses, lightweight cast aluminium body, built-in tachometer and footage counter, 8 v. interchangeable motor for speeds from 2 to 48 f.p.s., fixed shutter with 1/57 second exposure at 24 f.p.s., capacity for 100 ft. film spools.

Various accessories are supplied by the makers, amongst them 400 ft. magazines, rewinding device for producing double exposures, adjustable sunshade and filter holder, pistol grip with built-in switch, portable 8 v. battery and charger, synchronous motor, governor controlled motor, barney and a bracket for the zoom lens.

*Aäton Model 7*

The Aäton Cinematographie company, of Grenoble, France, which is headed by the well-known expert Jean Pierre Beauviala, has produced a very interesting 16 mm camera. The Aäton 7 camera is a lightweight easily carried and well balanced instrument, particularly suitable for hand held shooting. It is designed to take full advantage of the latest developments in lenses and emulsions by good registration. Moreover the reflex viewfinder makes focusing extremely precise. This instrument, which is equipped with rapidly interchangeable magazines and with a built-in television pick-up tube, could well make Super 16 a "standard" format.

INTERMITTENT DRIVE. The positive claw movement (Aäton patent) produces a low noise level which does not increase significantly with time. The absence of vibration contributes to high image definition. High efficiency energy distribution ensures low wear and high longevity, according to the manufacturer's claims.

VIEWFINDER. Wide rotating mirror (185° fixed opening) for reflex viewing. Bright 11 × magnification eyepiece in the nodal plane of standard zoom lenses. Field of observation 20% larger than Super 16 frame.

162

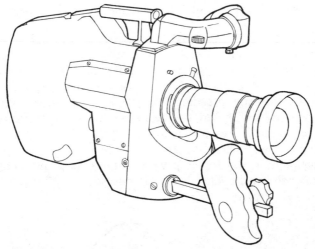

Fig. 17. The Aaton Mod. 7 camera, a light instrument manufactured in France and adaptable for the Super 16 system.

MOTOR. Crystal servo-controlled 12 v. DC motor for 24/25 f.p.s.

MAGAZINES. Clip-on 400 ft. (120 m.) coaxial magazines.

LENS MOUNT. Universal lens mount for Arriflex, Eclair, Canon, Aäton & "C" mounts, with lens locking system. Standard lens: Angenieux 12–120 mm.

OTHER FEATURES. Starting time: 0·6 sec; unaffected by gyroscopic effects. Chronometric marking; light measurement in central field, temperature range (0 to 140°F), reflex video viewing 625 lines, video modulation according to CCIR "L" Standards, adjustable hand-grip carrying handle, matte-box and filter holder, Super 16 model with (0·293 × 0·484 in. format), weight 12 lbs. without lens.

*Pathé Electronic "Duolight"*

The Pathé company of France has been world-renowned since 1896 for their film studios, their newsreels, laboratories, their film production and distribution and for the many items of equipment they manufacture both for amateur and professional cinematography, thus covering all fields of the industry. Their main contribution to the 16 mm field is an all purpose instrument, the Pathé Electronic "Duolight", which shows a fairly wide range

163

of improvements over their previous model, the PR 16-AT/BLT.

CAMERA BODY. The body is of diecast hydrallium, lightweight, yet extremely solid. It includes the electric motor and electronic circuits, the mechanism, the sync signal generators, the start and stop device, counters, etc. It consists of: 1. *Plate* with spool spindle, single sprocket, automatic threading device: 2. *Optical unit* with three lens turret, servo motor, optical reflex system, photo-electric cell, variable shutter, pressure pad claw assembly; 3. *Cover* with viewfinder, photo-cell calculator, speed selector, electronic circuit for servo-motor; 4. *Handgrip* with thumb release and detachable shoulder belt, which holds 0·5 A/H battery; 5. *400 ft. magazine*, as an optional accessory.

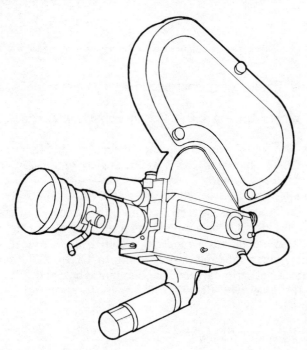

Fig. 18. Pathé Electronic "Duolight" camera with 400 ft. film magazine and built-in battery in the handgrip.

MOTOR. The camera is driven by a brushless 12 v. electric motor with integrated Hall-effect generator (Siemens Model 1 AD 3000 OA). The motor is controlled by an electronic circuit, with rotating field generator, voltage comparator and speed governor.

164

FRAME RATE. The Pathé Electronic camera can operate at frame rates of 8, 18, 24, 32, 48, 64 and 80 f.p.s. Frame rates are selected by a dial on the cover of the camera. Each speed can be adjusted separately.

VIEWING SYSTEM. The through-the-lens viewing system is flicker-free. The glass pellicle behind the lens, set at 45° deflects 20 per cent of the rays to the viewing screen. The optical system offers a 20 × magnification. Eyesight correction is possible by moving the eyepiece with the knob after unlocking the screw. The photo-cell is located behind the glass pellicle. The ground glass has a crosshair reticle and TV safe action frame line.

SHUTTER. Variable shutter from 180° to 45°.

"DUOLIGHT" EXPOSURE CONTROL. Exposure control can be automatic or manual. Over- and under-exposure is indicated in the viewfinder by the large and small red light-emitting diodes (LED). The CdS photo-cell is located in the optical unit. Light passing through the lens and the pellicle glass is reflected to the photocell by the film or the shutter whether the camera is running or not. Special treatment of the shutter surface assures light reflection analogous to the film emulsion, for correct exposure.

SYNC SIGNAL. The Pathé Electronic camera is equipped with two sound sync signal generators. The "Pilot-tone" signal is 60 Hz for 24 frames and the flash contact is made by one hermetically sealed switch driven by a rotating magnet with a maximum permissible load of 100 v. 0·25 A.

LENSES. All "C" mount lenses, and all lenses with "C" mount adapters fit the Pathé Electronic camera. The camera has a triple turret for 3 standard lenses. A servo motor screws into the lens opening above the taking lens.

OTHER FEATURES. 100 ft. internal film spools, alarm signal for battery, reverse drive, automatic threading system, handgrip which holds the 0·5 A/h battery, weight of camera and 400 ft. magazine: 10·4 pounds (4·7 kgs.).

*Canon Scoopic 16 M*

The 16 M model is the latest camera made by this firm after their success with the Canon Scoopic 16. This model includes some refinements and considerably increases the possibilities of the original camera. The manufacturers have introduced all possible advantages of automation within an attractive, functionally shaped body conceived for hand-held shooting, which makes it ideal for news coverage.

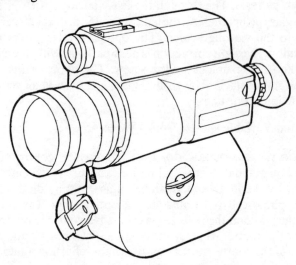

Fig. 19. The Canon Scoopic 16 M; new model with many refinements.

The body holds 100 ft. spools, which are automatically loaded. The operator need only to cut the spool's trailing end and introduce it into a slot in the mechanism, which automatically forms the loops. this is a great advantage to the newsreel reporter.

The reflex viewfinder is set on one side of the camera body, and the image is very bright. An all-matte screen with TV frame line makes for faster focusing and allows for checking out multiple focusing points in advance, for faster and accurate zooming once the action starts.

The lens is a macro-Canon zoom with focal lengths ranging from a wide angle 12·5 mm to 75 mm telephoto (zoom range 5·85: 1) with $f$1·8 diaphragm opening. A large portion of this lens is recessed into the camera body so that only a short length protrudes outside. This reduces the bulk and improves the instrument's balance.

A servo-controlled automatic exposure system (20 to 640 ASA) frees the operator from the need to change exposure in fast-changing situations. In the finder a T stop indicator allows complete visual exposure control. The exposure cell is fed from the power source driving the motor. Diaphragm regulation can be either automatic or by hand. A built-in 12 volt NiCad battery system supplies power for 1600 feet of film at 24 f.p.s. on a single charge.

Among other facilities offered by this camera, are: filming speeds with a range of 16 to 64 f.p.s., socket for connecting sound synchronization systems, a device for checking state of batteries, built-in small size motor, single frame operation, special grip for hand-held shooting, lens hood, etc. The manufacturer provides several accessories such as set of filters, light-tight aluminium case and an acrylic, water-tight, small-size shell for underwater filming. The weight of the unit is $7\frac{1}{2}$ lb.

## Sound-on-film cameras

During the past few years, the simultaneous recording of picture and sound on a single film has become an urgent requirement in covering news events. Long before the advent of TV, several camera manufacturers in America and Europe met this need with satisfactory 35 mm models. But these were heavy and took a long time to get ready, which made them unsuitable for rapid recording.

When 16 mm film began to replace 35 mm the size of equipment was immediately reduced, and an opportunity arose for creating more functional designs. The first attempts to produce simultaneous image and sound recording equipment for 16 mm film are already more than 40 years old. But it was TV which encouraged the development of 16 mm as most suited to many kinds of film reporting.

Optical recording in sound systems of this type was very popular up to about twenty years ago, and great improvements were made in the design of galvanometers, or modulators, which are their most critical components. Siemens-Klangfilm, Zeiss-Ikon's Ikophon, Mouillard et Deshayes' MD16, Meopta Somet, and Sonoretta in Europe; RCA, Maurer and Berndt-Auricon in the USA, were pioneers in this field.

But today, optical recording is obsolescent, having been largely replaced by magnetic. Portability is constantly being improved by using light alloys for camera and recorder bodies, by incorporating solid-state amplifiers, and by applying improved drive mechanisms and viewing systems.

### Auricon Cine-Voice

The American firm of Berndt-Bach has been a pioneer in this field

167

for many years, producing for TV news reporters a series of cameras capable of efficiently covering any type of filmed journalism with minimum effort. Their present range comprises four models progressing from the small Cine-Voice to the Super Auricon 1200. The Cine-Voice is designed for short duration reporting where ease of transport and rapid installation have precedence over all other factors.

The Auricon Cine-Voice was adapted by many companies to work with a large film capacity. For this purpose, a 400 ft. magazine has been added, as well as special devices for supporting the instrument on the shoulder, grip with trigger-switch, 12 v. AC motor and others. Some such adaptations leave the camera body intact, but others include a new special body to facilitate hand-held shooting. Among American firms who are specialists in these adaptations are F. & B. Ceco, General Camera Corp, S.O.S. Cine Optics Inc. and Frezzolini Electronics Co.

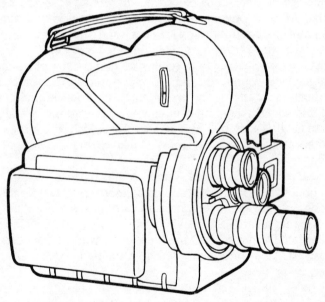

Fig. 20. Auricon Cine-Voice sound-on-film with side viewfinder and 100 ft. spool chamber.

DRIVE MECHANISM. The intermittent drive is of the sinusoidal type, which is of very simple design and provides excellent picture steadiness. There is a patented pressure system with steel balls round the aperture edges and a removable pressure plate ensures the

168

smooth passage of the film. The continuous drive is by a single sprocket with suitably positioned guide rollers and a pressure roller opposite the sound recording head. The whole mechanism is mounted on Neoprene bearings in a compact light-alloy body with lined internal walls to silence noise. Two 100 ft. spools of film are accommodated in the camera body.

MOTOR. This camera can be supplied with either a constant speed or a synchronous motor. Both are of the noiseless running type, 115 v. AC, either 50 or 60 Hz as required.

SHUTTER. This is of the fixed opening type at 173°. A special model for recording TV images can be installed on request.

LENS TURRET. This camera can be supplied either with a three-lens C type, or single mounting for zoom lenses.

VIEWFINDER. Viewing is through a side viewfinder, with parallax correction device, which gives a bright image covering the field of a 13 mm lens. Amber colour plastic masks can be inserted at the front to frame fields corresponding to various lenses: 17 mm, 1 in., 2 ins. and 3 ins.

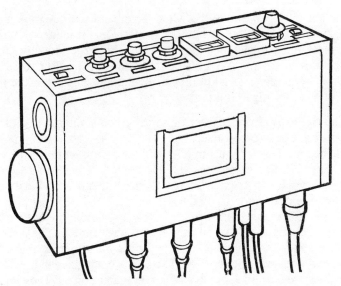

Fig. 21. A typical transistorized amplifier for magnetic sound-on-film cameras.

SOUND RECORDING SYSTEM. The makers supplied years ago this equipment with galvanometers for either variable-area or variable-density optical sound recording. A Filmagnetic magnetic recording head is also easily installed for use on raw stock with pre-striped magnetic track. The amplifier system is fairly compact and works from a battery source. The model for magnetic recording is fully transistorized and is very easy to carry. The cable connection system between camera and amplifier is foolproof, and in the latest models the connectors are of the Canon type to avoid faulty contacts. A wide range of accessories considerably extends the range of this instrument.

Several American accessory manufacturers for cinematography have built transistorized amplifiers for use with optical sound recording on Auricon cameras. They are all small-size units for installing between the camera and the tripod head, thus dispensing with the bulky amplifiers supplied with the camera.

### Auricon Cine Voice Pro-400

This is a new development based on the same premises as previous cameras, but now cordless, with external magazines, new Soundrive XTL motor and reflex viewfinder. The prototype of this camera is now ready to be put into production.

### Auricon Pro 600 and Pro 600 Special

The Pro 600 is based on the Cine-Voice, but the design is more sophisticated to facilitate shooting of professional standard. The film drive mechanism is identical to that of the Cine-Voice, together with the aperture plate and most of the threading system. But there are important changes and additions in the camera body and the film loading and viewing systems.

CAMERA BODY. In its general lines the body is similar to that of the Cine Voice, but larger in size.

The connections for the amplifier and the motor are placed on one of its sides. The other side carries the camera access door, which opens sideways on special hinges allowing a quick and easy interchange of door and viewfinder.

The lens turret takes three lenses with C type mounting, as well as the corresponding three small lenses for the viewfinder. The turret is 4 in. in diameter and the lenses are mounted wide apart so that their respective fields will not interfere. The film is not carried in the body, as on the smaller model, but in a 600 ft. magazine on top allowing 16 minutes continuous shooting.

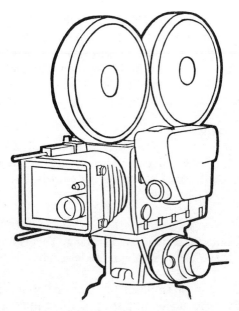

Fig. 22. Auricon Pro 600 with separate 600 ft. magazine, three-lens turret and three systems for viewing.

However, in the Pro 600 Special the film capacity is reduced to 400 ft., and the lens turret has been replaced by a single mounting to allow for the installation of zoom lenses. Both features contribute to reduce the weight of the instrument.

VIEWING SYSTEM. These cameras are provided with three systems for checking focus and framing. A bright image viewfinder can be looked through with both eyes; it allows for parallax correction, and masks are inserted to delimit the fields corresponding to different lenses. Another viewfinder uses small auxiliary lenses on the turret equivalent to those for taking; it gives a ten times magnified image which is helpful when using telephoto lenses. Third is a side-placed viewfinder for critical focusing; it is brought into use by rotating the turret until the taking lens is placed before it.

MAGAZINE DRIVE. These cameras are provided with independent magazine drive (called Electromatic) which starts operating at 1/3 power rating when the camera is connected to the power source, even when the camera motor switch is in the off position. This provides a constant tension on the film and prevents it slacking off when the camera is not running.

171

OTHER CHARACTERISTICS. The Auricon Pro 600 Special has been conceived as light equipment for newsreel work and is 30% lighter in weight than the standard model; its magazine is smaller and can take daylight loading spools. As both the standard and the Special models run so noiselessly, they are provided with a safety device to stop the camera should anything go wrong with the threading.

*Auricon Super 1200*

This model of the Auricon sound camera series is a heavy piece of equipment with all the refinements of a studio camera. Its basic characteristics are those of the preceding models, but it has several important additional features.

LARGE CAPACITY MAGAZINES. Magazines of 1200 ft. capacity provide 33 minutes of continuous shooting. This is a great help in covering conferences, shows, long interviews, etc.

FILM GATE. To prevent emulsion build-up on the film gate, polished sapphire inlays are used and they also minimize wear. The removable pressure plate system is the same as in the other models.

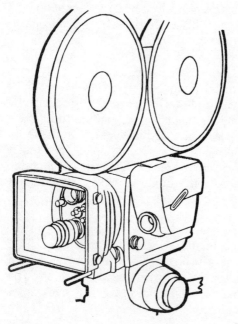

Fig. 23. Auricon Super 1200 camera designed for studio use, with large capacity magazines and through the lens viewing.

172

CONTINUOUS DRIVE. The extra large magazines call for a somewhat larger diameter sprocket to drive the film effectively. The smaller sprocket located beside the sound recording head has undergone no change.

DIRECT VIEWING THROUGH TAKING LENS. Accurate framing and critical focusing through the taking lens is effected in this camera by means of a device which, before shooting, inserts a mirror at 45° between the lens and the aperture. The viewfinder optical tube magnifies the image ten times. Before the camera is started, the mirror must be withdrawn from the viewing position, after which the optical tube acts as a side viewfinder working through small auxiliary lenses installed on the turret, and equivalent to those used for taking.

VARIABLE OPENING SHUTTER. The control is mounted on the right-hand side of the camera and allows for in and out fades, or for shutter speed variations from 1/50 to 1/200 sec. The higher shutter speeds are extremely useful when shooting with highly sensitive emulsions.

THREADING FAILURE INDICATION. As the Super 1200 runs so silently, failures in the threading or take-up systems are indicated by sound and lamp alarms.

OTHER CHARACTERISTICS. Two red lights go on when the camera is operating. Footage and frame counters are self-lighted. Another light indicates when the camera is connected to the power source and the take-up motor is running at one third power rating.

There are also connections for plugging in earphones, a device for automatic shutter opening when focusing, and withdrawing shuttle automatically when threading.

Other features are push-button starter, framing position safety device, special design sunshade, electric heater with light indicator.

## Canon Sound Scoopic Mod. 200 E & S

The features of this camera are similar to those of the Canon Scoopic Model M, especially the lens, the film supply system, the shape, the built-in power source, the method for holding and the controls. But it differs in the film load capacity, the drive mechanism and in other features. Here are the most important variations:

BODY. There is a relatively lightweight body with capacity for 200 ft. rolls (60 m.), low profile, quieter running design and hand held shooting suitable for the press and TV cameraman.

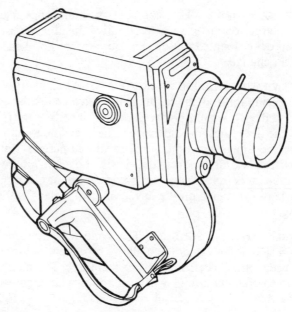

Fig. 24. Canon Sound Scoopic 200 E & S camera. Instrument similar to the silent line of Scoopic, but with 200 ft. film capacity and designed for single system sound.

MOVEMENT. Registration pin movement for high quality steadiness.

VIEWFINDER. Reflex viewing is effected through a rotating mirror shutter. The viewfinder contains T-stop scales, over/under exposure warning indications. The image is bright and clear and it is seen on a ground glass screen. The eyepiece has a special light shutter, adjustment ring and eye cup. The TV frame is visible but only in the 200 E model.

MOTOR. Small size, built-in DC motor of electronic speed control system for 24 f.p.s. filming is fitted. There is a film transport knob for manual operation.

SHUTTER. Fixed, 170° aperture, 1/50 sec.

FILTER HOLDER. Gelatin filter holder within optical scope of taking lens.

SOUND SYSTEM. The amplifier is designed for automatic and manual recording control. Unidirectional microphone. There is provision for monitoring the sound recording while shooting. A shoulder strap is attached to the amplifier for portability. The built-in

174

24 v. NiCad battery serves as the power source for camera and amplifier. Recording frequency: 200–8000 Hz; 3 Db. Dynamic headphone as monitor. There is an automatic gain control for recording volume and manual control is also possible.

## Beaulieu "News 16"

This is undoubtedly one of the most all-embracing items of equipment designed by the Beaulieu Company for news and general

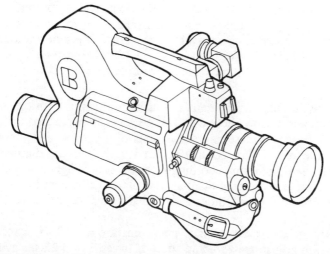

Fig. 25. The Beaulieu "News 16" instrument with the most modern concepts in design and automation and conceived for recording image and sound within the camera body.

professional cinematography. It uses the most up to date methods of automation for a camera designed for simultaneously recording image and sound. The Beaulieu "News 16" is very easy to handle and to carry, is fully automatic, allows for supporting on the shoulder and is provided with many extra refinements.

CAMERA BODY. Modular construction, silent running, very low profile, capacity for internal coaxially mounted 200 ft. (60 m.) spools. The unit is very well balanced for on-the-shoulder shooting. Dimensions: $8\frac{1}{2} \times 10 \times 20\frac{1}{2}$ in. ($215 \times 245 \times 512$ mm). Weight: 16 lb. (7·170 kg.) with Angenieux power zoom lens and crystal control module.

VIEWFINDER. This is a reflex optical construction of 14 elements and four prisms. It gives 22 × image magnification. There is a

"divided grain" focusing screen and etched TV frame area, 180°
swivelling eyepiece with eyesight correction.

SHUTTER. Guillotine reflex shutter which always stops in viewing
position. The frame exposure time at 25 f.p.s. is 1/60 sec.

MOTOR. The motor is interchangeable. Two models are available:
Type S motor (not suitable when using the crystal-pilot module) and
Type C motor. Both are instantly interchangeable without tools.
Speeds are fixed by means of an electronic governor and there is a
two position speed-range converter for 24 or 25 f.p.s. position and a
12–40 f.p.s. position (for variable speed). A tachometer situated on
one side of the camera provides a speed check.

EXPOSURE METER. The camera has built-in exposure meter control by means of CdS photo cell. The ASA sensitivity setting range is
from 12 to 400 and setting corrections of $\pm 1$ f-stop are possible.
Automatic diaphragm control is fitted with the lens diaphragm
driven by a micromotor according to the amount of light entering the
camera, but also optional manual control for the diaphragm. A needle is visible in the viewfinder with scaled indication.

ELECTRIC ZOOM CONTROL. The zoom is powered by a micro-
motor with adjustable zooming speed between 3 and 25 sec. with a
Angenieux 12–120 mm zoom lens. An automatic pre-focus control
automatically sets the zoom lens to the telephoto position and
maximum diaphragm opening.

LENS MOUNT. This is a "C" mount. There is a choice of two
powered zoom lenses: Angenieux 12–120 or Angenieux 9·5–57
mm, with the basic unit.

APERTURE. Made of chromium-plated brass with a stainless steel
removable pressure plate and "Sapphire" corundum edge guides.

POWER SUPPLY. Screw-in Nicad interchangeable battery-pack
(9·6 v. 1·2 Amp/hr.) High speed recharge in 40 min. Or external 7
Amp/hr. battery pack. Three position trigger switch for normal
filming position, off and safety catch and continuous filming settings.

SYNC-SOUND RECORDING CAPABILITIES. The camera comes with a silent module as standard equipment. In addition, the "News 16" offers six sync-sound recording assemblies:

(i)   1 Single System module (to be used in combination with the Beaulieu single system amplifier),

(ii)  3 Synchro-Pilot modules (60 cps for 24 f.p.s.; 50 and 100 cps for 25 f.p.s.),

(iii) 2 Crystal control modules (C24 for 24 f.p.s.; C25 for 25 f.p.s.).

SOUNDTRACK. Two positions (slide-switch selection):

(i)  large band position: 40–14,000 cps (3 dB),

(ii) narrow band position: 165–3000 cps (3 dB)

OTHER FEATURES. A signal lights when the camera is running. There is an end of film indicator in the viewfinder. The footage counter is graduated in feet and meters. There is a built-in film cutter, a fully automatic self threading facility including sound module and a complete line of accessories.

## Mitchell SSR

This camera is the result of a research project started by the Columbia Broadcasting System to produce a new type of camera intended for all kinds of work with 16 mm gauge film. The goal they set themselves was to achieve a versatile instrument which would also record on a magnetic track with highest fidelity to the original sound.

For this purpose they joined forces with the Mitchell Camera Corp., who designed the mechanical parts of the camera, while the sound system was handled by CBS and RCA. The result was the New Mitchell SSR-16 (Single Sound Reflex 16 mm).

The camera's main body is a magnesium alloy casting, housing the film drive and the reflex viewfinder, on which a divergent-axis three-lens turret, as well as the main controls, are installed. The magazine is attached to the top of the camera body, and the interchangeable motor is mounted on the right hand side.

The silent running intermittent mechanism is based on the famous Mitchell shuttle and register pin movement. The reflex viewfinder makes use of a highly polished stainless steel shutter, which is separate from the focal-plane type shutter used to close the aperture. The shutter opening is fixed at 170° and produces a shutter speed of 1/51 sec. at 24 f.p.s.

The finder's optical tube produces a very bright, ten times magnified image whose field is larger than that taken through the aperture, and shows objects just outside the frame.

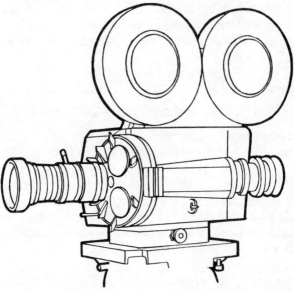

Fig. 26. Mitchell 16 mm SSR model. (Single System Reflex) with magnetic sound unit and lens mounted on divergent axis turret.

At the back of the camera are the tachometer, footage and frame counters, starting switch, and connections to the power source and the amplifier for the built-in magnetic sound recorder. The easily interchangeable motors supplied for this camera are: 12 v., DC, standard model with transistorized constant speed control; and a single-phase, synchronous model for 110 v. AC.

The sound unit consists of an RCA portable transistorized amplifier with interchangeable heads built into the camera.

Many accessories are offered by the makers, including magazines of up to 1200 feet, built-in generator, monitor viewfinder, and special battery power source.

*Cinema Products CP-16*

This is one of a new line of cameras made by the Cinema Products Co. of California. The CP-16 is a lightweight professional 16 mm

178

movie camera designed for either single-system or double-system cordless sound recording. Features of the camera include interchangeable self-contained battery packs, "C" type lens mounts with modified Angenieux lens cup, and a highly accurate crystal controlled DC servo drive motor system.

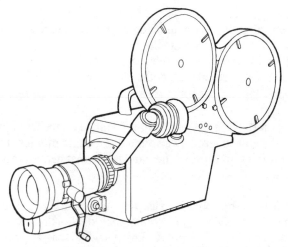

Fig. 27. Cinema Products CP-16. Popular camera designed for either single or double system cordless sound recording.

CAMERA BODY. The camera body is an assembly consisting in one side cover with battery mount, loading door, film transport movement, mount for the magazine, lens mount, carrying handle, control panel, footage counter and hand grip. The loading door is covered on the inside with sound-proofing material.

INTERMITTENT DRIVE. The film transport mechanism is shock-mounted inside the camera body. It is of semi-modular construction, with the drive system built into the motor, control electronics, and wiring harness installed as a pre-assembled unit. The intermittent drive employs the well known sinusoidal single claw Auricon movement utilizing self-engaging claw of hardened and tempered steel.

FILM GATE. Steel balls round the aperture edges and removable pressure plate.

SHUTTER. Rotary disc shutter with fixed aperture, 1/50 sec. at 24 f.p.s. 180° or 144° aperture can also be provided.

179

FILTER SLOT. This is behind the lens, accepting an 1·180 × ·740 in. ingelatine filter holder.

CAMERA SPEED. The camera may be ordered in the following configurations:

(i)   24 or 25 f.p.s.;
(ii)  either of above, with quick change pulley stored on main gear cross brace, to provide alternate speed;
(iii) either of above, with selector switch on upper front of the camera to provide an additional speed of 35 f.p.s. or 37·5 f.p.s.

LENS MOUNT. "C" type lens mount installed on the front plate with a locating pin and covered by a sound dampening muffler. The lens is mounted on the C-mount of the camera by means of a modified C-cup adapter.

VIEWFINDER. The camera uses the Angenieux zoom lens short zero viewfinder or a Cinema Product's 2½ in. short reflex viewfinder with an incorporated TV reticle. This viewfinder is appropriate for shoulder supported camera work.

MOTOR. A crystal controlled DC servo motor drives the main shaft via a belt at either 1440 rpm (24 f.p.s.) or 1500 rpm (25 f.p.s.).

MAGAZINE. There are double chamber, Mitchell type film magazines for 400 ft. (120 m.) or 1200 ft. (360 m.), top mounted.

SOUND RECORDING SYSTEM. The CP-16 camera has been designed to accept the Crystasound 5XL magnetic head (designed and manufactured by Cinema Products), as well as other Auricon type magnetic heads. The head plugs directly into the CP-16 centre plate. The 8-pin sound cable connector, located at the rear of the CP-16 camera is compatible with Auricon-type amplifiers.

OTHER FEATURES. Adjustable and removable front handgrip with power switch built-in, "out-of sync" warning light, compact NiCad battery inserted in the camera body and removable, very low noise level (31 dB at 3 ft.), Crystasound built-in amplifier (CP-16/A Model), camera weight for CP-16 complete 15 lbs. (7·2 kg.), Model CP-16/A 16 lb. 3 oz. (7·6 kg.).

180

## Mitchell/Wilcam W-2+4 Sound Camera

In March 1974 the Mitchell Camera Corporation announced the acquisition of the manufacturing and sales rights to a new lightweight 16 mm camera recently introduced by the Wilcam Photo Research, Inc of California. The new camera is a 16 mm single/double system sound camera with mirror reflex shutter featuring all magnesium construction.

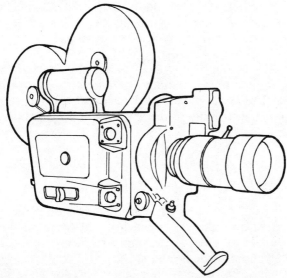

Fig. 28. Mitchell/Wilcam W-2+4 sound camera for 16 mm single/double system sound and with many refinements.

VIEWFINDER. With the viewfinder as an integral part of the camera body all primary functions of the camera can be monitored without removing the eye from the finder. Below the viewfinder image is a built-in match-pointer through-the-lens light meter which at full zoom of 120 mm is equivalent of a 1 degree spot meter. A flick of a switch on the front of the camera converts this to an audio VU meter so that a single operator can monitor the sound level while following the action. Above the viewfinder image is an analog footage counter showing feet remaining in the magazine.

FILTER WHEEL. A four position filter slide is fitted in front of the mirror shutter giving finger tip control to selection of a clear filter plus any three filters desired. The filter slide is instantly removable and any combination of filters can be fitted. The filter in use can, of course, be identified when looking through the viewfinder.

181

LENS MOUNT. Single lens mount with quick release bayonet mount. An adaptor can be supplied for the use of Arriflex lenses.

MOTOR. The Mitchell/Wilcam W-2+4 is driven by a 12 v. DC motor, which is speed-controlled by a crystal oscillator through a phase lock circuit. Due to its unique design it will maintain its speed lock from a no load condition to many times the required load. The 24/25 f.p.s. is accurate to within one frame per 1200 foot of film. The drive motor is capable of very high torque giving ultra rapid acceleration; there is also an electric magnetic brake.

MOVEMENT. The film transport is a long proved eccentric drive pull down with a short in/out motion to minimize sawing of the film by the claw. The in/out motion of the claw is perpendicular to the aperture plate and parallel to the lens axis to provide outstanding picture steadiness.

MAGAZINES. Standard Mitchell type magazines for 400 ft. and 1200 ft. are used.

SOUND UNIT. The W-2+4 16 mm sound-on-film camera can be supplied with its own integral amplifier or with three-channel external amplifiers. In all cases these amplifiers are supplied complete with the Wilcam magnetic head unit.

The amplifier with two microphone inputs is contained in a high impact plastic moulding, MU metal line, that fits to the side of the camera. The connector locates itself as the amplifier is placed on the camera body and a single knurled screw holds it in place.

OTHER FEATURES. NiCad batteries housed in the camera top handle, very low noise level, 24/25 and 35 f.p.s. crystal controlled, single frame inching control, rotating mirror shutter that always stops in closed position, very compact design, it weighs 16 pounds with the integral amplifier attached and a loaded 400 ft. magazine.

### Other 16 mm cameras

*General Camera TGX-16*

General Camera Corporation of New York initiated in 1972 a programme to design a single system/double system camera for TV and documentary work. The result was the proposed TGX Model, an instrument with many refinements and very original design.

**BODY.** Constructed of "Hi-Rez" a virtually indestructible plastic with the following dimensions: 5 in. wide, 15 in. long and 8 in. high. Weight 7 lb. 10 oz.

**MOVEMENT.** Half-heart cam movement providing straight film engagement for quieter and more efficient operation. A floating ball gives positive registration and eliminates scratching.

**MOTOR.** Crystal motor. Constant and variable speed (18/24 – 36/48). Click stop allows to change speed accurately while shooting. Optional speed: 24/36 – 48/72.

**MAGAZINE.** Internal 400 ft. (120 m) coaxial cassette magazine. Top load 1200 Mitchell magazine available.

**VIEWING SYSTEM.** Reflex viewfinder, rotating, adjustable diopter gives upright image (360° rotatable, optional). Multi-information as: digital footage counter, sound level on the VU-meter and red warning when the camera is out of sync.

**LENS MOUNT.** Heavy duty flange mount that accepts all 16 mm format lenses.

**HANDLE.** Of special design with on-off switch and viewfinder display button.

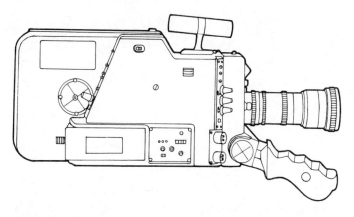

Fig. 29. The proposed General Mod. TGX sound-on-film camera with internal film cassettes and removable solid state amplifier.

183

AMPLIFIER. ("Astrosonic" Solid State amplifier with integrated circuitry with filters for music and voice and an automatic squelcher in AGC. Multifunctional VU selector with five point control. Magnetic head removable. The amplifier unit weighs only 1 lb. and is also easily removable.

## 3. REFERENCES

[1] Still, R., Fletcher, J., *Television Newsfilm Standards Manual*, Time/Life Broadcast, New York (1964).

Fletcher, J., *J'ai tourné dix mille metres en 16 mm en 1960—Vers Une Releance du 16 mm*, Le Technicien du Film. No. 69 p. 8 (1961).

[2] Ham, D., The Arriflex 16, *U.S. Camera Magazine*, p. 92 (March 1954).

Forbes, J., Single System sound for the Arriflex 16, *American Cinematographer Magazine*, p. 491 (August 1958).

[3] Henry, J., The new Arriflex 16 M, *American Cinematographer Magazine*, p. 28 (January 1964).

[4] Bronson, G., *The candid photography of "The Fabian Story"*, *American Cinematographer Magazine*, p. 582 (October 1964).

[5] Connaissance des cameras 16 mm, *Le Technicien du Film*, No. 72 p. 9 (May–June 1961).

[6] Mitchell New SSR16, *American Cinematographer Magazine*, p. 218 (Apr. 1964).

# SPECIALIZED CAMERAS

The development of cinematography towards techniques such as matting, animation, scientific work, etc., gave rise to the need for cameras of specialized design. The basic mechanical principles of these instruments are the same as those of standard cameras, but they differ in certain important characteristics, and thus require separate discussion.

## Low- and high-speed cameras

### Low-speed cameras

At one end of the speed scale is the "time-lapse" process, and the adaptations of it used in animation. All these processes employ standard equipment, and none requires structural changes in the camera itself but only in the drive motor.

TIME LAPSE CAMERAS. The time lapse system is based on the automatic printing of a few frames at preset intervals (minutes, hours, days). When projecting the film at normal speed (24 or 16 f.p.s.), the time elapsed appears to be more or less contracted according to the frequency of the takes. This process is a great help in all sorts of scientific research, medicine, biology, astronomy industry, etc.

Time-lapse cameras can be either spring or electric-motor driven. Those with spring drive require a special trigger device to operate the camera automatically, frame by frame. The system works under the action of a solenoid switch on an armature which stops the camera's mechanism. Each time the solenoid receives electric power, the armature is withdrawn from its position and the mechanism is thus free for a fraction of time enough to expose one or more frames. A spring

185

drives the armature back to stopping position as soon as the solenoid ceases its action. This is the principle used on many 16 mm cameras like the Cine Kodak Special, the Bolex Paillard, the Pathé and others. But the problem with spring driven cameras is that the spring requires periodic windings without the slightest framing modification. Therefore such instruments must be firmly seated on a rigid base.

Electric motor driven cameras work with a special time-lapse (or animation) motor designed to rotate only once each time it receives an electrical pulse. Thus the camera is operated frame by frame by adequately coupling the motor shaft with the camera's main shaft.

There are also other frame-by-frame devices using a "Bodine" type synchronous motor connected to a gearbox and working on the Geneva Movement principle.

INTERVALOMETER. Whether the camera is spring-driven or electric the fundamental item is the electrical pulse which shoots off the camera or acts on the electric motor. The instrument producing pulses at pre-set intervals is known as an intervalometer.

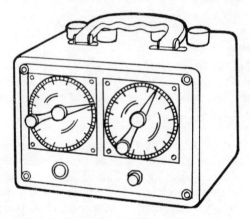

Fig. 1. Time-lapse device made by John H. Waddell Inc., suitable for programming a camera to operate according to specific requirements.

There are many types of intervalometer. Some operate by clockwork, others act under synchronous motors, and some models work by the action of electronic circuits based on the properties of certain gas discharge valves or on the accumulation of electric power in condensers. Whichever the process, the intervalometers must be capable of:

186

(i)    supplying electric pulses at intervals ranging from one second to several hours, to act on solenoids to trigger off the camera;

(ii)   operating the animation motor, at intervals from one second to 25 minutes, for frame-by-frame takes;

(iii)  regulating the exposure time of a take from one to ten seconds;

(iv)  acting synchronously on special shutters in co-ordination with the camera;

(v)   starting off a system for lighting up the scene to be shot, so that it goes on a few seconds before exposure and goes off immediately after;

(vi)  indicating the number of exposures actually effected.

Among a wide range of intervalometers made for various purposes we should point out the one made by Arriflex for their 16 and 35 mm cameras; the Roger, used extensively for time-lapse, animation and slide film; the multi-purpose Seco: those manufactured by the Eastman Kodak Co. for their Cine Kodak Special or Kodak Reflex Special; and the motor intervalometers made by the Industrial Timer Company, of the USA.

DESIGN CHARACTERISTICS. Although most cameras may be adapted to time-lapse work, there are some points to bear in mind. Reflex viewing is a great help, as it allows for easy checks on the exact framing and on sharp focusing. But the shape of some reflex shutter blades may allow light to leak in during long periods between each exposure. In such cases a separate shutter unit is placed in front of the lens and is synchronized with the camera's reflex shutter. This allows for long exposure takes by the double-pulse process: a pulse opens both the camera and the secondary shutters, and after exposure another pulse recloses both shutters.

Time-lapse work often requires exposure adjustments for each frame. Cameras with variable opening shutter allow for exact exposure time control disregarding whether it works at a wide range of speeds or not.

ANIMATION CAMERAS. Except for the mechanism and the motor drive, cameras for animation are of a very similar design to standard cameras. Their mechanism design must include:

(i)    fixed pilot pin intermittent mechanism;

(ii)   interchangeable mechanism for 16 mm and for 35 mm gauges;

187

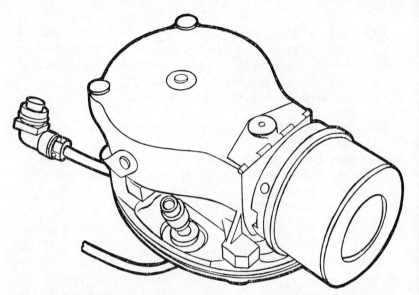

Fig. 2. S.D.S. 16 mm 6050 camera. A typical instrument for aerospace or missile test photography. Used on drone aircraft during test firing to photograph the missile for trajectory determination, miss-distance and relative velocity to drone.

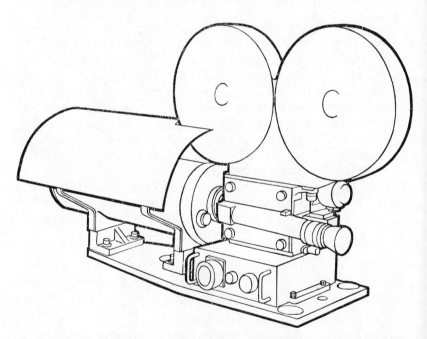

Fig. 3. 35 mm Cameraflex Radar Boresight camera. Used to photograph targets being tracked by radar. The Mirrotel lens is rigidly mounted and the whole unit is aligned with the radar antenna.

(iii)   automatic safety switch in case of threading failures;

(iv)   direct through-taking-lens viewing system (either reflex prism or sideways rack-over), with device for projecting the frame into the animation bench;

(v)   automatic fade-in and fade-out device;

(vi)   exposed frame counter, whether forward or reverse motion;

(vii)   magazine with individual mechanical drive to each chamber to keep constant tension and allow for effective take-up running forward or reversing;

(viii)   lens with linear displacement for focusing (non rotating), in order to be interconnected for automatic focusing during vertical displacement at the animation bench;

(ix)   possibility for adjusting the lens centre for adapting to the different formats in use or for special zoom effects;

(x)   they must allow for adapting both the magazines and the pressure plate to work with a bipack system;

(xi)   rechargeable film gate aperture for special systems, such as anamorphic, panoramic, full aperture, etc.

The drive motors must have the following characteristics:

(i)   they must be interchangeable;

(ii)   selector switches for forward and reverse motion;

(iii)   operating speeds of 1, 2, 3, 4 or more f.p.s.;

(iv)   remote control starting switch;

(v)   capacity for continuous operation (for titles or for winding film).

(vi)   exposure time selector device (from $\frac{1}{4}$ sec. to 4 seconds);

(vii)   selector switch for working at speeds from 1 to 3 f.p.s. (for shooting in black and white or colour film with tripack system),

Among the best known animation cameras are the American made Richardson-Bowlds R-500, the Acme Animation, and the Oxberry, working both with 16 and 35 mm film, the Czech Trick Type TK 3, the German 35 mm "Trick-Kameras" made by Askania and Crass, the French instrument designed by Armand Roux of the SAMOPRA, and in Japan two instruments of more recent design—one for 35 mm by Seiki, and one for 16 mm by Doi Works Co. Besides these instruments specifically conceived for animation benches, many American studios use the Bell & Howell 2709 for this purpose, while in Europe and Latin America the Debrie Parvo L and the Askania Z are used.

## Intermediate-speed cameras

Intermediate-speed cameras are those relying exclusively on a conventional intermittent drive system to attain speeds above the standard 24 f.p.s.

Most of the commonly used cameras can reach maximum operating speeds around the 80 f.p.s. mark. To work at higher speeds, specially devised intermittent mechanisms must be used, but mechanical limitations, together with the breakage resistance qualities of film base, set a maximum of approximately 300 f.p.s. for 35 mm and 600 f.p.s. for 16 mm.

Generally, the operating characteristics of intermediate-speed cameras are quite similar to standard ones; their difference lies mainly in the extra strength of the mechanical parts, and in the elimination of refinements unnecessary for scientific applications.

Among the film formats on intermediate-speed cameras are the following:

(i)   16 mm full frame (perforations on both edges)
(ii)  35 mm half frame
(iii) 35 mm full frame
(iv)  35 mm frame with margin for recording additional data

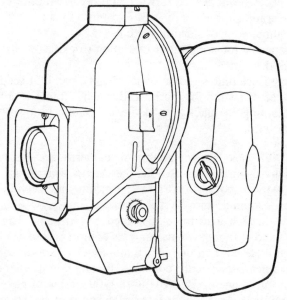

Fig. 4. Arritechno 35, camera designed for special requirements in medicine, industry and research. 90 or 150 f.p.s., 172° shutter aperture and running with minimum vibration.

(v)   35 mm double-height frame
(vi)  70 mm half frame
(vii) 70 mm 4/10 frame
(viii) 70 mm full frame.

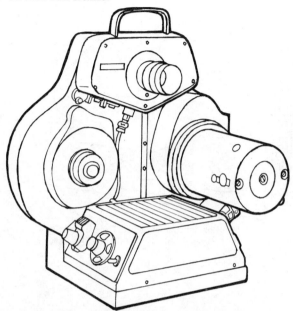

Fig. 5. Red Lake Hycam, general purpose camera available for instrumentation work in the field of research, design, product development, production engineering, and quality control.

The shape of intermediate-speed cameras is often the result of adapting them to specific requirements, such as installation in reduced space, or subjection to extreme vibrations or pressures. Moreover some models must undergo very high or very low temperatures and rapid accelerations or decelerations without detriment to their performance. It is often essential that these instruments allow for the simultaneous recording of additional data such as time and speeed, temperatures, distances, and other information necessary to analysing the recorded images.

Some 16 mm cameras have been made which, while suitable for standard work can also handle "slow motion" sequences in order to cover sporting events or the scientific study of subject movement. These cameras substitute the costly equipment previously used which was designed specifically for high speed shooting. The range of possibilities and applications of the later cameras is much wider, and their cost appreciably lower than complex scientific instruments.

191

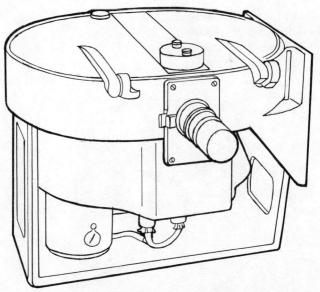

Fig. 6. Red Lake Hytax 35 mm instrumentation camera for high speed work. It is completely self-contained and provides electronic regulation over its full recording range of 30 to 250 feet per second.

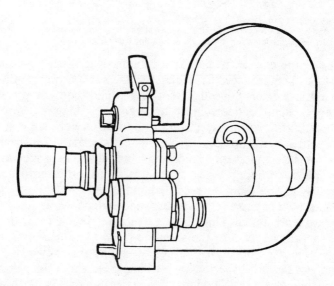

Fig. 7. Eclair Camematic GV 35 mm camera. A recording camera for speeds from 24 to 120 f.p.s.

Two outstanding specimens design are the Mitchell Sportster 164 and the Photo-Sonics 1PD Documentary camera.

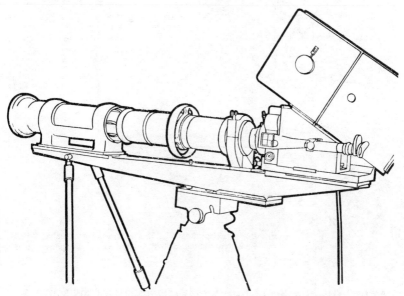

Fig. 8. Debrie Speedex high-speed camera for industrial applications.

## Mitchell Sportster 164

This is a sports photographer's ideal camera. The box shaped body measures $1_1\frac{1}{6} \times 9\frac{1}{2} \times 7\frac{1}{2}$ in. Inside the camera are 400 ft. (120 m.) daylight load spools and coxially mounted. The film transport is based on dual pin-registered film movement which provides rock-steady pictures. The film used must be 16 mm double perforated black & white or colour with a pitch of ·2994 or ·3000.

SHUTTER. The shutter is of interchangeable disc type, 140° standard. Other available openings are: $7\frac{1}{2}°$, 10°, 15°, 20°, 30°, 45°, 60°, 72°, 90°, 105°, 120°. The lens mount is for one single lens, "C" ... type.

SPEED CONTROL. Mounted on the back of the camera is the speed control panel which is easy to read and operate. A wide scope of low and high speed pairs are offered to the operator, with a range of 16 to 240 f.p.s. on the "S" (Standard) model or 16 to 500 f.p.s. in the "H" (High Speed) model. A dual-potentiometer, solid state control provides an accurate and rugged speed selector.

193

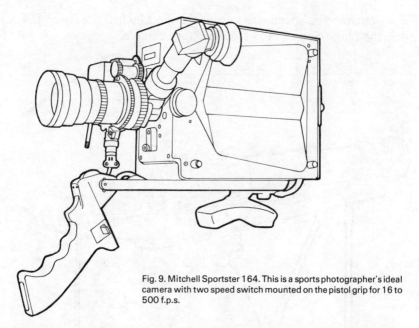

Fig. 9. Mitchell Sportster 164. This is a sports photographer's ideal camera with two speed switch mounted on the pistol grip for 16 to 500 f.p.s.

AUTOMATIC IRIS CONTROL. A totally unique, electrically activated iris drive automatically and simultaneously adjusts to pre-selected $f$ stops in unison with the camera speed changes. In addition, a master stop ring indexer permits the operator to retain the pre-set stop combinations during the minor adjustments of a half to a full stop to allow for quickly changing light levels caused by passing clouds or the desire to shoot into the shady side of a stadium or ski slope.

VIEWFINDER. The viewfinder is based in the Angenieux V30 coupled reflex viewfinder.

TWO-SPEED SWITCH. Mounted on the pistol grip is the high-low speed switch. Pulling back the thumb, the camera instantly accelerates to the preselected high speed index. Relaxing the thumb the camera speed returns to the normal pre-selected low speed. The quick switch also automatically triggers the iris stop changes required to match the speed combinations. The pistol grip is adjustable to the most comfortable hand position, and the shoulder support adjusts towards the front of the camera for additional comfort and balance of the unit.

MOTOR. Built-in 28 v. DC motor operated from a conventional 30 v. DC battery.

OTHER FEATURES. Footage counter in the front of the camera; semiautomatic threading; heater blanket and thermostat; variable power Boresight; weight 14 lb. (6·6 kg.) fully equipped.

## Photo-Sonics 1PD documentary camera

Photo-Sonics Inc., of Burbank, California, have specialized in producing instruments for high speed cinematography. Their 1PD is a precision 16 mm camera, specifically designed and constructed for obtaining high speed, high quality motion pictures at frame rates of 16 to 500 f.p.s. These pictures are valuable in detailed engineering and research studies as well as providing documentary information. In addition to being used for general purpose photography, the 16 mm 1PD camera is also suitable for combat documentation, sports, strike and gunsight type photography.

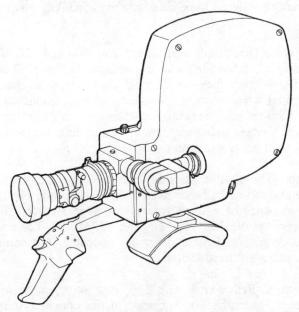

Fig. 10. Photo-Sonics 1PD Documentary Camera. This is a precision camera specifically designed for obtaining high speed rates from 16 to 500 f.p.s.

GENERAL DESCRIPTION. The unique features of the 1PD include: compactness, ease of handling, high frame rate capabilities, single integrated unit construction with the film movement completely packaged within the magazines to ensure excellent quality and high resolution motion pictures.

195

INTERMITTENT DRIVE. The film transport is a precision mechanism, dynamically balanced, with the pull-down movement mounted totally on permanently lubricated ball bearings. It provides dual register and pulldown pins for positive film control at all times.

APERTURE PLATE. The aperture plate is located in the camera body and is mounted directly in front of the film plane. This permits accurate and constant positioning between the lens and film format. The aperture may be equipped with either two fiducials, one on either side of the film format, or four.

LENS MOUNT. The camera front plate is designed to accept "C" mounted lenses. The front plate is also provided with threaded holes to allow the mounting of the rugged Photo-Sonics lens supports. This camera is designed to be used with modified Angenieux Zoom lenses.

MAGAZINES. Three basic magazines: 200, 400 and 1200 ft. (60, 120 and 360 m.) are available for use with the 16 mm 1PD camera system. These magazines are daylight loading spools and incorporate features which allow film threading to be accomplished in less than one minute. Each magazine contains its own film transport mechanism, footage indicator, runout switch actuator, inspection port, light-tight cover and data card.

SHUTTER. The shutter assembly has two openings with each opening equal to one-half the selected shutter opening. The shutter assembly consists of a fixed rotary disc type shutter. Effective shutter openings of: 7·5, 15, 22·5, 30, 45, 60, 90, 120 and 160 degrees aresvailable. Unless otherwise specified, the camera is equipped with a 90° fixed shutter.

VIEWFINDER. Reflex view with 360° rotation eyepiece with interchangeable ground glass. Included in the optical system is a removable gelatin filter holder located between lens and film plane.

MOTOR. Single drive motor 28 v. DC. Power is transmitted from the camera to the magazine by means of a coupling that ensures proper shutter to film transport timing. Frame rates are: 16, 24, 32, 48, 64, 96 and 200 f.p.s. These rates are electronically controlled. Any seven special rates between 16 to 500 f.p.s. are available upon request from the manufacturer.

OTHER FEATURES. Camera heater, timing lights, manual drive knob, runout switch inspection port, shutter correlation pulse, overrun indication lamp, automatic exposure control, adjustable handle and shoulder pod.

### Photo-Sonics Action Master 200

This instrument is a more recent development than that described above but resembles it in many ways. The main features of this model are: speeds from 24 to 200 f.p.s., zoom lens with a motorized variable speed zoom control, variable zoom rate, special mount housing and grip assembly with thumb actuated run button; internal rechargeable battery pack and tripod adaptor.

### High-speed cameras

This term is applied to cameras in which film is exposed at speeds higher than those attainable by intermittent drive systems. They have an application in countless scientific studies where the subject matter moves far too rapidly for direct human observation. Among these are: ballastics (missiles and satellites), aerodynamics (flight testing and rocket tracking), atomic fission and thermonuclear

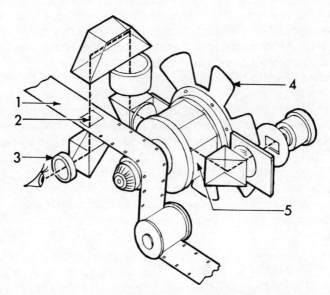

Fig. 11. Diagram showing the operation of the Hycam high speed camera and the light path from the lens through the rotating prism to the eyepiece. (1) Film strip. (2) Finder light path. (3) Finder. (4) Shutter blades. (5) Rotating prism.

energy, electrodynamics, hydrodynamics, biology, medicine, instrumentation, and even sports analysis and similar subjects.

High-speed cameras may be classified thus according to their mechanism:

(i) rotating prisms,
(ii) rotating lenses or mirrors,
(iii) cameras synchronized with intermittent light flashes,
(iv) extreme high-speed cameras.

ROTATING PRISM SYSTEM. The working principle of rotating prism cameras is a prism synchronized mechanically to the continuous film drive, so that its speed of rotation coincides with the displacement speed of the film.

Behind the lens is placed the rotating prism which refracts the image to "follow" the continuous displacement of each frame as it is exposed.

This method of alternation of exposure and blanking off is effectted by the different positions of the prism. The characteristics of this type of camera are determined by the size of the frame, the number of faces on the prism, and the refractive index of the glass.

Some manufacturers have added a supplementary shutter to the system just described; this is a rotating disc placed between the prism and the film. This gives a very steady image of better quality at all speeds. As the aperture of the rotating disc can be regulated, there is effective control of thee exposure time on the film.

Speeds of up to ten thousand frames per second can be attained with rotating prism cameras, and as the mechanical system employed is relatively simple, the camera can be of small size and light weight. These two factors are naturally of very great importance when cameras must be installed on missiles or in crowded aircraft cockpits.

It is worth noting at this point that a camera has been specially designed and built for TV interview coverage, based on the principle of the rotating prism which provides not only the advantages listed above, but also that of running noiselessly.

CAMERAS WITH ROTATING LENSES OR MIRRORS. Rotation of a ring made up of lenses or mirrors is another means of achieving high speeds in recording images on film, and enables speeds of up to forty thousand frames per second to be reached with 16 and 35 mm film.

The German Pentazet 35 is typical. It makes use of a rotating ring

198

of mirrors, which are interchangeable and can be varied in number from a minimum of 30 to a maximum of 120.

The subject is filmed through the lens and the image cast on a prism which, in its turn, deflects it on to the mirror ring. The film is displaced continuously behind a frame placed at the rotating axis of the ring, where the mirrors produce an upright image correct from left to right.

CAMERAS SYNCHRONIZED WITH LIGHT FLASHES. The application of the stroboscopic principlee to motion pictures has extended the possibilities of high-speed cameras. Intermittent flashes of light at pre-established intervals record an image on a film which is moving continuously. The gaps between each flash correspond to the period the shutter is closed. With such cameras as Dr. Ing. Frank Frungel's Stroboskin, up to 300,000 flashes per second can be electronically produced, each having a duration of $1/1,000,000$ sec.

Recent stroboscopic cameras incorporate a rotating prism to give appreciably better image quality.

EXTREME HIGH-SPEED CAMERAS. The highest speeds are attained by very elaborate instruments whose distinguishing characteristic is that the film remains stationary while the image is recorded on sensitive surfaces of $4 \times 5$ in. or larger. The operating principles vary considerably, but in most cases a mirror scanning system is used, applied in different forms and sometimes combined with a number of lenses (up to 94 in one French camera). The rotating elements are frequently driven by turbines running in helium gas.

The speeds reached with specialized equipment of this kind range from one to forty million frames per second. These instruments are as a rule very heavy, extremely expensive and are not built on a commercial basis.

Often their technical characteristics are well kept secrets.

An analysis of the images obtained is effected by transferring them to a conventional motion picture film by means of a special printing process in which each image is repeated several times before passing on to the next one.

## Multiple Film Cameras

*Bipack system*

The bipack filming process derives from some of the multiple image experiments carried out in the early days of colour cinematography. Its operating principle is simple, and consists of the simultaneous passage through the aperture of two films in close contact. These two films must be threaded with their emulsion sides inwards and touching, so that focus is the same on both. Hence, light entering through the lens must also pass through one film base.

Bipack films were employed in early colour processes to obtain a chromatic selection of the scene being taken. This was achieved by placing one film with orthochromatic emulsion face to face with another coated with panchromatic emulsion. The first film was tinted to act as a selecting filter so that a different region of the spectrum was recorded on each emulsion. Nowadays, the standardization of colour monopack films has made the bipack system obsolete, and it is now used only for process matting and similar special techniques. The technical requirements of bipack filming necessitate that the camera be adapted to the simultaneous travel of two films, have good registration steadiness, and take double magazines.

Suitable cameras are: the Acme Process, the Askania Color, the Bell & Howell 2709, the Mitchell NC, the Newall, the Oxberry, the Debrie Super Parvo, and others.

The adaptation of some instruments requires only minor adjustments (e.g.: the Super Parvo, whose normal 1000 ft. magazines must be changed for special ones with double capacity chambers but of smaller capacity), while the B & H 2709, the Mitchell and the Newall must undergo major modifications. By way of example we detail here under the adaptations that must be effected on Mitchells and Newalls.

CONTINUOUS DRIVE. The sprocket component called the "stripper" must be replaced by a device known as a "cutaway".

APERTURE. It is of vital importance that the pressure plate should work efficiently when two films travel in the film gate. Apart from the constant and even pressure needed for film steadiness, the pressure must be sufficient to eliminate any air bubbles formed between the two films. For Mitchell and Newall cameras, it is advisable to replace the standard pressure plate with two guide rollers with a 4-roller plate similar to that patented by Cinecolor Corporation.

LENS MOUNTS. As the two films travel through the aperture with their respective emulsion sides in contact with both film bases outwards, the frontmost film base displaces the image plane backwards a distance equal to the thickness of the base. The lens must therefore be mounted 0·0045 in. behind its normal position. Lenses with S.L. mountings need not have their position altered.

VIEWFINDER. As a result of the backward displacement of the image plane, the viewfinder ground glass of the Mitchell camera must also be displaced backwards by 0·0045 in.

MAGAZINES. The typical magazines for these cameras must be exchanged for a special four-chamber model. The Mitchell Corp. and the Rank Precision Industries (who sold the Newall) provide such "double" magazines, placing two chambers on top of the others, which are easily installed.

## Tripack system

Like bipack, the origins of the tripack system go back to the early days of colour cinematography. Apart from the difficulties of film drive and registration steadiness, this system presents the additional problem of how to obtain three identical and equally sharp images. If the three films face the same way and are superimposed in the same aperture, the focal plane will coincide with the emulsion of only one of them, and the other two will record images slightly out of focus. If two of the films are placed with the emulsion face-to-face (as in the bipack system), the third film is inevitably out of focus. If more than one aperture was to be used, there would be parallax errors. These problems were solved with the invention of the beam-splitting prism.

The beam-splitter principle, as originally used in Technicolor, Dufaychrome, and other cameras, works in the following way. Three images are obtained through two apertures by the use of a special optical system. It will be seen that the printing of three images through two apertures implies the use of the bipack system in one of them. The apertures are placed at right-angles to each other, and so of course are the corresponding drive mechanisms.

The beam-splitter optical system consists of a glass cube made up by two cemented half-cubes whose diagonally joined faces are treated with gold so as to form a semireflecting mirror at 45°. The optical system is assembled in a metal casting installed in the space between the lens and the angle made by the two aperture plates. The prism must be precision centered behind the lens and at the angle of the two apertures, so that the image reflected by the mirror to the bipack aperture at 90° is identical to the one formed on the aperture placed on the axis of the lens.

The insertion of a glass cube behind the taking lens means a considerable increase in the minimum space between the plane of the film and the rear elements of the lens. Lenses for this camera with short focal lengths of 25 and 35 mm had to be designed specially to have the characteristics of an inverted telephoto lens, i.e., their real focal length was greater than their effective focal length.

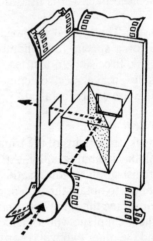

Fig. 12. Diagram showing the basic principle of the Technicolor beam-splitter system.

Another point to take into account in tripack cameras is the drive mechanism. The use of a bipack system and a separate single pack film necessitated two shuttle and register pin movements, synchronized in their motions, at 90° to each other. Since the requirements of colour register demanded maximum steadiness, the register pins had to be either of the full fitting or of the fixed type, while the apertures needed constant pressure plates, one of which had to be of special bipack type.

THE THREE-STRIP TECHNICOLOR CAMERA. Tripack Technicolor cameras were first used in 1932, and some years later, after a thorough programme of testing, they were produced at a cost of $25,000 each. They were very sturdily built with a high degree of precision. The body was box shaped, and the mechanical and optical systems were based on the principles described in the preceding paragraphs. Several innovations were included to ensure maximum film steadiness and to establish a more perfect contact of the film in the bipack aperture.

The lenses were made by Taylor & Hobson of Leicester, England, and were carefully corrected for colour and calibrated photometrically according to an arithmetic scale; the lenses supplied

202

were of 25, 35, 40, 50, 70, 100 and 140 mm focal length. Viewing was possible either by a direct finder or by a special monitor finder, affording parallax-corrected viewing with both eyes. Film had to be threaded through both sections of the camera, one section with monopack and the other with bipack film. The compact magazines were arranged to hold the three films side by side; take-up was by belt.

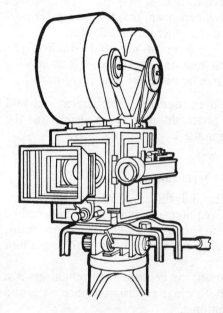

Fig. 13. Three-strip Technicolor camera (now obsolete) many of which were later adapted to the Technirama system.

The camera was driven by a motor mounted at the back; the motor was of the interchangeable type and eight separate models were supplied for different speeds and voltages, as well as for reverse drive.

As the Technicolor camera was too noisy for direct sound recording, it had to be blimped, and since the blimp was very large, special blimp mounts were needed. The camera was provided with a sunshade and matte-box, and could be furnished with remote focusing control operated by Selsyn motors, special lens mounts for aerial filming, watertight shell for submarine takes, etc.

The Technicolor tripack cameras were made in a wide range of models (C, D, E, F and G) to cover all the requirments of three-strip colour cinematography. They have, of course, been out of use now for many years. Some were later adapted to the Technirama system.

DUFAYCHROME TRIPACK CAMERA. The now abandoned
Dufaychrome process was created by Jack Coote, a British expert in
colour techniques, and operated by Dufay Chromex Ltd. some
years ago; it made use of a special tripack camera, designed by the
creator together with Gilbert Murray, which was very similar to the
Technicolor tripack, but with the following differences:

(i)  the beam-splitter was removable,
(ii) film storage was in two independent magazines, one for nor-
     mal monopack film and the other for bipack film,
(iii) direct viewing through mirror at 45° and Mitchell-type
     monitor viewfinder with automatic parallax correction,
(iv) remote control of focusing by means of Magslip motors.

Dufaychrome cameras have been used by some laboratories and
studios for special effects or processing filming, especially for the
type known as the "travelling matte".

## Special effects cameras

Effects or process filming demands the use of instruments properly adapted to the many special requirements of these techniques. The
camera is mounted on a stand in front of what is in effect a projector,
and the two together carry out work very similar to that of a film
printer.

No fundamental modifications to he camera mechanisms are
necessary, but they must meet very high precision requirements and
incorporate various special features.

*Intermittent movement*

In these cameras, the intermittent drive mechanism must achieve
the highest possible degree of registration steadiness. This is vital for
special optical effects, where the image is continuously modified as a
result of combining takes with masks and multiple exposures. The
shuttle claws are therefore made to act on both sides of the film in
synchronization with register pins, which can be either moving or
fixed to the gate.

Two of the best known special effects cameras, the Oxberry and
the Acme, have individual register pin systems working on similar
principles.

The Oxberry makes use of fixed register pins similar to those
devised for Bell & Howell 2709 cameras. Two pins are provided: one
with a cross-section exactly the same size as the film perforations

while the other fits the vertical dimension of the perforation but allows a clearance in the horizontal dimension to allow for film shrinkage or expansion. Both pins together adjust the exact positioning of the frame, vertically and horizontally.

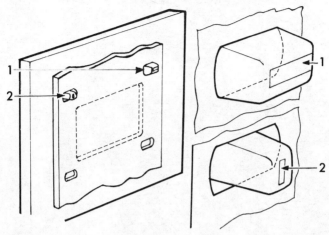

Fig. 14. Detail of the action of the registration pins in the film perforation. (1) Horizontal registration, (2) vertical registration.

The two-pin registration method of the Acme camera is similar: one pin fits the perforation exactly while the other fits vertically but leaves a clearance horizontally. These pins are made to penetrate the perforations in synchronization with the intermittent vertical drive of the shuttle and with the spring action of the pressure plate, so as to avoid damaging the film perforations. The pressure plate design permits the use of bipack film.

*Viewing system*

The Acme camera is provided with reflex viewing through a mirror set at an angle of 45° which operates as in the cameras previously described. Through a right-angled optical tube, the finder produces a sharp upright image, correct from left to right and twice magnified. Subsequent improvements include the provision of two pins on the finder window in order to fit a previously processed film frame in exact registration, for use as a reference when inserting mattes and masks. It is now possible to dismount the optical tube from the viewfinder window, and install in its place a housing with a light source so as to project a film which is to be used as a matte through the taking lens. This also allows for painting-on a mask in exact registration.

205

In the special effects model of the Oxberry camera, viewing is effected by the reflex method, and in the animation model, by the sideways rackover displacement method.

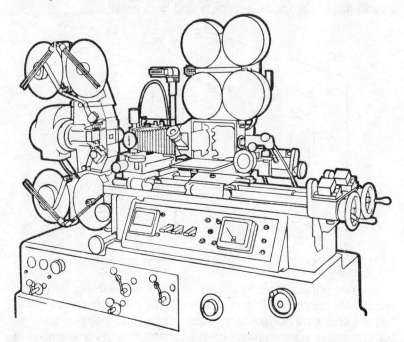

Fig. 15. Oxberry process camera mounted on an optical printer. Note the bipack magazine and the numerous controls.

### Shutter

The variable shutter is an essential accessory in special effects cameras. It can be either manual or automatic, but must have a wide range of openings. The Oxberry camera is equipped with a 170° shutter whose control allows for selection of the number of frames in a fade from 8 to 120. The Acme camera shutter has the same opening angle and is adjusted by two controls allowing for automatic fades over film lengths of 1, 2, 3, 4 and 8 feet.

### Magazines

Special effects cameras take 400 and 1000 ft. magazines, which admit couplings for working with the bipack system. They are driven by two sets of gears for forward and reverse drive, and for different speeds at a constant tension.

206

*Motors*

The motor is an important element in special effects cameras, and its constant speed regulation must be extremely accurate. It must be capable of working at minimum speeds of one frame per second, as well as at very high speeds in order to produce a slow-motion effect, and furthermore must be capable of reversing. As it is normally difficult to obtain such a wide range in a single motor, motors are generally furnished in interchangeable units.

*Other features*

Other notable features on special effects cameras are:

(i)   disc for inserting filters between lens and aperture. Different types of filters are supplied for colour shooting, and by means of a lever the disc can be synchronized with the shutter rotation, so as to facilitate the recording of three frames exposed in succession;

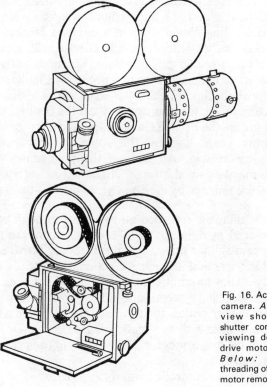

Fig. 16. Acme process camera. *Above:* side view showing the shutter control knob, viewing device and drive motor at right. *Below:* showing threading of film (drive motor removed).

207

(ii) because of their special design, effects cameras do not permit the use of wide angle lenses. The minimum focal length adaptable to the Acme camera is 62 mm while the Oxberry admits lenses of 47 mm focal length, when using 35 mm film. When the camera is installed on a special effects stand or animation table, focusing is controlled either by hand or automatically;

(iii) interchangeable movements which allow the same camera to be used with either 35 mm or 16 mm film (this feature only in Oxberry cameras).

(iv) footage counter, exposed frames counter, and totalizing counter, with discounting effect for reverse drive.

*Other special cameras*

The above cameras are used exclusively in the laboratory. But process filming often requires the use of adequate equipment in the studio itself. Thus cameras were designed with the characteristics necessary for special effects as well as those demanded by direct shooting. The special effect most commonly used is the travelling matte, i.e. the addition of a background to separate scenes with actors, by combining filmed shots in a complex laboratory process. This requires the "two-strip" system, effected with a camera incorporating a beam-splitter prism and two apertures at right-angles to each other to take the scene on two negatives simultaneously.

In Hollywood, this process is effected with the old Technicolor Tripack camera, while in Europe they use the British JARO made by the Rank group, the French Camé Twin, and a few cameras built in Spain some years ago by the Aragonés brothers for their Cinefotocolor system. An idea of the possibilities of these instruments may be gained from the characteristics of the Camé Twin, designed some time ago by the French engineers Coutant and Mathot:

(i) the image is recorded on two films through two apertures placed at right-angles to each other, by means of a fixed beam-splitter prism; the film gates are provided with a slot for filters and intermittent action pressure plates;

(ii) two-claw intermittent movement and fixed register pin;

(iii) two viewing systems, one direct through film with magnified image for critical focusing and framing, and a side monitor viewfinder with automatic parallax correction;

(iv) double magazines for 1000 ft. film in each compartment or receptacle;

(v) externally controlled variable shutter;

(vi)   lenses for various focal lengths from a minimum 35 mm;
(vii)  special synchronous motor;
(viii) correct threading safety device;
(ix)   soundproof blimp.

## Cineradiology cameras

Cineradiology is the cinematographic recording of images produced by X-rays on a phosphorescent screen. It allows for a careful analysis of the moving subject, either by projection, or by frame-by-frame study.

For some years now, manufacturers have been able to adapt their cameras to X-ray equipment, thanks to the development of image intensifiers. Some firms, Arnold & Richter for example, adapted their instruments to suit Philips equipment with 15, 21 and 27 cm diameter image intensifiers.

For this work the Arriflex 35 is fitted with a 22 × 18·67 mm aperture, and it works with small, 200 ft. magazines; it can be reversed and generally used with medium focal length lenses. The 16 mm Arriflexes have similar characteristics including reverse motion, a periscope designed specifically for this work, and 35 to 75 mm focal length lenses, according to the diameter of the image intensifier they must be aligned with.

One of the most serious problems of cineradiography is the poor quality of the images on the intensifier, due to their limited capacity for reproducing all the details on its phosphorescent screen, with the required definition and symmetry. It is therefore necessary that the cinematographic reproduction of such images should not have appreciable losses which could impair a subsequent correct analysis. With this end in view a special 35 mm gauge camera was built in Australia some time ago by the National Heart Foundation, making full use of possibilities afforded by this gauge. As this instrument comprises several concepts which may guide those interested in the subject, we detail hereunder its main innovations:

(i)    square frame covering the height of six perforations, allowing for full coverage of all of the circular surface of the image intensifier at the appropriate magnification;
(ii)   180° angle shutter opening synchronized with pulses emitted by the X-ray equipment;
(iii)  specially designed drive mechanism, with double claw shuttle and register pins;

(iv)  magazine with easily-removable, independent chambers, and a maximum 400 ft. load;

(v)  working speed up to a maximum of 100 f.p.s. for studies with slow motion projection;

(vi)  variable speed motor, separated from the camera but connected to its mechanism by means of a flexible shaft;

(vii)  speed and exposed-frame counters.

The NHF camera is part of a group of instruments for improving the recording and reproduction of images in the field of cineradiology as well as for electrocardiograms and phonocardiograms. Negatives can be viewed either frame-by-frame or in specially devised viewing apparatus. The processed film can also be projected for large audiences if it is reduced to 16 mm, which requires a special reduction optical printer.

Several cameras were designed specially for recording X-ray images. The most complete of such instruments is the British made Acmade. It prints images from a Marconi intensifier on to 16 mm film. The unit was designed to operate with a fast pull-down and is installed on top of the X-ray equipment itself, with large film-load capacity chambers.

### Kinescope cameras

Nowadays it is frequent practice to shoot scenes di:ectly from a television kinescope tube for a wide field of applications. It allows for recording permanently all sorts of transmissions, both in black and white or in colour, and whether they are sent out from a station or in closed circuit. It affords reference records of all sorts of transmitted events, as well as of educational, industrial and commercial applications of TV. Moreover it allows for retransmitting the same programme through one or several stations.

Electrical current is supplied in either of two frequencies: 50 or 60 Hz (hertz, or cycles per second), depending on the electrical standards adopted by each country. The established frequency determines the characteristics of TV transmission stations and of closed circuit systems. This imposes design characteristics on motion picture cameras for taking images from a kinescope tube (generally known in Britain as telerecording).

The image on a TV screen is produced by phosphoresence when its surface is scanned by an electronic beam. The beam sweeps the screen from left to right and from top to bottom forming a certain number of lines. The combination of these lines and the resulting contrasts produce the image. The screen is scanned twice during each TV picture. Of the total number of lines, half are used in one *field* and half in another *field*. Thus a complete TV picture is composed of two fields. Both scans of the beam are interconnected so that the even number lines are used on one field while the odd number lines are useed on the other field. The combination is made during the lapse of each cycle and each time a scan is completed the screen is blacked-out so that it should not show the beam going up to start the next scan.

The number of cycles per second (frequency) determines the fraction of time in which the complete image is formed. One half of this value is the time taken by the beam to scan two fields. For example, if AC is supplied at 50 Hz each complete image is formed in 1/25 sec. and only one field in 1/50 sec.

When printing kinescope images with a motion picture camera, its sound film standard speed (24 f.p.s.) must be adapted to the above values. In the case of 50 Hz, since each complete image formed by two half-fields is obtained in 1/25 sec. it suffices to increase camera speed to 25 f.p.s. to make each film camera frame coincide with a complete TV image. However, where 60 Hz is used the problem is not so easily solved. In this case the image is produced in 1/30 sec. Consequently during one second, 30 TV images are shown while the camera is printing 24 frames, thus one out of every five TV images is "palmed off". This may form a bar across the frame (known as a "splice") produced by printing the top part of one frame and the bottom part of another.

There are several means to reconcile these two sets of values. For one method the camera is fitted with a shutter with 144° opening which at 24 f.p.s. renders an exposure time of 1/60 sec. Thus only one half field is taken, eliminating the problem of the "splice". But this solution renders images of poor definition in the vertical section, since only one half of the lines of a complete scan are taken.

Another solution is to increase the vertical shuttle travel on the intermittent mechanism, so as to make the most of the short shuttering time and lose no more than one half field. This solution can be achieved either with an electronic or mechanical shutter. The electronic shutter blanks out the image on the kinescope after each complete scan and it can be synchronized with any camera speed by means of pulses coming from the receiver. The mechanical shutter must provide an exposure time of 1/30 sec. to expose the complete image, and blank out the aperture in 1/120 sec. so that the shuttle

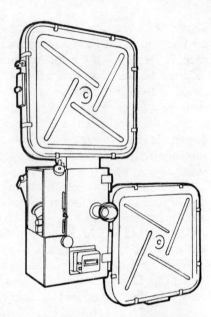

Fig. 17. Debrie Kinescope recording camera. Designed for recording images from a kinescope picture tube onto 16 mm film.

can pull down the exposed frame in that extremely short fraction of time. For such timing, shutters must have an opening of 288° and a closing (blacking out) sector of 72°. In some cameras these shutters are driven by a separate synchronous motor working independently of the camera's intermittent drive mechanism.

Various models of cameras for shooting from kinescopes are made according to the above requirments. In America the best known makes are: Acme, Auricon, GPL (General Precision Laboratories), Harvey, Milliken, Palmer, Mitchell and RCA, all for 60 Hz frequency and 24 f.p.s. camera speed. In Europe where the frequency is generally 50 Hz, several special cameras have been built for this work, among which one should note the British-made Moy (four models) and the Marconi, and the Eclair Cameflex Television and the Debrie Kinescope, both made in France; all European models run at 25 f.p.s.

In the instruments like the RP-15 made by Ernest Moy in the U.K., the intermittent movement is designed so that the vertical action of the shuttle is effected in 0·0014 sec. The complex mechanism of the Marconi camera designed by Arthur Kingston achieves a time of 0·0013 sec. These values were attained in order to adjust the 25 f.p.s. camera speed to British TV standards, using 50 Hz, 405 lines.

Of all special features of these instruments, the following are noteworthy:

212

(i)   large load capacity to cover long duration programs;
(ii)  high precision intermittent mechanism with maximum reduction of vertical insteadiness, typical shortcoming of this cinematographic medium;
(iii) synchronous motor drive;
(iv)  special system to facilitate fast phase adjustment;
(v)   critical framing and focusing devices.

### Underwater cameras

The growing interest in submarine films over the last few years has induced manufacturers to produce instruments to meet the exacting requirements of underwater shooting. As far back as 1954, several Hollywood studios had to tackle the construction of special shells to hold cameras for shooting "Twenty Thousand Leagues Under the Sea", "The Big Rainbow" and "Jupiter Darling". Intensive research and practical trials produced underwater camera covers for R.K.O., Metro Goldwyn Mayer and Walt Disney Studios, but they demanded an effort and investment which only the larger studios could afford.

At the special request of the U.S. Navy, Birns & Sawyer, one of

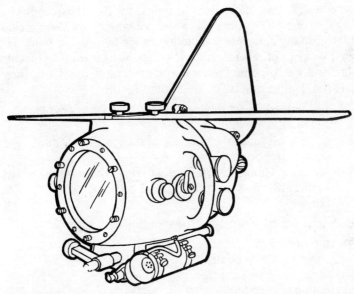

Fig. 18. Eclair Aquaflex underwater camera with stabilizing fins and special handgrips for underwater control.

213

the American companies specializing in studio equipment, built an underwater cover for Arriflex cameras. This was a big step forward, because it allowed for the use of an already widely accepted hand-held camera, easily operated in this type of work. This cover (or shell) was soon put on the market as an accessory for Arriflexes. Since then many accessory makers have produced different watertight shell models in aluminium, glass fibre, and other materials, both for light and medium weight cameras. The best known are probably those by Milliken, Gordon Enterprises and Jon Hall.

In Europe and especially in France, there was a widespread development of underwater documentaries and scientific films, among which the work of Commander Jacques-Yves Cousteau was outstanding, specially in his film "Le Monde du Silence" (The Silent World). This expert's name had already been associated with a camera, the Cousteau-Girardot, made by the Compagnie de Travaux Mecaniques which won deserved renown.

The Cousteau-Girardot underwater camera is distributed in USA by Gordon Enterprises and uses a modified LeBlay camera in its interior. Commander Cousteau's initiation in motion pictures was a documentary "Par Dix-huit métres du Fond" in 1943

For his film "Le Monde du Silence" Louis Malle, the well known director, was retained as cinematographic consultant, and he used another well known camera of this type—the Aquaflex, made by the Eclair Co. of Paris. It obtained wider recognition and was included in the company's normal production range in order to fulfil orders from the navies of several countries. This instrument is of ingenious design and has become the favourite camera of many underwater specialists. It thus deserves a fuller description:

(i) egg-shaped metal shell, measuring $27\frac{1}{2}$ in. overall length, by $13\frac{1}{2}$ in. maximum diameter;

(ii) all controls located on outside of shell to allow for any type of underwater operation;

(iii) houses a Cameflex with special long-shaped magazine (see Figure 18), 6–8 volt motor, and adapted reflex viewfinder tube;

The various controls provided for shooting operations are:

(i) motor switch,
(ii) shooting speed control,
(iii) distance setting control,
(iv) diaphragm setting,
(v) indicator of focal length of lens being used;

other controls included are:

(i) tachometer,
(ii) footage counter (in metres),
(iii) built-in photoelectric cell,
(iv) gauge for checking pressure inside shell;

bouyancy control system comprising:

(i) compressed air bottle,
(ii) de-compressive valve,
(iii) air distributor;

other characteristics of the camera are:

(i) facility for framing and focusing through special reflex viewfinder which can be observed through diver's mask,
(ii) stabilization fins,
(iii) special grips for handling the camera,
(iv) pressure-resisting, specially treated optical front glass,

Total weight, 86 lbs.

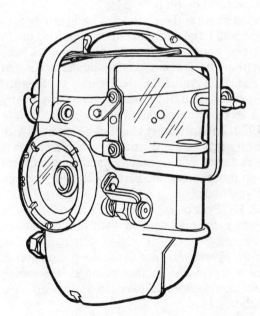

Fig. 19. Underwater shell for Bolex 16 mm cameras.

## The 65/70 mm wide screen systems

Several years ago the 70 mm gauge earned a very wide acceptance from both technical and commercial points of view. Multi-million dollar productions especially, both in Europe and the U.S.A., were filmed to an increasing extent in the 70 mm format, which was for some time the standard for very large screen presentation.

But when 70 mm is referred to in feature films, it is to be noted that this is a gauge exclusively for projection in theatres; 65 mm negative is nearly always used in the camera. An exception is Super Technirama 70, filmed on 35 mm film (see Table). Thus when the copy is printed on to 70 mm film, space is gained for the sound track.

Another exception is provided by the Russian motion picture industry, which makes use of 70 mm film both for shooting and projection. Several cameras have been built in the U.S.S.R. for this gauge, of which the foremost is the heavily built but noiseless Rossiya studio model.

The 70 mm positive copy is contact-printed from the 65 mm negative, since the dimensions of and distances between the perforations are identical on both films, the difference lying in the width of the edge beyond the perforation on both sides.

In the history of motion pictures there are a few early attempts to use 65 mm film, with the well known Magnafilm system tried out in 1929 by Paramount (then known as Paramount Famous Lasky Corporation). At that time Paramount commissioned a 65 mm camera from the French firm of André Debrie. Debrie first designed and built a 65 mm printer, and then after overcoming many difficulties, developed a very compact camera which was first put to work on October 23, 1930. This instrument had been conceived with the latest design developments in mind, such as double chamber magazine attached to the back of the camera (and thus different from this firm's classical model), special shutter with 230° opening and a projected image viewfinder.

About the same time, Mr. Fear of the Fearless Camera Company in the U.S.A. developed a 65 mm camera with a top-mounted magazine, a noiseless film-drive system of original design, and other refinements. This instrument was intended for series production at the rate of one per week, and provided the then new and outstanding characteristic of having interchangeable parts so as to work also with standard 35 mm film.

This was the first era of popularity of the "wide film," in which the contending gauges of 65 mm and 70 mm (the latter in Fox

Grandeur) vied for public preference. The Mitchell Camera Corp. had built an instrument for 70 mm which was very similar in its characteristics to its later and now well-known Standard model.

But the fantastic success of sound films, the development of fine-grain emulsions which improved the quality of large screen projection, as well as the effects on the motion picture industry of the world economic crisis in the late twenties and early thirties, led to the abandonment of wide-gauge film.

Twenty-five years later, spurred by the competition of TV, the 65 mm gauge re-appeared. One of its most enthusiastic early promoters in this second period was Michael Todd, the American producer, who patented the Todd-AO system in 1954. At present, 65 mm negative film is standard for large-screen systems such as Panavision 70, Ultra-Panavision, MGM Camera 65, Cinerama and Dimension 150. The 65 mm cameras most widely used were made by two American manufacturers, the Mitchell Camera Corp. and Panavision Inc.

The Mitchell Company has long-standing experience with wide film, dating back to the times of Fox Grandeur. Besides scientific and industrial instruments, they manufactured several cameras for 65 mm gauge: the 65-BFC, an adaptation of their popular 35 mm BNC, and a lighter model, the 65 FC, also similar to the 35 mm NC.

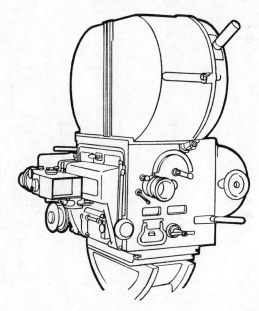

Fig. 20. Mitchell 65-BFC camera.

217

Both instruments have been tried out in several Hollywood and European feature films and adapted for reflex viewing.

## Todd-AO AP-65 camera

Todd-AO Co., producers and distributors of technical media for making 65 mm gauge films, commissioned the Mitchell Camera Corp. to design and manufacture a camera which should be light and adequate for hand-held shooting. The result was the new AP-65, of streamlined appearance, which incorporates many recent developments in the field.

The intermittent mechanism of this camera works on four perforations; its adjustable type register pins can be withdrawn to facilitate threading through the film gate. Its shutter has a fixed, 175° opening. The single-unit 250 ft. film-load magazines are easily coupled mechanically to the camera. Reflex viewing is effected by means of a bright-image beam splitter prism covering a larger field of view than the aperture; the viewing system affords facilities for focusing and inserting filters for studying illumination. The AP-65 can run at 12, 18, 20, 22, 24, 28 and 32 f.p.s. and it is driven by a built-in, 28 v. motor with electronic, constant-speed governor. The motor can be interchanged for others such as: synchronous model (110 or 220 v. AC), multi-duty motor (96 v. DC) a variable speed one (110 v. AC) and a motor for animation (110 v. AC).

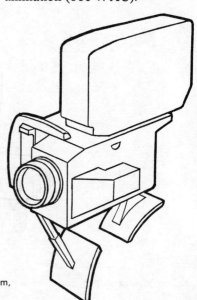

Fig. 21. The new Mitchell-made, Todd-AO system, AP-65 camera.

# TECHNIRAMA PROCESS

## Camera with anamorphic prism 1.5/1 Sq. ratio

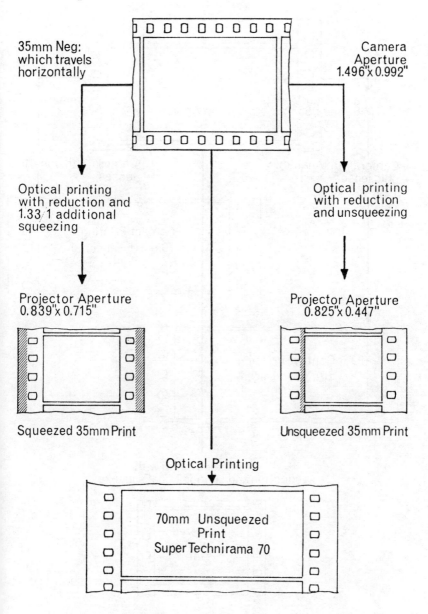

35mm Neg:
which travels
horizontally

Camera
Aperture
1.496"x 0.992"

Optical printing
with reduction and
1.33/1 additional
squeezing

Optical printing
with reduction
and unsqueezing

Projector Aperture
0.839"x 0.715"

Projector Aperture
0.825"x 0.447"

Squeezed 35mm Print

Unsqueezed 35mm Print

Optical Printing

70mm Unsqueezed
Print
Super Technirama 70

65mm Neg: film.

Camera Aperture 2.072"x 0.906"

Ultra Panavision &
M G M Camera 65

Panavision 70

Camera with Anamor-
phic lenses
1.25/1 Sq. ratio

Camera with Spherical
lenses

Contact Printing
70mm Unsqueezed
Print

Contact Printing
70 mm Squeezed
Print

Optical printing with
reduction and 1.6/1 additional squeeze

Squeezed
35mm
Print

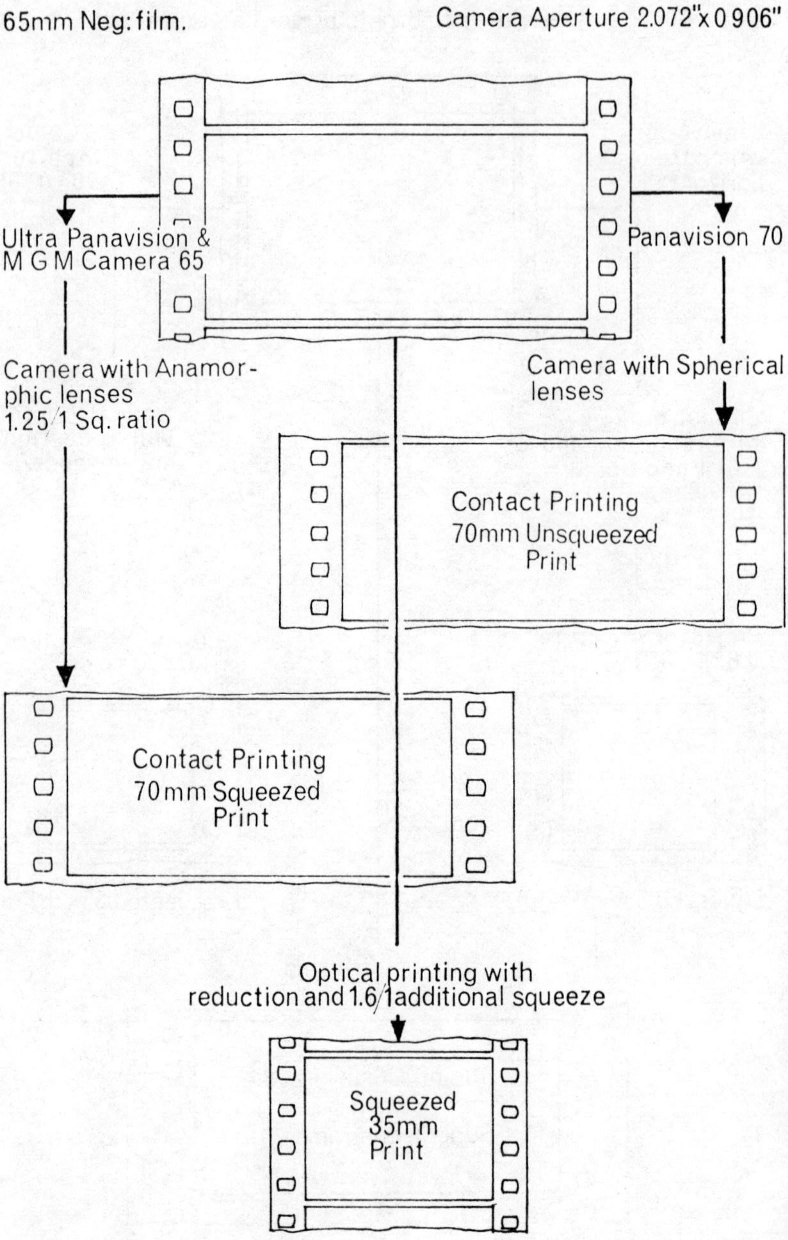

Other features of the AP-65 are: exposed film counter behind the camera; available raw-stock indicator placed on the magazine; slot in front of film gate for inserting gelatin filters; built-in heater; sockets for remote control connections; signal generator for sound synchronizing; special design lens hood; grip with starting switch and automatic zoom; total weight of the instrument including film-load 16 lb. Among the many accessories designed for the AP-65 are watertight shell for underwater takes, 1000 ft magazine, monitor viewfinder allowing adjustments of focus and field of view, belt supported battery with special charger; focus control device; and several lenses including a zoom.

### German 70 M.C.S. camera

Other 65 mm cameras have been built in the German Federal Republic. Their designer was Jan Jacobsen, who conceived two models: a lightweight one for hand-held shooting, and a more elaborate model. The latter item was proved in many European productions. It has a very compact body on top of which 500 or 1000 ft two-chamber magazines are seated slant-back.

Viewing is effected by the reflex method and the tube is attached to the camera body access door, in a fashion similar to the Arriflex. The simplified design movements include a high efficiency intermittent mechanism. The camera can run at speeds from one to 40 f.p.s., and is driven by interchangeable motors: either variable speed (16 v. DC), synchronous or high speed. Lenses for this camera are supplied in nine different focal lengths and are single mounted. The long-bellows lens hood allows for the insertion of filters.

### Panavision cameras

Panavision Inc., well-known as specialists in anamorphic lenses, have developed their own 65 mm cameras for Panavision 70 and Ultra-Panavision. This company was already well advanced when it reached an agreement with Metro-Goldwyn-Mayer to join forces in the development of a high quality image recording process for spectacular productions. During these investigations, new lenses were developed for the 65 mm negative, which achieved appreciable improvements in image quality and in freedom from distortion. The new system was called MGM Camera 65 and was first used in the production of the film "Ben Hur". The first instruments for this system were built by other makers to specifications by Panavision. Subsequently the design was totally revised and the cameras built at Panavision's own plant.

The 65 mm cameras built by Panavision are hired to producers for shooting with their Panavision 70 and Super-Panavision processes. Panavision 70 is for shooting directly on 65 mm film with spherical lenses, while Super-Panavision is the application of anamorphic lenses to 65 mm film while shooting. Both systems use the same types of camera, which this company supplies in two models: the heavily-built, noiseless-running studio model, and the lighter, hand-held, multi-purpose model.

## Studio model

This has a noiseless intermittent drive designed by the makers, with dual registration pins, a shutter with variable opening ranging from 50 to 200° and focusing by means of reflex viewing system with built-in contrast filters and variable magnification, top-mounted, 1000 ft., double chamber magazine. Motors are various 110 v. and 220 v. models, either synchronous or variable speed from 8 to 24 f.p.s. There is a parallax-corrected side view-finder and an adjustable sunshade with matte-box. The anamorphic or spherical lens is single mounted by a bayonet system.

## Portable model

This model is very useful for complementary takes and has recently been re-designed. The 500 ft. magazine is mounted at the rear at an angle of 45°. Other features are intermittent mechanism which produces rock-steady images, mirror type reflex viewfinder, wide assortment of interchangeable motors and a focus control device which corrects parallax of auxiliary viewfinder. The camera is supported on the operator's shoulder for hand-held shooting and can also be mounted inside an underwater shell.

## Soviet 70 mm cameras

In 1959 the Soviet motion picture industry adopted 70 mm negative film for shooting their wide screen productions. Several cameras were immediately manufactured for this gauge, among which the best known are the 70 SK and the Rossiya, both for studio work, and the KSRSH hand-held model, of very functional design. For special effects they have also built the high-speed 70 KSK camera, which can run up to 90 f.p.s. and the 70 KCK model for travelling mattes by the infra-red process. All these instruments are very well built and include several accessories to increase their scope.

The latest development for this gauge in the Soviet Union is the

Varioscope system, making use of a larger than standard image (48·5 × 46 mm), to which masking can be applied subsequently according to frame requirements. Several of the above mentioned cameras have been adapted to this new process, and a few experimental models have also been built.

## The 8 mm format

Over the last few years important progress has been made in the evolution of better quality 8 mm gauge filming, long popular with amateurs. The Eastman Kodak Co. pioneered a means of gaining more area for recording the image by fundamentally modifying the perforation dimensions. The old 0·172 × 1·29 in. frame thus became 0·211 × 1·58 in.

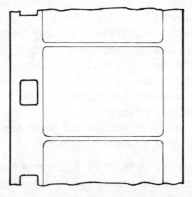

Fig. 22. Super 8 frame size with 50 per cent greater area than Standard 8 mm.

This system, called Super 8, has opened a vast field for the utilization of 8 mm film for certain types of sales promotion, industrial control , and even TV news.

Super 8 is today universally accepted, and many makers besides Kodak are manufacturing cameras for this gauge, incorporating the latest developments in mechanics, optics and automation, and thus meeting the need for easy-to-operate equipment. Such cameras are still destined for amateur use, but they are provided with some of the latest refinements, enabling them to rival and sometimes surpass professional equipment. Among these are:

(i) miniature electric motors for camera and zoom lens driven by three to eight dry cell batteries or rechargeable built-in nickel-cadmium batteries;

(ii)    50 ft. (15 m) cartridge to 200 ft. (60 m) and 400 ft. (120 m) magazines of double Super 8 film capacity;

(iii)   3–1, 4–1 or up to 12–1 zoom ratio super fast lenses with maximum apertures from $f$ 1·2 to $f$ 1·8, with manual or automatic zooming, one or two speed zoom control and macro-focusing facilities,

(iv)   manual or fully automatic exposure control with CdS through-the-lens meter, ASA speeds from 10 to 320 and exposure indicator in the finder,

(v)   reflex viewing with microprism focusing, 27 times image magnification, reflecting surface in front of lens diaphragm and control indicators in the finder such as end of film, low light level, camera not loaded, battery condition;

(vi)   wide aperture variable shutter;

(vii)  single frame exposures, T exposures, built-in intervalometer for 6 f.p.s. to one frame every 4 min, 12, 18, 24 or 40 f.p.s. to automatic slow motion effect with exposure correction;

(viii) self-resetting footage counter, automatic lap-dissolve, film rewind, cable release socket, film advance indicator, pulse synchronization device, built-in synchronization device for cassette or reel-to-reel magnetic recorder, sunshade, power supply condition indicator,

(ix)   small size, minimum weight and permanent or folding grip handle with trigger and trigger lock.

Over the last few years, some Super 8 cameras have appeared for shooting with direct sound recording. Two methods are used: the

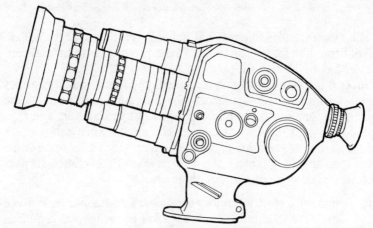

Fig. 7. Beaulieu 4008 ZM II refined Super 8 camera with a wide range of facilities and automation.

single system direct sound-on-film recording inside the camera using magnetic prestriped Super 8 film cartridges, or the double system, whereby the camera is synchronized either to a cassette or to a reel-to-reel magnetic tape recorder.

Since the market for 8 mm is already very large and is constantly growing , the effect of competition will undoubtedly be to widen the professional scope of Super 8, and compel manufacturers to bring their 16 mm cameras into line with these latest 8 mm advances.

## 4. REFERENCES

[1] High Speed Photography, S.M.P.T.E., New York (1949).

[2] Garrec, J., Connaissance des Caméras Ultra-Rapides, *Le Technicien du Film*, Nos. 64, 65, 66, 67, 68, 69, 75 (1960–1961).

[3] Garrec, J., Eclairage en Cinematographie Ultra-Rapide, *Le Technicien du Film*, No. 70–71 (March–May 1961).

[4] Cornwell-Clyne, A., *Colour Cinematography*, 3rd ed., Chapman & Hall, London (1951).

[5] Ball, J. A., The Technicolor Process of Three-Color Cinematography, *Journal of The Society of Motion Picture and Television Engineers*, Vol. XXV, No. 2, pp. 127–138 (1935).

[6] Hoch, W., Technicolor Cinematography, *Journal of The Society of Motion Picture and Television Engineers*, pp. 96–108 (August 1942).

[7] Kiel, J. P., A 35 mm Process Camera, *Journal of The Society of Motion Picture and Television Engineers*, pp. 551–558 (May 1951).

[8] Palen, V. W., The New Oxberry Combination 35/16 mm Process Camera, *American Cinematographer* (May 1956).

[9] Coutant, A., La Camera de Prise de Vues Double-bande, *Bulletin de L'Association Francaise des Ingenieurs et Techniciens du Cinema*, No. 17 (1958).

[10] Delaye, J., La Camera Sous-marine Aquaflex, *Cine-Sciences Photographie*, No. 31 (1956).

[11] Moon, A., Everest, F. A., Time-Lapse Cinematography, *Journal of the Society of Motion Picture and Television Engineers*, pp. 81–87 (February 1967).

[12] Hood, J. H., Jones, P. R. W., Cinematographic Instrumentation in Cine radiology, *Journal of The Society of Motion Picture and Television Engineers*, pp. 1090–1094 (November 1967).

# HOW TO OPERATE THE CAMERA

The purpose of this chapter is to provide detailed information on how to operate a number of actual camera models. Obviously not all cameras can be so described. The present selection includes some of the cameras most widely used in America and Europe, with emphasis on lightweight models popular with newsreel cameramen, documentary film crews, and low-budget production units. Moreover, these are the cameras with which newly initiated professionals usually start their careers, and the information presented here may help to give them a more comprehensive knowledge of their equipment.

## Operation of Mitchell S35R (Mark II) camera

LOADING THE MAGAZINE. Magazines must be loaded in a dark room or changing bag. In order to become familiar with the different operations, it is advisable to rehearse them previously in daylight with a roll of exposed film.

Before loading it is advisable to clean out the magazine chamber thoroughly, taking special care with the light-trap rollers. Every so often these must be checked by placing them before a light, and adjusted if they allow the passage of light which may fog the film.

The following sequence must be adhered to when loading the magazine:

(i)    remove both lids and place the magazine with its base towards you;

(ii)    insert the roll of film in the left-hand side magazine chamber, with the film unrolling clockwise;

(iii) thread the end of the film through the opening in that chamber, so that it will go round the first guide roller and run through the two plush rollers (see Fig. 2);

(iv) leave a free length of film of about 20 in.;

(v) close the lid of the film supply chamber and complete the operation in daylight;

(vi) reverse the process described under (iii) when threading the film into the take-up chamber, taking care that the film is threaded round the upper roller;

(vii) insert the contracting spool on the shaft of the right-hand side chamber. Insert the end of the film in the slot on the spool hub, and to obtain a more effective grip of the film end, fold it once or twice so that it fits the slot tightly. Finally, rotate the spool anticlockwise a few turns so that it starts winding the film;

(viii) rotate the pulley behind the magazine, by hand, a few turns, to check that film is properly adjusted and wound;

(ix) close the lid on the film take-up chamber.

MOUNTING THE MAGAZINE ON THE CAMERA. Open the camera door thus gaining access to the camera drive mechanism. To avoid accidental tripping, disconnect the buckle trip by swivelling the trip plate to the side. Place the front end of the magazine base on the front end of the magazine attachment recess plate, on top of the camera. Tilt the magazine until the small film loop can be slid through the slot which leads to the interior of the mechanism. Lower the magazine, taking care that the edges of its base and the camera top plate do not pinch the film. Secure the magazine firmly by turning the screw at the rear of the recess plate.

MOUNTING THE MAGAZINE ON THE CAMERA. This can be effected by one of three methods:

(i) on top of the camera;

(ii) on a side, slant back on the camera, by means of a special adapter;

(iii) under the camera, for hand-held shooting, for which only the special, 400 ft capacity magazine can be used.

THREADING THE CAMERA. Whichever the position of the magazine, the threading of the camera is the same. The Mark II is threaded in a very similar method to the other Mitchells. The main difference is that the sprocket is placed somewhat further below and somewhat nearer the intermittent mechanism.

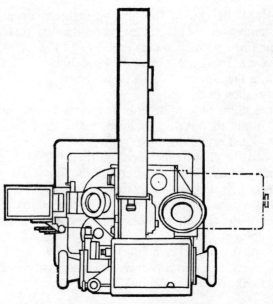

Fig. 1. Rear view of Mitchell S35-R with base-plate attachment and large matte box and sunshade

SETTING UP THE UNIT. The Mark II can be used in five different set-ups:

(i) as a hand-held, lightweight camera, in which case the magazine is mounted on the instrument's underside. The monitor viewfinder and special sunshade cannot be attached;

(ii) as a semi-portable camera, mounting the magazine on top and permitting the installation of the monitor viewfinder;

(iii) for more exacting requirements, use is made of a base plate attachment to take the lens hood; the camera is mounted thereon and is secured with two screws and the monitor viewfinder is then attached; this method affords a variation; the magazine can be installed slant-back by means of a special adapter;

(iv) as a noiseless instrument for studio work, for which the magazine is installed on top (but without the lens hood base plate) and over this the blimp, after which the monitor viewfinder can be installed;

(v) "System 35"; this is a special device added after installing the blimp which turns this camera into a complex instrument with remote control of the image by means of a closed TV circuit connected to the reflex viewfinder.

228

SHUTTER OPENING CONTROL. The shutter can be opened from 0 to 170° in both directions (increasing or decreasing the angle), and with the camera either stopped or running, just by turning a knob placed on top of the camera.

LENS MOUNT. Either a single mounting or a three lens turret can be used. Removal of the turret unit is effected by releasing locks placed at each end of the assembly. When changing the single mounting for the turret or vice versa, the viewing system's ground glass can also be exchanged.

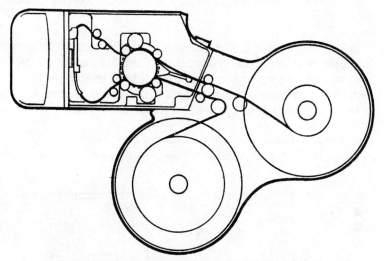

Fig. 2. Threading path of Mitchell S35-R with 400 ft rear magazine.

MOUNTING LENSES. Super Baltar lenses are used. To install, place focus indicating arrow in 6 o'clock position and fit lens to orifice, rotating clockwise until the bayonet seats home. To remove lens, press on the lever placed on the turret, above the lens and rotate it in the opposite direction (anticlockwise).

CONTROLS. The built-in tachometer, and footage and frame counters are placed side by side on the top rear of the camera.

MOTORS. These are installed on the camera's right hand side, by means of four screws. The variable speed motor, with rheostat for speed regulation, is the model most used for general purposes. Its body includes sockets for power supply and remote control.

MONITOR VIEWFINDER. Is installed the same as for the model described above. It makes use of a special finder clamp and harness for coupling to the automatic focus and parallax control.

SPECIAL LENS HOOD. This unit is supported on twin booms for extension and retraction. Its left-hand side has a hinged sector for permitting the use of the monitor viewfinder. The lens hood is supplied with a special based support for seating on the tripod platform, and on which the camera and the focus control system is installed.

OTHER OPERATIONS. The insertion of gelatin filters in front of the film gate and the operation of contrast filters for lighting study built into the viewing system, are very much the same as for the other Mitchells. The magnification control of the viewing system is placed between the two knobs operating the contrast filters.

*Operation of Eclair Cameflex CM3 and Scope model*

MOUNTING THE CAMERA. To mount the camera on an Eclair

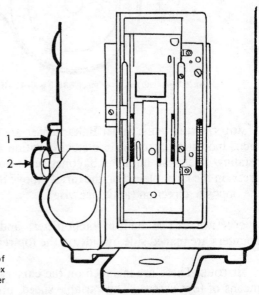

Fig. 3. Aperture plate of Cameflex showing: (1) reflex shutter regulator, (2) shutter knob.

230

tripod, mate the end of the flat dovetail base of the camera to the appropriate end of the slide on the tripod, then push the camera on to the slide, making sure that the dovetail is inserted correctly.

SHUTTER ADJUSTMENT. The following sequence must be followed to alter the shutter opening:

(i)   rotate the lens-turret so as to place it in an intermediate position;

(ii)  slightly loosen the screw which secures the adjustment of the shutter blades; this screw can be seen and reached through the opening for mounting the taking lens;

(iii) press the knob marked "reflex" and turn it until the shutter shows through the lens orifice;

(iv)  press the knob marked "obturateur" and turn it to obtain the desired shutter opening value marked at the edge of the reflex mirror.

Care must be taken that neither the "reflex" nor the "obturateur" knobs are touched while operating the camera.

MAGAZINE THREADING. Loading and threading the film on to the magazine is the most important operation in the handling of Cameflex cameras. As this loading and threading requires some

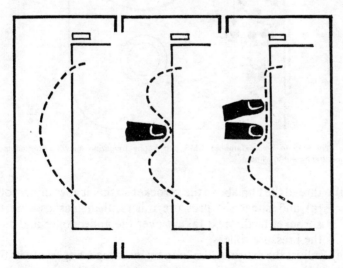

Fig. 4. Method of forming internal magazine film loops and flattening film against magazine plate.

practice, it is advisable to rehearse the procedure several times in daylight with blank film before carrying out the operation itself in the darkroom or changing bag:

(i) take off the lid of the magazine and keep it within easy reach;

(ii) release the pressure rollers above and below the sprocket by lifting the clips;

(iii) insert the film (wound emulsion out) on the top shaft, so that it will unwind anticlockwise (see Fig. 5);

(iv) insert the end of the film through the upper slot and draw out some 32 inches;

(v) insert this end through the lower external slot of the magazine;

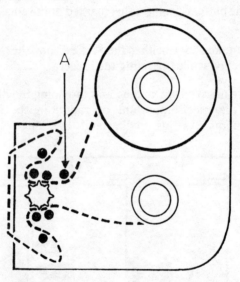

Fig. 5. Film path in Eclair Cameflex CM3 and Scope magazine showing formed loops, ready for attachment to camera.

(vi) thread the film above the sprocket so that it goes under roller (a) and under the pressure rollers, then meshes with the sprocket teeth; next take it over the upper roller and close the pressure rollers;

(vii) adjust the external film loop by inserting a finger into it (Fig. 11), and pressing down the film until it touches the magazine attachment knob;

232

(viii)  hold the film inserted through the lower magazine slot by pressing it with a finger, so that the length of the loop is not changed accidentally;

(ix)  thread the film over the remaining two pressure rollers, and mesh it to the lower side of the sprockets, checking that the sprocket teeth penetrate the film perforations fully;

(x)  close the lower pressure rollers;

(xi)  insert the film in the core so that it winds anticlockwise;

(xii)  replace the magazine lid;

(xiii)  in daylight, look at the footage counter reading and verify that it corresponds to the length of the unexposed roll of film;

(xiv)  the extended loop must now be pushed into the camera; this is done by pressing the rear of the loop with the finger, and flattening first one end and then the other with the other hand; when doing this, push the film through the light-trap slots so as to form two internal magazine loops (see Fig. 4); when the film is flat against the magazine base plate, the magazine is ready to attach to the camera.

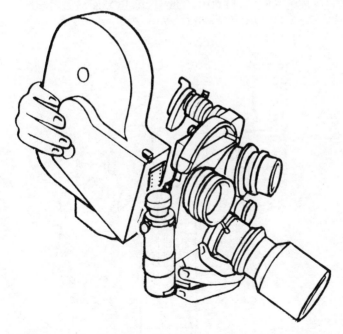

Fig. 6. Attaching Cameflex magazine to camera. Once in position it is automatically secured by a catch.

MAGAZINE MOUNTING. This is a very simple operation. Take the camera body in one hand, place the magazine on its slot and push it home with a jerk. To position the magazine correctly it is advisable to present it to the slot using the edges of the tachometer and speed indicator as guides. Once the magazine is pushed home, it is automatically secured by means of the catch placed on the upper right-hand side.

CAMEFLEX 16/35. In the Cameflex 16/35 mm model, when changing from 35 mm to 16 mm film, set the 16 mm aperture plate in the film gate and fix it by means of a retaining plate inserted through the filter slot.

Use 16 mm film magazines. Lenses need not be changed.

HAND DRIVE. The Cameflex can be crank-handle driven by means of a unit comprising an externally controlled gearbox which allows for regulation at three speeds: 1, 8 or 16 frames per turn. The crank-handle drive unit is installed in the same position for coupling the electric motor and is secured by the same means.

INSTALLING THE CAMEBLIMP. The specially designed blimp for the Cameflex can be installed either with 200 or 400 ft magazines,

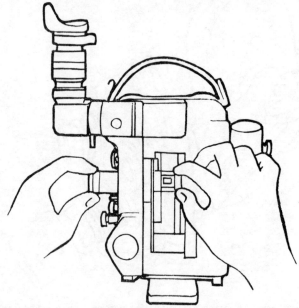

Fig. 7. Method of inserting aperture plate when using 16 mm film in Cameflex 16/35.

though the latter are normally used. Access is afforded by a single door on the blimp's right hand side; its lock is on the curved top sector. The camera is placed on a plate sliding along rubber guides which is pulled out of the blimp; this not only facilitates installing but also gives the operator access to all parts of the instrument. When the camera is pushed home, it will be automatically in line with, and connected to, the inside portions of the blimp's extrnal controls, such as viewfinder, diaphragm control, main drive shaft control, focus control, etc. A device for installing glass filters or 3 × 3 inch masks is provided on the sliding plate, in front of the camera.

The blimped Cameflex is generally used with synchronous motors, either 220 v. 3-phase, AC or 110 v. 60 Hz AC. All internal circuits are 6-wire throughout in order to take any type of electrical current.

The Cameblimp can be illuminated inside by means of special lamps for observing the camera's operation, installation, etc. from the outside. The external controls on the Cameblimp are:

(i)     reflex viewfinder eyepiece;
(ii)    starting switch;
(iii)   shutter opening control;
(iv)    knob for operating shutter by hand;
(v)     internal light switch;
(vi)    focus control;
(vii)   diaphragm control with two retaining catches and three observation windows, respectively for:
(viii)  lens setting;
(ix)    speed counter; and
(x)     exposed footage counter.

*Operation of Arriflex Models IIC and IICV*

THREADING THE MAGAZINE. Arriflex magazines require careful threading. Before loading, check that the roll of raw stock does not exceed the stated magazine capacity (a longer length of film may rub against the magazine walls, or cause the footage counter to stick, or the camera to run irregularly). Make sure that the film has been wound emulsion side in, and that the roll is tight and its surfaces perfectly flat.

To remove the magazine from the camera body, loosen the catch by turning it clockwise and pulling it out; the magazine can then be withdrawn.

To open the magazine, set the latch to position "A" and then remove the lid. Next, take the footage-counter roller seated on the left-hand core, and shift to the right as indicated by the arrow. Subsequent operations must be carried out in a darkroom or changing bag. As with the Cameflex, it is advisable to practice loading with blank or exposed film before attempting the following operations with raw stock:

(i) take the end of the roll and cut the perforations by means of the special template provided by the manufacturer; should this template not be available, cut the end of the film straight between two perforations;

(ii) push the prepared end of the film through the slot on the left-hand side of the magazine, taking care that the film is kept parallel to the magazine walls, so that the sprocket teeth mesh correctly with the perforations;

(iii) mount the film on the left side of the magazine, making sure that the core seats firmly on the spindle;

(iv) check that the roll of film rotates freely on its spindle, then draw the free end out of the magazine base and wrap it round the magazine until the end reaches the engraved marking (this ensures the right length of loop);

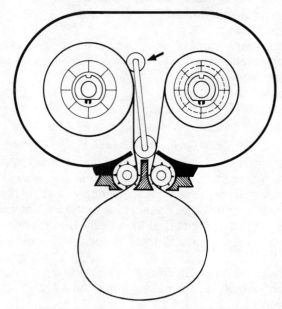

Fig. 15. Proper threading of Arriflex magazine. Arrow shows how footage counter arm must be seated on film roll.

(v) holding the film roll steady, insert the end of the film through the slot on the right-hand side of the magazine taking care that the sprocket teeth mesh correctly with the film perforations;

(vi) secure the end of the film to the take-up core with one turn, so that it will not slip;

(vii) return the arm of the footage counter to its working position (otherwise the magazine cannot be closed), and fasten the magazine lid by turning its catch; make sure that the lid edges are properly seated to avoid fogging.

THREADING THE CAMERA. To avoid the risk of accidental starting, disconnect the camera from its power source. Next, open the camera access door by turning the lock to position "A". Remove the door and put it in a safe place to avoid damage to the optical system built into it. Then,

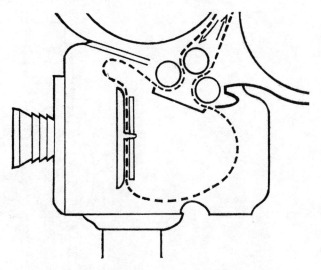

Fig. 9. Threading diagram of Arriflex 35 camera.

(i) rotate the inching knob until the claw is moved completely away from the aperture plate to the top of its cycle; open the film gate and check that the aperture and pressure plates are thoroughly clean;

(ii) place the magazine on the camera, taking care that the loop passes completely through the slot on the camera top. The best way to position the magazine is to tilt it first and place it

237

on the rear end of the magazine housing slot, and then seat it completely until the lock snaps back into position; finally turn the lock;

(iii) insert the film into the film gate; with a finger, carry the film over the aperture plate until the loop thus formed reaches the indicating mark on the camera wall; this upper loop must comprise 15 perforations from the top position of the claw to the magazine slot;

(iv) turn the inching knob by hand and check that the claw engages the film perforations;

(v) close the film gate, turn the inching knob and so make sure that the film is moving freely; connect the camera to its power supply and with the switch run a few feet of film;

(vi) replace the camera access door and secure it by turning the lock to position "Z".

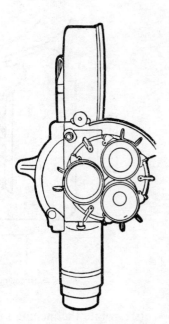

Fig. 10. Front view of Arriflex camera showing locking grips for changing lenses and external grips for rotating turret.

INTERCHANGING LENSES. The turret has three lens positions and the taking lens is the one just beneath the plane of the magazine base. To rotate the turret, press on one of three strips which are placed halfway between the lenses.

To remove a lens, press simultaneously on two locking grips placed at each side of the lens mount, and at the same time withdraw the lens very carefully from the turret. When installing a lens on the turret, check that the slot on the lens mounting is in line with the protruding pin which will be inserted into it.

The standard lenses on the Arriflex are 30, 50 and 75 mm. These are the markings jutting out of the turret edge to inform the operator which lens is in the taking position. If other lenses are used, be careful they do not interfere with each other's fields of view. The 25 mm wide-angle lens must be used without the rigid sunshade and without the 85 mm lens.

VARYING SHUTTER OPENINGS IN MODELS IIBV AND IICV. In models IIBV and IICV the shutter openings can be changed by a knob placed at the side. To alter the shutter opening, stop the camera and for safety's sake disconnect the power source. Next withdraw the taking lens from its mounting. Then press the shutter knob and turn it until the desired aperture angle appears in the lens mounting orifice. Finally replace the lens. The camera is again ready for shooting, but the makers recommend that the shutter knob *should not be pressed* while the camera is running, since this may damage the mechanism. To avoid accidents due to the shutter knob action, the knob is provided with a spring to return it to position after it has been pressed; however, it is advisable to check the positioning of this knob before restarting.

USE OF ANAMORPHIC LENSES. To use the camera with anamorphic lenses, the standard size aperture must be changed for one of the required dimensions: 18·67 × 22 mm (0·735 in. × 0·937 in.).

The aperture plate must first be replaced by one specially supplied for use with this lens. Since the photographed image will be squeezed by the anamorphic lens it is advisable to replace the normal viewfinder tube, which is integral with the camera access door, by another designed to unsqueeze the image. Model IIC is equipped with a door already prepared to accommodate this device, which takes the form of a prism. The unsqueezing viewfinder gives an upright image correct from left to right with an aspect ratio of 2·66 to 1. Anamorphic viewing can be changed back to normal by pressing a lever.

CHANGING VIEWFINDER FRAMING. The framing graticule is on a ground glass placed at right-angles to the lens mount orifice. In the IIC cameras the ground glass can be easily changed to adapt the

239

viewfinder to Cinemascope, widescreen or television frames. The ground glass is removed by hooking a piece of wire or paper clip in a perforation and drawing it out.

VARIABLE SPEED MOTOR. This motor works at 12–16 v. and is provided with a lever at the power socket to change from forward to reverse drive. It must be used in combination with the appropriate 400 ft. magazines, designed to work with reverse drive.

PERISCOPE ATTACHMENT FOR VIEWFINDER. This accessory can only be used with the latest IIC model Arriflex. It is installed on the standard eyepiece of the viewfinder and can be swivelled in any direction, to allow the camera operator to view from any angle, in relation to the camera and the subject. The periscope attachment gives a circular field of view, of approximately 22 mm diameter. This attachment is installed at the rear of the finder eyepiece system by means of a retaining ring.

## Operation of the Arriflex 35 BL

As is usual in most other cameras, especially in those of this make, the most important steps in preparing the camera for shooting are the loading of the film on to the magazine and the threading of the film loop on to the film gate. Loading film in the magazine takes place in the dark.

## Loading the magazine

(i)    Open the door giving access to the inside of the camera, by turning the lock at the middle to position AO.

(ii)    Turn the lock on the magazine throat clockwise to position AO.

(iii)    withdraw the magazine from its housing on the camera and lay it down with the loading side upwards.

(iv)    Move the loading lid lock in the direction of the arrow "A"; the lock is on the top part of the magazine. Open the magazine and put the lid aside.

(v)    Move the footage counter arm to the magazine edge until it clicks into a retainer. Place the edge of the film roll in the slot beneath the footage counter window. The film should unroll clockwise. The emulsion side of the film on the roll should be inwards. Insert the end of the film until you feel the resistance of the sprocket teeth on the corresponding side of the magazine throat.

(vi)    Engage the film in the sprocket by rotating the drive coupling counterclockwise by hand, and make it advance until the end comes out of that side of the throat. After placing the roll on the shaft of the raw stock chamber and checking that it is properly seated there, close the lid of the raw stock chamber. Once the lid is firmly in position the footage counter arm returns automatically to its position over the film roll. The following operations can be carried out in the light:

(vii)   Turn the magazine upside down so that the take up chamber faces upwards. Open the take up chamber lid in the same way as the raw stock chamber lid.

(viii)  By rotating the drive coupling pull out a length of film enough to reach the mark on the top part of the magazine. This trailing end of film should be about 9 in. long.

(ix)    Insert the film in the slot corresponding to the take up chamber in the magazine throat. By rotating the drive coupling engage the film on the sprocket and make it come out into the takeup chamber. Fix the end to the collapsible core. Make sure that the loop has maintained a constant length while rotating the drive coupling. Check that the locking lever of the collapsible core is in the correct position. Finally, close the lid of the magazine take-up chamber.

*Mounting the magazine on the camera*

(i)    Place the camera body in a firm position.

(ii)   Open the film gate by pulling the release lever out towards the doors casting with the left index finger. The lever must be pulled only for the initial releasing of the transport mechanism, you then let it return to its original position. This mechanism reaches its first stop after the initial pulling. By pulling again the film gate back plate would be further separated, but only for cleaning purposes, and in this position the magazine throat cannot be placed inside the camera.

(iii)   Rotate the knurled inching knob of the shutter system until the red marking is in line with the printed mark. In this position the shuttles should be withdrawn approximately 1/16 in. (2 mm).

(iv)   Place the loaded magazine on the back of the camera body so that the dovetail mount fits perfectly on to the steel rail. Guide the film loop with the hand until it reaches the film gate. Fit the magazine in position and close its lock to position "zc".

(v)   Adjust the film loop in the film gate so that it follows the printed indicating mark. A reference pin maintains the film in the desired position. Close the film gate back plate. An audible "click" indicates that the shuttle claws have engaged in the film perforations correctly.

(vi)  Turn the safety switch to the "on" position, swinging it to the position counter-clockwise.

Other steps to make the camera ready:

(i)    Set the footage counter to zero.

(ii)   Connect the camera to a 12 v. DC battery with a capacity not lower than 5 Ah.

(iii)  Select the operating speed 24/25 f.p.s. This is effected with a switch placed at one end of a small built-in panel at the rear of the camera.

(iv)   The on/off camera switch is on the hand grip.


## Operation of 16 mm cameras

*Operation of the Arriflex 16 M camera*

The 16 M Arriflex is designed to provide very rapid adjustment and operation. The magazines are of the type in which most of the threading is internal, so that they can be mounted on the camera with only a few moments' loss of shooting time.

THREADING THE MAGAZINE. The magazines supplied for the 16 M are for 200 or 400 ft. darkroom-loading rolls, or for 100 or 200 ft. daylight loading spools. Film is wound emulsion inwards.

The film spindles in the magazine incorporate a device which accepts either the square hole in a spool or the round hole in a normal core.

The following are the operations required to load and thread a magazine. Unless daylight loading spools, are used, they must be carried out in a darkroom or changing bag.

(i)    Open the magazine and lay the lid aside keeping it handy; place the open magazine before you, with its base nearest to you;

(ii)   lift the arm of the footage counter;

(iii)  place the film roll or spool on the left-hand spindle in such a way that it will unroll clockwise (film perforated on one side only has its perforations next to the magazine wall);

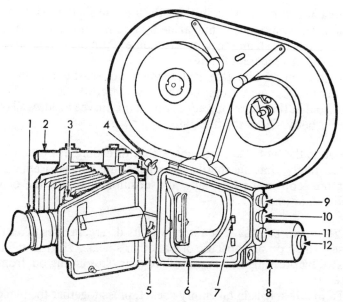

Fig. 11. Arriflex model M showing threading path. (1) Reflex eyepiece, (2) matte-box boom, (3) start switch, (4) magazine release lever, (5) optical system, (6) film loop, (7) switch connection, (8) variable speed motor, (9, 10, 11) external electric connections, (12) motor hand-knob.

(iv) insert the end of the film through the left-hand slot in the magazine base; rotate the sprocket making sure the teeth penetrate the perforations, until the end of the film comes out of the magazine base;

(v) pull out a length of film long enough when curved round the magazine to just reach the engraved mark; then insert the end into the magazine through the right-hand slot, rotate the sprocket, making sure the teeth penetrate the perforations, until the film goes in, thus ensuring that a 39-frame loop has been formed;

(vi) insert the end of the film into a core or spool and place it on the take-up spindle; rotate the sprocket a few turns to check that threading has been done correctly;

(vii) replace the lid, making sure that it is seated properly so as to avoid fogging.

Mounting the magazine on the camera takes only a few seconds. First turn the magazine lock to the left, so as to detach the plate protecting the magazine housing. Release the catch beneath the viewfinder on the access door by pressing it to the left, then open the

243

camera access door. After pushing the loop through the slot into the camera body, mount the magazine by tilting it slightly, so that the rear end rests first, and then press it home. Turn the magazine catch to the right to secure it firmly.

Next, open the film gate. Rotate the motor shaft until shuttle and register pin are away from the film gate. Insert the loop in the film track so that the lower loop edges round the curved inside wall of the camera body. Close the film gate.

Rotate the motor shaft to check that threading has been carried out correctly, that the shuttle claws penetrate the perforations, and that the loop keeps its shape and position. Replace the camera access door and lock it.

CHANGING LENSES. The turret with its divergent axes takes three lenses which do not obscure one another's fields. The turret can be rotated by pressing on one side of the wing clips jutting out from the edge.

To mount a lens in an empty socket, press together the two clips on the lens, and when inserting it make sure that the slot on the mounting is uppermost.

MOTOR. Dismounting and interchanging the motor is a simple operation. Turn the side lever to the left. Withdraw the motor carefully. If another motor is to be installed, check that the pin at its side coincides with the hole at the side of the motor housing. A ring at the back of the motor can be turned to reverse its rotation, and thus, the direction of film travel in the camera. The motor speed can be altered over a range of 5–50 f.p.s. by turning the black striped band on the top.

STARTING THE CAMERA. In order to start the camera proceed as follows:

(i)    connect feed cable end with Canon connector to lower, three-pin male contact, and the other end to 8 v. battery terminals;

(ii)   adjust motor speed by turning the rheostat until the chosen speed is shown on the tachometer;

(iii)  press down lever switch placed above reflex viewfinder; this locks automatically, so that, to stop the camera, the retaining clip must be released.

REFLEX VIEWFINDER. If, before starting the camera, no image

appears in the viewfinder, rotate the motor shaft until the image appears. There is an adjuster ring on the viewfinder eyepiece to correct for the operator's eyesight. To avoid fogging the film by light seeping in through the viewfinder tube, the eye should be placed closely against the eyepiece when shooting with strong backlight. When the viewfinder is not in use, the eyepiece should be closed. The latest models are equipped with an automatic device which opens up when the eye is pressed against the eyepiece, and closes again when pressure is withdrawn.

INSTALLATION OF SUNSHADE AND MATTE-BOX. These are mounted on a boom which is inserted in a slot located above the turret close to the magazine lock. The boom is secured by turning the fixing thumbscrew at its forward end. The bellows are then adjusted to suit the field of view of the lens in use.

*Operation of the Eclair NPR*

As already explained, the Eclair NPR (Noiseless Portable Reflex) makes use of a coaxial magazine, which houses the continuous drive mechanism and the footage and frame counters. The magazine consists of two side-by-side chambers (instead of the usual fore-and-aft arrangement, and the supply and take-up rolls are mounted on the same spindle which is supported by the internal wall separating the two magazine chambers. The magazine takes 100 or 200 ft. daylight

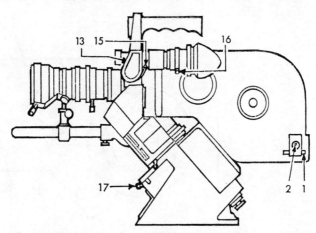

Fig. 12. Eclair 16 NPR self blimped camera. (1) Safety lock, (2) button catch, (13) finder retaining ring, (14) friction adjuster for finder, (15) finder position lock, (16) eyepiece magnification adjuster, (17) Motor Switch.

loading spools, or rolls of film up to 400 ft. loaded in the darkroom. These are wound emulsion in.

LOADING

(i) Place the magazine flat on a table with the base to the right, and the lock of the top lid nearest to you;

(ii) press the safety lock (1) and push-button (2) simultaneously and remove the magazine lid to give access to the supply chamber;

(iii) raise the arm of the footage counter, until it locks in the "up" position;

(iv) if daylight loading spools are to be used, the plate (3) must be removed; if the film is perforated on one side only, the perforations must be nearest the magazine lid;

(v) open the pressure roller (4) by pushing its retaining catch and feed the film on to the sprocket, checking that the teeth penetrate the perforations on the first inch of film;

(vi) close lid on upper side of magazine, but do not lock it and push safety catch back; the footage counter arm will then jump into position automatically;

(vii) turn the magazine upside down and remove what is now the top lid, and rotate take-up shaft (5) anticlockwise to make about 4 in. of film pass from the supply chamber to the take-up chamber;

(viii) edge the film end along the loop-marking engraved on the magazine wall;

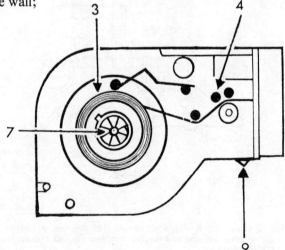

Fig. 13. Eclair 16 NPR Magazine supply chamber and film path. (3) Film spooling plate, (4) pressure roller, (7) Film drive shaft, (9) magazine release.

246

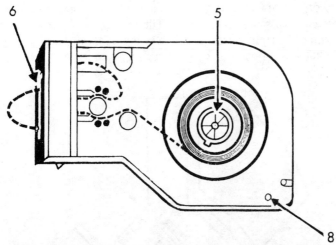

Fig. 14. Magazine take-up chamber of Eclair NPR camera showing film path. (5) Take-up shaft, (6) Base plate, (8) Operating pin.

(ix)   open guide roller and insert film on to sprocket and then close pressure roller;

(x)   keep rotating shaft (5) until film comes out of base-plate (6) and pressing it against the base-plate to facilitate the next steps;

(xi)   insert film end in through lower slot; open lower pressure roller; and insert film on to sprocket again, leaving a loop comprising about twelve perforations (approximately enough to allow the insertion of two fingers); this loop should protrude from the magazine base-plate;

(xii)   clip the lower pressure roller back into position and keep rotating the shaft until there is enough film inside the take-up chamber to insert the end into the slot in the spool core; check that the film goes over the guide roller;

(xiii)   after completing threading on the take-up side, check it by rotating drive shaft (7) [never use take-up shaft (5) for this purpose after the film end has been secured to it];

(xiv)   close lid on magazine, engaging the left-hand side first, thus pushing in pin (8); adjust lid firmly and push back safety lock (1);

(xv)   using your fingers (see Fig. 4), divide film loop into two halves, and push one into the upper and one into the lower slot in the magazine base (this is important and must not be neglected).

ATTACHING MAGAZINE TO CAMERA. Place magazine baseplate against camera's magazine-plate. Tilt magazine slightly and seat lower end of baseplate first, and then swing it forward until the upper catch clicks into position. To detach magazine from camera, press button (9).

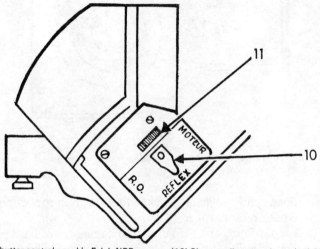

Fig. 15. Shutter control panel in Eclair NPR camera. (10) Shutter adjustment lever, (11) Shutter inching knob.

ADJUSTING THE SHUTTER. Shutter opening can be adjusted from 5° to 180°. Proceed as follows:

(i)   rotate turret until it is in horizontal position;
(ii)  turn lever (10) up to "Reflex" position;
(iii) turn knob (11) until shutter edge shows through lens opening;
(iv)  turn lever (10) to "Shutter Adjustment" position (R.O.) and push in;
(v)   rotate shutter control (12) until the desired shutter opening setting can be read on shutter edge through lens opening;
(vi)  release lever (10) on which its spring will return it to its neutral "Motor" position, thus unlocking the pull-down mechanism.

MOUNTING LENSES. The Eclair NPR takes lenses with three types of mounting; bayonet mounting, C type mounting, and Cameflex and Arriflex mountings.

(i)   insert the bayonet mounting so that the narrow flange is nearest the turret shaft, and then turn clockwise;

248

(ii) screw C type mounting lens into central orifice of turret mount;

(iii) lenses with Cameflex or Arriflex mountings must be fitted with an adapter which is then screwed in like a C type mounting.

The turret is rotated by pressing on the central shaft in the direction of arrow "D", and then pulling out and rotating the turret clockwise. After fitting the desired lens return the turret to its shooting position by rotating the central shaft in the direction of arrow "S".

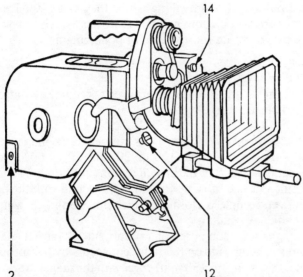

Fig. 16. Eclair NPR 16 mm camera mounted on a tripod adaptor. (2) Button release for magazine lid, (12) Shutter control, (14) Friction adjuster.

ADJUSTING VIEWFINDER. The viewfinder can swivel 360°, thus allowing for framing from any position, which is often a great convenience. This finder is removed by loosening the ring (13). It swivels on an axis which is parallel to the sides of the frame, and button (14) regulates the friction on the swivelling action. The thumbscrew (15) fixes the finder firmly in any desired position.

The eyepiece is provided with an automatic closing device, which opens up when the eye is pressed to the eyepiece, and closes down again when pressure is released. The eyepiece can also swivel so that the operator can use either his right or left eye. Thumbscrew (16) adjusts the eyepiece diopter reading to suit individual eyesight.

249

STARTING. The motor is started by means of a built-in switch (17). A pilot light is lit when the motor is running at the right speed, thus allowing the operator to check the state of the battery charge.

HOLDING INSTRUCTIONS. The Eclair NPR has been designed for hand-held shooting, with the back of the magazine resting on the operator's shoulder. It weighs 18 lb complete with magazine and motor. If it should be necessary to mount the camera on a tripod, a special hi-hat adapter must be used.

SUNSHADE. The matte-box and extendible bellows sunshade are mounted on a rigid boom, along which they can slide. This is also useful for supporting zoom and telephoto lenses. Also provided is a rotating disc allowing for insertion of polarizing filters.

*Operation of the Eclair ACL*

According with the manufacturer's recommendations the operational procedure is as follows:

THREADING THE MAGAZINE. The snap-on coaxial magazine of this camera is designed to take 100 or 200 ft. (30 or 60 m) daylight loading spools or 200 ft. darkroom loading rolls on a 2 in. (50 mm) core. You can use double perforation film wound with the emulsion in or out, and single perforation films emulsion-in (B winding) or emulsion-out (A winding).

The magazine is composed of a supply side on the left (viewfinder side) and a take-up side on the right, connected by lightproof guide. To load a film on a 2 in. (50 mm) core, with the magazine on its side, nose to the left, proceed as follows:

*A. Supply side*
  (i)   Turn the supply lid latch anti-clockwise (the latch covers the magazine number) and lift the part of the latch that projects over the edge of the magazine. At the same time pull the lid backwards to clear it from the magazine.
  (ii)  Lift the counter-arm which locks up automatically.
  (iii) Holding the film reel in the left hand, position the end of the film between the two rollers at the entry of the guide.
        *Note: The emulsion must be towards the exterior of the magazine between these rollers.*
  (iv)  Push approximately 6 in. (15 cm) of film into the guide.

250

(v) Place the core on the support flange.

(vi) Replace the lid.

    (a) Insert the spring strip, at the left of the lid, into the magazine body.
Push the lid down and forward to locate it in the body and turn the catch clockwise to lock the lid.

(vii) The counter-arm drops into place automatically as the catch is released by the lid.


## B. Take-up side

The take up side can be loaded in (preferably shaded), daylight. Turn the magazine and lay it on its side with the nose to the right. Then proceed as follows:

(i) Remove the lid.

(ii) Pass the film between the rollers according the threading diagram.

(iii) Place the end of the film into the upper film guide of the nose; if necessary press on the pressure guide.

(iv) Pull the film through sufficiently to introduce it into the lower film guide.

(v) Pull 20 in. (50 cm) of film into the magazine.

(vi) Open the two guide shoes by simultaneously pressing the two catches.

(vii) Place the film between the sprocket and upper guide shoe. Check that the perforations are engaged and push the guide shoe toward the sprocket, it locks automatically.

(viii) Place the film between the sprocket and the lower shoe.

(ix) Adjust the loop size by pulling the film outside the magazine until the loop is level with the magazine locking tongues.

(x) Close the shoe against the sprocket.

(xi) Spread the film equally in the magazine nose.

(xii) Wind the film on to the core and place it on the flange.

(xiii) Replace the lid.


## Loading a daylight loading spool to the magazine

(i) Pull and lift the flange catches on the supply and take-up sides.

(ii) Remove the flanges.

(iii) Load the film as for a core load.

(iv) Lock the spools in place with the catches, ensuring that they are pushed firmly home.

*Note:* In order to ensure the lowest noise level check that the spools are not warped and that they are firmly locked into the axle.

MOUNTING THE MAGAZINE ON THE CAMERA. Before snapping on the magazine check the loop and ensure that the aperture plate is clean and the side pressure guide is working correctly.

(i) With the magazine tilted backwards place the lower part of the magazine nose to the bottom of the aperture plate; the magazine drive shafts are aligned.

(ii) Pivot the magazine on its lower locating points and push it home. The lock operates automatically and a sharp click indicates that the magazine is firmly in place.

(iii) Push the safety catch inwards. This will ensure that the magazine will not be accidentally released by a knock on the lock release lever.

*Note:* The lock is so designed that the magazine will remain on the camera under all transport conditions.

*To remove the magazine*
(i) Slide the safety catch outwards.
(ii) Hold the magazine at the top with one hand and camera body with the other.
(iii) Press the lock release lever with the index finger.
(iv) Pull the magazine down and back to clear it from the camera.

*Starting the camera*
Having placed a lens and the magazine on the camera and adjusted the viewfinder:

(i) Connect the battery to the camera with the cable.
(ii) Adjust the mirror to the viewing position using the knurled knob on the motor.
(iii) Set the clapper to the required position.

central: no clapper,
to the left or right: automatic clapper,
vi) manual clapper is operated when the switch is moved from the center to a side position. The clapper duration is 0·3 seconds.

(iv) Starting the camera:

    (a) push the button in, which closes the test circuit;

    (b) slide the button to the left (towards the motor), which closes the motor circuit and starts the camera. The button locks in place.

(v) If the lamp on the motor body lights up, the battery is flat.

(vii) To stop the camera push the button to the right. The switch returns to the "off" position.

*Operation of Auricon Sound cameras*

The various Auricon models differ considerably from one another, and the following points are intended to bring out only the most important features for handling these instruments. A detailed description of their operation, as well as recommendations for sound recording techniques, will be found in the exhaustive manual supplied by the manufacturers.

CONNECTIONS. The camera operator may perhaps be baffled by the profusion of cables supplied with these instruments. But he should remember his camera works in combination with an amplifier and other electronic equipment, and the foolproof characteristics of all connectors, which ensure there will be no mix-up, should set his mind at rest. The cables are:

(i) from power source to camera, to provide the drive;

(ii) from galvanometer or magnetic recording head in the camera to the sound amplifier;

(iii) from microphone to amplifier;

(iv) from camera or amplifier (according to sound equipment or camera model being used) to earphones, to monitor the recorded sound quality.

THREADING. The Auricon Cine Voice is supplied with a threading chart engraved on the camera body; in the other Auricons, this chart is stuck on the camera access door. The instructions on these charts must be strictly adhered to. Threading models 600, 600 Special and Super 1200, requires prior loading of the magazine in darkroom or changing bag. The Cine Voice uses 100 ft. daylight loading spools.

These cameras take 16 mm film with perforations on one side only. If magnetic sound is to be recorded, the raw stock must be supplied with magnetic track already striped on the edge in accordance with ASA Standard PH 22.28–1958.

Before threading, it is advisable to clean the film gate; also check that loops are the proper size and shape, and that the film passes correctly over the compensating sprocket near the recording head.

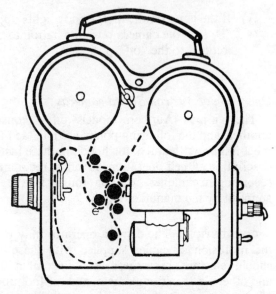

Fig. 17. Threading path for film in the Auricon Cine Voice.

In the Cine Voice model, the spools must be pushed right back on to the shaft, after the footage counter arm has been swung away. First complete threading and insert the film end into the slot on the hub of the take-up spool, and only then mount the take-up spool on the take-up shaft.

Models 600 and 1200 are equipped with a safety device which cuts the power supply if anything goes wrong with the take-up belt; the camera will run only if the take-up belt is working properly. When threading the 1200 bear in mind that two sprockets are used in this camera to drive the extra large load of film.

After threading the 600 and 1200 models, make sure to slip the magazine belt drive into place. Before closing the camera access door, start up the camera for a few seconds to check that it runs properly.

FRAMING AND FOCUSING. Viewfinding is by a different method in each Auricon model. The Cine Voice is provided with a side viewfinder allowing for parallax correction. But if a zoom lens with

254

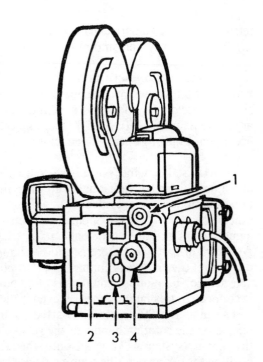

Fig. 18. Rear view of Auricon Pro 600. (1) Warning light, (2) footage counter, (3) on-off push button, (4) telefinder eyepiece.

built-in reflex viewfinder is used, the camera door with built-in side viewfinder must be replaced by a special tubeless door. The finder on the zoom lens will permit very accurate framing, and focusing will be by means of the attached rangefinder.

The same side viewfinder can be employed on the two 600 models, but these cameras are also equipped with two additional systems. One is a small eyepiece at one side of the camera, which makes direct focusing possible when the turret is rotated until the taking lens is placed in front of it. The other is an optical tube with ten times magnification, working through auxiliary lenses mounted on the turret, which are equivalent to the taking ones. This latter system is useful with telephoto lenses.

As explained previously, focusing and framing with the Super 1200 is effected by a rackover ground glass system which, before shooting, inserts mirrors at 45° behind the taking lens. This device is controlled from behind the camera by a rotating handle. When this handle is in the "g.g. focus" position, framing can be carried out through the taking lens and focus adjusted, but the camera cannot be operated. When the control handle is in the Telefinder position, the viewing system sights through the auxiliary lens, the mirror system is

255

retracted and the camera can be operated. The control-handle can be rotated very easily and smoothly even with gloved hands.

VARIABLE OPENING SHUTTER. The Super 1200 model is equipped with a shutter whose variable opening is adjusted by a control at one side. This allows for fade-ins and fade-outs and for shutter speed adjustments from 1/50 to 1/200 sec. The calibrations on the control are: open, $\frac{3}{4}$ open, $\frac{1}{2}$ open, $\frac{1}{4}$ open, closed.

STARTING. The Cine Voice is started by means of a lever switch and a neon lamp beneath it lights up when the motor is running. The two 600 models are provided with two push-buttons, one above the other, for starting and stopping, respectively. Two lamps on the camera front and one at the back go on when the motor is running. At the right-hand side there is another lamp which lights up to indicate that the camera is connected to the power source and that the "electronic" take-up is running at $\frac{1}{3}$ of its power rating; when power is connected, this lamp comes on even if the motor is not running.

The model 1200 camera is started by means of a push-button placed on the rotating handle of the rackover framing device. Thus the start-up system will operate only when the bar is in the telefinder position for taking, and the framing device has been withdrawn from the viewing system. When the control-handle is in the "g.g. focus" position, the instrument cannot be started, thus avoiding mishaps. Should it be necessary to look through the taking lens when the camera is running (e.g. when checking shutter synchronization for back projection), the handle must be rotated to "g.g. focus" after the camera has been started, but it must be remembered that no image is being recorded on the film while the rackover system is in the viewing position. The instrument is stopped by pressing the red button above the rotating handle.

SPECIAL CHARACTERISTICS

(i)   No means of correcting parallax is provided in the telefinder supplied for the Pro 600 and Pro 600 Special when using telephoto lenses, since the error is negligible.

(ii)  In the Cine Voice, the footage counter is on the left-hand side of the camera, while on the other models it is at the back and is illuminated.

(iii) When working under very low temperatures, it is advisable to connect the camera to the power source some 30 minutes before shooting, so that the heater will be turned on. It will

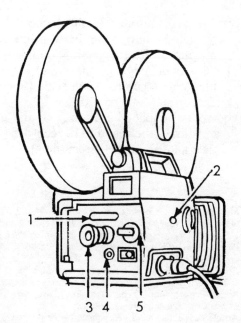

Fig. 19. Rear view of Auricon Super 1200. (1) Footage counter, (2) cameraman's headphone plug, connection (3) telefinder eyepiece, (4) power line indicator light, (5) shift-over device with on-off push button.

3  4    5

then gradually build up to a temperature adequate to free the lubricant. When the camera motor is started, the heater is automatically switched off. The heater is controlled by a thermostat working at a minimum of 65°F and a maximum of 70°F.

(iv) When rolls of film larger than 400 ft. are employed, the makers recommended the use of the 3 in. Auricon centres.

OPERATION OF AMPLIFIERS. This varies considerably according to type and model, as well as to choice of magnetic or optical recording. The Auricon company publishes a manual with precise instructions on the steps to follow in each case. A summary of the main points is given here so that the reader may get a general idea of how to proceed.

(i)   Check the charge of the batteries feeding the amplifier, by means of the controls provided for this purpose (optical or magnetic amplifier).

(ii)  Check that the frequency reading of the "record bias" is correct (61 kc/s) (magnetic sound amplifier).

(iii) Turn on the amplifier and adjust the intensity of the exciter lamp in the galvanometer according to the sensitivity of the film to be used (optical sound amplifier).

257

(iv) Establish a sound quality control channel, either directly from the microphone, or from the recording on the film's magnetic track (magnetic sound amplifier).

(v) Check volume by means of the volume indicator meter or by the volume control knob scale (sound amplifier for optical and/or magnetic recording).

(vi) Adjust amplifier according to the quality and/or characteristics of the sound to be recorded (sound amplifier for optical and/or magnetic recording).

## 5. REFERENCES

[1] Mitchell Camera Corporation, *Handbook M-202* (Calif. Jan, 1957); U.S. Navy Department, *Navy Training Courses: Photography*, Vol. 1 (1951).
U.S. Navy Department, *Navy Training Courses: Photographers Mate 1 & C* (1962).

[2] Pittaro, E. M., *TV and Film Production Data Book*, Morgan & Morgan, New York, pp. 249–253 (September 1959).

[3] Couthant, A., Mathot, J., A Reflex 35 mm Magazine Motion Picture Camera, *Journal of The Society of Motion Picture and Television Engineers*, pp. 173–179 (Aug. 1950).

[4] British Broadcasting Corporation, Eng. Div., *Arriflex 35 mm Camera Technical Instructions*, London (May 1960).
Arnold & Richter, K. G., *Handbook of the Arriflex 35 System*, Part 1, Instruction Manual, Munich (Dec. 1961).
Cinepress, *Repair and Parts Manual for Arriflex 35 mm Cameras*, Vol. 1, Hollywood (June 1966).
*See also:* Cameraflex Corp., *Instruction Book for Camera PH-330-K*, New York.

[5] U.S. Air Forces, *Handbook of Instructions with Parts Catalogue for the Type (A-3.35 mm) Aircraft Camera*, Washington (Sept. 1942).

[6] British Broadcasting Corporation, Eng. Div., *Arriflex 16 mm Camera Technical Instructions*, London (May 1960).

[7] Bach Auricon, *How to use your Auricon 16 mm sound-on-film equipment: recording equipment*, Hollywood (Nov. 1960).

# CHOICE, MAINTENANCE AND INSPECTION
# OF CAMERAS

Very often the choice of a motion picture camera, whether for buying or renting, is the responsibility of the professional cinematographer. Film companies and independent producers usually consult the photography director on the advantages of certain equipment as against others, or on which is the most adequate instrument for a specific task. Correct advice can only be given after analyzing various factors in their corresponding scale of value.

Normally, film companies either use their own instruments or rent them from camera and equipment rental firms. In the former case the company must be economically very solvent, usually with studios and laboratories, in order to afford investing a large capital in equipment; this must therefore be made to work continuously, either producing, or even sometimes renting equipment to others. On the other hand, cameras and accessory equipment are normally rented only by independent producers, who tackle films one at a time, each being an individual business transaction, and the rental fees are included in each film's budget; such independent producers generally avoid being tied up with long-term actors' contracts, maintenance of premises, or permanent personnel salaries.

A company will invest capital in costly equipment, especially cameras, only when they can programme a continuous output, when they want to be free from third parties for the material they shall use, and when their administration policy tends towards capitalization through such equipment. The absence of specific equipment for rental, and others, may sometimes be complementary factors.

For example, some TV newsreel companies do not rent cameras. The continuous use of the instruments would make rental too expensive and unpractical. The same occurs with institutions specialized in scientific films, who are continuously using instruments which are difficult to obtain for rental.

## Choosing a camera

Before selecting a camera it is essential to determine the specific task in view. This brings us back to the subject of film production. Throughout the world there are four basic types of film: the feature film, the short (documentary or scientific) film, the news coverage film and the theatrical or TV commercial. Each of such main classifications is broken down into a series of sub-groups which define precisely each type of production.

### Shooting methods

According to technical requirements or shooting methods, the above classified films can be shot as follows:

(i) direct sound recording on the film's own track (single system);

(ii) direct sound recording on a separate strip (double system);

(iii) silent printing of the image to add the sound track later (dubbing).

The first system is used for newsreels, especially for TV and has been mentioned before (see p. 167). The second system is used for feature films or for newsreels by means of special devices. The soundless image recording for adding sound later is mostly used for "shorts", publicity films, or low-cost feature films where fast shooting and low-cost media are essential.

### 35 mm Studio cameras

When using the double system, a silent camera must be used, which must work synchronized with the sound recorder. Such instruments are used for shooting feature films or commercial film with a dialogue, and are called "studio cameras", which are noted for the following characteristics:

BULK AND WEIGHT. The body of the camera is designed to dampen the noise made by the movements and to house a large synchronous motor. Therefore the instrument needs a rolling pedestal or dolly for displacements round the studio and it must be dismantled and reassembled each time the scene is changed when shooting outdoors.

PRECISION INTERMITTENT. Being provided with register pins, these instruments provide rock steady images, thus producing better quality photography with improved relief and definition. They also allow for special effects such as multiple exposures, travelling mattes, background projections, etc. which cannot be effected by other means.

EFFICIENT FOCUS CONTROL. Focus regulation by means of external controls or by cable connected remote control is essential when shooting scenes with continuous displacements of actors or combined actors and cameras. Studio cameras are generally the only instruments with suitable built-in facilities for such scenes.

HANDLING AND OPERATION. Studio cameras are very complete and complex instruments which require more than one operator to work them.

HIGH COST. Instruments for studio work are very expensive: international prices range from US $20,000–40,000, according to make, model, and accessories wanted. The daily rent varies from one country to the other, but it will usually be found in the order of US $150 for the simplest models and US $450 for the most complex items.

It will be appreciated that studio cameras must be used when shooting by the double system; but on the other hand they necessitate complex accessories, shooting time per day is reduced by delays in readying for shooting, they require a larger number of technicians and consequently increase daily shooting costs in addition to rental or capital amortization costs.

Therefore, when planning a production, the excellent efficiency of direct sound recording must be weighed against its higher cost and slowness, in comparison to soundless shooting for a later dubbing.

*Lightweight cameras*

Shooting for postsynchronization is usually effected with lightweight cameras, whose characteristics are as follows:

SIMPLE INTERMITTENT MECHANISM. The intermittent movements of most lightweight cameras generally do not include register pins and in some models the shuttles work with only one claw on only one side. Such mechanisms provide acceptable images, but they are not sufficiently steady for special effects.

261

NOISY OPERATION. The running noise of this type of camera sometimes disturbs non-professional actors, who feel camera-shy as soon as they hear it, especially when shooting documentary films.

MOBILE AND PORTABLE. This type of camera is easy to move assembled from one point to another of the set or location. It can even be kept in a carrying case, completely ready for immediate use. This avoids a great loss of time in assembling, etc.

RESTRICTED FOCUSING FACILITIES. Few lightweight cameras are provided with devices for following focus continuously. Focus adjustment by camera assistant is difficult as the scales are not easily visible. Sometimes this work must be carried out by the camera operator himself. This is a point to consider when planning to shoot scenes with continuous displacements of camera and actors.

MINIMUM CREW. Since these instruments lack elaborate refinements and are simple to operate and easy to carry, they can be operated by a minimum camera crew.

LOW COST. The international price of these cameras is from approximately US $6,000–10,000, according to make, format and accessories, and they are rented for about US $30–50 a day.

From the production point of view, therefore, though lightweight cameras have certain technical shortcomings, they bring about appreciable savings which can be summarized as follows: large number of takes during each working day, lower salary costs and lower rental or capital amortization costs.

## Summary of factors

The above considerations on the advantages and shortcomings of equipment as applied to different types of shooting are only intended as a guide for selecting the best suited item, whether for purchasing or renting. Care must also be taken with the individual technical characteristics of each instrument, with its working conditions and state of conservation.

If the purchase of a camera is contemplated, besides the above considerations, attention should be paid to the following:

(i) uniformity of make(s) used by the production company or group;

(ii) availability of spare parts;

262

(iii) experience of the company's operators and servicing technicians with the chosen instrument;

(iv) range of available accessories allowing for future improvements;

(v) suitability for use with the latest techniques;

(vi) possibilities of re-sale in the market where the purchaser works.

### Camera equipment rental

The renting of camera equipment is a very usual practice in professional motion picture making today. The independent producer will find many advantages in this system: he can use the most up-to-date equipment and that which is most suited to the different shooting requirements of each of his films. He need not invest large sums in aquiring a wide variety of equipment and accessories which soon become out-dated, lose value with wear, and have to be maintained and insured. Moreover, with purchased equipment he may even have to adopt a production policy which will ensure the amortization of the capital outlay involved.

There are many companies all over the world specializing in renting shooting equipment. Some are large, with branches in many countries, and can thus ensure their clients an adequate service in whichever country they may be shooting. Since the people responsible for camera equipment must be acquainted with this aspect of production, we will analyze some of the points to take into account when renting camera equipment:

(i) Equipment should be hired per day or per week. Weekly rentals are generally at a lower rate than daily rentals. The weekly rental is applied only from week-end to week-end. The daily rental is often near 0·5% of the cost of rented equipment.

(ii) Camera equipment generally comprises the camera itself, two or more magazines, a set of lenses, a motor, a sunshade and matte-box-filter-holder, a tripod, batteries, and some accessories. Zoom lenses and other kinds of equipment are generally rented individually and separately.

(iii) When a production team intends to rent equipment it is advisable to warn the rental company sufficiently in advance what equipment they intend hiring, in order to ensure it will be available and will be properly examined beforehand.

(iv)   When receiving the equipment from the rental company it is essential to test it carefully and examine the material and to point out to the rental company any irregularity in the instruments, even though they do not affect their proper operation. This is simply to avoid being blamed for it when returning the equipment.

(v)   When rental companies hire equipment to users who are not normal clients, they usually demand a deposit as a garantee of the safety and return of the equipment.

(vi)   When estimating rental budgets, one must take into account any days which might be necessary for transit. Some rental companies do not charge rental for this time, but in order to save time, they dispatch the material by air express or air freight and include the cost of same in their invoice.

(vii)   Many rental companies stipulate that hired equipment must be returned before 10.00 a.m., otherwise they will charge the rental for that day.

(viii)   Certain accessories such as filters, which come in a set, are not rented as individual units but as a set. Moreover, all types of filters, electronic lamps, and other similar articles must be replaced by the user if during their use or transit they should be damaged or wear out.

Besides these basic considerations, the agreement between the parties will materialize in a contract which generally comprises the following clauses:

(a)   the hirer assumes responsibility for the care and safe keeping of hired equipment and must replace any stolen, lost or damaged items with equivalent instruments or pay the current prices for same;

(b)   the hirer undertakes to insure the hired equipment in order to cover the total replacement value of same during all the time the equipment is withdrawn from the rental firm: the insurance policy must establish the owner of the hired effects as the beneficiary and the policy as well as the payment receipts must be delivered to the renting firm. Rented equipment must be insured against all risks with a sound, well known insurance firm; should the hirer receive any amount of money as insurance payment from such policy, such amount shall be applied to replace or repair the affected goods;

(c)   the hirer must withdraw the hired effects from the owner's premises and return them to the same place, at the hirer's

264

expense and risk; the applicable rent will run as from the withdrawal of the hired effects from the owner's premises until they are returned, no discounts are allowed for unused items;

(d) the hirer undertakes to indemnify the owner for time lost due to repair or replacement of equipment due to damage, loss, theft and so on;

(e) the owners or their representatives will be allowed access to the places where hired effects are being used in order to verify that they are in good working condition;

(f) the hirer undertakes that he shall not lend or sub-rent the hired equipment to third parties and to keep each item of equipment under his care all the time;

(g) the hirer accepts that the owner has the right to cancel the rental agreement with 24 hours notice in writing, by cable, etc. and undertakes to return the hired effects at his own expense and risk, and in the same condition in which they were hired; the owner will reimburse the hirer for paid rental covering the unexpired period;

(h) the hirer undertakes to reimburse the owner for any reasonable lawyer's fees and legal expenses incurred in protecting his right to the rented equipment or in action arising from a breach of the rent agreement;

(i) acceptance of the hired effects by the owner will not impair his rights to claim from the hirer for latent or evident damage to the returned goods.

## Maintenance and lubrication

One of the main chores of the camera operator is to check that his camera and its accessories are at all times, working properly. In a studio this check is normally the responsibility of servicing personnel from the camera department, who are in charge of cleaning, inspecting and making ready all the cameras in the studio.

When shooting on location, far from the facilities provided by organized servicing, the task of inspecting, cleaning and lubricating the cameras is sometimes the responsibility of the camera assistant, who must carry out all this work with available facilities, and must report any difficulty to the camera operator.

### General cleaning

To avoid breakdown and delay when shooting, it is highly desirable to clean out the camera and its accessories at the end of each day's work. The external parts of the camera most liable to get dirty are the camera body, the sunshade, the magazine and the front surfaces of the lenses.

Except for glass surfaces, all these items can be very easily cleaned. The dust should first be removed with a long-haired brush, and the component then wiped with a cloth soaked in petrol or cigarette lighter fluid.

## Cleaning lenses and viewfinder optical surfaces

Before cleaning, lenses should be dismounted from the camera. Dust is the first thing to eliminate, and this is best done with a rubber-bulb blower, a fine camel-hair brush or a high pressure air supply. Dust tends to build up at the rim formed by the glass and the metal mount. If removal proves difficult, try an orange stick with its point protected by a soft linen cloth folded several times.

Should there be spots on the glass, clean by rubbing lightly, but only with special optical cleaning paper. If the spots resist this treatment rub with a very soft (preferably linen) lintless cloth soaked in a special fluid for optical surfaces. However, do not rub hard or long, as this may affect the antireflective coating.

After cleaning the external lens surfaces (never even try to clean the internal surfaces), replace the lens caps, and put the lenses in their cases or mount them on the camera. The optical surfaces of viewfinders or reflex shutters are to be treated in the same way as lens surfaces.

## Cleaning inside the camera

The inside of the camera must be cleaned out daily. The dirt that must be eliminated is generally emulsion deposit, dust and dried up lubricating oil. The implements needed are: camel-hair brush, long-hair brush, rubber bulb blower, high pressure air and soft cloth. Cleaning procedures can be classified thus:

INTERNAL SURFACES OR CAMERA BODY. The internal walls of the camera are exposed to dust each time the camera is opened for threading. This causes an accumulation of dust in areas near the film path. Every trace of dust must be removed by means of the long-hair brush and the rubber bulb blower. The operation can be completed with a petrol soaked cloth, provided the walls are not lined with corduroy.

APERTURE AND PRESSURE PLATES. In most cameras these two

266

plates can be removed or at least opened up to afford easy access. In either case the maker's instructions must be strictly observed. Before removing a plate from its mounting, care must be taken that the shuttle claws and the register pin are fully withdrawn, i.e. that they are away from the plates. The dirt collected by these parts is mostly emulsion deposit, and therefore must be removed at short intervals to avoid scratching the film. Normally a check is made after each take, while a thorough cleaning is made each time film is threaded into the camera, or after each 1000 ft. has been exposed.

This cleaning can be done with the camel-hair brush, or with an orange stick if too much emulsion has accumulated. Never use hard materials for this purpose. Some makers recommend spreading paraffin thinly on the edges of the film track, others advise a light film of oil. In all cases the operator or assistant should follow closely the manufacturers' instructions for every camera he is handling, since each model is built of different materials and with different structural characteristics.

SPROCKETS AND FILM TRAVEL GUIDE ROLLERS AND GROOVES. All these parts, like the aperture and pressure plates, suffer from a build-up of emulsion deposits. However, cleaning may be rendered difficult by emulsion sticking in inaccessible recesses, as between sprocket teeth, on the curves of the rollers, and in the edges of grooves. These must be cleaned with the same devices as for the film gate, but it is advisable to finish off the operation with a soft cloth wiped over the cleaned parts. Take care, however, that no thread or particle of the cloth remains in the camera.

*Cleaning the magazine*

In Arriflex and Cameflex cameras, the continuous film drive mechanism is housed inside the magazine. Other magazines, such as those for the Mitchell, the Cinema-Products XR-35 and the Auricon, have different characteristics which require special care for each chamber or compartment.

The points which must be carefully checked for cleanliness are the inlet and outlet slots (light traps), internal rollers and surfaces which may come in contact with the film, such as magazine walls. These zones must be inspected and cleaned each time the magazine is loaded, using the following procedure:

(i) removal of dust by means of an air squirt and long-hair brush, especially from chinks, crevices, and light traps;

(ii)  removal of emulsion deposits on rollers;

(iii) general cleaning of the whole magazine with a soft cloth.

*Lubrication*

Here the operator is advised to follow closely the manufacturer's instructions. The following information has been compiled for easy reference but may not be exhaustive.

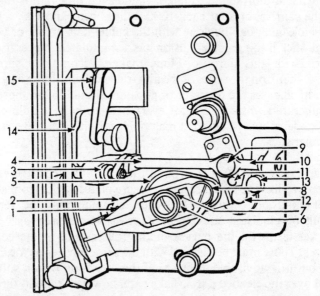

Fig. 1. Lubrication points of Mitchell intermittent mechanism. Lubrication of all points shown after every 2,000 ft, except point 9, which should be lubricated after every 5,000 ft.

LUBRICATION OF MITCHELL & NEWALL CAMERAS

Type of oil:
   Mitchell camera oil;

Grease:
   light neutral bearing grease;

Lubricating points:
   movement: every 2000 ft.:
   eccentric arm bearing, timing clock unit, register pin bearings, eccentric arm bearing, eccentric shaft sliding-block bearing, top and lower sides of sliding block, rear bearing, pull-down claw arm, rear bearing of register pin arm, rear pivot arm bearing, front bearing of toggle arm, rear bearing of toggle arm;

268

Every 5000 ft.:
swivel block on register pin arm;
Every 10,000 ft.:
pressure plate (two rollers);
Every 50,000 ft.:
pressure plate retainer arm. Film rollers must be oiled according to manufacturer's instructions.

### LUBRICATION OF DEBRIE SUPER PARVO REFLEX CAMERAS
Type of oil:
Huilfrigor or Mobiloil Arctic in case of aerial shooting, in the mountains or in polar regions, uiltropic for cameras working in tropical regions;

Lubrication points:
two oil holes in front part of camera and in the shutter oil housing. Bearing housing situated inside camera, between magazines. Oil must be poured in until it reaches the mark on a special indicator.

### LUBRICATION OF ECLAIR CAMEFLEX CM 3 CAMERAS
Type of oil:
high quality watch oil or Huilfrigor or Huiltropic as above;

Lubricating points:
oil holes are marked in red. All moving parts must be oiled when necessary. In the magazine the red screws must be removed and no more than two drops of oil introduced.

### LUBRICATION OF ARRIFLEX CAMERAS
Type of oil:
Esso Clock Oil 8119;
Grease:
Arriflex Spezialfett;

Lubricating points:
(i)   grease hole on the right-hand side, next to the plate indicating the length of the loop;
(ii)  claw shaft and guide (use oil);
(iii) bearing of the single-frame shaft situated behind the inching knob. Never lubricate in excess. The few lubricating points should be lubricated after 15,000 to 20,000 feet.

LUBRICATION OF EYEMO CAMERA
    Type of oil:
    Bell & Howell camera oil;

Lubricating points:
    six oil holes in the front of the mechanism plate (two of them on
    the sprocket shaft). One drop every 3500 feet will be sufficient.
    A seventh oil hole is situated in the centre of the camera head.
    Two drops each 1000 feet of film run.

LUBRICATION OF AURICON CAMERAS
    Type of oil:
    Singer sewing machine oil;
    Lubricating points:
    oil holes marked in red in all models;
    Rate:
    one drop in each hole every five days of use.

## Maintenance of Mitchell cameras

As the Mitchells are the most widely-used cameras in large-scale
studios, a few more details about their maintenance may prove
helpful.

CLEANING THE APERTURE PLATE. The aperture and pressure
plates (the film gate) should be cleaned each time before threading as
follows:

(i)   prepare the camera for threading (see page 227);
(ii)  introduce a length of film between aperture and pressure
      plates to check that shuttle claws and register pin are com-
      pletely away from the plates; perform the operation carefully
      since even slight mishandling may cause serious damage;
(iii) turn the two aperture latches at top and bottom of the film
      gate upwards, then draw the aperture plate very carefully out
      of the camera;
(iv)  clean it with a camel-hair brush, and then reinstall it; great
      care must be taken in all these operations to avoid scratching,
      since this will damage the film and necessitate replacement of
      the damaged part.

CLEANING THE PRESSURE PLATE. Each time the aperture plate is
cleaned, the pressure plate should also be inspected and cleaned. The
latter is removed by swinging away the retaining frame behind it.

Clean out all deposits of emulsion or gelatine with a camel-hair brush; check that the pressure rollers rotate freely; if they tend to stick, immerse the part in a highly refined thinner and rotate the rollers until they turn freely; remove from liquid and wait till it evaporates. Next apply a little of the special oil supplied by the makers and clean off the excess. Finally, reinstall pressure plate.

WARMING UP THE CAMERA. The operator should never forget to run the motor for a few minutes before threading the film. This warming will ensure steady running at the proper speed.

AFTER-THREADING CHECKS. Make sure that all guide rollers have been returned to position, and have not been left open after threading film round the sprocket. Also verify that the shuttle and register pin are in the correct position. If any of these parts are out of place, the camera access door cannot be secured.

Check the threading visually, and test that the movements run properly, by turning the motor flywheel. The upper loop should comprise about 22 visible perforations, from the sprocket to the film gate inlet, and the lower loop from the film gate outlet to the sprocket, 30 perforations.

CHECKS BEFORE SHOOTING. Never forget to remove the protective caps from the lenses. Check the position of the adjustable mattes by looking through the focusing tube. Verify that the shutter is either fully open, or in the setting fixed by the operator. Also make sure that the side monitoring viewfinder corresponds with that of the lens to be used, and that the proper parallax correction has been set.

Just before shooting set the frame and footage counters to zero, and check that the camera is properly levelled. Make sure that the power supply for the motor is correct.

## Operation and maintenance of batteries

Batteries are a common source of power for driving cameras when working out of the reach of mains supply lines. There are four types of batteries used by the motion picture industry; the non-rechargeable, dry-cell battery; the rechargeable wet-cell battery; the rechargeable dry-cell battery; the nickel-cadmium battery.

Dry-cell batteries are used only for standard power supply of Super 8 cameras, built-in exposure devices or sound amplifiers. They also afford packaged electricity on expeditions or wherever nightly battery recharging is impossible or undesirable. They cannot be charged and their life is limited by internal chemical action, and also depends on the motor's power rating and the use made of the camera. Many specialized firms manufacture units for up to $7\frac{1}{2}$ v in parallel or 15 volts in series to cover the standard requirements for 16 or 35 mm cameras.

Accumulators can be either the wet-cell type, with cells of 2 v. each or the solid electrolyte type, with cells of slightly lower voltage. The former are normally used in the industry; their plates are made of lead peroxide and the electrolyte is diluted sulphuric acid. The materials employed make them heavy items of equipment; their load is measured by the density of the electrolyte.

Solid electrolyte batteries are based on a principle of alkaline solution developed by Thomas A. Edison. Though the voltage of each cell is less than that of wet-cell batteries, they have other advantages making them very practical and are now used increasingly in the motion picture industry. The principal characteristics of solid electrolyte batteries are:

(i)   they can be used, recharged or stored in any position even upside-down;
(ii)  they do not need care other than recharging;
(iii) they have an extremely low self-discharging rate;
(iv)  fully loaded, solid electrolyte batteries allow long time storage without loss in capacity

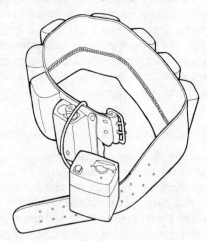

Fig. 2. Belt type battery manufactured by Cine 60 Inc. USA, and ideally suited for the news cameraman.

## Choice of battery

The battery must be chosen according to the type of camera to be used, the characteristics of its motor and the footage to be shot. The nature of the job on hand—news coverage, documentary, feature film, etc.—must be also considered.

The power consumption of large cameras like the Mitchell BNCR, Cinema-Products XR-35, Camé 300 Eclair, etc. is considerable and they therefore require batteries of a high ampere rating. In the case of the wet-cell type motor-car batteries are used on such occasions. Their power provides drive for many thousand feet of film. However, they are excessively heavy, which is an important consideration when planning shots demanding frequent moving about.

Lightweight cameras are driven by small-consumption motors which therefore need smaller sized wet-cell accumulators or dry-cell batteries. Besides those made specifically for this purpose, motorcycle batteries or electronic flash wet-cell batteries can also be used. The important factor in such cases is small bulk and light weight, since they will usually be strapped to the operator's shoulder. Solid electrolyte batteries show these qualities best. The ampere rating of batteries for lightweight cameras is never more than 7·5 amp/hr. which allows for shooting up to 5000 ft. of 35 mm film and 8000 ft. of 16 mm.

## Checking battery charge

Normally the electricians on the production unit are responsible for maintaining and checking batteries, but it is just as well for all the camera crew to know about their care and maintenance.

At the end of each working day, the batteries used during the day's operations must be recharged. It is a good idea to number the units so as to determine at a glance which batteries have been used and must be recharged, and which are ready for service.

Wet-cell battery charge may be checked as follows:

(i) unscrew the stoppers from the cells and observe whether the electrolyte covers the plates; if the latter show up above the surface of the liquid, top up with distilled water until the plates are immersed to a depth of $\frac{1}{4}$ in.

(ii) clean the terminals with a wire brush, and apply a volt-meter under load to the poles of each cell; the reading for each under full load should be 2 v.;

(iii) use a hydrometer to measure the density of the acid solution in each cell; when fully charged the reading should be 1·25–1·30; portable batteries are generally provided with floats painted in different colours to indicate at a glance the state of the charge.

## Recharging the battery

Before recharging, make sure that the charge can be adjusted to the voltage of the battery, and so adjust it; then verify the ampere-hour rating of the battery, which will probably be given on the name or rating plate. The time required for recharging can be roughly estimated from this information. For example, if the battery is rated at 180 amp/hr. and it is to be connected to a charger supplying 18 amps. it will be recharged in about 10 hrs.

From the operator's point of view, the three most important elements of a battery charger are: the ammeter to indicate the rate of charge, the selector switch to regulate the current rating, and the two connecting cables, the red one of which corresponds to the positive pole, and the black one to the negative pole. These two cables are connected to the respective battery terminals and must be securely clamped on to make a resistance-free contact. The stoppers must be removed from the cells before charging begins, and naked lights must never be brought near a battery under charge.

The end of the recharging period is indicated by hydrogen bubbling from the cells. The density of the electrolyte should now be measured again; a faulty cell will be revealed by a low reading on the hydrometer. Batteries not in use should be given a topping-up charge every week or so.

## Recharging dry-cell batteries

As stated above, solid electrolyte batteries have many advantages over wet-cell batteries in their ease for handling, storing and conservation. They also offer advantages with storing, since dry cell batteries have a very low self discharging rate and can be kept for up to sixteen months without any loss at all, as long as they are stored at an ideal temperature of +41°F (5°C). A higher temperature reduces this stored capacity proportionally to a minimum of three months in tropical conditions with temperatures of +104°F (41°C).

A further advantage over wet-cell batteries is that there is no need to add distilled water to the dry cell or to check the level of the acid when charging for the first time. Generally, dry-cell batteries are provided with special self-lubricating valves which allow any excess

274

gas which may have resulted from a faulty recharging to be released. Undoubtedly, all these advantages simplify their attention and maintenance considerably, but the key to their life duration is correct recharging. Care must be taken to use only the charger supplied or indicated by the maker of the battery in order to avoid damaging the battery or the charger. Besides being designed specially for the characteristics of each battery these chargers usually indicate automatically when the battery reaches maximum load.

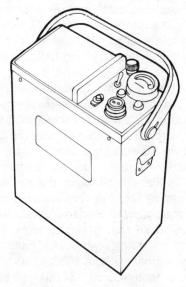

Fig. 3. Nickel Cadmium battery of modern design, manufactured by Frezzolini Electronics Inc. of USA

*Nickel-cadmium batteries*

Solid electrolyte batteries of the nickel cadmium type have an extremely long life; they have been tested over more than five thousand recharging cycles without loss of capacity. Moreover, they retain 70% of their charge after being laid up for more than a year, and the maintenance they require is negligible.

According to the manufacturer, the nickel-cadmium battery can be made with positive plates based on small diameter steel cells, and negative plates in similar cells filled with cadmium hydroxide. Also the plates are designed as rolled sheets with two separators and a porous plaque with the electrolyte that consist of a 30% solution of potassium hydroxide. Each cell has a rated voltage of 1·5 and a

275

capacity of 6 to 10 amp/hr. They can stand temperatures from −20°F to more than +140°F. No gases are produced and they can, moreover, be stored completely discharged without harm.

### Recommendations for use and charging

However, nickel-cadmium batteries also require careful handling and operation. Their life duration depends on the characteristics of the charger, the system used in consuming the power load, and the maintenance. These batteries are very sensitive to incorrect recharging, and are therefore manufactured with their own, built-in charger, designed specifically for the characteristics of each unit. It is advisable not to allow the battery load to fall below 60% of its rated capacity.

One must remember that the life duration of the battery depends on a determined amount of charge/discharge cycles and therefore this life is duplicated on shallow discharges. Moreover, by combining the battery capacity adequately with the camera motor consumption, a comfortable working schedule for the power source may be achieved which will not consume battery power down to dangerous levels while still shooting the estimated footage. For example, if the shooting schedule requires a battery of 2 amp/hr. for the estimated footage, using its load to the end, it is advisable to use a battery of 4 amp/hr. so that it should work with a wide safety margin; it would thus last longer and would have sufficient power left for contingency situations without affecting its life duration.

Finally, it must be remembered that this type of battery retains its load in better form if it is stored in rooms at a low temperature: best results are obtained at temperatures near +32°F (0°C), whereby 90–95% of the load is retained. When storing nickel-cadmium batteries at much higher temperatures, it is advisable to recharge them to maximum load before using.

## Checking the camera

In the vast and complex technical-economic organization for producing motion pictures, one of the most crucial elements is undoubtedly the instrument for carrying out the plans and efforts of countless men. Should this instrument fail costly shooting will have to be repeated or, in the case of newsreels, will be irreparably lost.

It is vital that the camera should work efficiently, free from technical accidents which might spoil the filmed material. Consequently it is essential that production companies or teams should check carefully all cameras they use and schedule periodic inspections and overhauls.

This section sets out to describe concepts and methods to trace different mishaps and control performance of all camera types. Such checks have been simplified as much as possible, for the benefit of those who may not have available all recommended technical means. However, it is highly advisable to carry out this work with great care, so that faulty appreciation should not lead to distorted results, nor cause misadjustments of the checked instrument.

The checks hereunder are a summary of the tests normally carried out by the manufacturer before delivering equipment. The checks should be scheduled according to how much the instrument has been used, the conditions undergone, and the task to be carried out.

Complementary to the explanations hereunder, a "trouble shooting chart" is given at the end of the section, with the more typical difficulties that may arise while operating a camera. From a careful study of both, the newly initiated operator will know what to expect while working with his instrument, the reasons for any failures, and the possible immediate solutions.

## Checking for film damage

One of the main functions of a cine camera is to allow film to pass through its mechanism and compartments without damaging it physically in the least. That is to say that after shooting the film must not show the least scratch on base or emulsion, nor any breakage, deformation, etc. of the perforations.

The first step of the check is to thread 15–20 ft. of raw stock and run it from one magazine to the other. Remove the film and place it on a table with a strong side lighting and examine it by reflection and very carefully, first the base and then the emulsion side. If no faults are found, the perforations must then be examined with a 10 × magnifying glass to check their physical conditions. If the shuttle of the camera being checked works on only one side of the film, bear this in mind and examine the perforations that were acted upon.

### LOCATING CAUSES

Should a fault appear, proceed to locate it in the part of the camera producing it. Effect this by threading the camera again, but before making it run, remove the lens from its socket and mark the aperture frame on the film with a crayon. Run the camera until the crayon mark reaches the inlet slot of the take-up magazine chamber. Make another crayon mark at the outlet slot of the raw-stock chamber, and withdraw the filmlength from the camera for a very close examination. Locate the fault again and its distance from the crayon marks will determine the exact point on the mechanism which produces it.

Damages on the film surface are generally due to emulsion build-up on some parts of the mechanism, specially on the film gate. This is frequently the only part directly in contact with the film; the faces of other parts are machined so that contact with the film is effected only at the edges. Therefore, when scratches etc., appear on the emulsion or the film base, the first places to inspect should be the aperture and pressure plates. A small build-up of emulsion or celluloid dust from the film base will gradually adhere firmly to the parts by the pressure of the film's constant passage. Besides the film gate, build-up may occur on the sprockets or on the guide rollers.

If no defect is found inside the camera, the damge may be produced inside the magazines. They must therefore be carefully inspected, specially at the sections where the film issues from the raw-stock chamber and enters into the take-up chamber. Emulsion or celluloid build-up may also occur at the guide or plush rollers that are found there. Such inspection must be made on all magazines used with the camera being inspected.

DAMAGE TO PERFORATIONS. Perforation breakage or deformation may occur in certain cameras, due to alterations of the film itself or to faulty operation of the shuttle and/or register pins, Sometimes, after long and heavy use, shuttle claws wear and, among other impairments, may cause perforation breakage or deformation. Some camera manufacturers have allowed for easy exchange of damaged claws; in other cameras the shuttle complete must be removed for repairing or replacing with a spare part.

Shuttle claws may also damage the perforations if they are mis-aligned. This may occur if the main shaft of a lightweight camera should be accidentally knocked. Under such conditions, the shuttle claws would not work into their correct position and, besides scraping the film edges, they would also slightly miss the perforation. If this misalignment is very slight, it may be remedied with slight pressure on the centre of the intermittent mechanism, to return the shuttle to its correct position, but if it is serious it should be repaired by an expert mechanic at a workshop.

Register pins may also produce perforation injury, as they are designed to work to very close tolerances. When affected by atmospheric conditions a film contracts or expands and the perforation position varies in relation to the action of the register pin. The pin meets resistance in locating the film firmly and steadily, thus producing injury.

The action of shuttle and register pins must be minutely inspected, first at the camera's normal speed, then at slow speed and then, if possible, in reverse motion.

*Image steadiness control*

Another essential condition of a cine camera is to provide a high degree of steadiness of the images printed on the film. The quality of the image obtained on projection depends on this steadiness. The image printed on the film frame is magnified about 500× when projected on the screen.

Image steadiness is a quality depending closely on the camera's intermittent drive mechanism. We have already seen that there are simple mechanisms, in which only the shuttle acts on the film, and more complex movements using register pins to place the frame exactly behind the aperture. With the naked eye it is difficult to tell the difference between images printed by one system or the other, but when the register pin system is used there is better definition and multiple exposures can be effected without blurred edges.

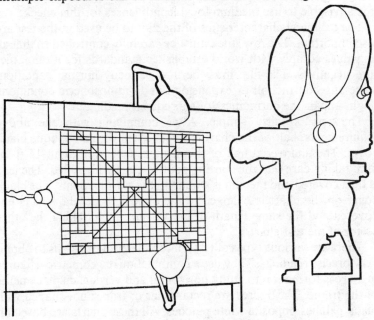

Fig. 4. Method of aligning a camera to an unsteadiness test chart.

According to existing standards, limit values by which one frame may differ from another are 0·015 to 0·02 mm for material shot with instruments without register pins, and 0·008 to 0·012 mm for films taken with cameras having register pins. Therefore, when there are doubts that an instrument does not meet such requirements image steadiness checks must be made on the basis of such values.

Procedures for checking the steadiness of images produced by a camera are generally based on effecting takes with double exposures of a special test chart. However, there is a very simple method providing excellent results without recurring to the double exposure system. In both systems, the main difficulty lies not on how the test is carried out, but on the correct evaluation of the readings obtained.

DOUBLE EXPOSURE METHOD. For this method there are several procedures which differ only in the design of the test charts. The way to shoot these charts and the evaluation of results are very similar. In all of them the camera must be firmly installed on a rigid support so that the unit is completely motionless. The chart is then seated on a firmly placed board and correctly lit. Whichever the type of chart, it is fundamental to present its surface squarely to the optical axis of the taking lens, in order to avoid deformations at the ends. Therefore it is advisable to use medium focal length lenses for this check.

The technical characteristics of the film to be used in the test are also important. The raw stock must be carefully controlled so that all its values comply with world established standards for motion picture negatives. The film must be in a perfectly normal condition, since any contraction or expansion due to atmospheric conditions might impair the correctness of subsequent readings.

The test is fairly simple. After complying with the above requirements, half of the chart is screened off with an opaque black cover. The uncovered half of the chart is shot with about 15 ft. of film, taking care that the starting point is clearly identified. The lens is then covered and the film is wound to the starting point. The black cover on the chart is changed to the opposite side, the lens is uncovered and the same length of film is shot again taking the other sector of the test chart.

There are various types of test chart with special designs to obtain very precise readings. They use a combination of geometrical figures in a cross-formation to study horizontal and vertical displacements of the frame. The figures are rectangular or trapezium-shaped with black patches opposite white patches. All these charts are based on the vernier principle in order to facilitate the subsequent evaluation from their position in relation to each other. In some cases these figures are composed of the separately exposed halves, so that when the two halves are combined, a white wedge is obtained against a black background, and the length of the base of this triangle-shaped wedge will vary in direct ratio to the registration unsteadiness.

When such charts are not available, some manufacturers propose a very simple check. A large cross is made with $\frac{1}{4}$ inch white masking tape on a surface of approx. 35 × 50 inch, black solid background. The camera is placed so as to cover the complete figure exactly and two exposures are made with the same film. Any differences existing between the superimposed images would show the unsteadiness values produced by the camera's mechanism. The vertical arm of the cross will show image steadiness in one direction and the horizontal arm will show unsteadiness in the other direction.

All these tests can be evaluated by studying each frame through a microscope. A displacement measurement is established for each frame and the sum of the maximum values in each direction will determine the unsteadiness value. Generally these processes are not more exact than 0·004 to 0·005 mm. But this is sufficient to comply with requirements of most cameras. If image unsteadiness does not exceed $\frac{1}{4}$ of one per-cent of the dimensions (length and height) of frame, image steadiness may be considered acceptable.

SINGLE EXPOSURE METHOD. The double exposure method demands that the camera should be reversed, which motion not all

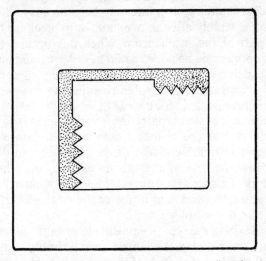

Fig. 5. Characteristics of a mask for measuring image unsteadiness in a camera.

instruments are capable of effecting. In such cases the single exposure method may be used, with a fixed matte. By this method, instead of measuring misadjustments of two exposures, the position of the ends of the matte are compared. This is effected by placing a matte in the filter shot of the film gate, with indentations on one horizontal and one vertical side of the frame.

The test is made as follows: remove lens from its socket, place a lamp at a certain distance from and directed towards the camera; start the camera. After developing the film thus exposed, frames are obtained with clear cut shadows which duplicate the dimensions and outlines of the matte. This film length is then installed on a bench with special registrations; each frame is viewed through a microscope and the positions of such indentations, both horizontal and vertical, are measured to a fraction of an inch. The maximum differences should be those allowed by the unsteadiness standards.

## Checking the shuttle/shutter synchronization

The function of the shutter is to blank out from the sensitive film the light rays coming through the lens, while the former is driven by the shuttle claws to place a new frame behind the aperture. The shutter's work is synchronized with the shuttle travel, to allow light through only when the film is rock-steady. If such synchronization should become misadjusted, the image would be printed with a number of evident faults, such as: incorrectly exposed frames, uneven spacing, vertical displacements (ghost images), etc.

Generally, shutter and shuttle may become unsynchronized due to incorrect assembly after an overhaul, or to breakage or loosening of some part of the mechanism. When this occurs, perfect synchronization must be achieved again in order to eliminate such unacceptable defects. Procedures vary according to each camera's mechanical characteristics. After re-adjusting the mechanism, a critical synchronization check must be made.

When the lack of synchronization is very slight, it shows up by an evident blurring at the printed frame corners. Consequently this specific point must be checked on inspecting an unsynchronized camera. There are several methods for effecting this: the simplest is to take shots of a special test chart for lenses; an open filament lamp is placed at each corner and in the centre of this chart, facing the camera and fed at a low voltage.

After estimating the type of emulsion to print the filament without overexposing or blurring, the camera must be firmly seated on a rigid base and framed so that each of the lamps is very near each of the corners of the frame. Shoot about twelve to fifteen feet of film taking the chart and the lamp filaments.

Study the processed negative with a 10× magnifying glass to check the definition of the filaments in the corners, and verify if there are blurred or ghost images there. The central lamp serves as a comparison standard. This test must be effected with maximum shutter opening and then repeated with smaller openings to establish rendition in each case.

*Checking coincidence of aperture and reflex viewfinder fields*

Work requiring critical framing often demands that the operator should check if the camera complies with the fundamental condition that the frame on the reflex viewfinder should cover exactly the same field that is included by the aperture.

Present day wide-screen systems with different sized apertures often need the use of masks on the reflex viewfinder to reproduce the dimensions of the frame being printed. But a slight misplacing of the mask or a slight mistake in its dimensions may cause very serious framing errors, especially when effecting takes for multiple exposure and other special effects.

Therefore, cameras without direct-through-the-film viewing must be checked that their viewfinder and aperture fields coincide. This is verified by determining the aperture outline (perimeter) on a test chart and then adjusting the viewfinder mask to this outline.

Place a test chart with a ground-glass bulb at each corner of a firm board. The position of each lamp should be easily adjusted and each should have a clearly visible black cross on its front surface, made with a vertical and a horizontal line. The camera is placed before the chart so that the inner angle of the cross on each lamp coincides with the edges of the corresponding corner on the aperture. This coincidence must be made through the aperture itself, with the camera stopped, the shutter open, and the lens diaphragm at full opening.

After effecting this critical framing, view through the reflex finder and check that the crosses are in identical position. Should there be any differences, the mask must be adjusted or changed for another one with the correct dimensions. This method can also be applied to monitor viewfinders, fixed side-viewfinders and other viewing systems.

*Checking that the camera is light-tight*

Light leaks into the camera may be due to dropped-off screws, cracks in the walls, door misadjustment, dents due to wear and tear, etc. But they may also be caused by carelessness in closing doors or cover-plates, and in installing the magazine, shooting while the direct or reflex viewfinder eyepiece is exposed to direct sunlight, or forgetting to fit protection lids on empty lens sockets in a turret. Checks must also be made to determine whether film fogging is due to causes other than the camera: light leaks in the darkroom, changing bag or faulty seals in film cap.

Some manufacturers recommend a light-tightness test consisting of threading highly sensitive film in the camera and after carefully closing all doors and covers, exposing it for about fifteen minutes to direct sunlight, moving it about different positions. A more methodical control is effected by individual tests of the most critical parts, threading each time a different film length, removing lenses from the turret, opening viewfinder eyepiece, etc. and then processing each film length separately.

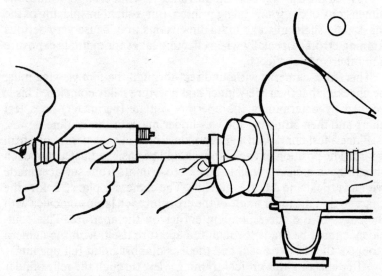

Fig. 6. Method of checking the rendition of a lens by means of an autocollimator.

### Checking exactness of lens focus and values on scale ring

The markings on the lens focus ring occasionally do not correspond to the real values, due to the harsh treatment and extreme temperatures that cameras must sometimes undergo.

This correspondence can be checked by a careful analysis of focus definition of the image produced on the plane of the film when the lens is set at infinity. But this study is very difficult due to the grain of the ground glass, the small size of subjects in an image produced by a short focal length lens, and other optical factors.

Focus exactness of a lens and its correspondence with markings on the focus ring is nowadays controlled by a device known as an autocollimator. It consists of an optical tube coupled to a special projection system called a collimator, which emits a light beam from a small lamp inside it. The beam goes through a mask and produces an image on a reflecting surface in the optical tube; the image is of similar conditions as if it comes from infinity. When the camera is adequately aligned with the autocollimator, the image from the optical tube reaches the plane of the film, where it is reflected, either by the film's bright surface or by a mirror placed at the aperture, back to the checking instrument where it can be precisely measured in the exact form it was produced by the camera lens.

Autocollimators are light, portable instruments, usually with their own battery power source which can be used for fast checks that the infinity setting of a lens is exact. But when installed on test benches they allow for complex studies in optics, and with a special test chart optical problems can be analyzed, such as: aberrations of lenses, transmission quality of filters, photographic resolution of the optical unit, contrast, and various others.

These instruments are built in Europe and in America. Those made by von der Gonna in Munich (Friedrich), Kinoptik in France and Zoomar or Richter Cine Equipment in USA, are among the best known.

## 6. REFERENCES

[1] Brosio, V., *Manuale del Productore di film*. Edizione dell'Ateneo, Roma (1956).
[2] Gordichuk, I. S., *Sovietscaia kinosiomochnaia apparatyra*, Iskusstvo Ed. Moscow (1966).

# SHOOTING TECHNIQUES

### Focusing

To focus an object on the plane of the film, the distance from the camera to the object is measured and the lens is adjusted to the corresponding figure. This simple method ensures that the image obtained is sharp—or at least sufficiently so to satisfy the spectator in the cinema. But present day styles of shooting based on editing within the frame and dynamic movement of the actors, frequently combined with dollying or travelling shots, have necessitated the development of more sophisticated focusing techniques.

For many years past, however, quite elaborate methods of following focus have been commonplace in the studios, and this in turn has been reflected in the evolution of camera design. The Mitchell camera, and types based on it, provide knobs and dials for both side and rear operation, with white scales on which focusing distances can be temporarily marked. The Technicolor Corporation pioneered the use of interlocked electric motors for remote operation of focus controls, so that the operator was able to change focus when physically distant from the camera itself, which might be perched on a highcrane while he was on the ground. Vinten of England, in their Everest camera, tried to popularize a built-in rangefinder which freed the operator from the need to use mental estimations or external markings, but this innovation did not meet with success.

### *Focus puller*

The importance of follow-focus techniques meant that a special place in the camera crew was assigned to the focus puller, whose job it became to measure the distance to significant points in a travelling shot—wherever, in fact, alterations of focus were required—and so mark these that during the actual take, the lens focus could be smoothly altered or "pulled" as changes in the relative position of camera, actors and scene demanded it.

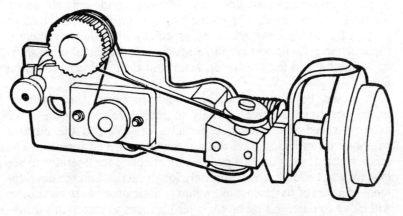

Fig. 1. Newman Sinclair follow-focus device. Can be fitted to many professional cine-cameras as well as Newman Sinclair models. Dials can be engraved for lenses of various focal lengths.

To make matters more difficult, movement of the focus control is not simply proportionate to change of distance, but becomes much greater as the distance lessens. Thus the angular rotation of the focus knob is the same from 4 to 5 ft. as it is from 10 to 20 ft., and from 20 ft. to infinity. This sort of variable movement requires a good deal of practice on the part of the focus puller.

Some camera techniques, however, tend to mitigate these difficulties. Among these are the use of extreme wide-angle lenses with their inherently large depth of field; faster emulsions and higher studio lighting intensities, which permit the use of greater stopping down and zone focusing in which the plane of sharp focus is suddenly shifted from one part of a scene to another.

But the normal practice is still to use reference marks on the studio floor, which the actors must sense if they cannot look directly at them, and which the focus puller must follow as the camera moves past them. Often many rehearsals are needed until all the relative speeds of movement have been synchronized and firmly established. For instance, if the actor moves too fast and arrives at one of his marks too quickly, the crane or dolly pusher will have to accelerate unexpectedly to keep the right distance relationship. This will throw the focus puller off balance, since he will not be able to twirl his knob fast enough, and a long take will have to be done again.

*Modern conditions*

But the latest shooting techniques make this sort of careful rehearsal impossible; and in television it is often uneconomic. The modern free-swinging use of the camera has, however, made critically sharp focusing less essential. The public has now grown accustomed to large out-of-focus areas in a scene, especially when the movement is rapid or violent, and will even tolerate it when the cameraman shifts on to the blurred features of an actor and then sharpens focus on him.

It would be quite wrong to imply, however, that focusing techniques have become slovenly in recent years. The need for extreme speed in shooting, especially for TV, and the modern emphasis on mobility, have put a premium on rapid focusing. The reflex shutter has made this possible by enabling the operator to see exactly what is on his film. But only long practice and the development of a sort of sixth sense allow him to anticipate where his subject will move to next, so that he can alter his focus to match this movement precisely. In this kind of situation, where movements must be spontaneous, the one-man crew is much more effective than a team which must rehearse and repeat the action.

## Composition

In motion pictures, composition is the art of correctly placing the various moving or static elements of an image within the frame. The quality of composition or framing determines the aesthetic values of the picture and constitutes the visual balance.

Although the gift of good composition is an intangible quality, there are certain elastic rules to such factors as balance, harmony, discord, symmetry and pace. Among the guides to good composition are the following:

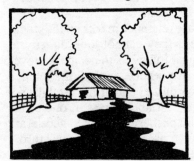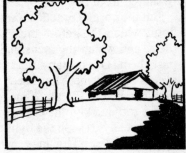

Avoid symmetry and try to balance the masses within the frame.

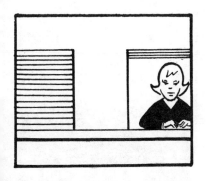 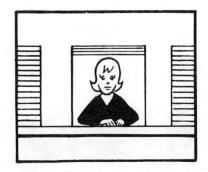

Elements which should be seen complete, must never be partially within and partially outside the frame.

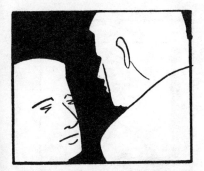 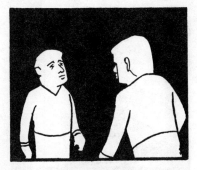

The subject should always be framed with adequate space; it should not be so small as to be lost in the frame, nor so large that vital parts of it must be cut off and lost.

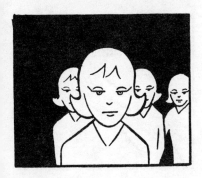 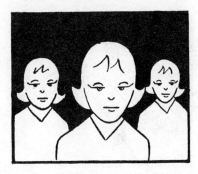

Dispose your subjects over the various field depths so that they neither conceal one another, nor produce a confused composition.

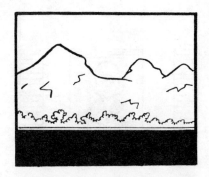 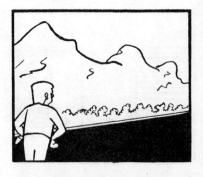

When the main subject is in the background or in medium shot try to frame some secondary subject in the foreground to accentuate depth.

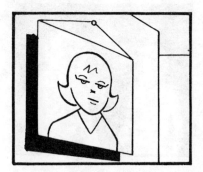 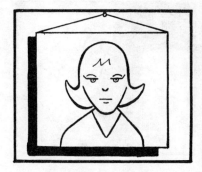

Paintings, tapestry, and similar subjects with no relief should never be shot from one side, as this will produce a deceptive perspective.

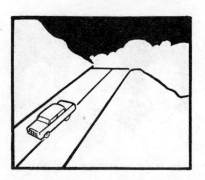 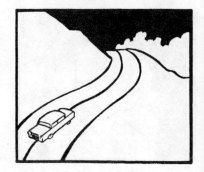

Landscapes will be more dramatically rendered by avoiding straight lines and by enhancing curves.

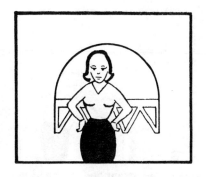 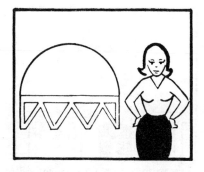

Never place an important subject behind an essential element in the scene, as this will diminish the value of both.

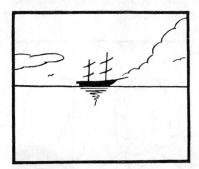 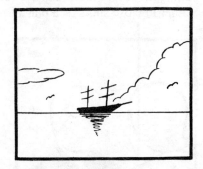

Avoid horizontal symmetry; in particular, place the horizon above or below the horizontal mid-line of the frame.

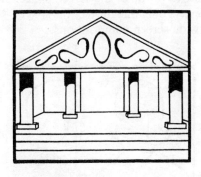 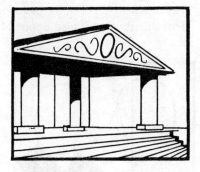

The masses in a frame should never be equidistant from each other.

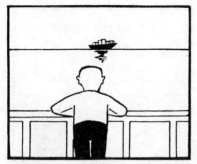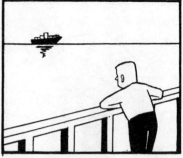

Try to avoid straight parallel lines when they attenuate perspective and reduce depth of field.

*Composition for reverse shots*

Dialogue scenes are usually covered from reverse camera positions, either in close shots or a pair of medium shots.

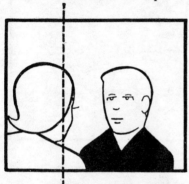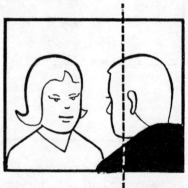

The subject facing the camera gets two thirds of the screen space. The one with his back to the camera gets only one third of the space. This distribution is also applied to wide screen compositions.

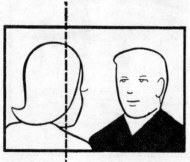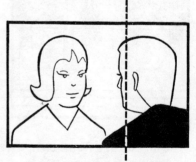

Medium shots on a wide screen get a slightly different treatment.

The screen is divided into three equal parts and the subject facing the camera is placed in the centre of both main and reverse shots.

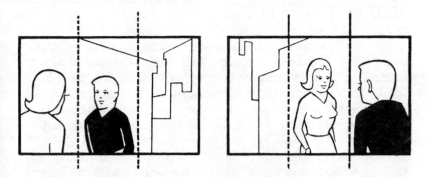

*Different cutting heights for framing the human figure*

In professional cinematography there are standard cutting lines applied to the human body when different types of shot are desired. These lines are shown on the illustration below.

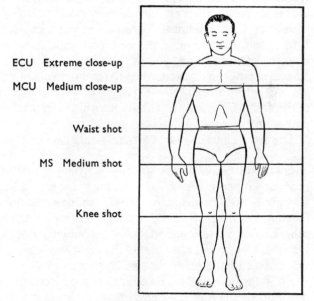

ECU  Extreme close-up

MCU  Medium close-up

Waist shot

MS  Medium shot

Knee shot

**Film Language**

In the course of his professional career, the cinematographer is sometimes faced with the complex task of personally directing a film.

This occurs when the cinematographer must act as operator-director in films such as newsreels, shorts, documentaries, etc. For such events it is essential that, besides sound technical know-how, he should also know the basic rules of cinematographic language in order to make the resultant product smooth flowing.

Effective cinematographic language is based on two main factors: control of movement on the screen and the previous preparation of material to be filmed bearing in mind its subsequent editing. With this in mind and applying some of the narrative techniques created during motion pictures' 80-year history, a highly professional level will be attained in line with highest world-accepted motion picture standards.

From the point of view of filmed narrative, there are two typical techniques used nowadays: one is sometimes known as "editing within the frame" and the other is "cut-editing".

### Editing within the frame

This method consits of long-sustained takes with the actors moving continuously and being followed by a mobile camera. It requires professional actors who are accustomed to making exact movements, who know the correct position to stop, and can memorize long dialogues. These takes must be planned in detail beforehand, to determine the best positions, stopping points, and how the camera should follow. To maintain fluidity, directors use several arrangements, according to requirements of the script, of the specific actors and of the set. These allow for background variation of the scene, for alternating characters in the frame, for variations of planes and of zones of interest.

The most characteristic of these arrangements are:

COMBINED MOVEMENTS BY THE ACTORS. When two characters face each other in a long dialogue, the scene would be too static if it was not broken by the actors moving in the scene one at a time and meeting again at different points. For example: A and B face each other in a conversation. Suddenly, without interrupting the dialogue, B moves away to another part of the scene, and the camera, which at first covered both, now follows B with a pan.

From the new position B continues his conversation with A who is now outside the frame. After a predetermined time, B returns to A's position and the camera frames both of them again. Quite often this is repeated by the other character.

This simple resource affords pictorial variation in the image: the

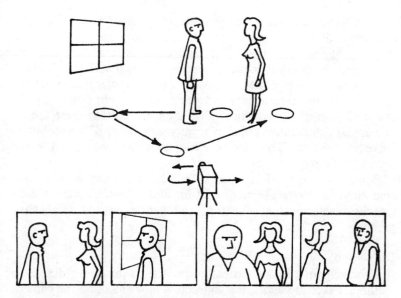

Fig. 2. Editing within the frame. A player who moves from zone to zone on the set and is followed by a panning camera will present successive and different pictorial arrangements on the screen. This method is smoother than a cut editing pattern, where the player moves in and out of each shot to obtain the same effect. Long takes using this technique of combined camera and performers' movement allow a more realistic approach to dialogued scenes.

pan and the change of plane of action when the characters move from and return to the original position, as well as the modification of the number of characters in the frame.

DISPLACEMENTS FROM ZONE TO ZONE. This device is also very much used on the stage and it consists of the displacement of actors during a dialogue, one in front of the other, to modify their position in the scene. This change is repeated by the various actors and produces a constant change of framing and a gradual movement to another zone.

The change from zone to zone is normally effected by panning or by travelling takes. Sometimes an actor moves away from a group towards another group in a distant zone of the scene. This changes the zone of interest, and the character links the two areas without need for cutting. For example, when a large scene must be shown at the beginning of a sequence and an important area therein must be pinpointed, a character moves within such scene and the camera follows him until he passes in front of or through the zone of interest; there the camera stops and the "decoy" moves out of the frame.

Combined actors' movements and changes of zones are basic principles of editing within the frame; many variations afford efficient filmed narrative. The above cases are the simplest. Analyzing the possibilities carefully, we realise that the character's displacement can be either depthwise (from or towards the camera) or from side to side, that the moving actor's body position can be changed to emphasize or neutralize a character, that there are innumerable combinations of displacements of actors with a mobile or a fixed camera, etc. Thus, we have an infinite variety of resources for each specific requirement.

Editing within the frame tends to help filmed narrative to flow smoothly, due to the absence of cutting and the combination of continuous displacements of actors and camera within established premises.

## Cut-editing

This technique is diametrically opposite to the above described method. Takes are short, the characters move less and the camera displacements are smaller. From the production point of view, this type is of much lower cost, because expensive rehearsals are not needed to prepare the combination of movements of cameras and actors. Furthermore, the actors do not need to remember long lines, or effect very precise movements. However, this technique demands extreme care in conceiving each individual take, because its efficiency depends on how it links with the next take. It is based on the principle of shooting in order to edit afterwards. This requires that the director should continuously observe several rules which ensure continuity.

CUTTING ON THE MOVEMENT. If two static shots of a subject are joined the result is a jerk, caused by the sudden change in the dimensions of the elements in the image. It has long been realised that this jerky effect is decreased by effecting the change while the subject is moving within the frame. At the critical movement, the attention of the audience is centered on the movement and does not notice the change of shot so much, thus achieving smooth flow.

The cutting technique requires that in each take the subject should effect the movement complete and at the same speed. Later, on editing, $\frac{1}{3}$ of the movement of the first take is used, together with $\frac{2}{3}$ of the second take. Another requirement to make this method of cutting work is to place the subject in the same sector of the frame, but to shoot from a different angle in each take.

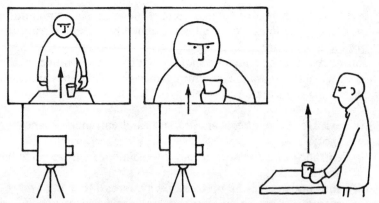

Fig. 3. Cutting on movement. The best way to join two takes featuring the same players is to have them repeat the last motion of the first take at the beginning of the second shot. Thus, part of the action ending the first take is matched with its completion on the second take. Smooth pictorial transition is then obtained.

Cuts on movement are very much used nowadays in all sorts of films. The director should plan such cuts beforehand every time he intends editing that way, specially when shooting dialogue scenes. If extreme focal length lenses are used in each take (for example: wide angle and telephoto), a careful watch must be kept on the speed at which such movements are made, because these extreme lenses modify the real speed on the screen.

CUTTING BY INTERPOSITION. The action to draw audience attention away from a cut need not always be carried out by the subject. Two shots with a passive subject can be joined by using a 'decoy' action. The moving subject is the decoy whose secondary action must smooth out the cutting. If the decoy crosses the screen in front of the main subject we can change the shot distance at the precise moment at which the passive subject is hidden away by the decoy: when the main subject reappears he is seen in close up and the audience does not notice the cut. Cutting by interposition can also be effected by making the decoy move behind the subject. In both cases the action must be shot complete in both shots and then spliced at the correct spot on editing, the same as for "cutting on the action".

ENTRANCES INTO AND EXITS FROM THE FRAME. Cut editing necessitates entrances of subjects into the frame and exits therefrom. If this is applied adequately, dynamic effects are produced. It also covers zone to zone displacements, and characters alternating in the frame. In usual practice, screen entrances and exits are used to

297

shorten the movement of subjects across the frame, in combination with a change of shot. Continuity is attained by cutting during the subject's movement.

Entrances and exits must be shot so that the subject moves at the same speed and in the same direction. Among the different variations the following are usual:

(i)   exit from the screen on one shot and entrance on another shot;

(ii)  entrance into the screen and immediate exit, to re-enter on another take;

(iii) entrance into frame up to half way across, then cut and re-entrance again on another shot up to mid-frame.

Entrances and exits of subjects are always combined with a change of shot. Usually, in the case of entrances into a zone, a long or medium shot is first shown, and then a close shot. Exits are shown the other way round.

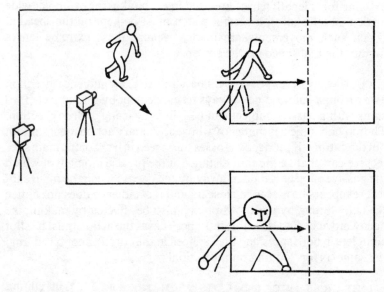

Fig. 4. Another form of cutting on the movement. A player's movement to a predetermined end position can be planned to cover the travelling distance in two different takes. The first one will show most of his movement along the path, while on the second, the final part of his movement is recorded by the camera as he re-enters the screen and stops at his destination. This solution features the repetition of the screeen zone in the two parts into which the movement is broken down.

PLACING CHARACTERS IN THE FILM FRAME. Cinematographic continuity necessitates that the characters maintain their topographic position in the frame. This is attained by the camera's location in relation to the actors, so that they keep their position in the correct sector of the frame. For example, "B" faces the camera on the right hand side of the frame, while "A" is on the left hand side with his back to the camera; on effecting the reverse shot the camera must be placed so that the characters maintain the same position, i.e.: "A" must still be on the left hand side but facing the camera, and "B" still

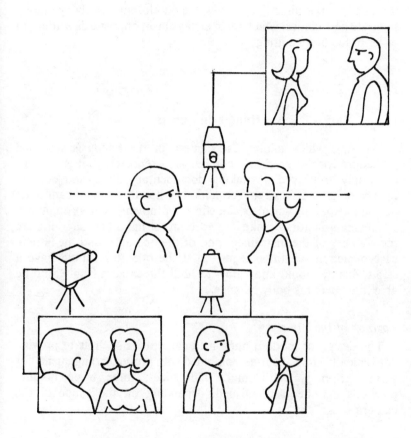

Fig. 5. Direction of gaze. The direction of the gaze exchanged between two players forms a line between both performers. One side of this line must be chosen to locate the camera sites that will cover the scene. Constant screen position of the players is then ensured. If a camera site is placed on the other side of this line the positions of the players on the screen will be reversed, and the take will not cut properly with the others.

on the right hand side, but with his back to the camera. Thus the audience will appreciate the situation correctly, otherwise a jerk would be produced, confusing the audience and reducing continuity.

It is therefore essential to study the camera position for each take in order not to break this premise. Generally, the camera's point of view is determined on the basis of eyesight direction of the main characters, and the projections thereof; the camera should always be placed on the same side of such imaginary line.

A careful camera positioning in relation to actors is also fundamental for a proper direction of sight, because on the shots near to the camera, the direction of eyesight on closeups is always along separate half-planes, which must always be in opposite directions, in order to facilitate cutting.

## Hand-held camera

Shooting while holding the camera in the hands is standard procedure for newsreel and combat area reporters, but is now increasingly employed in making documentary films, and even in feature films under extreme conditions when the camera cannot be put on a tripod or when special effects of movement are sought.

The main factors to take into account for hand-held shooting are the stability of the instrument and of the operator, and the latter's ease of action; all three require that the operator should have a steady hand, should know how to hold the camera firmly, and be able to control his body balance.

### Position of the camera

The design of modern hand-held cameras is such as to provide conveniently shaped curves combined with proper arrangements for secure gripping. With minor differences, three basic holding positions can be distinguished, depending on the shape of the camera:

(i)   holding by hand from underneath the camera;
(ii)  holding the camera from above or from the side, while supporting part of its weight on the shoulder;
(iii) supporting all the weight on the shoulder.

300

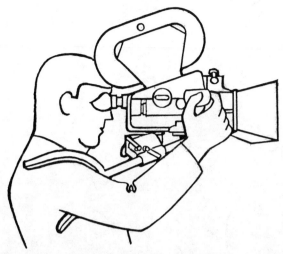

Fig. 6. Correct position for holding the Arriflex 35 camera with shoulder attachment.

CAMERAS HELD ONLY BY THE HAND. These cameras are provided with a hand grip situated beneath the instrument: among them are the Bell & Howell Filmo and Eyemo, the Arriflex 35, the Cameraflex and the Sputnik. The operator's wrists and forearms bear the weight of the camera. Additional support can be supplied by a shoulder attachment (Fig. 6).

HAND-AND-SHOULDER HELD CAMERAS. The idea was evolved after research by the US Government on a combat camera during World War II; and the resulting instrument, the Cunningham, showed the advantages of using the shoulder as a main support. This is facilitated by the shape of some cameras, in which the magazines are attached at the rear and are rested on the front part of the shoulder, which thus acts as a support. This takes some of the weight off the wrists and forearms and distributes it over the shoulder and the full length of the arm, thus affording greater steadiness. This type includes the Cameflex, the Sinclair Model P/400, and the Konvas Automatic.

SHOULDER SUPPORTED CAMERAS. This is the latest development, based on the principle adopted in 1935 by Askania Werke for their lightweight Askania Schulter by which most of the weight is borne by the shoulder, while the arms only act as a complementary

301

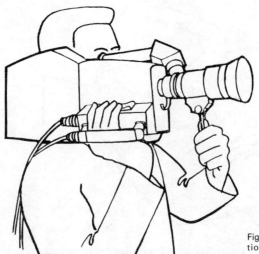

steadying element, by gripping either beneath or at a side of the camera. A large number of instruments conceived for hand held shooting, have applied and improved on this method.

When describing the original concepts which led to the design of the Askania Schulter, one of the designers, Dr. Ing. P. Heinish, chief engineer of the well-known Berlin manufacturers, pointed out that many hand-held cameras demanded operators to be athletes when having to run with a heavy instrument to effect a take which should be free of unsteadiness due to gasped breathing.

This led to adopting the shoulder as support for the magazine and thus the whole instrument, freeing it of throbbing from the chest and pulse. It was also verified that the major portion of a camera's weight is its film load and the magazine housing it. The Askania Schulter has a body at right angles, with one side resting on the operator's shoulder and the other covering half of the operator's face. This allows for easy holding and handling.

*Position of operator's body*

From the point of view of a steady take, there is another factor just as important as holding the camera: the positioning and balance of the operator's body. Unless these techniques are learned the full potentialities of the camera will not be realized.

302

When shooting, the operator's body must be perfectly balanced so as to produce a minimum of sway. Although specific circumstances may sometimes require the operator to shoot while sitting or lying down, the normal position for hand-held takes is standing up, since this has been proved to afford greater ease of operation and camera steadiness.

The way the operator stands is also important to his stability. Balance for this type of shotting is best obtained by standing with the right foot some ten inches in front of the body's vertical line, and the left foot about four inches to one side. The weight of the body must be distributed on both feet but slightly more on the left foot. This not only affords great stability but also ease of action. An operator standing thus will be able to effect 100° angle pans without moving his feet; he will also be able to tilt 90° with ease while maintaining his stability.

When special shots or situations require the operator to shoot from a sitting or lying down position, there is little advice to give. If the operator is sitting, it would be well that he rest his back against, or his elbows upon, some prop. If he is lying down on his face he may rest his elbows or the camera on the ground. If on his back, he will evidently need a good prop to help support some of the weight of the camera.

GORDON-ECLAIR SHOULDER BRACE. This is a special camera support designed for the Eclair NPR camera. The shoulder brace distributes the weight evenly and permits hours of filming without fatigue. The cameraman can use the viewfinder without having to strain his neck forward. It also allows him the use of both hands since he does not have to hold the camera.

PRENZEL DOUBLE SHOULDER POD. A fully adjustable camera support that brings any camera exactly to eye level for ease of viewing. Camera weight is evenly distributed on both shoulders. It affords complete mobility leaving both hands free for necessary functions while filming. Available in two versions: A & B. Type B has additional reinforcement and a tilting head.

ARRIFLEX SHOULDER-POD. This accessory, designed for use with the Arriflex 35 or 16, can also take other makes of camera. It consists of a chromed-metal frame which is fitted over the shoulder and under the armpit. The camera support can be adjusted in extension and inclination to give greater flexibility in use. Some models include a pistol grip with trigger release mechanism.

S.O.S. BODY BRACE. Manufactured of aluminium alloy to afford a rigid and strong frame of light weight, it allows for fitting the camera with 200 or 400 ft. magazines. The design of the frame distributes the weight of equipment over the shoulder and the waist.

KENYON GYROSCOPIC STABILIZER. This device was originally designed for use with high magnification binoculars, but has proved its efficiency in hand-held motion picture shooting. The high speed gyroscope it contains produces a very effective resistance to jerky camera movements, which makes possible the use of telephoto lenses on hand-held cameras with minimum image oscillation. This accessory is very compact and is attached to the camera base by means of a threaded pin. There is a special model for heavier,

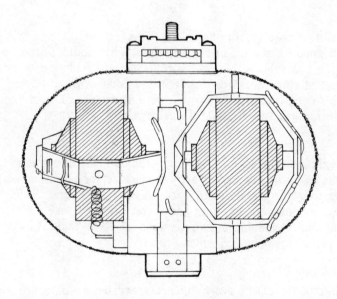

Fig. 8. Kenyon gyroscopic stabilizer.

medium-weight cameras. A nickel-cadmium battery and inverter unit provides the necessary power for the Kenyon Stabilizer for a minimum of three hours continuous running.

## Anamorphic systems

*Background and fundamentals of the anamorphic system*

The visual characteristics of the higher animals are such that their field of view is much more extended horizontally than vertically. In man, the eyes are placed side by side in such a way that their fields of view complement each other and overlap. This leads to a strong emphasis on the horizontal.

The standard motion picture frame, with its four horizontal to three vertical units, is unanimously accepted in preference to square or circular forms which have sometimes been advocated.

When the motion picture industry felt the need for a change in the standard frame ratio to increase audience attention, it was a horizontal widening of the image frame which was proposed, changing the aspect ratio from 4 : 3 to 8 : 3 or thereabouts.

The process by which this was to be done was an old one: Fresnel had used cylindrical lenses as far back as 1825, and during the 1930s Professor Henri Chrétien used what he called an anamorphic lens to compress the image while filming and to expand it afterwards during projection.

The term "anamorphic" is applied to any optical system capable of compressing a normal image, and subsequently projecting it back in its original proportions without apparent distortion.

The first practical anamorphic lenses consisted of cylindrical adaptors mounted in front of a normal camera lens. A concave cylindrical lens with a vertical axis of curvature acts as a wide-angle attachment in the horizontal plane only (the image in the vertical plane being unaffected). The lens constants were set so that the anamorphic factor was 2. Thus, when used in combination with a standard camera lens, an anamorphic lens acts as an optical transformer, doubling the horizontal field of view of the standard lenses, and compressing the image within the standard 3 : 4 frame. A similar converter is used in the projector to return the image to its original 3 : 8 proportions.

The first really practical anamorphic lens was Professor Chrétien's Hypergonar. It comprised two achromatic systems, one convergent and the other divergent, and its elements were calculated to reduce aberrations to a minimum. Two forms of the lens were designed, one for use on the camera, one on the projector.

In 1952 Twentieth Century Fox acquired the rights to the Hypergonar lens, and commissioned the American optical firm of Bausch & Lomb to manufacture improved lenses based on this design. This was no easy job, for intricate mechanical problems in connection with the focusing system had to be solved. After much research, improved anamorphic optical systems for coupling to standard lenses were produced, and these were followed by units combining the standard spherical lens and the anamorphic system in a single mounting.

Subsequent improvements attained a high degree of perfection in correcting distortion at the ends of the frame, where vertical lines tended to converge and horizontal lines to curve, thus lowering the quality of the image. The lenses commissioned by Twentieth Century Fox from Bausch & Lomb were made under the registered name Cinemascope which also designates the complete system developed by that studio. In recent years, many other anamorphic systems have been developed, and some of these are listed in a later section.

Modern anamorphics follow the original pattern: either an anamorphic adapter is fitted in front of the standard lens, in which case both elements require separate focusing; or the anamorphic and the basic spherical lens are fully integrated, when only a single focusing control is needed. When an adapter is employed with a standard lens, the focal length in a horizontal plane will effectively be halved. Thus for purposes of calculating the horizontal angle of field, a 35 mm lens will become an 18 mm, a 75 mm a 38 mm, and so on, while in the vertical plane the acceptance angle will remain unchanged.

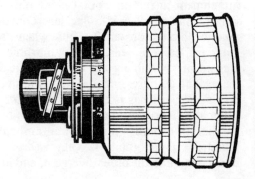

Fig. 9. Integral anamorphic lens.

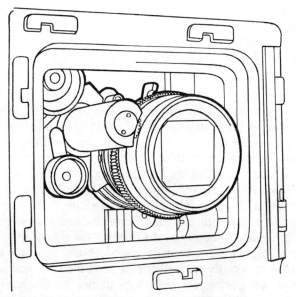

Fig. 10. Totalvision anamorphic block unit mounted on Came 300 Reflex camera. Note the geared connection with the focusing ring.

Integral or block anamorphics have effective focal lengths of 15 up to 600 mm, and anamorphic zoom lenses are coming into use. Most of these lenses are available with mountings for Mitchell, Debrie, Arriflex, Eclair and other well known makes of camera.

*Image quality of anamorphic lenses*

There are various factors which determine the optical quality of the image formed by an anamorphic lens unit.

DEFINITION. The definition of an image taken through an anamorphic lens can be tested by checking that focus is maintained all along the horizontal and vertical lines. This can be carried out with acceptable accuracy by the help of the focusing chart provided by some makers which can be placed on the edges of the "lily" or colour chart shot at the start or end of each take.

When integral block anamorphic systems are used, focusing is adjusted with only one ring; but with coupled lenses, focus adjustments must be carried out simultaneously on the two rings corresponding to the primary and secondary lenses respectively. This requires either a high precision mechanical adjusting device, or the help of two camera assistants. In the latter case it is desirable that the scales on the rings of the primary and secondary lenses be calibrated identically. Finally, when focus is controlled visually, directly through the taking lens, it is better to view the squeezed image rather than the unsqueezed image seen through many viewfinders.

DISTORTION. A faulty proportioning and forming of shapes in the image is one of the most important factors to look for and correct when using anamorphic lenses. When checking distortion, the operator should concentrate on vertical and horizontal lines extending from side to side of the frame. Image distortion often results from lack of precision in mounting and centring the anamorphic lens on the camera. A practical method of checking consists of critical examination of the outline of an anamorphic image as seen through the camera's direct focusing tube through the taking lens. For this purpose a plumbline can provide a vertical line, while the long pan handle of a previously levelled tripod head may be used to set the horizontal line. For more critical tests, there is no alternative to setting up the lens and camera on an optical bench.

ANAMORPHIC COEFFICIENT. The anamorphic coefficient of a system can be checked by the experienced eye, observing whether the subject going across the frame from side to side maintains the same compression factor throughout its travel. In older anamorphic systems, the compression factor tended to become less as the subject approached the camera, producing unpleasant distortions in close-up. If modern anamorphics give rise to distortion, it is probably due to incorrect setting up.

*Techniscope*

In mid 1963 Technicolor introduced a new shooting technique, which brings about a saving of 50% in raw stock and film processing costs. This system, developed at Technicolor Italiana by Dr. Giulio Monteleoni and Mr. Giovanni Ventimiglia, uses a frame which is one half the height of the standard frame (two perforations instead of four). By a special printing process, this two-perforation-high frame is changed into a standard four-perforation frame with an anamorphic image of 2 to 1 squeeze ratio, ready for projection. To film in Techniscope, the camera requires some modification.

(i) the aperture must be changed to the new frame size;

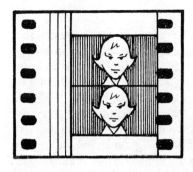

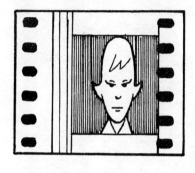

Fig. 11. Techniscope format. *Above:* size of the two-perforation frame. *Below:* the four-perforation frame with a 2:1 anamorphic compression applied during printing.

(ii)  the intermittent drive must be modified to make the film travel the height of the reduced frame;

(iii)  the viewfinder has to be adapted to the new image shape.

Arnold & Richter, German makers of the Arriflex, have produced a model for Techniscope shooting with 200° shutter opening and 9·5 × 22 mm. In the USA the Mitchell Camera Corp. and Birn & Sawyer Cine Equipment have specialized in adapting various cameras to the new system. Other manufacturers have followed suit, among which Eclair have introduced a Cameflex model (CM-3T) which can be easily and rapidly adapted by exchanging aperture plates and adjusting shuttle travel.

The advantages of the new technique mean that the shooting time per foot of film is doubled, so that a 1000 ft. magazine provides the same shooting time as 2000 ft. of film by the standard method. With the improvement in grain and resolution of modern integral tripack materials, Techniscope gives excellent picture quality on large screens. But the small size of the negative area does introduce some limitations when projecting on to the very largest screens.

## Super 16

Experiments made by a Swedish cinematographer, Rune Ericson, recently led to the adoption of a new shooting system called Super 16 which allows for reducing film production costs. This method uses 16 mm film with a larger frame, which is then enlarged to 35 mm by the liquid gate printing method. The area taken up by the sound track is used for the image, gaining 24% image area, which brings about a smaller drop in image quality when enlarged to 35 mm. An advantage of Super 16 is the use of much lighter running cameras. Although Super 16 does not achieve the image quality obtained with 35 mm, it provides an acceptable substitute for documentaries and certain feature films where a low budget is of paramount importance over other factors.

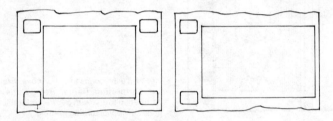

Fig. 12. Comparison in relative image areas of 16 mm and Super 16 formats.

### Technical data

Original raw stock gauge: 16 mm (single perforation);
Frame dimensions: $0.492 \times 0.296$ in. ($12.30 \times 7.47$ mm);
Exposure speed: 24 f.p.s.;
Enlarging ratio to 35 mm frame: 3 to 1;
Aspect ratio: $1.85:1$ or $1.33:1$.

### Camera requirements

The basic requirements for a camera for Super 16 is that it should work with registration pin(s) to make sure that the printed image is rock steady so that definition values should be as high as possible. Some cameras are available nowadays which run with this system: the Aaton, the Arriflex SR and the Vinten-Coutant (now out of production). Among the instruments which can be adapted, the Eclair NPR and ACL seem to be most suitable. The necessary modifications are as follows: the aperture must be increased to the new dimensions: the lens mount must be centered to suit the new aperture: magazine rollers and film guides must be relieved and the viewing system adjusted.

310

Several firms in the USA, UK, France and Sweden has specialized in adapting cameras and many rental firms in some film centres have Super 16 cameras and sound recording equipment for an average rental of US $250 a week.

## Lenses

The foremost characteristic of lenses for Super 16 is that they must cover the larger image dimensions adequately and that they render a high definition image. Most cinematographers working with Super 16 prefer Cooke Kinetal lenses for these qualities and also the new Canon line. Zoom lenses can be used but specialists recommend they should be used only for zooming. Among the many available makes, the Canon and Angenieux 12–120 have been successfully used, but the latter must be adapted (unadapted it can be used only for focal distances from 20 to 120 mm).

## Zoom or vari-focal lenses

### General

When shooting a film, the camera operator must be able to vary the field of view without changing his position, and consequently must be equipped with several lenses covering an ample range of focal lengths. Well aware of the advantages there would be in combining a wide range of focal lengths in a single optical system, lens designers developed a lens with variable focal length, which came to be called a zoom lens. The new lens had to meet the most exacting optical and mechanical requirements, and many difficult technical problems could only be solved when advanced electronic computers became available.

However the success achieved by this new type of lens was not so much due to the fact that it could replace several others of different focal lengths, but that it opened up a new possibility to the camera operator of continuously changing the focal distance of his lens, thus obtaining the effect known as optical travelling or zooming. Zooming creates the illusion, at least in part, that the camera is moving towards or away from the scene. It is carried out by gradually changing the focal length and thus the magnification of the lens, so that the subjects in the scene increase or decrease in size.

The principle of construction of zoom lenses is the controlled displacement along the optical axis of a set of elements in relation to another set which remains stationary. All the elements and movements must be calculated and constructed with such high precision that during the displacement of the mobile unit, the diaphragm and focus settings are maintained constant, while only the focal length changes.

Some zoom lenses are equipped with a beam-splitter reflex viewfinder with a prism and semi-reflecting glass at 45°, built into the lens, to afford exact framing throughout the range of focal lengths. As the beam-splitter is placed in front of the last set of elements, focusing cannot be checked by means of this viewfinder. To compensate for this, many models of zoom lens are provided with a rangefinder or telemeter.

Originally, variable focus devices were available only for substandard cameras, and they became increasingly popular. Subsequent improvements have put them on a level of quality which meets most of the exacting requirements of the professional motion picture industry. Among the latest models for 35 mm are the Canon K-35 Macrozoom, the Cine Varotal 25–250 of Taylor Hobson and the 10 × 25 of Pierre Angénieux. A survey of zoom lenses can be found in the table section at the end of the book.

*Recommendations for zooming*

The widespread use of zoom lenses in professional motion picture production has highlighted the importance of the following:

(i) whenever a zoom lens is used on a camera with a lens turret, make sure that the lens is well seated and the turret lock works properly;

(ii) when working with a hand-held camera, mount the camera whenever possible on a tripod before shooting with a zoom lens, since the inevitable lack of rock steadiness in hand-held shooting will show up unfavourably when the lens is in the telephoto position;

(iii) when focusing a scene before the take, adjust the lens focus to the telephoto position, where it can be accomplished more critically; the focus of shorter focal lengths will then be automatically correct;

(iv) when zooming with the hand wheel or lever, bear in mind:

(a) to use the long control lever whenever possible;
(b) move the lever by holding it lightly with forefinger and thumb;
(c) allow for inertia at the beginning and momentum at the end of the run by respectively increasing and decreasing the speed gradually;

(v) when zooming towards a scene, frame it beforehand at the final zoom position, since the initial framing will not remain constant if not properly centred;

(vi) when effecting a slow zoom towards a static subject, the camera speed may be increased;

(vii) at the end of a zoom keep on with a static take of the scene, so that it can be adequately appreciated and will be long enough to allow for subsequent editing.

## Special devices for zoom lenses

Servo controls for operating zoom lenses have now become available. Some years ago studios developed systems for remote control zooming, but the use of these was limited to the individual companies. More recently, manufacturers have introduced devices which can be attached to any handle or lever-controlled zoom lens. Their main characteristics are:

(i) very smooth movement;

(ii) working speeds from $2\frac{1}{2}$–10 seconds for the total zoom range;

(iii) can be installed on the lens or in the tripod-head handle;

(iv) some work with dry-cell batteries as power source;

(v) different models for sound and silent cameras;

(vi) finger-tip starting and stopping control;

(vii) rheostat for adjusting working speed.

## The photographic report

In all organized motion picture production there should be strict control of the work to be carried out each day. This allows for keeping a continuous, step-by-step watch on the film, so that cost fluctuations can be closely checked. The most efficient and complete method for carrying this out is the printed form. Usually the production department of a studio has forms printed for its own use in production, and for the sound recording crew, for the art staff and cast, and one for the camera crew, which is known as the photographic report. This form permits full control of shooting, and this is of great use not only for the camera crew itself but for the production unit as a whole. The photographic report will be carboned in triplicate and all the technical characteristics of each take must be noted, as well as the necessary indications for the processing

313

CAMERA REPORT

## PATHE LABORATORIES, INC.
## — NEW YORK

105 EAST 106TH STREET ·· TRAFALGAR 6-1120
NEW YORK 29 N Y

Date_____

Director_____ Cameraman_____

Company_____

No. or
Name of Picture_____

PRINT CIRCLED TAKES ONLY

| Scene No. | Day or Night | TAKES | | | | | |
|---|---|---|---|---|---|---|---|
| | | 1 | 2 | 3 | 4 | 5 | 6 |
| | | | | | | | |
| | | | | | | | |
| | | | | | | | |
| | | | | | | | |
| | | | | | | | |
| | | | | | | | |
| | | | | | | | |
| | | | | | | | |
| | | | | | | | |
| | | | | | | | |
| | | | | | | | |
| | | | | | | | |
| | | | | | | | |
| | | | | | | | |
| | | | | | | | |
| | | | | | | | |
| | | | | | | | |
| | | | | | | | |

IMPORTANT
FILL OUT INFORMATION ON REVERSE SIDE OF ORIGINAL COPY

No. Cans to Lab._____ Bal. Neg. on Hand_____

Good Footage_____ Received_____

N. G. Footage_____ Exposed_____

Waste Footage_____ On Hand_____

Emul. No._____ Total Footage_____

Form L -7

Fig. 13. Photographic
or camera report.
(*Courtesy of the Pathe
Laboratories Inc.*)

314

laboratory. At the end of the day's shooting the three copies are distributed as follows:

Copy 1 to the laboratory with the film negatives,
Copy 2 for the production department,
Copy 3 for the files of the camera crew.

From the filled-in data, the production people can determine how many takes were made, which were repeated and how many times, which takes will be printed, as well as the daily and total amounts of raw stock used. The camera crew, on their side, will be able to determine all the technical conditions under which the takes were made, which cameras and other equipment were used for each take, in order to be able to go through the same takes again, or to trace the source of any fault.

### The mobile camera

All professional and many amateur films make extensive use of the mobile camera, the basis of a technique sometimes called "editing within the frame". Though the travelling truck and dolly are the most commonly used devices for shooting with a mobile camera, there are occasions when travelling shots are required which cannot be taken in this way. This section describes the mounting of cameras on various vehicles, and suggests ways of obtaining an image free of jerkiness and unsteadiness, defects which often occur as a result of inexperience.

*Mounting the camera on a motor car*

Many silent films reveal that the camera was often mounted on a car to follow or lead other vehicles in motion, or for long sustained takes of moving subjects. The films of Mack Sennett, Buster Keaton and other comedians of the time are examples of perfection in this technique. The method used was very simple, the mere setting up of a tripod-mounted camera in an open car.

With the advent of hand-held cameras, many cameramen resorted to shooting from inside a car, but the results are seldom satisfactory. In the first place, the human body is not well suited to absorb the vehicle's vibrations, which are thus transmitted to the operator's wrist; but worse than this, the operator, in trying to keep his eye constantly to the viewfinder, transmits the swaying and unsteadiness of his body to the camera. In the silent film era this did not happen as cameras were too heavy for hand-holding, and moreover were crank-handle driven, thus requiring a tripod mounting which produced excellent results.

In consequence, most professional operators nowadays mount their cameras rigidly when shooting from a car. Methods are:

(i)   the camera is mounted on a hi-hat securely fixed to a base mounted across the car's bonnet;

(ii)   the camera is mounted at the end of a long board passed under the seats and jutting out through the open door (this is for shooting a car in side view);

(iii)   the camera may be installed behind the car's front seat, for taking the actors' backs, or for shots showing a car coming up from behind; "baby" tripods are very useful on these occasions;

(iv)   the camera may also be installed in special camera mounts or platforms with rubber suction cups for use on the hood of a car.

Many Hollywood studios make use of specially designed cars provided with improved suspension and facilities for installing cameras and lighting equipment at different levels and positions.

### Mounting the camera on aircraft

Air shots are frequent in professional film making. Besides the aeroplane, the helicopter is the favourite type of aircraft, because of the wide range of movements it allows. In both types of aircraft, the camera is always rigidly mounted. For shooting from a helicopter experts advise that the aircraft should be flying at speeds between 15 and 25 knots, and that the flying manoeuvre known as autorotation should be used if possible. During the autorotation, power to the rotor is cut off so that the blades turn freely and the aircraft descends gradually with a slight forward motion towards the target. Other factors for obtaining good footage are: sufficient forward speed to provide lift to aircraft, and an adequate wind blowing with force against it.

### New anti-vibration devices

We have seen that a rigid mounting is recommended in all cases when shooting from a vehicle in motion. The following factors are also a help:

(i)   use wide-angle lenses to reduce the effect of vibration;

(ii)   increase of camera speed up to 32 frames per second if allowed by the character of the shot;

316

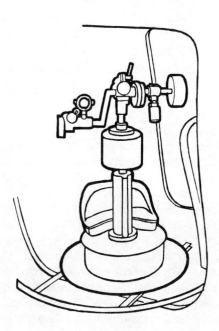

Fig. 14. Aero-Vision anti-vibration mount installed in a helicopter.

    (iii) the camera should be mounted away from the vibration centre.

More recent devices intended to subdue vibrations include a camera stabilizer designed by French engineers for use in a helicopter, called Helivision, which was first used in the film "Voyage en Ballon" by Albert Lamorisse. This achieved sensational results, as it made steady shooting possible with telephoto lenses from a helicopter, together with zooming as the aircraft moved towards or away from the subject.

Another device of similar characteristics, Ceco's Aero-Vision, has appeared on the American market, working on the same principles as Helivision. Its main characteristics are:

(i)    weighs only 120 lbs.;
(ii)   allows for quick mounting on helicopter or other vehicle with only four bolts;
(iii)  permits the use of 10 : 1 25/250 mm zoom lenses;
(iv)  provides a seat for the operator.

A small mount developed some time ago by Danelan Ltd. of England, is of a shape similar to a spider, which allows for placing a tripod in it, and thus eliminates vibrations. This useful accessory weighs no more than 22 lb. and is very practical for takes from un-

317

steady travelling trucks, or indeed from any sort of vehicle of the kind described above.

Tyler Camera Systems Company have produced an automatically controlled portable unit with seat for operator, power source and other facilities, devised specially for installing on aircraft, helicopters, motorcars, boats, wheelchairs, and all types of vehicle.

Another device conceived for compensating vibrations is the Dynalens a revolutionary image stabilizing system conceived by the Spanish engineer Juan de la Cierva and developed by Dynasciences Corporation in 1968. The Dynalens was winner of an Academy Class II Scientific Award from the Academy of Motion Picture Arts and Sciences.

The Dynalens system performs its function by "bending" light rays as they enter the camera lens, by an angularity proportional and opposite to the camera deflection angle. The instrument consists of a volume of liquid enclosed between two optical flats and bellows forming a "liquid lens". The prism angle is controlled, providing exact orientation of the image. Vibratory motions of the camera are detected and measured by sensing gyroscopes within the optical head. Signals generated then program the liquid lens to the prism angle required in compensation for the image movement.

The Dynalens has no focal length, no exposure compensation, no loss of resolution.

*Electrical specifications*
Model S-038
Voltage input: 24–32 v. DC or 12–14 v. DC.
Power input: 100 W. average, 225 W. peak.
Warm-up time: 2 min.
Controls: Power on-and-off switch,
Compensation on-and-off switch.

*Mechanical specifications*
Model S-038.
Size: Head diameter elliptical shape 9 × 7 in.
Length: 5 in.
Power supply: 8 × 8 × 6 in.
Weight: head: 5·5 lb.
control unit: 7 lb.

Model S-038 compatible with Arri 16 and 35 mm with 12/120 mm, 12/240 mm, 25/250 mm, 50/500 mm Zoom lenses

Model S-023 compatible with 35 mm Arriflex camera and 35 mm–140 mm zoom lens.

In 1975, a new device was introduced by Dynasciences with the name of Vibra Stop for compensating for vibrations in motion picture cameras, TV and still photography. The Vibra Stop is a very compact instrument being of the size and format of a supplementary lens, and is mounted in front of the camera lens. Its main characteristics are: length $4\frac{1}{2}$in, (113 mm); diameter $4\frac{3}{4}$in. (120 mm); weight 3 lb. (1.360 kg); maximum camera lens outside diameter required $2\frac{7}{8}$in. (73 mm); light transmission 95%; lens fully coated achromatic optics; power requirements: none.

## On the spot coverage

The shooting of news items where they occur is the most characteristic task of the newsreel cameraman. It calls for a wide range of shooting techniques, both to help the operator and to turn out a more vivid final product.

These technical rules range from the correct way of holding the camera to how the story must be told. Adherence to these rules is indeed the hallmark of professionalism.

### Hand-held operation

Though it is advisable to use a tripod whenever possible, there are many situations which can only be covered with a hand-held camera. In these cases it is obvious that the framing will not be as steady as if the operator were shooting from a tripod; the human body is not a rigid support and its stability depends on its positioning (both natural and with artificial aids), on its balance system, and on the normal functioning of the operator's breathing and blood circulation.

After a run, the faster heart beats will produce an abnormal throbbing of the pulse and consequent unsteadiness. Therefore, avoid physical exertion before hand-held shooting. If this is unavoidable, make the first takes with wide-angle lenses, so as to give the pulse time to return to normal. After this has slowed down, change to other lenses with a longer focal distance better suited to the shot in question.

The use of telephoto lenses with hand-held shooting should be avoided whenever possible, and when essential should be confined to the 50 mm on 16 mm cameras for close-ups.

## Framing

This is the cameraman's most important preoccupation when shooting an item of news interest or telling a story in images. Among the many points of view from which a scene can be shot, he alone has the responsibility of choosing that angle that will be seen by the audience. His choice should be based on sound technical reasoning to show the event.

The rectangle of the standard motion picture frame, longer than it is high, is an excellent medium for producing good composition. The operator will be constantly placing subjects at all distances from his camera: background, medium shot, close-ups, so that they show up and help to describe the action as vividly as possible.

## Panning and tilting

Panning is swivelling the camera in a horizontal plane, while swivelling in the vertical plane is known as tilting. Both are an aid to filmed narrative and give freedom in four important respects:

(i) following the movements of a subject over any depth range;
(ii) viewing a scene too wide to embrace with the field of view of the lens, and covering it with a movement very similar to that of the head when observing the same scene;
(iii) allowing for a smooth change in subject distances, if the camera movement is combined with the displacements of the subject in a determined direction;
(iv) smoothing the passage from one scene to the next one, or bringing out an important detail in one of the scenes.

However, panning is the Achilles heel of many camera operators, who do it either inaccurately or too often. In view of the fast pace and short duration of TV newsreels, panning should be on a strictly functional basis. This is because panning slows down the pace and panned shots cannot be shortened. Many of the panned shots rejected in the cutting room reach the waste bin because they are inaccurate or unplanned. The commonest mistakes are listed in the panning trouble chart on page 334.

## Zooming

The zoom lens is undoubtedly one of the most important innovations in modern motion picture technique. It affords a new and valuable aid to imaginative film narrative. It makes reflex viewing possible when using cameras without this built-in. But, most important, it combines in a single lens all focal lengths necessary to cover a

320

story, and furthermore adds the dramatic effects of drawing near the subject or moving away from it, by the mere action of a small lever. But these remarkable powers lend themselves readily to misuse, and exaggeration will turn the advantages of the zoom lens against the cameraman and spoil his story rather than improve it.

A wide range of zoom lenses is available for 16 mm cameras. Some cover a 10:1 to 20:1 span of focal lengths, while others range only from a medium wide-angle lens to a medium telephoto lens. In practice it is advisable not to use the full range, unless the scene specifically requires this.

## How to tell the story

When time is short, as in TV coverage, there is only one way to tell a story: as directly and effectively as possible. The image on the TV set must portray action fast and vividly, in order to keep audience attention centered on the small screen. In the newsreel, responsibility is shared between the editor and the camera operator. No matter how expert the editor, the final product will lack the quality and interest demanded by the audience if the cameraman's coverage is not good enough.

Very often there will not be time to edit the story in such a way as to bring out the necessary qualities of fluidity and pace. Consequently it is essential that the operator should as far as possible edit in his camera, so that his footage is almost ready for going on the air.

Every day of our lives all of us tell some story or other. But only the cameraman has the responsibility of telling the story with realistic images, from a specific point of view and for a vast audience. For this task he must combine technical discipline with sound journalistic know-how and intuition. The cameraman should be working out the structure of the news item in his mind from the moment he receives the assignment; and it is essential for him to know as much as possible about the event in question so that his coverage is fully adequate and, if possible, in its proper sequence. Moreover he will need to be nimble-minded enough to foresee the development of events he is covering, and thus be ready to shoot them as they occur.

## Continuity

When telling a story, the narrator must go through three successive stages: in the first the audience is placed in the setting where the event occurred; next the characters or elements which make up the story are introduced, and last the images should unfold the event or action or conflict on which the whole news story is centred. These stages must be shot in this specific sequence, and each may comprise one or more shots as may be needed to portray the event fully. The takes should be long shot or medium shot, to include the most significant components of the scene and of the participating characters or elements. Once the main theme is reached, its details should be covered with medium shots and close-ups. If the action being taken is long, it may sometimes be advisable to re-identify the characters or elements with quick establishing shots, and then return at once to the main points of interest. It may also be helpful to insert cut-away shots showing the reactions of non-participants, to accentuate the importance of a scene and avoid any feeling of monotony.

## Pace

The main factor determining the pace of a news story is the length of each take. A minimum time is required to depict an event which varies according to the distance from the camera at which it occurs. For close-ups, a take should last about two seconds. For medium shots, each take should last some three to four seconds. Long shots should be held longer, as they generally include several elements which claim audience attention; four to five seconds is a reasonable length. Of course, the length of a take will vary according to the elements included in it and the time taken by the action being covered, but the above figures are values which may be used as a guide.

Another point to take into account is the climax of each shot; for example, when shooting a plane about to take off, the camera must continue until the undercarriage effectively leaves the ground, as the footage up to this point shows action which is merely passive. It is also important to remember that each take must have action within the borders of the frame to hold audience attention; two consecutive takes with internal action of this kind are more effective and fluid from the editing point of view than two passive takes.

The golden rule of the news reel cameraman—constant change of field covered and continual change of angle—gives the narrator that forward impetus and momentum which is needed for TV news.

### 7. REFERENCES

[1] Marcelli, J. V., The Technique of Follow-Focus, *American Cinematographer Magazine*, p. 34 (Jan. 1961).
[2] Nilsen, V., *The Cinema as a Graphic Art*, Hill & Wang, New York.
   Kraszna-Krausz, A., *La Composicion*, Foto Bibliotecta. Ed. Omega, Barcelona.
   Faveau, P., *La Perspective*, Ciné Memo Prisma, Prisma Ed., Paris.

[3] Chretien, H., La Cinematographie Panoramique par le procedé Hirègonar, *Bulletin de l'Association Francaise des Ingenieurs et Techniciens du Cinema*, No. 11, pp. 13–23 (1952).

[4] Bendford, J. R., The Cinemascope Optical System, *Journal of Society of Motion Pictures and Television Engineers*, pp. 64–70 (January 1954).

[5] Pohl, W. E., Techniscope, *Journal of the Society of Motion Picture and Television Engineers*, Vol. 74, No. 2, p. 121 (Feb. 1965).

[6] Shappert, V., Gli Obiettivi da ripresa a distanza focale variabile. Differenti principi ed evoluzione delle forme, *Bulletino Tecnico della Associazione Italiana Cineoperatori*, No. 5 (Aug. 1960).

Shappert, V., Progres de L'Optique Francaise, *La Technique Cinematographique*, No. 160. Dic. (1955).

Kingslake, R., What makes the zoom zoom, *Modern Photography*, p. 76 (June 1961).

# Trouble Shooting Chart

*Camera operation mechanical trouble chart*

### TROUBLE: *The motor will not run*

| PROBABLE CAUSES | | REMEDIES |
|---|---|---|
| (i) | internal safety switch in "off" position; | (i) open camera and check that safety switch is in "on" position; |
| (ii) | insufficient power from source; | (ii) check line voltage under load; |
| (iii) | faulty contact in connections; | (iii) check that plug is pushed home into socket; |
| (iv) | damaged power feed cable; | (iv) examine motor and power feed cable all along its length; check that cable feeds power continuously; |
| (v) | damaged switch; | (v) check continuity with tester; |
| (vi) | excessively low temperature; | (vi) check that motor runs adequately when detached from camera and at normal temperatures; |
| (vii) | damaged part jamming drive mechanism; | (vii) rotate the motor flywheel by hand and verify whether intermittent drive works properly or is jammed; if motor flywheel does not rotate, detach motor from camera and check that coupling is not faulty; |

## TROUBLE: The motor will not run

| PROBABLE CAUSE | | REMEDIES |
|---|---|---|
| (viii) | damaged motor; | (viii) send motor to specialist workshop; |
| (ix) | piece of broken film jamming the mechanism; | (ix) examine intermittent drive mechanism, shuttle, register pins, and sprocket; also check aperture plate and pressure plate seat; |
| (x) | in spring-driven cameras, breakage of the spring or jamming of winding mechanism. | (x) in spring motor, check tension of springs, and verify that the winding key works properly. |

## TROUBLE: Faulty image framing

| PROBABLE CAUSES | | REMEDIES |
|---|---|---|
| (i) | monitor viewfinder not corrected for parallax; | (i) adjust monitor viewfinder for parallax according to distance from camera to subject; |
| (ii) | incorrect viewfinder field in relation to type of lens being used. | (ii) check the focal length and lens field and place proper mask in viewfinder. |

*Camera operation mechanical trouble chart—continued*

### TROUBLE: *Obstruction in lens field*

| PROBABLE CAUSES | REMEDIES |
|---|---|
| (i) sunshade not mounted correctly or too small for the lens; | (i) check mounting of sunshade by direct viewing through taking lens; |
| (ii) faulty insertion of mask or filter; | (ii) push mask and filters home when inserting them; |
| (iii) telephoto lens in field, when using wide-angle lens. | (iii) remove telephoto lens when using wide-angle lens. |

### TROUBLE: *No image on film*

| PROBABLE CAUSES | REMEDIES |
|---|---|
| (i) shutter fully closed; | (i) check shutter opening before shooting; |
| (ii) lens cap left in place; | (ii) remove lens cap before shooting; |
| (iii) camera in focusing position. | (iii) when using rackover type camera, always return to taking position after framing. |

## TROUBLE: *No image through reflex viewfinder*

| PROBABLE CAUSES | | REMEDIES |
|---|---|---|
| (i) shutter in image recording position; | (i) | rotate inching knob until the image appears; |
| (ii) viewfinder protector in closed position; | (ii) | open viewfinder protecting device. |

## TROUBLE: *Blurred or jerky images*

| PROBABLE CAUSES | | REMEDIES |
|---|---|---|
| (i) tripod unsteadiness; | (i) | make sure the tripod is steady before shooting; |
| | (ii) | send camera to repair workshop; |
| (ii) damaged intermittent drive mechanism; | (iii) | protect camera from direct sunrays; store film in cool place or refrigerator, when shooting in tropics; keep magazines under shade and protected by white bag; if possible use adjustable register pin cameras and adjust the pin to maximum steadiness value, which will also produce minimum camera noise; |
| (iii) film shrinkage due to working under excessively hot ambient conditions; | | |
| (iv) use of telephoto lens on hand-held camera; | (iv) | when using telephoto lens, mount hand-held camera on tripod; |
| (v) camera used on vibrating vehicle for travelling shot. | (v) | on unsteady vehicles, fix camera very firmly, use wide-angle lenses and/or vibration absorbing devices. |

## TROUBLE: Camera runs too slow

| PROBABLE CAUSES | REMEDIES |
|---|---|
| (i) power system terminals make faulty contact, or are worn or dirty; | (i) clean and/or tighten the terminals; |
| (ii) the battery charge is too low; | (ii) check voltage of power source; change batteries; if there is no spare battery, the charge may be momentarily raised by exposing run-down battery to sun; under extreme conditions use motor-car battery by connecting camera terminal to cigarette-lighter plug, but check beforehand that car battery voltage and that of camera motor are the same; |
| (iii) very cold weather affects mechanism lubrication. | (iii) use grease or oil supplied for the purpose. |

## TROUBLE: Camera runs too fast

| PROBABLE CAUSES | REMEDIES |
|---|---|
| (i) voltage greater than it should be; | (i) use adequate voltage for camera motor; |
| (ii) speed control not in correct position; | (ii) check tachometer for proper speed; |
| (iii) wrongly adjusted speed control; | (iii) rotate speed control to proper value; |
| (iv) damaged motor rheostat; | (iv) send camera to repair shop; |
| (v) damaged camera mechanism. | (v) send camera to repair shop. |

## TROUBLE: Excessive camera noise

| PROBABLE CAUSES | | REMEDIES |
|---|---|---|
| (i) | lack of adequate lubrication; | (i) makers instructions regarding lubrication schedule should be strictly followed; |
| (ii) | wrongly adjusted pressure plate; | (ii) check whether shuttle or register pins graze or scrape film track between pressure and aperture plates; |
| (iii) | shutter running off-centre; | (iii) send camera to specialist workshop; |
| (iv) | damaged mechanism. | (iv) rotate motor flywheel by hand and check if noise comes from drive mechanism; send camera to specialist workshop. |

## TROUBLE: Loops are lost

| PROBABLE CAUSES | | REMEDIES |
|---|---|---|
| (i) | loops too short; | (i) check threading in camera; adjust film loops to correct size; |
| (ii) | damaged shuttle claws or register pins; | (ii) verify that there is no damage to any of the faces of the shuttle claws and/or register pins; |
| (iii) | faulty perforation in raw stock. | (iii) check perforation of raw stock, if necessary by return to supplier. |

## TROUBLE: Film damaged while travelling through camera

| | PROBABLE CAUSES | | REMEDIES |
|---|---|---|---|
| (i) | dirty or scratched aperture plate; | (i) | remove aperture plate and clean it carefully; if its surface is scratched it must be replaced by a new one; |
| (ii) | dirty or scratched pressure plate; | (ii) | remove pressure plate, clean rollers and edges as well as front face; |
| (iii) | faulty threading; | (iii) | check that threading has been effected correctly; |
| (iv) | film scratched in magazine or in its travel through camera. | (iv) | check that magazine is clean and verify the state of rollers. |

## TROUBLE: Fogged film

| | PROBABLE CAUSES | | REMEDIES |
|---|---|---|---|
| (i) | wrongly adjusted magazine light-traprollers; | (i) | check seat of light-trap rollers on magazines; after loading magazine keep film inlet and outlet slots from direct light; |
| (ii) | faulty sealing of magazine lids; | (ii) | after loading magazine check that lids seal effectively and that they fit properly into their flange seats; |
| (iii) | camera access door not correctly sealed or misadjusted; | (iii) | check that camera access door seals correctly: |

| PROBABLE CAUSES | REMEDIES |
|---|---|
| (iv) faulty attachment of magazine to camera top; | (iv) check that magazine is correctly seated on camera; |
| (v) reflex viewfinder with open eyepiece while taking; | (v) while shooting, always keep reflex viewfinder eyecup covered by the eye; when shooting with both eyes away from finder, close the tube with the protection device; |
| (vi) light leaking in through faulty mountings on lens turret; | (vi) when using only one lens on a turret, cover the other lens housings with their protection caps; |
| (vii) shutter remains open for too long at the end of a take. | (vii) when working with reflex camera, at the end of each take close the shutter to the viewing position to avoid bright light filtering through to the film, thus fogging the first few frames of the next take. |

*TROUBLE: Unsteady images or uneven running*

| PROBABLE CAUSES | REMEDIES |
|---|---|
| (i) loops are too small; | (i) adust loops to dimensions specified by makers; |
| (ii) line voltage drops (fluctuations); | (ii) check voltage with voltmeter when camera is running under full load; verify AC frequency with a frequency meter; |

## TROUBLE: *Unsteady image or uneven running*

| PROBABLE CAUSES | REMEDIES |
| --- | --- |
| (iii) damaged motor; | (iii) before shooting, run motor separately from camera to make sure that it is working properly; |
| (iv) camera running in cold conditions; | (iv) run camera for a few minutes without film since many cameras need warming up before shooting; |
| (v) film roll wound too tightly; | (v) check that film roll in magazine is neither too tightly nor too loosely wound on core; |
| (vi) magazine take-up belt too tight; | (vi) loosen or change belt; |
| (vii) faulty loading of magazine; | (vii) check the loading of raw stock into magazine; check that roll seats properly on core; check that length of film roll is not greater than magazine capacity as this may cause grazing against magazine walls; |
| (viii) film roll edges grazing magazine walls. | (viii) if film has to be rewound in darkroom before loading, take special care that the side faces of the roll are perfectly flat and smooth, as any ridges are likely to graze against magazine walls. |

## TROUBLE: *Image intermittently out of focus*

| PROBABLE CAUSES | | REMEDIES |
|---|---|---|
| (i) | some fault in the exposure mechanism; | (i) send camera to a specialized workshop to check that the aperture and pressure plates, and the intermittent drive, are properly adjusted; |
| (ii) | film base has shrunk; | (ii) check camera with another type of film; |
| (iii) | faulty lens mounting or seating. | (iii) examine lens mountings and seats carefully. |

## TROUBLE: *Film intermittently fogged*

| PROBABLE CAUSES | | REMEDIES |
|---|---|---|
| (i) | magazine not loaded in complete darkness; | (i) check light seal of darkroom or changing bag; |
| (ii) | light allowed in through reflex viewfinder; | (ii) take care to close reflex viewfinder tube after each take; when shooting with the sun behind the camera, be extremely careful that light does not penetrate through eyecup; |
| (iii) | camera lets light in when stopping. | (iii) at the end of a take, many cameras overexpose and fog the last few frames as the motor freewheels to a stop; to avoid this effect spoiling a take, wait a few seconds after the order to cut before switching off the camera. |

333

## TROUBLE: Ghost images

| PROBABLE CAUSE | REMEDY |
|---|---|
| (i) shutter is out of synchronism with intermittent movement. | (i) send camera to specialist workshop. |

*Panning trouble chart*

## FAULT: Pan travel jerky throughout

| PROBABLE CAUSES | REMEDIES |
|---|---|
| (i) inadequate or faulty tripod head; | (i) check working condition of head, if possible use gyro or gear head; |
| (ii) unsteadiness of operator during pans. | (ii) maintain body stability throughout pan, balance turning of body with camera rotation. |

## FAULT: Pan travel jerky at the beginning or end

| PROBABLE CAUSE | REMEDY |
|---|---|
| (i) inertia is overcome jerkily. | (i) start panning slowly and increase speed gradually; at the end of pan reduce panning speed gradually; to overcome inertia effects, use a gyro head. |

## FAULT: Frame out of level at end of pan

| PROBABLE CAUSE | REMEDY |
|---|---|
| (i) tripod out of level. | (i) when setting up the tripod, rotate the camera 180° and check levelling of head throughout rotation. |

## FAULT: Stroboscopic effects during panning

| PROBABLE CAUSE | REMEDY |
|---|---|
| (i) exposure time incorrect in relation to panning and to position of elements in scene; excessively narrow taking angle. | (i) shoot the same take from a wider angle. |

## FAULT: Pan stops short

| PROBABLE CAUSE | REMEDY |
|---|---|
| (i) static scene at end of pan not shot. | (i) before and after a pan, shoot a static scene to allow the spectator's eyes a rest; this also facilitates editing. |

## FAULT: Image distortion at edge of frame

| PROBABLE CAUSE | REMEDY |
|---|---|
| (i) use of extreme wide-angle lens. | (i) avoid panning with very wide-angle lenses. |

## FAULT: Blurred pans

| PROBABLE CAUSE | REMEDY |
|---|---|
| (i) camera was panned too fast. | (i) when panning on a static scene, e.g. a landscape, rehearse the shot beforehand to obtain the most natural panning speed; if a poor tripod head makes smooth pans impossible, raise camera speed to 32 f.p.s. |

## FAULT: Subject goes out of frame during pan

| PROBABLE CAUSES | REMEDIES |
|---|---|
| (i) faulty framing; | (i) when panning on a fast moving subject, keep it framed so that half of the screen area remains empty ahead of it; |
| (ii) incorrect panning speed in relation to the speed of the subject; | (ii) keep panning speed proportional to the movement of the subject; |
| (iii) panning action not previously planned. | (iii) if the subject zigzags or moves in a complicated pattern, establish reference points and rehearse the scene before shooting. |

*FAULT: Unrealistic displacements of subject in frame*

| PROBABLE CAUSE | REMEDY |
|---|---|
| (i) excessive panning in following a subject over a uniform background. | (i) when panning on a subject moving over a uniform background (e.g. planes in cloudless sky), do not attempt to pan abruptly so as to keep the subject in frame, as this will only tend to produce an apparent unrealistic movement of the subject itself. |

# TABLES

## FORMULAE

*Weights and Measures*

| | | | | |
|---|---|---|---|---|
| Millimetres | × | 0·03937 | = | Inches |
| Inches | × | 25·40 | = | Millimetres |
| Feet | × | 0·3048 | = | Metres |
| Kilograms | × | 2·2046 | = | Pounds |
| Pounds | × | 0·4536 | = | Kilograms |
| Grams | × | 0·03527 | = | Ounces |
| Ounces | × | 28·3495 | = | Grams |

*Ohm's Law*

$$\text{Watts} = \text{Volts} \times \text{Amperes}$$

$$\text{Watts} = \frac{\text{Volts}^2}{\text{Ohms}}$$

$$\text{Volts} = \text{Amperes}^2 \times \text{Ohms}$$

$$\text{Volts} = \text{Watts} \times \text{Ohms}$$

$$\text{Amperes} = \frac{\text{Volts}}{\text{Ohms}}$$

$$\text{Amperes} = \frac{\sqrt{\text{Watts}}}{\text{Ohms}}$$

$$\text{Ohms} = \frac{\text{Volts}}{\text{Amperes}}$$

$$\text{Ohms} = \frac{\text{Volts}^2}{\text{Watts}}$$

*Exposure and lens formulae*

$$\text{Shutter Opening} = \frac{\text{Frames per second} \times 360°}{\text{Exposure Time}}$$

$$\text{Exposure Time} = \frac{\text{Frames per second} \times 360°}{\text{Shutter Opening}}$$

*Depth of field*

$$\text{Nearest Distance in focus} \ldots = \frac{H \times D}{H + (D - F)}$$

$$\text{Farthest Distance in focus} \ldots = \frac{H \times D}{H - (D - F)}$$

H = Hyperfocal Distance
D = Object–camera distance
F = Focal length

## CHARACTERISTICS OF CERTAIN ANAMORPHIC SYSTEMS
(*Note*. All focal lengths require division by 2 to give the effective horizontal angle.)

| Trade name | Country of origin | Characteristics |
| --- | --- | --- |
| Alexcope | Argentine | Uses aspect ratio of 2·55 to 1 with magnetic sound track and 2·33 to 1 with optical sound track. The system comprises 2 sets of Bausch & Lomb primary lenses coupled to anamorphic Cinepanoramic. Focusing is effected mechanically on both lenses. |
| Cinemascope | U.S.A. | 2·55 to 1 and 2·33 to 1 aspect ratios. Optical system designed by Bausch & Lomb comprising integral block lenses with 35, 40, 50, 75, 100 and 152 mm focal length. Focusing is effected by a ring on the mounting. |
| Cinepanoramic | France | 2·33 to 1 aspect ratio. Anamorphic lens for coupling to standard primary lens. The focusing ring admits the insertion of a lever for hand adjustment. Employed in Europe under different patent names. |
| Dyaliscope | France | 2·33 to 1 aspect ratio. Anamorphic coefficient: 2. Integral block anamorphic optical system with focal lengths of 40, 50, 75 and 100 mm. There are also anamorphic models for coupling to primary lenses. Block systems are focused with only one lever. Coupled systems must be focused individually at primary and anamorphic. The makers of this lens have recently introduced a variable focus (zoom) anamorphic system with focal lengths from 35 to 140 mm, at $f3\cdot5$. |
| Naturama | U.S.A. | 2·33 to 1 aspect ratio. Standard primary lenses coupled to anamorphic "Cinepanoramic". Single control synchronized focus adjustment. |

339

| Trade name | Country of origin | Characteristics |
| --- | --- | --- |
| Panavision | U.S.A. | Anamorphic coefficient: 2. Aspect ratio of 2·35 to 1. Fairly recently developed anamorphic lenses with a high resolution, and distortions completely corrected. Block mounted for focal lengths of 35, 40, 50, 75, 100, 150 and 210 mm. Aperture f/2·3 except for 100 mm (f/3) 150 mm (f/3·2), and 210 mm (f/5·6). Supplied with mountings for NC and BNC Mitchells. |
| Pictoscope | U.S.A. | Optical system made up with normal primary lenses and anamorphic "Pictoscope" lens for coupling, supplied in three models: N° 600, 630 and 670. Each anamorphic model covers a certain range of primary lenses. |
| Scanascope | U.S.A. | Anamorphic system for coupling by means of special mount. Works with primary lenses from 40 to 100 mm. |
| Ultrascope | Germany | Anamorphic coefficient: 2. Block system for 50, 85, 135, 300, 400 and 600 mm focal lengths. Two focus adjusting rings calibrated in meters and in feet. There is also a 40 mm wide angle Ultrascope and a 300 m lens of 76–300 mm at f/5·6. |
| Totalscope | Italy | 2·33 to 1. Anamorphic coefficient: 2. This system consists of Taylor & Hobson primaries to which a Cinepanoramic anamorphic system is coupled. Either with individual focus adjusting, or equipped with special mechanical device for synchronizing focus adjustment. |
| Vistarama | U.S.A. | 2·66 to 1 aspect ratio. Anamorphic coefficient: 2. Optical system comprising standard primaries and Vistarama anamorphic system for coupling. |
| Iscomorphot | Germany | Block unit with focal lengths of 50, 75 and 100 mm. Focus adjusted with only one lever, and with minimum focusing distance of one metre (3 ft.) with use of attachments. |
| Totalvision | France | Anamorphic coupling lens. To be used with 40, 50, 75 and 100 mm primaries. Includes sunshade. Standard specifications. |
| Agascope | Sweden | Anamorphic factor: 2. Block unit, with focal length of 46, 75 and 105 mm. Focus and iris controls can be readily connected to control knobs. Excellent resolving power. |

340

## ARRIFLEX FITTING CHART GUIDE FOR TAYLOR HOBSON LENSES SERIES III COOKE SPEED PANCHRO

*This chart guide indicates any interference of the taking lens by the other lenses on the turret.*

| Lens in taking position | Fitting |
| --- | --- |
| 18 mm with filter holder | Must be used single mounting |
| 18 mm without filter holder | Ditto |
| 25 mm with filter holder | Ditto |
| 25 mm without filter holder | 75 mm must be used without filter holder and sunshade. 100 mm must be removed. |
| 32 mm | Ditto |
| 40 mm | Ditto |
| 50 mm | Ditto |
| 75 mm | 100 mm must be used without filter holder and sunshade. |
| 100 mm | 75 mm must be used without filter holder and sunshade. |

## 35 MM MITCHELL & NEWALL CAMERAS

## FITTING CHART GUIDE FOR TAYLOR HOBSON LENSES SERIES III COOKE SPEED PANCHRO IN TUFFET

*This chart guide indicates any interference of the taking lens by other lenses on the turret.*

| Lens in taking position | Fitting |
| --- | --- |
| 18 mm with filter holder | 25 mm with filter holder and 100 mm can only be mounted in the opposite (not adjacent) position. |
| 18 mm without filter holder | 100 mm can only be mounted in the opposite position. |
| 25 mm with filter holder | 18 mm and 100 mm with filter holder can only be mounted in the opposite position. |
| 25 mm without filter holder | Ditto |
| 32 mm | Ditto |
| 40 mm | No interference occurs at either the adjacent or opposite mounting positions. |
| 50 and 75 mm | Ditto |
| 100 mm | At the shorter focusing distances the gear of the 100 mm lens, if mounted in the position adjacent the 18 mm lens, will foul the filter holder of the 18 mm lens. |

## 35 MM CAMERAS COMPARED

| Make & Model | Source | Studio type | Field type | Hand held | Reflex viewing | Rack over | Variable shutter | Maximum shutter aperture | Pilot-pin movement | External 1000 ft. magazines | Internal 1000 ft. magazines | Built-in electric motor | Spring drive | Single lens mount | Divergent lenses turret | Side monitor viewfinder | Silent running | Other features |
|---|---|---|---|---|---|---|---|---|---|---|---|---|---|---|---|---|---|---|
| Ark 1-A Filmovy Prumysl | Czechoslovakia | × | | | × | | × | 170 | × | | × | × | | × | | | × | Binocular viewfinder; 3 × 220 volts 50 c/s. |
| Arriflex BL | Germany | × | | | × | | × | 180 | × | × | | × | | × | | | × | Pilotone generator; 12 volt DC motor |
| Arriflex IIC | Germany | | | × | × | | × | 180 | | × | | | | | | | | 400 or 1000 ft. blimp; 16 volt DC motor |
| Arriflex IIC-BV | Germany | | | × | × | | × | 165 | | × | | | | | | | | 0° to 165° shutter in stages of 15°. |
| Cinema Products XR-35 | USA | × | | | × | | × | 180 | × | × | | | | × | | | × | Variable stroke; 26–36 volt DC motor. |
| Convas Automatic | USSR | | | × | × | | | 150 | | × | | | × | | | | | Interchangeable spring motor; 6/8 elect. motor. |
| Camé 300 Eclair | France | × | | | × | | × | 180 | × | × | | | | | | × | × | Adjustable register pin; Back-projection device. |
| Cameflex CM3 | France | | | × | × | | × | 200 | | × | | | | | × | | | Gelatine filter slot; 6/8 volt DC motor. |
| Cameflex CM3 16/35 | France | | | × | × | | × | 200 | | × | | | | | × | | | Quick interchange of formats in one unit |
| Cameflex CM3 Scope | France | | | × | × | | × | 200 | | × | | | | | × | | | 0·937 × 0·735 in scope aperture |
| Cameflex CM3 T | France | | | × | × | | × | 200 | | × | | | | | × | | | Rapidly adapted Techniscope/standard unit. |
| Druzhba Mashpriborintorg | USSR | × | | | × | | × | 170 | × | × | | | | × | | | × | Automatic dissolve; 24 Db sound level. |

| Make & Model | Source | Studio type | Field Type | Hand held | Reflex viewing | Rack over | Variable shutter | Maximum shutter aperture | Pilot-pin movement | External 1000 ft. magazines | Internal 1000 ft. magazines | Built-in electric motor | Spring drive | Single lens mount | Divergent lenses turret | Side monitor viewfinder | Silent running | Other features |
|---|---|---|---|---|---|---|---|---|---|---|---|---|---|---|---|---|---|---|
| ERK-1 Filmovy Prumysl | Czechoslovakia | × | | | × | | × | 170 | × | × | | | | × | | | | Adapted for extreme temperatures; 12 v. DC motor |
| MIR 3KCC Mashpriborintorg | USSR | × | | | × | | × | 170 | × | × | | | | × | | | × | Special torque motor for film magazines |
| Mitchell BNCR | USA | × | | | × | | × | 175 | × | × | | | | | | × | × | Blimped front unit. |
| Mitchell BNC | USA | × | | | × | × | × | 175 | × | × | | | | × | | × | × | Automatic dissolve; Interchangeable motors |
| Mitchell NC | USA | × | | | | × | × | 175 | × | × | | | | | | × | × | 4-way matte device; 4-lens front turret |
| Mitchell S35R (Mark II) | USA | | | | × | | × | 180 | × | × | | | | × | × | × | × | Interchangeable front unit; variable configuration. |
| Mitchell Mark II | USA | × | | × | | | × | 170 | × | × | | × | | × | | | × | Coaxial 400 ft. magazine. |
| Newall Gaumont-Kalee | UK | | × | × | | | × | 175 | × | × | | | | × | | × | × | Same features as Mitchell Model NC. |
| Newman Sinclair P/400 | UK | | | × | × | | | 160 | × | | | × | | | × | | | Normal and reverse drive; Fixed registration pins. |
| Newman Sinclair P/100 16/35 | UK | | | × | × | | | 160 | × | | | × | | | × | | | Quick interchange of formats in one unit. |
| Newman Sinclair N | UK | | | × | × | | | 160 | × | | | | × | | × | | | Box shaped duralumin body; 200 ft. capacity. |
| Panaflex Panavision Silent Reflex | USA | × | | × | × | | × | 200 | × | × | | | | × | | × | × | Multipurpose camera; Variable configurations. |
| Panavision Studio | USA | × | | | × | | × | 175 | × | × | | | | × | | × | × | Remote focus control; Interchangeable motors. |

343

| Make & Model | Source | Studio type | Field type | Hand held | Reflex viewing | Rack over | Variable shutter | Maximum shutter aperture | Pilot-pin movement | External 1000 ft. magazines | Internal 1000 ft. magazines | Built-in electric motor | Spring drive | Single lens mount | Divergent lenses turret | Side monitor viewfinder | Silent running | Other features |
|---|---|---|---|---|---|---|---|---|---|---|---|---|---|---|---|---|---|---|
| Parvo Debrie 58 | France | | × | | × | × | × | 150 | × | | | | | × | | | | To be used in combination with reflex finder zoom lenses. |
| Rodina IIIKC Mashpriborintorg | USSR | | × | | × | | × | 160 | × | × | | | | × | | | | External focus control; Bellows sunshade and matte box. |
| Super Parvo Debrie AN | France | × | | | × | | × | 180 | × | | × | | | × | | | × | Multiple controls in back; Gelatine filter slot. |
| Super Parvo Debrie V | France | × | | | × | | × | 180 | × | | × | | | × | | | × | Focus and diaphragm controlled in rear. |
| Sputnik Mashpriborintorg | USSR | | | × | × | | × | 160 | × | | | × | | | | | | Totally controlled from the handgrips. |
| Twentieth Century Fox-Simplex | USA | × | | | | × | × | 200 | × | × | | × | | | | × | × | Automatic slating device; Back-Project. control. |
| Vinten Everest II | UK | × | | | × | | × | 170 | × | | × | × | | × | | | × | Built-in rangefinder; Self-lighted safety device. |
| Vinten Windsor | UK | | × | | × | | × | 170 | × | × | | × | | | | | | Interchangeable motors. |

## 35 MM SOUND-ON-FILM CAMERAS

| Make & Model | Single system | Double system | Optical sound | Magnetic sound | Reflex viewing | Rack over system | Side finder | Pilot pin registration | Lens turret | 1000 ft. external magazines | Other features |
|---|---|---|---|---|---|---|---|---|---|---|---|
| Akeley Audio | × | | × | | | | × | × | × | × | Lenses with matched lens finders. 225° shutter. Filtered sprocket unit. 12 v. motor |
| Arricord | | × | | × | × | | | × | × | | Combined Arriflex IIb 35 mm camera and 17½ mm magnetic film recorder in special blimp. |
| Debrie Parvo LS | × | | × | | | × | × | × | | | Silent running camera. Ebonite construction. Same features as Parvo "L". |
| Devry Sound Professional | × | | × | | | × | × | | × | × | Dual sound system camera. Single big unit or double compartment magazine. |
| Camereclair Sound | | × | × | | | × | | × | × | × | 110 v. synchronous 3-phase motor. Four lens turret. Two-top mounted magazines. |
| Newall Single System | × | | × | | | × | × | × | × | × | Same features as NC Mitchell camera. |
| Mitchell Single System | × | | × | | | × | × | × | × | × | Four-lens turret. Variable shutter. Monitor viewfinder. 4-way mattes. Magnification tube. Matte box and sunshade. |
| Vinten Combined Sound & Picture | × | | × | | × | | | × | × | × | Adjustable 10–170° shutter. Compact design. Sunshade and filter holder. 220/50 Hz motor. |
| Wall Single System | × | | × | | | × | × | × | × | × | 4-lens turret. Parallax corrected side viewfinder. Variable shutter. 12 v. DC motor. |

345

## 35 MM VINTAGE CAMERAS

| Make & Model | Max. film capacity | Hand-crank | Electric motor | Metal construction | Lens turret | Internal magazines | Film spools | Viewing on film | Shift-over device | Lateral finder | Reflex viewing | Hand-held | Spring motor | Other features |
|---|---|---|---|---|---|---|---|---|---|---|---|---|---|---|
| Akeley | 200f | × | | × | | × | | | | | | | | 240° focal plane shutter; Pre-loaded film magazine. |
| Arriflex I | 400f | | × | × | × | | | | | × | × | | | 120° mirror shutter; 12 v. variable speed motor |
| Askania Atelier | 1000f | | × | × | | | | | | | | | | Pilot pin movement; Sound insulated body. |
| Askania Schulter | 200f | × | × | × | × | × | | | × | × | | | | On-the-shoulder design; Interlocking focusing rings. |
| Askania Z | 400f | × | × | × | | × | | × | × | × | | | | 15–157° variable shutter; 12 v. DC motor. |
| Bell & Howell Eyemo K | 100f | | | | | | × | | | | | × | × | 12, 16 and 24 f.p.s.; 160° fixed shutter. |
| Bell & Howell L to Q | 100 or 400f | × | | × | × | × | × | | | × | × | × | × | 3-lens turret; greater speed range |
| Bell & Howell Standard | 1000f | × | | × | × | × | | | × | × | | | | Fixed pilot pins movement; 170° variable shutter. |
| Bell & Howell 2709 | 1000f | × | | × | × | × | | | × | × | | | | Dissolve shutter; Removable intermittent unit. |
| Box | 200f | × | | | | | | | | | | | | Wood construction; Very simple construction. |
| Bourdereau Cinex | 200f | × | | | | | | | | | | | | Internal or external film chamber. |
| Cameraflex Cineflex A-5 | 400f | | × | × | | × | × | | | | × | | | Gelatin filter slot; 12 v. variable speed motor. |
| Cinchro | 400f | × | | × | | × | × | × | | | × | | | Variable shutter; Controls grouped at rear. |
| Cinephon Slechta BH | 200f | × | | × | | × | × | × | | × | | | | Pilot-pin movement; Monitor viewfinder. |
| Cinephon Slechta BR | 1000f | × | | × | | × | | × | × | × | | | | Dissolving shutter; Built-in 6 v. motor |
| Cunningham Combat PH-530 | 200f | × | | | | | | | × | × | | | | Rifle stock body design; Pilot-pin registration |
| Debrie Parvo E & K | 400f | × | × | × | | × | | × | | × | | | | Wood construction (walnut); Built-in punch. |
| Debrie Parvo L | 400f | × | | × | | × | | × | | × | | | | Dissolving shutter; Sunshade, filter and matte box. |
| Debrie Parvo T | 1000f | × | × | × | | × | | × | | × | | | | Sound padding cover; Same features as "L" model. |
| Devry | 100f | | | | | | × | | | | | × | × | 135° rotary disc shutter; Reflecting device for focus. |
| Eclair Camé 6 | 400f | × | × | × | × | | | × | | × | | | | Six-lens turret; Pilot-pin movement. |
| Ernemann | 400f | × | | × | | × | | × | | × | | | | Newtonian lateral finder; Dissolving manual shutter. |

| Make & Model | Max. film capacity | Hand-crank | Electric motor | Metal construction | Lens turret | Internal magazines | Film spools | Viewing on film | Shift-over device | Lateral finder | Reflex viewing | Hand-held | Spring motor | Other features |
|---|---|---|---|---|---|---|---|---|---|---|---|---|---|---|
| Fearless | 1000f | | × | × | × | | | | × | × | | | | Variable shutter; 35/65 bi-format camera. |
| Gaumont | 400f | × | | | | | | | | × | | | | Very simple design; Square top mounted magazine. |
| Institut Standard | 400f | × | | × | × | | | | | × | | | | Modular multi-use unit; Four lens turret. |
| Moy-Omnia | 400f | × | × | | | × | | × | × | | | | | Wood construction; Fade-in and out device. |
| Newman Sinclair 4 | 400f | × | | × | | × | | × | × | × | | | × | Duralium construction; 180° variable shutter. |
| Newman Sinclair E | 200f | | | × | | × | | × | | × | | × | × | 10 to 32 f.p.s. film speed; Parallax control in finder. |
| Newman Sinclair D | 200f | | | × | × | × | | × | × | × | | × | × | Four lens turret; Lenses w/filter holders. |
| Pathé 1913 | 400f | × | | | | × | | × | × | × | | | | Wood construction; Small box shape. |
| Pathé Professionnel | 400f | × | | | | | | × | | × | | | | Top mounted square magazine; Dissolve shutter. |
| Prevost | 400f | × | | × | | × | | × | | × | | | | Adjustable lens mount; Side by side magazines. |
| Russell | 400f | × | | × | | | | × | × | | | | | Automatic dissolve; Recessed lens mounting. |
| Universal | 400f | × | | × | | × | | × | | × | | | | Finder on top of camera; film punch; Peep hole. |
| Wilart B | 400f | × | | × | | × | | × | | × | | | | Refined body design; Top mount compact magazine. |
| Zeiss-Ikon Kinamo ICA | 80f | × | | × | | | | × | | × | | × | × | Very compact design; Two speed shafts. |

| Make & Model | Electric motor | Spring motor | 400 ft. Ext. magazines | 100 ft. Internal spools | Reflex viewing | Monitor viewfinder | Rack-over device | Lens turret | Hand-held | Variable shutter | Built-in exposure meter | Snap-on magazine | Automatic threading | 200 ft. film capacity | Bellows sunshade & matte box | Other features |
|---|---|---|---|---|---|---|---|---|---|---|---|---|---|---|---|---|
| Aaton Beauviala | × | | | | | | | | | | | × | | | | Speed crystal controlled |
| Arriflex BL | × | | × | | × | | | | × | | × | | | | × | Silent running |
| Arriflex M | × | | × | | × | | | × | × | | | × | | | × | Three connector sockets |
| Arriflex SL | × | | | | × | | | | × | | | | | | | Divergent 3-lens turret |
| Arriflex ST | × | | × | | × | | | × | × | | × | | | | × | Built-in sync. pulse |
| Beaulieu R-16 | × | | | × | × | | | | × | | × | | | | | 2-64 variable speed range |
| Beaulieu R-16B (PZ) | × | | | × | × | | | | × | | × | | | × | | Reglomatic device |
| Bell & Howell Filmo HR | | × | | × | | | | × | | | | | | | | Critical focuser |
| Bell & Howell Filmo | | × | | × | | | | × | | | | | | | | Side viewfinder |
| Bolex Paillard H-16 EMB Elec. | × | × | × | | × | | | × | × | | | | × | | × | Built-in electric motor |
| Bolex Paillard H-16 REX-5 | × | × | × | | × | | | × | × | | | | × | | × | Gelatin filter slot |
| Bolex Paillard 16 Pro. | × | × | × | | × | | | | | × | × | | × | | | Controls in hand-grips |
| Canon Scoopic | × | | | | × | | | | × | | × | | × | | | Built-in batteries |
| Canon Scoopic 16B | × | | | | × | | | | × | | × | | × | × | | Single frame device |
| Cameflex Eclair 16/35 CM-3 | × | | | | × | | | × | × | × | | × | | × | × | Two formats in one camera |
| Debrie CS 16 | × | | × | | × | | | | × | | | × | | × | | Two compartment magazine |
| Debrie CX 16 | × | | × | | × | | | | × | | | × | | | | New compact design |
| Doiflex | × | | | | × | × | × | | | | | | | | | Special reflex system |
| Eclair ACL | × | | | | × | | | | × | | | | | × | × | Very compact camera |
| Eclair N.P.R | × | | | | × | | | | × | | | × | | | × | Silent running |
| Kodak Reflex Special | | × | × | × | × | | | × | × | | | | | | | "C" mount lens |
| Mashpriborintorg CIIM | × | | × | × | × | | | × | × | × | | | | | | 30-70° variable shutter |
| Maurer 16 | × | | × | | | | × | × | × | × | | | | | × | Blimp for studio work |

348

| Make & Model | Electric motor | Spring motor | 400 ft. Ext. magazines | 100 ft. Internal spools | Reflex viewing | Monitor viewfinder | Rack-over device | Lens turret | Hand-held | Variable shutter | Built-in exposure meter | Snap-on magazine | Automatic threading | 200 ft. film capacity | Bellows sunshade & matte box | Other features |
|---|---|---|---|---|---|---|---|---|---|---|---|---|---|---|---|---|
| Mitchell 16 | × | × | × | | | × | × | × | | × | | | | | × | Hand dissolve lever |
| Pathé PR 16-AT/BTL & Electronic 16/BTL | × | × | × | × | × | | | × | × | × | | | × | | × | Reversing drive |
| Pentaflex | × | | | × | × | | | × | × | × | × | × | | | × | Two position drive motor |
| Photo-Sonics 1PD | × | | × | | × | | | | × | × | | | | × | | High speed possibilities |
| Seiki | × | | × | | × | | | | | | × | | | × | × | Silent running studio camera |
| Vinten-Coutant | × | | × | | × | | | | × | | | | | | | Super 16 facilities |

349

## 16 MM SOUND-ON-FILM CAMERAS

| Make & Model | Magnetic sound | Optical sound | Hand held body | Reflex viewing | Lateral finder | Variable shutter | Lens turret | Studio type | Built-in amplifier | Removable sound unit | Internal film spools | External magazines | Very compact unit | Monitor viewfinder | Rack-over device | Multiple refinements | Other features |
|---|---|---|---|---|---|---|---|---|---|---|---|---|---|---|---|---|---|
| Arriflex BL | × | × | × | × | | | | | | × | | × | | | | | Built-in exposure meter; self blimped; Pilotone signal; pilot pin. |
| Auricon Cine Voice | × | × | | | × | | × | | | | × | | | | | | 100 ft. internal spools; 173° fixed shutter; 3-lens turret. |
| Auricon Special | × | × | | | | × | × | × | | | | | | | | | 30% lighter than Pro 600. |
| Auricon Pro-600 | × | × | | | | | × | | | | | × | | × | × | | 400 ft. external magazine. |
| Auricon 1200 | × | × | | | | × | × | × | | | | × | | × | × | | 3-lens turret with C mount. Three-viewing and focusing methods. 1200 ft. magazine; safety switch; push-button starter; light indicators. |
| Beaulieu News 16 | × | | × | × | | | | | | | × | | × | | | × | Built-in exposure device; automatic zoom drive; low profile. |
| Beckman & Whitley 16 | × | | × | × | | | | | | | | × | | | | | Prism intermittent drive system On-the-shoulder design. |
| Bolex Commag | × | | × | × | | | | | | × | | × | | | | | Three-servo motors; built-in exposure meter; special handgrips |
| Canon Sound Scoopic 200 | × | | × | | | | | | | | × | | × | | | × | Registration pin; 170° fixed shutter; gelatin filter holder |
| Cinema Products CP/16A | × | | | × | | | | | × | × | | × | | | | | 24/25 f.p.s.; "C" lens mount; 173° fixed shutter; gel. filter holder |
| Kodak Reflex 1 | × | | | × | | | × | | | × | | × | | | | | Removable magnetic unit for single system sound. |

| Make & Model | Magnetic sound | Optical sound | Hand held body | Reflex viewing | Lateral finder | Variable shutter | Lens turret | Studio type | Built-in amplifier | Removable sound unit | Internal film spools | External magazines | Very compact unit | Monitor viewfinder | Rack-over device | Multiple refinements | Other features |
|---|---|---|---|---|---|---|---|---|---|---|---|---|---|---|---|---|---|
| Mitchell SSR | × | | | × | | | × | | | | | × | | × | | × | Interchangeable motors; divergent lens turret; 170° shutter. |
| Mitchell-Wilcam W-2+4 | × | | × | × | | | | | | | | × | | | | × | Built-in amplifier; multiple indications into the finder. |
| Morton Soundmaster | | × | | | × | | × | × | × | | | × | | × | × | | Electronic tube sound recording system. 240° fixed shutter. |
| Orafon | | × | × | | × | | × | | × | × | | × | × | | | × | Three-lens turret; built-in-door optical sound recorder. |
| Tolana Sinchroflex | × | | | × | | | × | × | | | | × | | | | × | Pilot pin; 200° special shutter electronic viewing; sunshade. |
| Tolana Sonoflex | × | | | × | | | × | × | | | | × | | | | × | Pilot pin; 1000 ft. capacity; Synchronous 3-phase motor, 220 v. |

351

# REFINED SUPER 8 SILENT AND SOUND CAMERAS

| Make & Model | 50 ft. cartridges | 200 ft. rolls | Reflex viewing | Built-in battery | Built-in exposure meter | Electric film drive | Direct sound recording | Single frame exposures | Built-in time lapse | Other features |
|---|---|---|---|---|---|---|---|---|---|---|
| Bauer Royal 10E | × | | × | | × | × | | × | × | 7–70 f/1·8 two speed power zoom lens; four camera speeds; variable shutter; film rewind; instant slow motion 54 f.p.s.; end of film indicator in finder. |
| Beaulieu 4008ZM2 | × | | × | × | × | × | | × | | 6–66 mm f/1·8 macrozoom lens; automatic start/stop control; variable shutter; lap dissolves device; 27 × magnification in viewfinder; sound synch. |
| Bolex Paillard 160 | × | | × | | × | × | | × | | 8·5–30 mm f/1·9 Macrozoom; rangefinder prism focusing; self-resetting footage counter; 18–36 f.p.s.; end-of-film indicator; built-in batt. check. |
| Canon DS-8 | | × | × | | × | × | | × | | Double Super 8 film; 7·5–60 mm f/1·4 zoom lens; rangefinder prism focusing; self resetting footage counter; remote control; variable shutter. |
| Canon Autozoom 1014 | × | | × | | × | × | | × | × | 7–70 mm f/1·4 macro-zoom; central microprism in finder; film-end signal lamp; three film speeds; automatic lap dissolve and fades device. |
| Leicina Special | × | | × | | × | × | | × | | Interchangeable 10 mm macro f/1·8 standard lens; flicker free reflex viewing; fades and lap-dissolves device; exposure setting; conversion filter. |
| Nizo S-480 | × | | × | | × | × | | × | × | 8–48 f/1·8 zoom lens with two speed power zoom; instant slow motion button; automatic lap-dissolve device; variable shutter; film advance indicator. |

| Make & Model | 50 ft. cartridges | 200 ft. rolls | Reflex viewing | Built-in battery | Built-in exposure meter | Electric film drive | Direct sound recording | Single frame exposures | Built-in time lapse | Other features |
|---|---|---|---|---|---|---|---|---|---|---|
| Pathe Electronic DS8 | | × | × | × | × | × | | × | | Dual super 8. 8–64 f/1·9 zoom lens. 3-lens turret; 0–180 variable shutter; 4 to 100 f.p.s.; 200/400 ft. magazines; sound synch. matte box; flash synch. |
| Sankyo Super CM-880 | × | | × | × | × | × | | × | | 8–64 mm f/1·8 single speed power zoom; rangefinder prism focusing; 20 ft. remote control; under/overexposure control; self-resetting footage counter. |
| Sound-on-film Kodak Ektasound 140 | × | | × | | × | × | × | | | 9–21 mm f/1·2 zoom lens; automatic and manual Type A filter control; 230° shutter; automatic gain control; magnetic recording on film; 18 f.p.s. speed. |
| Sound-double-system Nizo S-800 | × | | × | × | × | × | × | | | Same features as Nizo S-480 but has also included a reel-to-reel or cassette sound synchronizer; 7–80 mm f/1·8 zoom lens and synch. cables. |
| Single/Double System Beaulieu 5008S | × | | × | × | × | × | × | | | Built-in sound amplifier; Angenieux 6–80 mm f/1·2 zoom lens; macrocinematography capability; synch. speeds 18/24 f.p.s.; electric power zoom; "C" lens mount; modulation indicator. |

## EVOLUTION OF THE STANDARD ARRIFLEX
## 35 MM CAMERA

| Model | Year of production | Features |
|-------|--------------------|----------|
| I | 1938–1945 | Circular claw movement; 120° shutter; film gate parts made in "plastic"; small size viewfinder tube; square shaft for matte box; 12 v. motor without rheostat; special mirror for lens scales. |
| II | 1950–1953 | Circular claw movement; 120° shutter; stainless steel film gate; large viewfinder tube; new camera body design; round shaft for matte box; 12 v. motor with built-in rheostat; louvre over ground glass. |
| IIA | 1954–1957 | New cardioid heart-shaped cam claw system; 180° shutter; new brighter optical system; new mechanical design. |
| IIB | 1957–1964 | 16 v. motor; new larger 400 ft. magazine; new viewfinder tube design; adjustable matte box. |
| IIC | 1964– | New brighter optical system; camera door with front finder closure; improved finder tube and eyepiece; interchangeable ground glass; 16 v. forward and reverse drive variable speed motor. |

## SPECIAL MODELS OF ARRIFLEX 35 MM CAMERA

| Catalogue number | Model | Special features |
|------------------|-------|------------------|
| 2030 | II C BV | Adjustable shutter (when camera is not running) from 0 to 165° in segments of 15°. |
| 2040 | II C HS | Designed for filming speeds from 22 to 80 f.p.s.; special balanced film movement; film gate and tachometer regulated for 0/80 f.p.s.; 32 v. motor with separate rheostat. Suitable forward operation only. It cannot be equipped with control signal generator and electric slate. |
| 2022-23 | II C BV (P & ST) | Built-in control signal generator and electric slate, consisting of: Signal generator for 50 cycles at 25 f.p.s.; electric slate for start marking on film and tape; adjusted start marking lamp holder; end-of-film and buckle switch and governor speed controlled 16 v. transistorized motor. |
| | II CT B | Designed for filming with the Techniscope system. Gate aperture: 22 × 9·4 mm; 200° shutter aperture; special two perforation pulldown; ground glass with Techniscope format markings. |

## NEW SOVIET CAMERAS

| Name & Model | Format | Purpose | Features |
|---|---|---|---|
| Mini-SK | 35 mm | Location shooting | 1000 ft. top mounted magazine; reflex mirror shutter; synchronous crystal controlled motor; 6, 12, 24, 25 and 32 f.p.s. speeds; 42 dB noise level; 30 kg. weight with film; built-in battery. |
| 1 KR | 35 mm | Hand held shooting | Reflex shutter; 400 ft. magazines; 8 to 36 f.p.s.; 40 dB noise level; 8 kg. weight. |
| Slavoutich | 35 mm | Studio shooting | 1000 ft. top mounted magazines; reflex shutter; TV signal output; synchronous crystal controlled motor; single lens mount; built-in exposure meter; zoom lens with remote control; 8 to 32 f.p.s. |
| 1 KSM | 35 mm | Animation | Double mirror reflex shutter; exposures of 1/24; 1/12; 1/4; 1, 2 and 4 of sec. |
| 1 SKL | 35 mm | High speed and normal shooting; hand held. | Mirror reflex shutter; 25 to 150 f.p.s.; 12 kg. weight; 400 ft. mag. |
| Kinor 16-SX | 16 mm | TV film production and factual films | Hand held; 30 meter capacity; 8 to 64 f.p.s.; 4·7 kg. weight. |
| Rouss 16-SK | 16 mm | TV film production | Reflex shutter; variable (0–170°) shutter; synchronous motor; 24 or 25 f.p.s. |

## NEW SPECIALIZED CAMERAS

| Make | Film mm | Max. speed | Max. capacity | Features |
|---|---|---|---|---|
| Arritechno R-90 | 35 | 90 f.p.s. | 200/300 | Registration pin; 172° single blade shutter; film marking device; built-in motor; single lens mount. |
| Arritechno R-150 | 35 | 150 f.p.s. | 200/300 | Registration pin; 172° single blade shutter; film marking device; built-in motor; single lens mount. |
| Photec IV | 16 | 10,000 f.p.s. | 400 | Built-in electronic speed control; built-in timing light; mechanical brake; electronic frame counter; rotating prism full frame system |

## WINDINGS AND TYPES OF CORES
## USED IN SOME 35 mm CAMERAS

| Make | Capacity | Type of core | Winding |
|---|---|---|---|
| Arriflex 35 | 200–400 ft. | 2 inch | emulsion in |
| Akeley Sound | 400–1000 ft. | 2 inch | emulsion out |
| Bell & Howell Eyemo | 100–400 ft. | 93 mm spool 2 inch | emulsion in |
| Cameflex | 100–200–400 ft. | 2 inch | emulsion out |
| Camé 300 Reflex Eclair | 1000 ft. | 2 inch | emulsion out |
| Mitchell BNCR, BNC, NC,Standard and Mark II | 400–1000 ft. | 2 inch | emulsion in |
| Newall | 400–1000 ft. | 2 inch | emulsion in |
| Newman Sinclair | 200 ft. | Special core (25 mm) | emulsion in |
| Parvo Debrie Mod. L. | 400 ft. | Special core (50 mm) | emulsion out |
| Super Parvo Debrie | 1000 ft. | Special core (78 mm) | emulsion out |
| Technirama | 1000–2000 ft. | 2 inch | emulsion in (1000 ft. magazine) emulsion out (2000 ft. magazine) |
| Twentieth Century Fox | 1000 ft. | 2 inch | emulsion in |
| Vinten Windsor | 400–1000 ft. | 2 inch | emulsion in |

## SURVEY OF ZOOM LENSES FOR
## 35 MM MOTION PICTURE CAMERAS

| Make | Zoom range | Full length | Maximum aperture |
|---|---|---|---|
| Angénieux | 1:4 | 35 –140 mm | F/2·2 |
| Angénieux | 1:4 | 35 –140 mm | F/3·5 |
| Angénieux | 1:4 | 25 –100 mm | F/3·5 |
| Angénieux | 1:10 | 25 –250 mm | F/3·2 |
| Angénieux | 1:10 | 24 –240 mm | F/2·6 |
| Angénieux | 1:15 | 10 –150 mm | F/3·2 |
| Canon | 1:10 | 12 –120 mm | F/2·2 |
| Canon Super 16 | 1:10 | 13·5 –135 mm | F/2·2 |
| Canon | 1:4 | 45 –200 mm | F/2·8 |
| Canon K-35 Macro-zoom | 1:4·5 | 25 –120 mm | T/2·8 |
| Som-Berthiot Pan Cinor | 1:4 | 38·5–154 mm | F/3·8 |
| Som-Berthiot Pan Cinor | 1:4 | 38·5–154 mm | F/2·4 |
| Taylor & Hobson Cooke Varotal | 1:5 | 20 –100 mm | F/2·8 |
| Taylor Hobson Cooke Varokinetal | 1:5·5 | 9 – 50 mm | F/2·2 |
| Voigtlander | 1:2·5 | 36 – 82 mm | F/2·8 |
| Zolomatic Zoom | 1:10 | 28 –280 mm | T/4·2 |

## SURVEY OF ZOOM LENSES
## FOR 16 MM MOTION PICTURE CAMERAS

| Make | Zoom range | Focal length | Maximum aperture |
|------|-----------|--------------|------------------|
| Angénieux | 1:4 | 17 −68 mm | F/2·2 |
| Angénieux | 1:4 | 17·5–70mm | F/2·2 |
| Angénieux | 1:4 | 12 −50 mm | F/2·5 |
| Angénieux | 1:4 | 20 −80 mm | F/2·5 |
| Angénieux | 1:10 | 12 −120 mm | F/2·2 |
| Angénieux | 1:20 | 12 −240 mm | F/4·8 |
| Som Berthiot Pan Cinor | 1:4 | 17·5–70 mm | F/2·4 |
| Som Berthiot Pan Cinor | 1:4 | 25 −100 mm | F/3·5 |
| Som Berthiot Pan Cinor | 1:5 | 17 −85 mm | F/2 |
| Som Berthiot Pan Cinor | 1:5 | 17 −85 mm | F/3·8 |
| Canon | 1:4 | 25 −100 mm | F/1·8 |
| Canon | 1:8 | 15 −120 mm | F/1·3 |
| Canon Zolomatic | 1:10 | 15 −150 mm | F/2·4 |
| Canon | 1:11·5 | 15 −170 mm | F/2·5 |
| Elgeet Zoom Navitar | 1:4 | 20 −80 mm | F/1·8 |
| Schneider Variogen | 1:5 | 16 −80 mm | F/2 |
| Traid Twenty-Eighty | 1:4 | 20 −80 mm | F/2·5 |
| Vario-Switar | 1:4 | 18 −86 mm | F/2·5 |
| Wollensak | 1:3 | 20 −60 mm | F/1·8 |
| Zeiss Vario Sonnar | 1:6 | 12·5–75 mm | F/2 |
| Angénieux | 1:15 | 10 −150 mm | F/3·2 |
| Canon | 1:10 | 12 −120 mm | F/2·2 |
| Canon Super 16 | 1:10 | 13·5–135 mm | F/2·2 |
| Taylor Hobson Cooke Varokinetal | 1:5·5 | 9 −50 mm | F/2·2 |

## RECOMMENDED PRACTICE FOR TELEVISION SAFE TITLE AND SAFE ACTION AREAS IN 16 & 35 MM MOTION PICTURE FILMS

|  | Width in. | Height in. |
|---|---|---|
| 16 mm Safe Title Area | 0·294 | 0·221 |
| 35 mm Safe Title Area | 0·633 | 0·475 |
| 16 mm Safe Action Area | 0·331 | 0·248 |
| 35 mm Safe Action Area | 0·713 | 0·535 |
| 16 mm TV Station Projector Aperture | 0·379 | 0·284 |
| (16 mm TV Transmitted Image Area | 0·368 | 0·276 |

## 35 MM CAMERA APERTURE SIZES

| Aperture | Width ins. | Height ins. |
|---|---|---|
| Academy Aperture | 0·868 | 0·631 |
| Full Aperture | 0·980 | 0·735 |
| Cinemascope Aperture | 0·868 | 0·735 |
| Panoramic Aperture | 0·868 | 0·447 |
| Techniscope Aperture | 0·868 | 0·373 |
| Vistavision Aperture | 1·485 | 0·991 |
| Technirama Aperture | 1·496 | 0·992 |

358

## APPROXIMATE WEIGHT OF SOME 35 MM EQUIPMENT

| Camera | Weight in lb. |
|---|---|
| *Mitchell and Newall* | |
| Camera, lenses and case | 50 |
| Accessory case with contents | 50 |
| Two 1000 ft. magazines and case | 49 |
| Synchronous motor in case | 37 |
| Standard tripod with friction head and pan handle | 39 |
| Newall Blimp, complete | 95 |
| | |
| *Arriflex* | |
| Camera, lenses and accessories in large camera case | 50 |
| Camera with variable speed motor for forward and reverse drive, lenses, matte box and 400 ft. magazine | 13 |
| 400 model Blimp | 47 |
| 1000 model Blimp with camera, motor and 1000 ft magazine | 129 |
| | |
| *Eclair Cameflex CM3* | |
| Camera, lenses, accessories and 400 ft. magazine in carrying case | 45 |
| Camera with motor, magazine and three lenses in turret | 13 |
| Cameblimp | 110 |
| | |
| *Eclair Came 300 Reflex* | |
| Camera case with camera and viewfinder | 193 |
| Camera ready for shooting | 177 |
| | |
| *Bell and Howell Eyemo* | |
| Model Q (less motor and magazine) | 12 |
| Model K (with one lens) | 11 |

## APPROXIMATE WEIGHT OF NEW 35 MM CAMERAS

| Camera | Weight in lb. |
|---|---|
| Arriflex 35 BL | 31 |
| Cinema Products XR-35 | 93 |
| Convas Automatic | 12 |
| Mitchell Mark III | 22 |
| Panaflex Silent (Hand-held configuration) | 25 |
| Panascope | 26 |

## APPROXIMATE WEIGHT OF SOME 16 MM
## CAMERAS (BASIC UNIT)

| Camera | Weight in lb. |
|---|---|
| Arriflex Mod. ST | 6·5 |
| Arriflex Mod. 16 M | 12 |
| Arriflex Mod. BL | 18 |
| Auricon Cine Voice | 12 |
| Auricon Pro 600 | 21 |
| Auricon Pro 600 Special | 15 |
| Auricon Super 1200 | 32 |
| Beckman & Whitley R-16.E | 11 |
| Bell Howell Filmo | 7·25 |
| Beaulieu | 4 |
| Paillard Bolex | 6·5 |
| Debrie CX-16 | 16·5 |
| Eastman Kodak Reflex Special | 24 |
| Eclair N.P.R. | 18 |
| Eclair Cameflex 16/35 | 13 |
| Mitchell SSR-16 | 18 |
| Pathe Webo | 4·5 |

## APPROXIMATE WEIGHT OF NEW 16 MM CAMERAS

| Camera | Weight in lb. |
|---|---|
| Aaton Beauviala | 12 |
| Arriflex 16 SR | 11 |
| Beaulieu News 16 | 16 |
| Bolex 16 Pro. 2500 | 23·7 |
| Bolex 16 Pro. 2510 | 21·7 |
| Canon Scoopic | 7·5 |
| Cinema-Products CP-16 | 15 |
| Cinema-Products CP-16/A | 17 |
| Eclair ACL | 7·7 |
| Gamit Pro 16 | 10 |
| General Camera | 7·9 |
| Mashpriborintorg CIIM | 10 |
| Mitchell/Wilcam 2+4 | 16 |
| Mitchell Sportster 164 | 14 |

## EXPOSURE TIMES OF BOLEX PRO CAMERA
(Shutter aperture: 132°)

| F.p.s. | 16 | 20 | 24 | 25 | 30 | 50 | 100 |
|--------|------|------|------|------|------|-------|-------|
| Times | 1/44 | 1/55 | 1/65 | 1/68 | 1/82 | 1/136 | 1/270 |

## EXPOSURE TIMES OF BEAULIEU R-16 CAMERA

| f.p.s. | Exposure time |
|--------|---------------|
| 2 | 1/5 |
| 4 | 1/10 |
| 8 | 1/20 |
| 16 | 1/40 |
| 25 | 1/62 |
| 32 | 1/80 |
| 48 | 1/120 |
| 64 | 1/160 |

## EXPOSURE TIMES OF BEAULIEU "NEWS 16" CAMERA

| f.p.s. | Exposure time |
|--------|---------------|
| 12 | 1/30 |
| 16 | 1/40 |
| 25 | 1/60 |
| 40 | 1/100 |

## COMBINATION OF FRAMES AND APERTURE STOPS FOR PRODUCING FADE-OUTS IN BOLEX PRO CAMERA

| Fade-out started at aperture | 2 | 2·8 | 4 | 5·6 | 8 | 11 | 16 | 22 |
|------------------------------|-----|-----|-----|-----|-----|-----|-----|-----|
| Number of frames to be rewound | 144 | 126 | 108 | 90 | 72 | 54 | 36 | 18 |

## EXPOSURE CORRECTIONS WHEN FILMING SPECIAL SCENES WITH BUILT-IN AUTOMATIC METER IN BOLEX PRO-CAMERA

| Subject/scene | without correction | Necessary correction | |
|---------------|--------------------|-----------------------|----------------------------|
| | | Suggested in F stops | Correction in DIN values |
| Snow without sun | Underexposed | +1 to 2 | −3 to 6 |
| Snow with sun | Underexposed | +⅔ to 1 | −2 to 3 |
| Bright beach scenes | Underexposed | +⅓ to 1 | −1 to 3 |
| Backlighted scenes | Underexposed | +1 to 3 | −3 to 9 |
| Titles (white writing on black background) | Overexposed | −1 to 2 | +3 to 6 |
| Grey overcast skies | Overexposed | −⅓ to 2 | +1 to 3 |

## SHUTTER OPENING AND EXPOSURE TIME FOR VARIOUS 16 MM MOTION PICTURE CAMERAS RUNNING AT 24 FRAMES PER SECOND

| Make | Shutter opening | Time |
|---|---|---|
| Arriflex Mod. ST | 180° | 1/48 |
| Arriflex Mod. 16 M | 180° | 1/48 |
| Arriflex Mod. BL | 180° | 1/48 |
| Auricon Cine Voice | 173° | 1/50 |
| Auricon Pro-600 | 173° | 1/50 |
| Auricon S. 1200 | 173° | 1/50 |
| Beckman & Whitely R-16E | 180° | 1/48 |
| Bell & Howell Filmo | 204° | 1/44 |
| Paillard Bolex H-16 Reflex | 130° | 1/65 |
| Eastman Kodak Cine Kodak Special | 165° | 1/52 |
| Eastman Kodak Reflex Special | 170° | 1/51 |
| Eclair N.P.R. | 180° | 1/48 |
| Eclair Cameflex 16/35 | 200° | 1/44 |
| Maurer Mod. 150 | 235° | 1/37 |
| Mitchell 16 | 235° | 1/37 |
| Pathe Webo & 16-AT/BLT | 180° | 1/48 |
| Tolana Sincroflex | 200° | 1/44 |
| Tolana Sonoflex | 200° | 1/44 |
| Triad 805 Fototracer | 204° | 1/44 |

## SHUTTER OPENING AND EXPOSE TIME FOR VARIOUS 35 MM MOTION PICTURE CAMERAS RUNNING AT 24 FRAMES PER SECOND

| Make | Shutter opening | Time |
|---|---|---|
| Arriflex IIB & IIC | 180° | 1/48 |
| Arriflex Techniscope | 200° | 1/44 |
| Bell & Howell M. 2709 | 170° | 1/51 |
| Bell & Howell Eyemo | 160° | 1/54 |
| Cameflex CM3 | 200° | 1/44 |
| Came 300 Reflex | 180° | 1/48 |
| Mitchell Standard & H.S. | 170° | 1/51 |
| Mitchell NC & BNC | 175° | 1/50 |
| Mitchell Mark II | 180° | 1/48 |
| Newall | 175° | 1/50 |
| Newman Sinclair A.K. | 160° | 1/54 |
| Technicolor Technirama | 175° | 1/50 |
| Vinten Everest II | 170° | 1/51 |
| Wall | 170–190° | 1/51–46 |

## SHUTTER EXPOSURE TIME AT 24 FRAMES PER SECOND FOR DEBRIE PARVO L AND 58, AND SUPER PARVO CAMERAS

| Shutter Opening Calibration | Angle | Exposure Time |
|---|---|---|
| *Parvo L and 58* | | |
| 1 | 20° | 1/432 |
| 2 | 41° | 1/220 |
| 3 | 62° | 1/141 |
| 4 | 83° | 1/106 |
| 5 | 104° | 1/84 |
| 6 | 125° | 1/69 |
| 7 | 150° | 1/57 |
| *Super Parvo V and AN* | | |
| 1 | 25° | 1/345 |
| 2 | 46° | 1/187 |
| 3 | 66° | 1/130 |
| 4 | 87° | 1/97 |
| 5 | 112° | 1/77 |
| 6 | 140° | 1/61 |
| 7 | 180° | 1/48 |

## INTERMEDIATE AND HIGH SPEED CAMERAS

| Make | Film mm | Max. Speed f.p.s. | Capacities ft. | Features |
|---|---|---|---|---|
| Eclair GV 16 | 16 | 200 | 100 | Pilot, variable shutter, numbering device, designed for research and industrial purposes. |
| Fairchild H.S. 108 | 16 | 14,000 | 100 | Rotary prism camera, eight side prism, two timing marker lamps, adjustable aperture (8 or 16 mm format), high speed motor, several speed ranges according to voltage applied. |
| Fairchild H.S. 401 | 16 | 8,000 | 400 | Rotary prism camera, magnetic brake, complete auxiliary equipment. |
| Fastair H.S. | 16 | 600 | 200 | Built to withstand acceleration forces. Choice of 3 film magazines: 50, 100 and 200 ft. |

363

| Make | Film mm | max. Speed f.p.s. | Capacities ft. | Features |
|---|---|---|---|---|
| Fastax WF1. | 16 | 16,000 | 100 | Rotary prism camera, two motors, neon timing light, automatic switch, direct viewing and focusing. |
| Fastax WF2. | 16 | 18,000 | 400 | Same as above. |
| Fastax WF3. | 16 | 8,000 | 100 | Same as above. |
| Fastax WF3T. | 16 | 6,000 | 100 | Same as above. |
| Fastax WF4. | 16 | 9,000 | 400 | Same as above. |
| Fastax WF4T. | 16 | 6,000 | 400 | Same as above. |
| Fotomatic Triad 560 | 16 | 200 | 200 | Governor-controlled 24 v. motor, built-in radio interference filters and heaters. |
| Fotoscorer Triad 200 | 16 | 200 | 400 | 28 v. DC or 115 v. AC. Rotary disc shutter, exposure 1/1,000 sec. |
| Fototracer Triad 805 | 16 | 64 | 1,200 | Designed for observing rocket test or long-run applications. Trip switch, four speeds, "C" type mounting, 200° shutter, 28 v. motor. |
| Hy-Cam | 16 | 6,000 | 100 | Rotating prism camera with disc shutter, "X" mount lenses, interchangeable film magazines, very portable unit. |
| Nova | 16 | 10,000 | 100 | Rotating prism camera, seven configurations, interchangeable aperture, 1,200 ft. external magazines, interchangeable prism. |
| Pentazet | 16 | 3,000 | 100 | Rotating prism camera, direct viewing, 35 mm, *f.* 2·8 standard lens, 125 mm *f.* 2·8 complementary lens, 220/380 V. special motors, 300 f.p.s. minimum speeds. |
| Photo-Sonics 16 mm 1a | 16 | 300 | 100 | Pilot-pin movement, 24 v. DC motor, very rugged design. |

| Make | Film mm | Max. Speed f.p.s. | Capacities ft. | Features |
|---|---|---|---|---|
| Photo-Sonics Mod. 1.D. | 16 | 3,000 | 1,200 | Rotating prism camera, reflex viewing, safety switch, timing lights, interchangeable shutter. |
| S.D.S. 6050 | 16 | 200 | 200 | 110° *f* 1·5 periphoto lens, two 12,000 rpm camera drive motors, rotary disc 36° shutter, GSAP lens mount. |
| Wadell, H.S. | 16 | 3,000 | 400 | Rotating prism camera, viewfinder with parallax correction, relay operated cut-off switch, supplementary gear trains for special motors, electronic flash synchronization, double timing lights, external magazines. |
| Triad Fotopak/15 | 16 | 100 | 50 | Developed especially for cramped spaces, 28 v. DC governor-controlled motor, variable shutter, weighs 2¼ lbs. |
| Bell & Howell 2709 | 35 | 200 | 1,000 | See Chapter II |
| Bourdereau U.R. | 35 | 1,000 | 1,000 | Disc shutter-rotating prism combination, two main sprockets, magnetic tachometer, removable aperture plate, 110 v. 2-phase, 4 H.P. AC drive motor. |
| Bourdereau GV | 35 | 300 | 1,000 | 140° variable shutter, three lens turret, registration pin movement, 400 and 1000 ft. interchangeable magazines, 110 or 220 v. AC motors. |
| Cinerama Mod. H-35 | 35 | 300 | 1,000 | Pin registration, reflex viewing, intermittent movement, variable speed transmission, modular design, remote control receptacles, timing lights, trouble free interlock system. |

| Make | Film mm | Max. Speed f.p.s. | Capacities ft. | Features |
|---|---|---|---|---|
| Debrie Cine Theodolite | 35 | 100 | 400 | Incorporated in a theodolite, with a very long focal lens, marking device, frame size of 24 × 36 mm, horizontal film travel. |
| Debrie Gux | 35 | 300 | 1,000 | Special design mechanism, top mounted magazine with meter counter, very compact construction. |
| Debrie Speedex | 35 | 240 | 1,000 | 16–240 f.p.s., 24 v. DC motor or 100 and 220 AC, registration pin movement, 132° interchangeable shutter. |
| Debrie Speedo | 35 | 240 | 1,000 | Very similar features. |
| Debrie G. V. | 35 | 240 | 400 | Electric motor or hand-crank option, interchangeable shutter, registration pins, direct focusing. |
| D.M.N. Milliken | 35 | 250 | 1,000 | Dual film movement, pilot pins, rackover viewing system, 120° adjustable shutter, electrical brake, 24 f.p.s. minimum speed, antivibration film transport system. |
| Eclair GV. 35 | 35 | 120 | 400 | Shutter adjustable between 0 and 160°, 24 to 120 f.p.s., viewing on detachable viewfinder, 2 double feeding claws movement, with 2 double pilot claws. 27 v. or 220 v. AC motor, neon marking device. |
| Fastax WF5 | 35 | 6,000 | 100 | Rotary prism camera, reflex viewing, two motors, double timing lights, bayonet lens mount, variable aperture. |
| Fototracker Triad 75A | 35 | 80 | 400 | Designed for airborne re-recorder, quick speed change gears, variable shutter, 28 v. DC motor, 100 ft. daylight spools. |

| Make | Film mm | Max. Speed f.p.s. | Capacities ft. | Features |
|---|---|---|---|---|
| Mitchell High Speed | 35 | 128 | 1,000 | Two-claw pulldown with two register pins, rising and falling front, rackover focusing system, viewfinder with parallax correction, etc. |
| Newman Sinclair H.S. | 35 | 120 | 200 | Electric motor drive, lens accommodation from 9·8 mm, approximate size 20 in. × 8 in. × 12½ in. |
| Photo-Sonics 2A | 35 | 200 | 100 | Very rugged design, pilot pin movement, 24 v. DC motor. |
| Pentazet 35 | 35 | 40,000 | 50 | Rotating mirror camera, variable aperture, 45 mm. *f.* 2 standard lens, 350 mm, *f.* 2·8 complementary lens very compact size. |
| Vinten H.S. 300 | 35 | 275 | 1,000 | Adjustable shutter between 0° and 170°, pilot pin registration, parallax-corrected viewing, two-speed gearbox to cover range from 50 to 275 f.p.s. |
| Photo-Sonics 1A | 70 | 400 | 80 | Pin-registered movement, 24 v. DC or 110 v. AC motor, frame height 0·218 in. |
| Photo-Sonics 1B | 70 | 400 | 1,000 | Pin-registered movement, 24 v. DC or 110 v. AC motor, frame height 0·218 in. top mounted magazine. |
| Redlake Hycam 41 | 16 | 4,000 | 400 | Rotating prism system; single lens "C" mount; 115 or 230 v. power requirements; built-in electronic speed control; dual timing lights; shutter speed: 1/50 to 1 n/sec. |
| Redlake Hytax 61 | 35 | 100 to 6000 | 500 | High speed continuous recording camera; electronic speed control; bi-directional film movement; dual timing lights; uses polyester triacetate film; full field viewing and focusing; 115/230 v. voltage requirements. |

367

| Make | Film mm | Max. Speed f.p.s. | Capaci- ties ft. | Features |
|---|---|---|---|---|
| Visual Instrumentation Cine-9 Hi-Speed SP.2 | 8 | 250 | 100 | Registration pin; 50 or 100' Kodak film cartridges; 10–160° variable shutter; 28 v. DC power requirements; single lens "C" mount; reflex viewfinder detachable unit; battery pack and pistol-grip with trigger unit; 3 lb. basic unit weight. |

## CAMERA OPERATOR'S CHECKING LIST BEFORE SHOOTING

1. Camera firmly installed and levelled.
2. Enough raw stock for the programmed take.
3. Connections effectively made and correct voltage.
4. Film correctly threaded.
5. Clean aperture plate.
6. Safety switch in *on* position.
7. Footage counters set to zero.
8. Selected lens properly mounted and adjusted.
9. Filter (if needed) in correct position.
10. Camera in taking (not focusing) position.
11. Monitor viewfinder corrected for parallax and adjusted to lens to be used.
12. Sunshade correctly selected for the lens to be used, and equipped with its proper masks.
13. Tripod head controls in position.
14. Shutter opening properly set (variable shutter models).
15. Motor selected for the required speed.
16. Motor and camera must have been warmed up.
17. Magazine belt adjusted.
18. Camera movement should have already been tested.

| Cameras | Available motors |
|---------|------------------|
| Mitchell BNC Model | Synchronous, 3-phase, 220 v. AC.<br>Interlock, 3-phase, 220 v. AC.<br>Multi-duty 220 v. AC or 96 v. DC.<br>Variable Speed (8 to 24 f.p.s.) 110 v. AC or DC. |
| Mitchell NC Model Standard and High Speed | Synchronous, 3-phase, 202 v. AC.<br>Variable Speed 12 v. LC.<br>Variable Speed 110 v. AC.<br>High Speed with theostat control (24–120 f.p.s.) 110 v. AC, 96 v. DC, 220 v. AC. 3-phase M.D. |
| Bell & Howell Standard | Westinghouse interlock, 32 v. DC.<br>12 v. DC.<br>24 v. DC.<br>110 v. AC or DC.<br>H.S. 110 v. AC.<br>Richardson (Animation) 115 v. AC. |
| Bell & Howell Eyemo | Synchronous, 110 v. AC–60 c/s.<br>Universal Var. Speed. 110 v. AC.<br>Field 12 v. DC.<br>Field 24 v. DC. |
| Cameflex CM3 | Synchronous, single phase 110 v. AC.<br>Synchronous, 3-phase, 220 v. AC.<br>Non-synchronous 3-phase 220 v. AC.<br>Non-synchronous 110 v. DC.<br>Transistor controlled. Constant speed (8 to 40 f.p.s.), 8 to 12 v. DC, and 24 v. DC. Manufactured by Kinotechnique, Paris.<br>220 v. AC. Model with magnetic circuit breaking.<br>24 v. DC. Field.<br>12 v. DC. Field.<br>6/8 v. DC. Standard (55 W). |
| Arriflex IIB, IIC | Standard Model, 18/16 v. DC. 20/24.<br>Synchronous 115 v. AC 60 c/s.<br>Animation 24 v. with special unit to adapt it to 110 v. AC.<br>Cinekad synchronous 220 v. AC.<br>N.C.E. Animation 115 v. AC.<br>Reverse Mod. 16 v. DC. |
| Debrie Super Parvo | Synchronous, 220 v. 3-phase AC.<br>Interlock, 220 v. AC.<br>Synchronous, 110 v. AC.<br>Field 24 v. DC. |
| Camé 300 Reflex Eclair | Synchronous, 3-phase, 220 v. AC 50 c/s (24 f.p.s.)<br>Synchronous, 3-phase, 220 v. AC 60 c/s (24 f.p.s.)<br>Field (variable speed) (22 to 26 f.p.s.) 25 v. DC. |

369

# CAMERA EQUIPMENT RENTAL DIRECTORY

UNITED STATES OF AMERICA

*West Coast*
Birns & Sawyer Cine Equipment Company, 6424 Santa Monica Boulevard, Hollywood 38, Calif.
F & B/Ceco Inc., 6446 Santa Monica Boulevard, Hollywood 38, Calif.
Gordon Enterprises, 5362 North Cahuenga Boulevard, North Hollywood, Calif.
Hollywood Camera Company, 6838 Sunset Boulevard, Hollywood 28, Calif.
Hollywood Camera Exchange Ltd., 1607 Cosmo Street, Hollywood 28, Calif.
Lloyds Camera Exchange, 1612 North Cahuenga Boulevard, Hollywood 28, Calif.
Mark Armistead Incorporated, 1041 North Formose, Hollywood 46, Calif.
Masterlites Cine Rentals Inc., 7277 Santa Monica Boulevard, Hollywood, Calif.
Tech-Camera Rentals Inc., 6450 Santa Monica Boulevard, Hollywood 38, Calif.
S.O.S. Photo/Cine Optics Inc., 6331 Hollywood Boulevard, Hollywood 28, Calif.
Traid Corporation, 17136 Ventura Boulevard, Encino, Calif.

*Mid-West*
Behrend's Rental Corporation, 161 E. Grand Ave., Chicago 1. 111.
Masterlite Rentals of Arizona, 834 N. Seventh St., Phoenix, Ariz.
Producers Services Incorporated, 2519 Maple Avenue, Dallas, Texas.
Jack Frost, 234 Piquette, Detroit, Mich.
Victor Duncan & Company, 234 Piquette, Detroit 2, Michigan.
Syncron Corporation, Wallingford, Connecticut.

*East*
Camera Service Centre, 333 West 52nd St., New York, N.Y.
F & B/Ceco Inc., 315 West 43 St., New York 36, N.Y.
F & B/Ceco Inc., 51 East 10th Ave., Hialeah, Florida.
General Camera Corporation, 321 W. 44th St., N.Y.
General Camera Corporation, 2945 N.E. 2nd Ave., Miami, Florida.
National Cine Equipment, 209 W. 48th Street, New York 36, N.Y.
The Camera Mart Inc., 1845 Broadway, New York 23, N.Y.
S.O.S. Cine Optics Inc., 602 West 52nd Street, New York.

CANADA
Jack A. Frost, 6 Shawbridge, Toronto, Canada.
Toronto Camera Exchange Limited, 293 Church Street, Toronto 2, Ontario.

UNITED KINGDOM
Don Long (Cinematography) Ltd., 11 Moxon Street, London W.1.
Samuelson Film Service Ltd., 303 Cricklewood Broadway, London N.W.2.
Mole-Richardson (lighting equipment only), Chase Road, London N.W.10.

FRANCE
Chevereau, 20 Rue de La Chine, Paris 20.
Mole-Richardson, 28–28 bis. Rue Marcelin-Berthelot, Paris.
Bogard, 185 Rue de Grenelle 75007, Paris.
Alga Cinéma, 162 Rue Saint Maur, Paris (11e).

ITALY
Mole-Richardson, Via del Velodromo 68–74, Roma; Via Pestalozzi 18, Milano.
Vicenzo Mariani, Via Baldo degli Ubaldi 226, Roma.

**SPAIN**
Mole-Richardson, Gustavo Fernandez Balbuena 13, Madrid (2)
Albiñana, Encarnacion 24, Barcelona.
Arturo Gonzalez P.C., José Antonio 66–2° Izq. Madrid 13.
General Organizacion, José Antonio 464, Barcelona (15)
Eduardo Perez Climent, Breton de los Herreros, 56, Madrid (3).
Felix Duran Aparicio, Pinos Alta, 3, Madrid (20).

**HOLLAND**
Samuelson International N.V., Building 67, Schiphol Airport, Amsterdam.
Filmpartners N.V., Duivendrechtsekade 86/, Amsterdam.

**GERMANY**
Mole-Richardson, Hofangerstrasse 78, Munchen 8.

**GREECE**
Mole-Richardson, 60 Vasilissis Sofias Ave., Athens.

**PUERTO RICO**
Wialliam Moraski, Film Center Bldg., San Juan.

**ARGENTINE**
Alex Film Laboratories, Dragones 2250, Buenos Aires
Estudios Lumiton, Bme Mitre 2349, Buenos Aires.
Servicine, Mendoza 975, Buenos Aires.

**URUGUAY**
Carrillon Films, Av. 18 de Julio 2196, Ap. 702, Montevideo.
Cinema, Andes 1382 2do Piso, Montevideo.
Tecnocine, Colonia 1171, Montevideo.

**HAWAII**
Motion Picture Service Center, 2424 Kalakaua, Honolulu.

**MEXICO**
Docam S.A., Calle Sur 64-A No. 3141, Viaduacto Piedad, Mexico 13 D.F.
Estudios Churubusco Azteca S.A. (Calz de Tlalpan), Mexico 21 D.F.
Laboratorios Cinematograficos Mexico S.A., Frias No. 1145, Col. del Valle, Mexico D.F.

**PERU**
Nova Estudios Cinematograficos, Bellavista 560, Miraflores, Lima.
Estudios Cinematograficos Roselló, Huiracocha 1548, Lima.

**BOLIVIA**
Producciones Interamerica Ltda., Casilla 2606. Tel 28921. La Paz.
Toussaint & Co., Potosi 1130 3er Piso Edif, La Paz.

## MANUFACTURER'S DIRECTORY OF PROFESSIONAL
## MOTION PICTURE CAMERAS

*Aaton 16. camera. Aaton Cinematographie 2 Rue Carnot—B.P. 31 38001 Grenoble, France.*
*Acmade X-Ray Cameras:* Acmade, The Rank Organization, Woodger Road, Shepherds Bush, London, England.

*Acme Process Camera:* Producers Services Co. 1145 NO. McCaddin, Hollywood 38, Calif., U.S.A.

*Arriflex 35, Arricord, Arriflex 16ST, Arriflex BL, etc.:* Arnold & Richter, A.G. Munchen, Turkenstrasse 89, W. Germany.

*Askania Z, Askania Schulter, Askania H, Speed, etc.:* Askania Werke, A.K. Berlin, Fridenau-Dundesalles 86–89, W. Germany.

*Auricon Cine Voice, Pro-600, Super 1200 etc.:* Bach Auricon Inc., 6950 Romaine Street, Hollywood 38, California, U.S.A.

*Beaulieu R-16; News 16 cameras; etc.:* Maison Brandt Freres, 16 Rue de la Cerisaie 94, Charenton-le Pont, France.

*Beckman & Whitley Model 339, 357, etc. High Speed Cameras, CM-16, Newsreel:* Beckman & Whitley, San Carles 3, California, U.S.A.

*Bell & Howell Filmo 16 mm cameras and Eyemo 35 mm cameras:* Bell & Howell Company, 7100 McCormick Road, Chicago 45, Ill., U.S.A.

*Bolex Paillard 16 mm cameras:* Paillard S.A. 1401 Yverdon, Suisse.

*Bourdereau High Speed Cameras:* Ets. A. Bourdereau, 262 Rue de Belleville, Paris, France.

*Cameflex 16/35, 35 mm, Came 300 Reflex, Aquaflex, Camematic, Cameraeclair, Cameraflex, Reflex Radar Boresight, Data recording cameras, etc.:* Federal Manufacturing & Engineering Corp., 1055 Stewart Ave., Garden City, New York, U.S.A.

*Canon Scoopic 16:* Canon Camera Co. Inc. 3,5 Chome Ginza, Chuoku-Tokyo, Japan.

*Cinema Products XR-35 and CP16 camera:* Cinema Products, 2037 Granville Avenue, Los Angeles, California 90025, U.S.A.

*Cinerama High Speed Cameras:* Cinerama Camera Corporation, 11930 W. Olimpic Blvd., Los Angeles, California, U.S.A.

*Eastman Kodak Special II and Kodak Reflex Special 16 mm cameras:* Eastman Kodak Company, 343 State Street, Rochester 4, New York, U.S.A.

*Eclair 16 mm (N.P.R.), etc.:* Eclair International Diffusion, 12 Rue Gaillon, Paris, France.

*Erk & Ark Filmovy cameras:* Filmovy Prumysl, Praha 5—Barrandov, Czechosolvakia.

*Fairchild High Speed Cameras:* Fairchild Camera & Instruments Corp., Robbins Lane, Syosset, L.I. New York, U.S.A.

*Fastax WF5, WF7, WF8, WF9, WF10, WF18, etc. High Speed Cameras:* Wollensak Optical Company, 850 Hudson Ave., Rochester 21, N.Y., U.S.A.

*Milliken High Speed Cameras, Underwater cameras, etc.:* D.B. Milliken, 131 North Fifth Avenue, Arcardia, Calfornia, U.S.A.

*Mitchell BNC, NC, Standard, H. Speed, Mitchell 16, SSR-16, BFC, FC, Mark II, E:* Mitchell Camera Corporation, 666 West Harvard St., Glendale 4, Calf., U.S.A.

*Newall cameras and studio equipment:* G. B. Kalee Limited, Rank Precision Industries Ltd., Mortimer House, 37–41 Mortimer Street, London, England.

*Newman & Sinclair P.400, Auto-Kine Mod. G, N.G.:* James A. Sinclair Co. Ltd., 3 Whitehall, London, England.

*Oxberry Process Camera:* Oxberry Corp., 25–15, 50th Street, Woodside, N.Y., U.S.A.

*Panascope Mini B:* Cine Precision Engineering Co, 1038 North Highland Ave., Hollywood, CA 90038, U.S.A.

*Panavision Silent Reflex, Panavision Studio, etc.:* Panavision Incorporated, 1917 Pontius Ave., Los Angeles, California 90025.

*Pathé Webo & Model AT/BLT:* Consortium Patheé, 14 Av. de la Place, Joinville-Le-Pont-Seine, Paris.

*Pentaflex:* Veb Kamera und Kinowerk, Dresden, German Democratic Republic.

*Photomechanism Cinefluorographic cameras:* Photomechanism Inc. 15 Stepar Place, Huntingdon Station, New York, U.S.A.

*Photosonics 1PD, Action Master 200:* Instrumentation Marketing Corp., 820 South Mariposa Street, Burbank, CA 91506, U.S.A.

*Red Lake High Speed Cameras:* Red Lake Labs. Inc., 271 Corvin Drive, Santa Clara, California, U.S.A.

*Rodina, Moskva, Mir, Druzhba, Convas Avtmat, Panorama, Era, Rossiya, etc.:* Mashpriberingtorg, Smolenskaia Sennaia 32–34, Moscow G-200, U.S.S.R.

*S.D.S. Instrumentation & Special works cameras:* Scientific Data Systems Aerospace Systems, 600 East Bonita Ave., Pemena, California, U.S.A.

*Strobodrum Ultra-High-Speed Cameras:* Impulsphysik, GmbH, 2000 Hamburg 56, Sülldorfer Landstrasse 400, Germany.

*Super Parvo Color, Mod, V, Parvo L & 58, High Speed cameras, Simmer, Debrie CS16, Debrie CX16, etc.:* Etablissements André Debrie, 111–113 Rue St. Maur, Paris, France.

*Twentieth Century Fox Cameras:* Twentieth Century Fox Studio, Camera Department, 10201 Pico Blvd., Los Angeles, California, U.S.A.

*Technirama Technicolor Camera:* Technicolor Corporation, 1033 N. Cahuenga Blvd., Hollywood, 38, Calif., U.S.A.

*Vinten Windsor, Vinten Everest II, Vinten H.S. 300, etc.:* W. Vinten Limited, Western Way, Bury St. Edmunds, Suffolk, England.

*Waddel High Speed Cameras,* John H. Waddel Inc., Syosset, New York, U.S.A.

# GLOSSARY

**A**  ABERRATION. Defect in the rendition of a lens due to non-convergence of light rays in the focus and producing in the image a loss of definition and of likeness to original subject.

APERTURE. (i) Opening in the aperture plate in contact with which the film runs through the film gate. Thus the aperture frames the image produced by the lens on the film. (ii) Effective size of the lens opening through which light passes to the film. (Also stop, *f*-stop, *f*-number, or T-stop.)

APOCHROMATIC. Lens designed for colour photography, in which the light rays of the three basic colours converge at the same focus.

AUTOCOLLIMATOR. Instrument for checking visually the rendition of a lens.

**B**  BARNEY. Flexible cover thrown over the camera as a substitute for a blimp, when sound filming. It reduces camera noise.

BEAM-SPLITTER PRISM. Used in some viewfinding systems to conduct a portion of the light away to the viewfinder while the remainder passes through to the film.

BIPACK SYSTEM. Method by which two films in contact run through the intermittent movement of a camera.

BLIMP. Rigid soundproof cover for a camera used when sound filming. Although camera noise is eliminated it allows full control from the outside.

**C**  CAMERA SLATE. Board, used at the beginning of takes, showing the shot number, number of take, and other details about the film.

CLAW. Metal tooth in the intermittent movement of a camera which engages with the perforation and pulls down the film frame by frame.

CRANE. A camera support of large size which carries the camera on a pivoted arm.

**D**  DIAPHRAGM. Variable control regulating light passing through the lens.

DISSOLVE. Where the end of one shot gradually merges into the beginning of another. A dissolve control is fitted to some cameras, but normally the effect is produced by optical printing in the laboratory.

DITTY BAG. Small bag hanging between tripod legs used for keeping accessories.

DOLLY, CRAB DOLLY. A wheeled vehicle for carrying the camera in tracking shots. Crab dolly allows oblique or sideways movements.

**E**  EMULSION. Light sensitive coating on one side of the film, identifiable as the dull side, which when inserted in the camera gate should face the lens.

EXPOSURE. Amount of light permitted to reach each frame while filming.

**F**  FILM PLANE. Position of the film in the gate indicated by the symbol-⊖-on the outside of the camera body.

FOCAL LENGTH. The distance from the centre of a lens to the surface of the film when the lens is focused on a distant object. This distance governs the angle of view of the lens—a short focal length has a wide angle of view, a long focal length lens has a narrow angle of view.

375

FOOTAGE COUNTER. Indicator showing footage run through camera while filming.

F.P.S. Frames Per Second. The number of pictures produced every second, as the film passes through the camera.

FRAME. A single picture on a length of cinematograph film. The frame line is the narrow line dividing frames.

FRAMING. Arranging the subject within the picture area.

**G** GATE. The part of the camera mechanism in which the film is held while each frame is exposed.

GIMBAL TRIPOD. Camera support providing stabilization of the camera independently of the support itself. It allows horizontally steady shots to be taken from a moving platform such as a ship at sea.

GRATICULE LINES. Lines engraved in the viewfinder to give a perimeter of the area covered by the camera lens, or measurements of screen proportions etc.

**H** HIGH SPEED CAMERA. Camera specially designed to film at shutter speeds much higher than normal.

HI-HAT. A small metal platform for mounting the camera a few inches above floor level.

**I** INTERCHANGEABLE LENSES. Lenses of fixed focal length which are dismounted and interchanged for those of other focal lengths.

INTERLOCKED MOTORS. Interlocking between two motors so that their rotors and stators are similarly positioned, thus providing constant synchronism of the intermittent movements of two cameras or one camera and a projector for rear projection work.

INTERMITTENT MOVEMENT. That part of the film drive mechanism which stops, positions, and advances the film frame by frame when the camera is running. It is the primary feature governing picture quality and steadiness, and must be of the very highest precision.

**L** LOOP. The film is formed into two loops, one either side of the intermittent movement to allow freedom of activity between that mechanism and the continuous film feed.

**M** MAGAZINE. Lightproof housing containing the film, usually detachable and holding 400 ft. (16 mm) or 1000 ft. of film (35 mm).

MATTE-BOX. Box shaped or bellows attachment fitted in front of the camera lens. It holds mattes (opaque cards) which mask off part of the image, and it also serves as a filter holder.

MONITOR TV VIEWFINDER. An externally mounted TV monitor attached to the viewfinder of a camera so that the image may be viewed by several persons simultaneously. A recording device may be employed to play back the take immediately after shooting so that the scene may be checked before processing and printing.

**O** ORTHOCHROMATIC. Film sensitive to all colours of the visible spectrum except red.

**P** PANCHROMATIC. Film sensitive to all colours of the visible spectrum.

PARALLAX ERROR. An error from displacement of a viewfinder above or to one side of the taking lens in certain camera designs. The view through the finder differs slightly from that on the film, but the difference is only apparent when working at short range.

PAN. An abbreviation of 'panoraming', swivelling the camera in a horizontal plane.

PAN AND TILT HEAD. Fitting on tripod for making pan and tilt movements (*TILT*). Swivelling the camera in a vertical plane.

PERFORATIONS. Holes in cinematographic film by which sprockets and claw mechanism drive it through the camera.

PILOT PIN. See REGISTER PIN.

PRESSURE PLATE. A plate behind the aperture which applies back pressure to hold the film accurately in the focal plane. The pressure plate incorporates rollers to minimize frictional contact with the film.

**R** RACKOVER. Method used on some cameras whereby the entire film mechanism is displaced to one side so that a viewfinder can come into position behind the lens. The lens is racked back before shooting begins.

RAW STOCK. Unexposed cinematograph film.

REFLEX VIEWFINDER. Optical system allowing viewfinding through the actual taking lens of the camera while filming.

REGISTER PIN. A precision pin in the film gate which engages with a perforation while each frame is being exposed, and withdraws when the film moves on. With the fixed pin (Bell & Howell system) the film seats itself on the pins for each frame. With the other system (Mitchell), the pins are inserted and withdrawn mechanically.

REGISTRATION. Ability to position each frame correctly and hold it steady while being exposed.

RHEOSTAT. An adjustable control used on 'wild' motors to vary the current and so the filming speed, over a continuous scale.

**S** SHUTTER. A device for obscuring light from the film while it moves on from one frame to the next. A variable shutter is one whose opening may be adjusted to let in more or less light.

SHUTTER ANGLE. A rotating shutter with an adjustable opening lets light through to the film according to any setting up to half its total area, i.e. 180°. The shutter angle is the size of that opening, e.g. 90° (half open), 45° etc.

SHUTTLE. The moving part which carries the claws and gives them their reciprocating motion.

SIXTEEN MILLIMETRE. Smallest gauge of cine film used in professional film production.

SPROCKETS. Toothed wheels inside the camera which drive the film by engaging with the film perforations.

STARTING SWITCH. Switch for starting the camera motor.

START-UP. Inertia of the film at the beginning of a shot.

STOP-FRAME EXPOSURES. Single frames exposed at longer intervals than in normal continuous running.

SYNCHRONOUS MOTOR. Motor deriving its constant speed from a 50 or 60 cycle alternating current.

**T** TACHOMETER. Film speed indicator alibrated in f.p.s.

TELEMETER. Rangefinder.

TRIANGLE. Metal plate with slots for tripod legs, placed beneath a tripod to prevent the legs from spreading.

TRIPOD HEAD. Fitting on a tripod to accommodate the camera. It may be of friction, fluid or gyroscopic type.

TURRET (*Lens*). Rotating plate on the front of a camera holding two or more lenses which may be interchanged without removing them from the camera.

**V** VARIABLE SPEED MOTOR (or 'WILD MOTOR'). Motor that can be operated over a range of speeds by adjustment of a built-in rheostat. It is only used for shooting silent sequences which will be post-synchronized.

VERNIER (OR NONIUS). Device for obtaining fractional subdivisions of a normal scale.

377

VIEWFINDER. Any viewing system which gives a framed representation of the image as it will appear on the film.

**W** WEAVING AND BREATHING. Faults in film movement. Weaving is a shift of the film up and down or side to side. Breathing is a movement of the film back and forth in and out of the image plane.

**Z** ZOOM LENS or VARI-FOCAL LENS. Lens which varies its focal length over a continuous range by operating a control, so giving a greater or less magnified image.

# INDEX